Haltonchesters

Excavations directed by J. P. Gillam at the Roman Fort, 1960–61

J. N. Dore

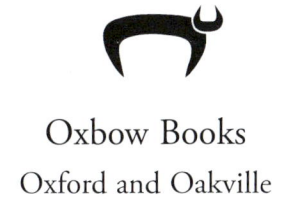

Oxbow Books
Oxford and Oakville

Published by
Oxbow Books, Oxford

© Oxbow Books and the individual authors, 2010

ISBN 978-1-84217-360-2

This book is available direct from

Oxbow Books
Phone: 01865-241249; Fax: 01865-794449

and

The David Brown Book Company
PO Box 511, Oakville, CT 06779, USA
Phone: 860-945-9329; Fax: 860-945-9468

or from our website

www.oxbowbooks.com

Front cover: left: Block C236 22, right: C219 Block 22
Back cover: Tea-break during the 1961 excavation season. The reclining figure wearing a jacket and red jumper in the centre of the photo is John Gillam. Other local archaeologists and members of the Newcastle Society of Antiquaries who can be identified are Jock Tait (back row standing wearing a beret), to the left in a white hat: Dorothy Bowes; to the left of DB with arms folded: Matthew Sadler; seated in front of Dorothy: Harold Bowes.

Printed and bound at
Gomer Press, Llandysul, Wales

Contents

Preface v
List of Figures vii
List of Tables viii
Acknowledgements ix
Summaries x

Chapter 1. Introduction 1
    Previous work 1
    The Excavations of 1960–61: Post-Excavation History 3
    The Archive 4
    Report Methodology 6
    Presentation of the Primary Archive 7
    Interpretation of the Primary Archive 8

INTERPRETATION OF THE PRIMARY ARCHIVE
Chapter 2. The Granary 9

Chapter 3. The Building Complex to the West of the Granary 15

Chapter 4. The Late Buildings 25

Chapter 5. The Other Structures 34

Chapter 6: Conclusions 38

THE PRESENTATION OF THE PRIMARY ARCHIVE
Chapter 7. Structural Synopsis 44

Chapter 8. The Coins
    Richard Brickstock 91

Chapter 9. The Decorated Samian and Potters' Stamps
    Brian Hartley and Brenda Dickinson 108

Chapter 10. The Other Pottery
    John Dore 126

Chapter 11. The Small Finds
    Lindsay Allason-Jones 143

Appendix I. Secondary Sources 161
Appendix II. Selected Finds Groups 164
Appendix III. Location of Finds 168

Bibliography 175
Index 177

Preface

John Gillam and John Dore

The publication of an excavation report is normally an occasion for some celebration amongst those involved in its production, particularly one so long awaited as this, which deals with the excavations in 1960 and 1961 at Haltonchesters. However in this case it is tinged with great sadness owing to the premature and unexpected death of John Dore (JND), the principal author and editor of the volume, during the final stages of its preparation. Hence neither the director of the excavations, John Gillam (JPG), nor the individual primarily responsible for steering the report through to the brink of publication will witness the volume's appearance.

The close association between these two began in 1974 when JND was appointed a research assistant at Newcastle University, having earlier in that same year participated in the excavations at the Flavian military base of Red House near Corbridge. In his capacity as research assistant, JND was involved in preparing reports on a number of excavations which Gillam had directed, either solely or in collaboration with others, and the result was a close working relationship between the two. As well as the Red House report, this resulted in joint authorship in 1979 of the monograph on excavations at South Shields fort from 1875 to 1975 and publication of the investigations at Corbridge directed by JPG and others between 1947 and 1980, which appeared a couple of years after Gillam's death in 1986 (authored jointly by JND and Mike Bishop).

JPG had for many years been at the forefront of Romano-British archaeology, and in particular the study of Roman pottery, with a series of seminal works on the subject, perhaps most notably *Types of Roman Coarse Pottery Vessels in Northern Britain* which went into three editions, but also 'Sources of Pottery found on Northern Military Sites' and 'Coarse Fumed Ware in North Britain and Beyond'. This knowledge of the dating evidence, coupled with experience of excavating at many of the key sites, in turn enabled JPG to write numerous authoritative and influential papers on the history of the Northern Frontier.

It was as a result of his close association with JPG that JND was to develop his own interest in Roman ceramics, which saw him become, in his turn, one of the subject's foremost scholars, with a detailed understanding of the pottery of Roman Britain and the Classical Mediterranean world, particularly North Africa. His works included joint authorship, with Roberta Tomber, of *The National Roman Fabric Reference Collection, A Handbook*, and pottery reports relating to many of the key sites on the Northern Frontier, including Elginhaugh, Carpow and Housesteads, in addition to his involvement in the excavation reports noted above.

JND openly acknowledged his debt to JPG and viewed him as one of the two individuals, along with Barri Jones at Manchester University, most responsible for shaping the direction of his career in archaeology. Such transmission of a breadth of expertise from one generation to another now seems more difficult to achieve in the compartmentalised world of modern archaeology, with its separate career paths and narrowly defined academic specialisms, and perhaps especially so in the disciplines associated with the analysis of material assemblages like pottery, where practitioners need to gain detailed familiarity with a broad range of material. This makes the premature loss of JND's expertise all the more tragic.

The intellectual partnership and close friendship between these two men made JND the natural person to assume responsibility for preparing the Haltonchesters excavation report from 1988 onward, the last significant piece of Gillam's corpus of work which remained unpublished. The detailed understanding of JPG and his system of excavation which JND brought to this task is eloquently demonstrated in the discussion, in Chapter 1, of the problems inherent in the primary archive (see p. 6). At the time of the JND's death the only significant task still outstanding was the completion of the photographic illustrations of the decorated and stamped samian vessels. Three overall phase plans of the fort have subsequently been prepared by the Archaeological Practice to satisfy English Heritage's refereeing process, whilst the opportunity has also been taken to integrate the photographs more fully with the text to meet the standards required of an Oxbow Monograph, and to make a few typographical and other minor editorial corrections.

In the obituary he wrote for JPG in *Archaeologia Aeliana* in 1987, JND noted 'it was, above all, the charisma of his personality which added an extra dimension to his skill and enabled him to communicate it to the benefit of others. It was his character with its warmth, enthusiasm and humour which made a great many people in many different countries deeply love and respect him'. In truth this statement could be applied with equal validity to both men and it is to be hoped that this volume will serve in some way as a permanent memorial to two charismatic, engaging scholars and teachers who did so much to help shape our current understanding of Rome's frontier in northern Britain.

Alan Rushworth
November 2008

Gillam. Photo take by John Dore, perhaps during the 1980 Corbridge excavation.

John Dore. Photo taken by Marta Lahr during a meeting at the Libyan Department of Antiquities in Tripoli during January 2008.

List of Figures

Figure 1.1 Location of the site; location and dates of the various campaigns of excavation

Figure 1.2 The excavations of 1960–61, trench layout in the central area

Figure 2.1 The granary: plan

Figure 2.2 Photograph M12: Labelled 'Haltonchesters 1960. East Granary'. Block 4 Trenches Fb14, Fc14, Fd14, Fe14

Figure 2.3 PhotographC241: Block 41 Trench Fc21 view looking south showing intersection between longitudinal sleeper walls and transverse wall

Figure 2.4 Photograph M13: Labelled 'Haltonchesters 1960. East Granary' Block 21 trench Fa24 and Fb24

Figure 2.5 Photograph M14: Block 24 Trench Fb23; the granary from the west with sleeper walls, robbed west wall and flagged base in view

Figure 3.1 The building complex to the west of the granary: plan

Figure 3.2 Gillam's schemes of interpretation for the area to the west of the granary in period I; A: 1960; B: 1961: plan

Figure 3.3 Photograph M17: Block 22 Trenches Ee25 Fa25 Fb25 from the west

Figure 3.4 Photograph M18: Block 15 trench Ed24 from the south, showing Period II wall 94 directly overlying Period I wall 92

Figure 3.5 Photograph C223: Block 22 Trench Ee25; the north-west corner of the trench with burnt daub deposit present in section

Figure 3.6 Photograph C206: Block 15 Trench Ed24, north-facing section showing a possible robber trench over Period I wall 92 and the destruction deposit in the south-east corner

Figure 3.7 Pottery from the destruction deposit; 1:4

Figure 4.1 The fragments of the late buildings: plan

Figure 4.2 Photograph M29: Block 7 trench Ea22 looking east; east end of late wall 49

Figure 4.3 Photograph M30: Block 7 trench Ea22 looking west; 'park-railing' blocks of wall 49 of late Building Fragment B

Figure 4.4 Photograph M25: Block 2 Trench Db25 Dc25 looking west

Figure 4.5 Photograph M26: Block 2 Trench Db25 Dc25 looking east,; wall bases and surface of late Building Fragment C

Figure 4.6 Photograph M28: Labelled 'Haltonchesters 1960. late fourth-century 'kerbs": Block 11 Trench Ea25/Eb25

Figure 5.1 The buildings to the south of the *via quintana*: plan

Figure 5.2 Photograph M27: Block 2 Trench Db25 Dc25 Dd25 from the east

Figure 5.3 Photograph M23: Block 29 Trench Db33 looking west

Figure 6.1 Period I Phase Plan

Figure 6.2 Period II Phase Plan

Figure 6.3 Phase Plan Period III/IV Phase Plan

Figure 7.1 Block 1: plan

Figure 7.2 Block 2: plan

Figure 7.3 Photograph M53a: Block 2 Trench Dc25

Figure 7.4 Block 4: plan

Figure 7.5 Block 5: plan

Figure 7.6 Photograph M32: Labelled 'Haltonchesters 1960. Corner of second-century building' Block 5 Trench Eb24

Figure 7.7 Photograph M33: Labelled 'Haltonchesters 1960. Fourth-century wall above second-century wall' Block 5 Trench Eb24

Figure 7.8 Block 7: plan of the early features

Figure 7.9 Block 7: plan of the later features

Figure 7.10 Photograph M1: Block 7 Trench Ea22, early structures from the west

Figure 7.11 Photograph M2: Block 7 Trench Ea22, early structures from the east

Figure 7.12 Photograph M3: Block 7 Trench Ea22, early flags 56–57 and wall 54 from the east

Figure 7.13 Photograph M34: Labelled 'Haltonchesters 1960. Early fourth-century wall above second-century wall'. Block 7 Trench Eb23 (?) south east leg from east

Figure 7.14 Photograph M35: Block 7 Ea22 north facing section at east end of block

Figure 7.15 Photograph C209 Block 7 Trench Ea22 north facing section – location of destruction deposit 240?

Figure 7.16 Block 8: plan

Figure 7.17 Blocks 9, 10 and 11: plans

Figure 7.18 Blocks 12 and 13: plans

Figure 7.19 Photograph M41a: Block 13, looking south

Figure 7.20 Photograph M42a: Block 13, looking north

Figure 7.21 Block 15: plan

Figure 7.22 Block 15 Trench Ed24: section of south face

Figure 7.23 M19: Block 15 Trench Ed24; from the east, showing Period II wall 94 overlying Period I wall 92

Figure 7.24 Photograph C213: Block 15 Trench Ed24 from the north

Figure 7.25 Block 16: plan

Figure 7.26 Photograph M44a: Labelled 'Haltonchesters 1960. Third-century flagging above 2nd century wall'. Block 16, looking north-east
Figure 7.27 Block 18: plan
Figure 7.28 Blocks 19 and 21: plans
Figure 7.29 Block 22: plan
Figure 7.30 Photograph M16: Block 22 Trenches Ee25 Fa25 Fb25 from east
Figure 7.31 Photograph M45a: Block 22 looking south
Figure 7.32 Photograph M46a: Block 22 Trenches Ee25 Fa25 Fb25 looking west showing late north-south wall 132
Figure 7.33 Photograph M47a: Block 22; wall 128 abutting granary west wall – secondary buttressing?
Figure 7.34 Photograph M48a: Block 22, looking north
Figure 7.35 Photograph M49a: Block 22 looking south
Figure 7.36 Photograph C220: Block 22 Trench Ee25 south facing section in north-west corner of trench with destruction deposit 133 evident
Figure 7.37 Block 23: plan
Figure 7.38 Blocks 24, 25 and 26: plans
Figure 7.39 Block 24 trench Fb23: section of east face
Figure 7.40 Photograph M37: Block 24 Trench Fa23 looking west; with foundation (137) revetted platform (143) and buttress for robbed granary west wall 136 in foreground
Figure 7.41 Photograph M39: Block 24 Trench Fa23; stone-revetted clay foundation 143 and buttress for granary west wall 136 with Period II wall 144 to west
Figure 7.42 Photograph M52a: Block 24 Trench Fa23; showing from left to right, late wall 145. Period II wall 144 and reveted clay foundation 143
Figure 7.43 Photograph M15: Labelled 'Haltonchesters 1960. East Granary'. Block 25 Trench Fd15, looking west showing granary sleeper walls 146 and 148
Figure 7.44 Block 28: plan
Figure 7.45 Block 29: plan
Figure 7.46 Photograph M36: Perhaps Block 29, Trench Da32 looking north?
Figure 7.47 Photograph M24: Block 29; Trench Db33 looking south

Figure 7.48 Block 32: plan
Figure 7.49 Photograph C235: Block 32 Trench Ea32 looking east
Figure 7.50 Block 35: plan
Figure 7.51 Block 36: plan
Figure 7.52 Blocks 37 and 38: plans
Figure 7.53 Block 39: plan
Figure 7.54 Block 39: section of west end of north face
Figure 7.55 Blocks 40, 41 and 43: plans
Figure 7.56 Photograph M20: Block 40; Trench Fa31 Fb31 from the west
Figure 7.57 Photograph M21: Block 40; Trench Fa31 Fb31 from the east
Figure 7.58 Photograph M22: Block 40; Trench Fa31 Fb31 from the south
Figure 7.59 Photograph M38: Block 43; Trench Fb15 looking north
Figure 8.1 Coins graph
Figure 9.1 Decorated samian: 8–40, 1:2
Figure 9.2 Decorated samian: 45–58, 1:2
Figure 9.3 Decorated samian: 61–70, 1:2
Figure 9.4 Decorated samian: 72–113, 1:2
Figure 9.5 Decorated samian: 114–132, 1:2
Figure 9.6 Samian potters' stamps: 1–8, 1:1
Figure 9.7 Samian potters' stamps. 9–20, 1:1
Figure 9.8 Samian potters' stamps. 21–30, 1:1
Figure 10.1 Other pottery: nos 1–41, 1:4
Figure 10.2 Other pottery: nos 42–74, 1:4
Figure 10.3 Other pottery: nos 75–101, 1:4
Figure 10.4 Other pottery: nos 102–132, 1:4
Figure 10.5 Other pottery: nos 133–164, 1:4
Figure 10.6 Other pottery: nos 165–192, 1:4
Figure 10.7 Other pottery: nos 194–202, 1:4
Figure 11.1 Small finds: nos 2–31, 1:2
Figure 11.2 Small finds: nos 32–58, 1:2
Figure 11.3 Small finds: nos 59–146, 1:2
Figure 11.4 Small finds: nos 159–211, 1:2

List of Tables

Table 2.1 Dating evidence for the granary
Table 3.1 Selected finds groups from the building complex to the west of the granary
Table 3.2 Dating evidence from the destruction deposit
Table 4.1 Finds associated with the late buildings
Appendix III Location of finds

Acknowledgements

Post-excavation analysis on the excavation archive was initially carried out by JND as a consultant funded directly by English Heritage. Subsequent editorial and drawing work was carried out by JND and Alan Williams in their posts of Director and Contracts Manager, respectively, of the Archaeological Practice, Newcastle University with funds provided by English Heritage. Final editing was funded by English Heritage through the agency of the Archaeological Practice Ltd.

Specialist reports were contributed by Lindsay Allason-Jones (Small Finds), Richard Brickstock (Coins) and Brenda Dickinson (Samian). Plans and sections were inked by Alan Williams (in a pre-digital era) and later scanned and enhanced by Mark Hoyle and JND. The small finds were drawn by Sandra Rowntree. Claire MacRae of the Archaeological Practice Ltd. undertook valuable copy-editing and repro work. Alan Rushworth of the same organisation provided equally valuable editing and management input including final editorial corrections and proofreading following the death of JND. Tony Wilmott and Mike Collins of English Heritage provided encouragement and editorial comment.

David Breeze, Beryl Charlton, Brian Dobson and other members of the Society of Antiquaries of Newcastle upon Tyne helped to identify the people in the back cover photo.

Finally, special thanks are due to David Sherlock of English Heritage who provided the initial impetus for the project shortly after the death of John Gillam, and then kept things moving with a gentle but insistent pressure.

Summary

This volume reports on the excavations at Haltonchesters Roman fort on Hadrian's Wall which were directed in 1960 and 1961 by John Gillam, one of the foremost northern frontier scholars of his generation. The excavations were carried out in the western part of the central range of the fort, a section of the west wall of the fort (including the *porta quintana*), the north end of the west half of the *retentura* and part of an annexe attached to the west side of the fort. The results obtained from this programme of investigation were to play a significant part in Gillam's highly influential writing and teaching in the years up until his death in 1987.

The opening introductory chapter provides the background to the investigation of the fort including a summary of earlier work. The nature of the 1960–61 excavation archive is described with an essential outline of the 'recording methodology employed and the problems this entailed in interpreting the data in the primary archive. The information contained therein has been reproduced here in a rationalised, intelligible and usable way in Chapter 7. This is presented as a Structural Synopsis supported by the plans and sections and a subset of the context information contained in the Finds Book. All the significant archaeological features are described within the framework of their respective Trench Blocks – groupings of one or more related trenches.

Chapters 2–4 interpret the information contained in the Structural Synopsis in relation to the principal recognisable structures investigated. These comprise the granary (Chapter 2), a building complex immediately to the west ultimately interpreted as a large courtyard building of two periods (Chapter 3) and a series of late Roman buildings, some displaying a distinctive construction technique involving the use of long slab sills with holes for (timber?) uprights which were colloquially labelled 'Park Railing' stones by the excavators (Chapter 4). A range of structures which were the subject of less extensive investigation in 1960–61, including parts of the fort's western defences and a set of possible barracks in the southern part of the fort, are described in Chapter 5.

Conclusions outlining the implications of the results for our wider understanding of the fort's development are set out in Chapter 6, providing the opportunity to reassess the preliminary interpretations of the results presented by Gillam. Amongst the issues considered are the date of the fort's initial construction, the evidence for a late second-century destruction level, the date and purpose of the western extension to the fort, the possible existence of a late third-century destruction episode, the phasing of the fourth-century buildings and the validity of Gillam's assertion that the fort was largely abandoned in the period *c.* AD 270–367.

Particular prominence is given in the report to consideration of Gillam's argument that much of the fort was destroyed as a result of an assault on the frontier defences at some stage during the late second century, which rested on the existence of a destruction deposit similar to that which he had previously uncovered during excavation at Corbridge. Examination of the primary archive provides clear confirmation that an *in situ* burnt deposit was encountered at a number of points in the area examined. However it is not possible to determine whether the destruction was the result of hostile action or accidental conflagration and it remains unclear whether the archaeological deposit should be associated with the turbulent events portrayed in the historical sources relating to the northern frontier in the late second century.

The specialist reports are incorporated in Chapters 8–11, describing the pottery (both fine samian tableware and coarseware), coins and small finds recovered. The coin report (Chapter 8) catalogues the full coin assemblage known from the site and assesses its implications. Amongst the small finds (Chapter 11), the amount and quality of jewellery discovered was especially noteworthy and there was some evidence that a jeweller's workshop was operating in the area of the fort. Of the military equipment, 50 percent could be specifically related to cavalry which would tend to support the identification of the third-fourth century garrison as the *ala Sabiniana*, based on the evidence of RIB 1433 and the *Notitia Dignitatum*.

Résumé

Ce volume rend compte des fouilles de Haltonchesters, fort romain sur le mur d'Hadrien, qui ont été dirigées en 1960 et 1961 par John Gillam, un des plus éminents savants de la frontière nord de sa génération. Les fouilles furent entreprises dans la partie ouest de l'alignement central du fort, une section du rempart ouest du fort (y compris la *porta quintana*), l'extrémité nord de la moitié ouest de la *retentura* et une partie d'une annexe attachée au flanc ouest du fort. Les résultats obtenus à la suite de cette campagne de fouilles devaient jouer un rôle significatif dans la forte influence des écrits et de l'enseignement de Gillam dans les années qui ont précédé sa mort en 1987.

Le premier chapitre d'introduction fournit l'arrière-plan aux fouilles du fort, y compris un résumé des travaux antérieurs. On y présente un descriptif de la nature des archives des fouilles de 1960–61 avec les grandes lignes essentielles de la méthodologie de répertoriage utilisée et des problèmes que cela a entraînés pour l'interprétation des données des archives primaires. Les renseignements qui s'y trouvent ont été reproduits ici d'une manière rationalisée, intelligible et utilisable au Chapitre 7. Ils sont présentés sous la forme d'un Synopsis Structural s'appuyant sur des plans et des coupes et un sous-ensemble de renseignements sur le contexte contenu dans le cahier de trouvailles. Tous les vestiges archéologiques significatifs sont décrits dans le cadre de leurs Blocs de Tranchées respectifs – des groupements d'une ou plusieurs tranchées apparentées.

Les chapitres 2–4 interprètent les renseignements contenus dans le Synopsis Structural dans leur relation avec les principales structures reconnaissables examinées. Celles-ci comprennent le grenier (Chapitre 2), un complexe de bâtiments immédiatement à l'ouest interprété finalement comme un grand bâtiment sur cour couvrant 2 périodes (Chapitre 3) et une série de bâtiments romains tardifs, certains révélant une technique de construction distinctive impliquant l'utilisation de longs seuils de pierre, percés de trous pour des montants (en bois ?), qui ont été familièrement nommés pierres à Grilles de Parc par les fouilleurs (Chapitre 4). On décrit dans le Chapitre 5 une série de structures qui ont fait l'objet de fouilles moins extensives en 1960–61, y compris certaines parties des défenses ouest du fort et un ensemble peut-être de baraques de cantonnement dans la partie sud du fort.

On expose, au Chapitre 6, les conclusions qui mettent en évidence les implications des résultats pour notre compréhension plus globale de l'évolution du fort, ce qui nous offre l'opportunité de réévaluer les interprétations préliminaires des résultats présentés par Gillam. Parmi les questions prises en considération, on trouve la datation de la première construction du fort, les témoignages d'un niveau de destruction de la fin du deuxième siècle, la date et le but de l'extension à l'ouest du fort, la possibilité de l'existence d'un épisode de destruction à la fin du troisième siècle, l'ordre d'apparition des bâtiments du quatrième siècle et la validité de l'affirmation de Gillam que le fort avait été en grande partie abandonné pendant la période vers 270–367 ap. J.-C.

On accorde, dans ce compte-rendu, une proéminence particulière à la considération de l'argument de Gillam selon lequel la destruction d'une grande partie du fort aurait été le résultat d'un assaut contre les défenses de la frontière à un certain stade vers la fin du deuxième siècle et qui reposait sur l'existence d'un dépôt de destruction semblable à celui qu'il avait mis au jour précédemment au cours d'excavations à Corbridge. L'étude des archives primaires vient clairement confirmer qu'on a bien constaté à certains endroits de la zone examinée la présence d'un dépôt calciné *in situ*. On ne peut pas, cependant, déterminer si la destruction était le résultat d'un acte d'hostilité ou une conflagration accidentelle et ce n'est pas clair si ce dépôt archéologique devrait être associé aux événements violents dépeints dans les sources historiques relatives à la frontière nord à la fin du deuxième siècle.

Les rapports spécialisés sont incorporés dans les Chapitres 8–11, ils décrivent la céramique (aussi bien la vaisselle samienne raffinée que la plus grossière), les monnaies et les menues trouvailles qui ont été découvertes. Le rapport sur la monnaie (chapitre 8) catalogue la collection complète de toutes les pièces connues du site et évalue son implication. Parmi les menues trouvailles (chapitre 11), la quantité et la qualité des bijoux découverts étaient particulièrement remarquables et des témoignages attestaient qu'un atelier de joaillier était en activité dans la zone du fort. Parmi les équipements militaires, 50 pour cent ont pu être rattachés à la cavalerie, ce qui tendrait à aller dans le sens de l'identification de la garnison du troisième-quatrième siècle comme étant l'*ala sabiniana*, sur la base des témoignages de RIB 1433 et de la *Notitia Dignitatum*.

Zusammenfassung

Dieser Band berichtet über die 1960 und 1961 am römischen Kastell von Haltonchesters am Hadrianswall durchgeführten Ausgrabungen, geleitet von John Gillam, einem der herausragendsten Erforscher der Nordgrenze des römischen Reiches seiner Generation. Die Ausgrabungen wurden im westlichen Teil des zentralen Gebäudekomplexes des Kastells durchgeführt, sowie in einem Abschnitt des Westwalles (inklusive der *porta quintana*), am nördlichen Ende der Westhälfte der *retentura* und in einem Teilbereich eines Anbaus an der Westseite des Kastells. Die Ergebnisse dieses Forschungsprogrammes sollten in den Jahren bis zu Gillams Tod 1987 in seiner einflussreichen Publikations- und Lehrtätigkeit eine bedeutende Rolle spielen.

Das Einführungskapitel berichtet über den Hintergrund der Forschungstätigkeit am Kastell und beinhaltet auch eine Zusammenfassung früherer Arbeiten. Die Eigenschaften des Ausgrabungsarchives von 1960–61 werden beschrieben und das Kapitel umfasst auch eine grundlegende Übersicht zur angewandten Dokumentationsweise, sowie der sich daraus ergebenden Probleme bei der Interpretation des Originalarchives. Die im Originalarchiv enthaltenen Informationen werden im vorliegenden Band in einer rationalisierten, verständlichen und nutzbaren Form in Kapitel 7 wiedergegeben. Dies nimmt hier die Gestalt einer Gebäudeübersicht an, die von den Plänen und Profilzeichnungen sowie einem Teil der im Fundbuch enthaltenen Befundinformationen ergänzt wird. Alle wichtigen archäologischen Befunde werden im Rahmen ihrer jeweiligen Schnittblocks – Gruppierungen von einem oder mehreren zusammengehörigen Grabungsschnitten – beschrieben.

In Kapiteln 2–4 werden die in der Gebäudeübersicht enthaltenen Informationen im Hinblick auf die wesentlichen erkennbaren Strukturen untersucht. Zu diesen gehören der Getreidespeicher (Kapitel 2), ein unmittelbar westlich davon gelegener Gebäudekomplex, der letztendlich als ein ausgedehnter, zweiperiodiger Bau mit Innenhof interpretiert wird (Kapitel 3) und eine Reihe spätrömischer Gebäude, von denen einige eine charakteristische Bautechnik aufweisen, die von den Ausgräbern scherzhaft als 'Parkgeländer'-Steine bezeichnet wurde: lange Schwellen aus Steinplatten sind mit Löchern für (hölzerne?) Pfosten versehen (Kapitel 4). Kapitel 5 beschreibt mehrere Gebäude, die 1960–61 weniger intensiv erforscht worden waren, darunter Teile der westlichen Befestigungsanlagen des Kastells und ein Reihe möglicher Soldatenunterkünfte im südlichen Teil des Kastells.

Kapitel 6 legt die wesentlichen Schlussfolgerungen dar, die sich aus den hier vorgestellten Ergebnissen für unser weiteres Verständnis der Entwicklung des Kastells ziehen lassen. Dies bietet auch eine Gelegenheit, Gilliams vorläufige Interpretation der Ergebnisse neu zu bewerten. Zu den hier behandelten Themen gehören die Datierung der Errichtung des Kastells, Hinweise auf eine Zerstörungsschicht aus dem späten zweiten Jahrhundert, Datierung und Zweck des westlichen Anbaus am Kastell, die mögliche Existenz einer Zerstörungsepisode im späten dritten Jahrhundert, die Abfolge der Gebäude aus dem vierten Jahrhundert und die Gültigkeit von Gilliams Behauptung, dass das Kastell im Zeitraum von *ca.* 270–367 n. Chr. weitgehend verlassen war.

Ein wesentliches Thema des Berichtes ist die Diskussion von Gilliams Argument, dass das Kastell im Zuge eines Angriffs auf die Grenzbefestigungen irgendwann im Laufe des zweiten Jahrhunderts zerstört worden sei. Diese Idee basierte auf der Existenz eines Zerstörungshorizontes, ähnlich dem, den Gilliam bereits früher, während der Ausgrabung in Corbridge, identifiziert hatte. Eine Untersuchung des Originalarchives bestätigt zweifelsfrei, dass eine Brandschicht an verschiedenen Orten des untersuchten Areals *in situ* angetroffen worden war. Es ist jedoch unmöglich zu klären, ob diese Zerstörung das Ergebnis feindlicher Übergriffe oder eines versehentlichen Brandes war. So bleibt es unklar, ob diese archäologische Schicht mit den turbulenten Ereignissen in Verbindung gebracht werden kann, die sich laut historischer Quellen im späten zweiten Jahrhundert an der Nordgrenze des Reiches abspielten.

Kapitel 8–11 beinhalten die Berichte verschiedener Spezialisten zu Keramik (sowohl feines Sigillatageschirr als auch Grobkeramik), Münzen und anderen Kleinfunden. Der Bericht zu den Münzen (Kapitel 8) umfasst einen Katalog aller auf der Grabung aufgefundenen Exemplare und wertet ihre weitere Bedeutung aus. Unter den Kleinfunden (Kapitel 11) lassen sich vor allem die Menge und Qualität der Schmuckgegenstände hervorheben und es gibt einige Hinweise, dass sich auf dem Gelände des Kastells eine Juwelierwerkstatt befand. Von den aufgefundenen militärischen Ausrüstungsgegenständen konnten 50% speziell der Kavallerie zugeordnet werden, was die auf RIB 1433 und der *Notitia Dignitatum* basierende Identifizierung der hier im dritten und vierten Jahrhundert stationierten Garnison als die *ala Sabiniana* unterstützt.

1. Introduction

This report presents the results of the excavations directed, in 1960 and 1961, by Mr J. P. Gillam within the fort at Haltonchesters. The work of each season lasted about six weeks, from early May to mid-June. It was carried out in the area to the south of the B6318 Newcastle to Carlisle road and to the west of the lane which runs from the B6318 to Halton village. Within the investigated area lie the western part of the central range of the fort, a section of the west wall of the fort (including the *porta quintana*), the north end of the west half of the *retentura* and part of an annexe attached to the west side of the fort. Fig. 1.2 shows the trench layout of the excavations in the central area of the fort.

Previous Work
Fig. 1.1 shows the location and dates of the various campaigns of excavation.

1823 and 1827
A substantial bathhouse was excavated, partly in 1823 and completely in 1827 (Birley 1961, 170). John Hodgson provided a detailed description with plan and sections by John Dobson (Hodgson 1840, 179, 316–20). Although it was definitely situated in the northern part of the fort (Hodgson 1840, 179), ambiguities in Hodgson's text gave rise to a degree of uncertainty regarding its precise position (summarised by Blood and Bowden 1990, 60). The argument that it was situated in the north-west corner, based on parchmarks visible on aerial photographs and the negative evidence provided by the 1936 excavations in the north-east quarter, seems to have been confirmed by the 1995 geophysical survey (Berry and Taylor 1997, 57; cf. Daniels 1978, 87). A fourth-century date has been attributed to this bathhouse on the grounds that the Hadrianic bathhouse probably lay outside the fort (beside Fences Burn perhaps; cf. Blood and Bowden 1990, 60–1) and the remains of a third-century bathhouse have been found in the south-west extension (Jarrett 1959, 187).

1935 and 1936
In 1935 the North of England Excavation Committee undertook trial trenching in the extension on the west side of the fort, at the junction of the extension wall with Hadrian's Wall. In 1936 the North of England Excavation Committee in collaboration with Durham University Excavation Committee excavated the east, west and north gateways of the fort and examined buildings in the east half of the *praetentura*.

The gateways exhibited varying degrees of preservation (Simpson and Richmond 1937). In each case most of the superstructure had been robbed, and a coal shaft had been sunk through the north carriageway of the east gate during the nineteenth century. However, the northern gatetowers of the east and west gates were built over the former ditch of Hadrian's Wall, requiring massive stepped foundations set on rubble platforms in the bottom of the ditch. The surviving condition of these substructures is impressive. A broken, Hadrianic dedication slab was found face down in front of the central pier of the west gate (RIB 1427), having fallen from the haunch of the pier at some stage (Simpson and Richmond 1937, 158). This remains one of the most significant Hadrianic documents from the Wall, demonstrating that work on the forts was already underway before the end of Aulus Platorius Nepos' governorship (Simpson and Richmond 1937, 161–2).

To the east of the north gate, in 1936, a solid base of pitched stone and clay was found set into the north rampart, (Simpson and Richmond 1937, 167–8). A similar feature may have existed on the west curtain of the *praetentura*, where the wall was found to be nine feet thick at one point, according to Bruce's informant, when it was revealed during the 1820s (Bruce 1851, 160; 1867, 106). These features were interpreted by both Bruce and Richmond as solid, elevated platforms for torsion artillery, and labelled *ballistaria*, adopting the term mentioned in two inscriptions from High Rochester (RIB 1280, 1281).

In the eastern *praetentura* two phases of barracks, stables and possible stores buildings were uncovered. Very few internal partitions were revealed in the primary building ranges, but the overlying ranges were more

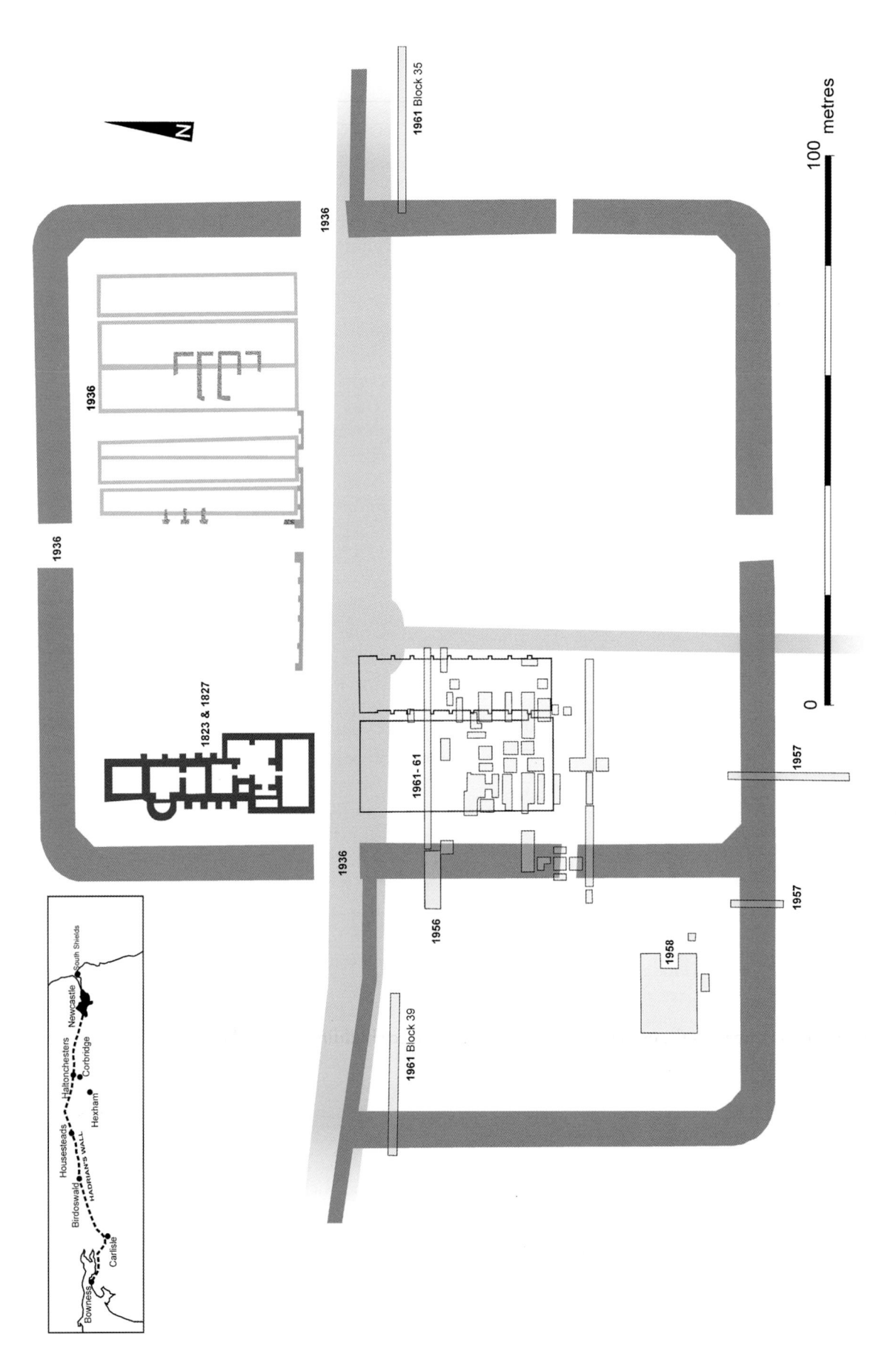

Figure 1.1. Location of the site; location and dates of the various campaigns of excavation.

informative, despite their patchy survival, and have gained added significance as a result of recent discoveries elsewhere on the Wall. The secondary buildings are divided into individual *contubernia*, each of which appears to contain a drain in its front half. They can be interpreted as stable-barracks, of the kind recently identified at Wallsend (Hodgson 1999, 86–8; and now 2003, 37–121) and known at a number of forts on the German frontier as a result of the work of Sebastian Sommer. These barracks are considered to have been for the use of cavalry, three troopers being accommodated in the back room, whilst their horses were stabled in the front room, where the central drain could carry away or collect the horses' urine. This probably represents the third-century barrack layout at Haltonchesters (cf. Hodgson 2003, 79, 119–20), but all evidence of any later Roman remodelling, overlying this phase, has been removed by the ploughing carried out this part of the fort since the early nineteenth century.

Although little is known of the core of the building, the 1936 excavations revealed a substantial forehall to the headquarters building, straddling the *via principalis* and supported on stone piers (Simpson and Richmond 1937, 168–70). Conventionally, this forehall has been interpreted as a cavalry drill hall (*basilica equestris exercitatoria*; cf. Simpson and Richmond 1937, 170), but see now Hodgson (2003, 176–82) for discussion of the forehall at Wallsend (esp. 181–2 for the possible function of such buildings as ceremonial assembly areas), and Wilmott (1997, 95–8; 2001, 70–72) for an example at Birdoswald of a different building type which represents a much more convincing *basilica exercitatoria*.

1956–58

Between 1956 and 1958 work was carried out under the direction of M. G. Jarrett within the south-western part of the fort including the extension. In 1956 a section was cut across the west rampart of the primary fort. In 1957 sections were cut through the south rampart of the fort and through the south rampart of the extension. Both of the trenches excavated in 1957 uncovered the remains of buildings set into the rampart area (Jarrett 1959, 187–8; 1960, 154–5, 157–8). In 1958 the west ditches of the primary fort, within the area of the extension, were examined, revealing a sequence of overlying buildings, beginning with a bath-house, apparently of Severan date. This was replaced by a large, clay-floored workshop, built around a paved courtyard, which was associated with numerous hearths with evidence of metalworking and was assigned to 'the reconstruction of Constantius Caesar' (*c.* AD 300). The workshop was replaced in turn by a further structural phase, which was associated with much late fourth-century pottery and comprised two long narrow buildings, separated by a narrow eavesdrip and featuring the use of stone sill-wall probably to support a timber-framed superstructure. Most of the results of the work on the defences were published (Jarrett 1959 and 1960). However, detailed publication of the 1958 season's results was held over, the intention being to undertake further work inside the extension.

The Excavations of 1960–61: Post-Excavation History

Following the completion of the work in 1961, JPG incorporated the principal conclusions of his interpretation into his ongoing round of teaching and research. Students, researchers, specialists and conference goers all came to hear of these conclusions and three, in particular, were absorbed into the broad canon (broad in the sense that it incorporates not only published, printed work, but also a constantly changing oral tradition derived on a more informal basis from personal contact in both academic and social contexts) of Northern Frontier Studies: firstly, there was evidence of a late second-century destruction on the site, which bore comparison with what was claimed as a similar destruction at Corbridge; secondly, an 80–100 year hiatus, or at any rate severe reduction in intensity of occupation, between *c.* 270–370 AD, was postulated; thirdly, the latest Roman buildings on the site employed an interesting and, at the time, a-typical constructional technique which was labelled "Park Railings" by the excavators. Beyond this, little work seems to have been done on preparing the records of the excavation for publication. None of the pottery seems to have been drawn and no finished plans were produced beyond general ones for synthetic works such as the Hadrian's Wall Handbook. No draft text or even preparatory notes are known to exist.

The finds were stored in Newcastle University (King's College, Durham, as it was at the time of the excavations), first in the Classics Department in rooms in the Percy Building and the Armstrong Building, then when the Archaeology Department came into being in 1972, partly in the new Department's rooms above the Museum of Antiquities and partly in the two former locations. Towards the end of 1978 the Department acquired an annexe, in Haymarket House (a block of mostly nineteenth-century buildings fronting on to the Haymarket and adjacent to an Odeon cinema) and most of the finds were moved there (apart from a portion which had already moved to the store of the Museum of Antiquities in the Daysh Building). In 1986 both Haymarket House and the Odeon were demolished and the portion of finds which had resided there moved with the Department Annexe to the immediately adjacent

Line Building. During all this time they remained largely untouched, although a small amount of pottery was reboxed sometime towards the end of the seventies. The one major exception to the foregoing was the decorated and stamped samian which was sent, soon after the excavations to Brian Hartley and Brenda Dickinson who examined it and wrote a full report before returning it to JPG. Evidently JPG then deposited the material in Corbridge Museum, probably as a matter of temporary convenience, where it remained until rediscovered in 2007. As a result the decorated vessels (and stamps) have been illustrated by means of digital photographs – which could be undertaken quickly at minimum cost at what was then a very late stage in the report preparation – rather than drawn illustrations in the conventional manner.

The plans, Finds Book and photographs were kept by JPG at his house in Corbridge. Following his death in 1986 these were transferred to the Archive of the Department of Archaeology in Newcastle (the photographs were held for a short time by Mrs V. G. Swan, RCHM, York). Copies of the plans are now held by the National Monuments Record.

Consultation with English Heritage about the possibility of producing a final report began in 1988. An evaluation of the archive material was carried out by JND in 1990. English Heritage approved grant aid to the project in December, 1993, with a supplement in 1995 for additional drawing work. The major part of the stratigraphic analysis and writing was carried out by JND in 1994 and a reasonably complete draft text was in existence by 1995. Between 1995 and its dissolution in 2002, JND was Director of the Archaeological Practice at Newcastle University and the project stalled due to pressure of other work. In 2004, English Heritage agreed to provide additional grant aid to bring the project to completion.

The Archive

Primary Excavation Archive

1) Documentary

i) Plans and Sections. These were drawn on graph paper to an imperial scale, mostly 1:24. Most sheets carry a number of drawings, usually of different trenches. By and large only stone structures are shown and these are usually coloured to indicate their period interpretation: green is usually used to represent Period I, blue is Period II and red is Period III/IV. There are very few sections.

As a reference tool during the production of the report each sheet was given a unique number with a prefix "PI" (for Plan Index).

ii) The Finds Book. The records of the finds groups from all the seasons from 1956 to 1961 are contained in one hard-backed foolscap cash ledger. The following details are recorded:

a) Date
b) Finds-group code. This is a two letter code which begins at AA and proceeds alphabetically: AA, AB, AC, AD and so on.
c) Trench identifier. In 1960 a site grid was laid out across the whole of the extension and the part of the fort which lay to the south of the B6318 and to the west of the minor road to Halton. Major intervals were every 50 feet and were identified on the x axis by capital letters and on the y axis by integer numbers; minor intervals were every 10 feet and were identified on the x axis by lower case numbers and on the y axis by integer numbers. Thus the full indentifier for a peg consisted on two letters and two integer numbers, *e.g.* Ea23. The part of the scheme which relates to the central area of the 1960–61 excavations is shown on Fig. 1.2. Trenches seem to have taken the identifier of the nearest grid peg. This system worked reasonably well in the 1960 season where there were comparatively few, reasonably well spaced trenches but increasingly broke down in 1961 as trenches proliferated and previously separate trenches were amalgamated.
d) A brief description of the level or feature from which the finds-group came, or the excavation process which resulted in the recovery of the finds-group (*e.g.*, Cleaning of surface, or removal of baulk).
e) A list of the classes of finds comprising the finds-group, *e.g.*, samian, coarse pottery, amphora, bone.

iii) Photographs
a) Black and White: Thirty-nine small prints (most of them 5 1/2" × 3 1/2") numbered 1–39, plus a further fourteen unnumbered examples contained in an envelope misleadingly marked 'Jarrett 1958', are known. The numbers on the prints (prefixed by "M") have been used in this report to identify the photographs. The unnumbered examples have been allocated an M number followed by "a" to indicate this was not a primary archive reference, but was added during the production of this report. The additional numbers continue the original sequence, beginning with M40a, and run in order of numbered trench block shown (see below). Nos M4–11 simply show stonework disturbed by a Newcastle and Gateshead Water Board trench to the east of the fort in 1961 and are not reproduced here. The whereabouts of the negatives is not known.
b) Colour transparency: Following the death of Charles Daniels in 1996, thirty-one colour transparencies were found among his papers in the Department of Archaeology at Newcastle University. These were held in two twenty-four pocket plastic slide wallets. Each slide was accompanied by a small square cut from an index card on which was written, in JPG's handwriting, the site code for Haltonchesters and a reference number.

1. Introduction   5

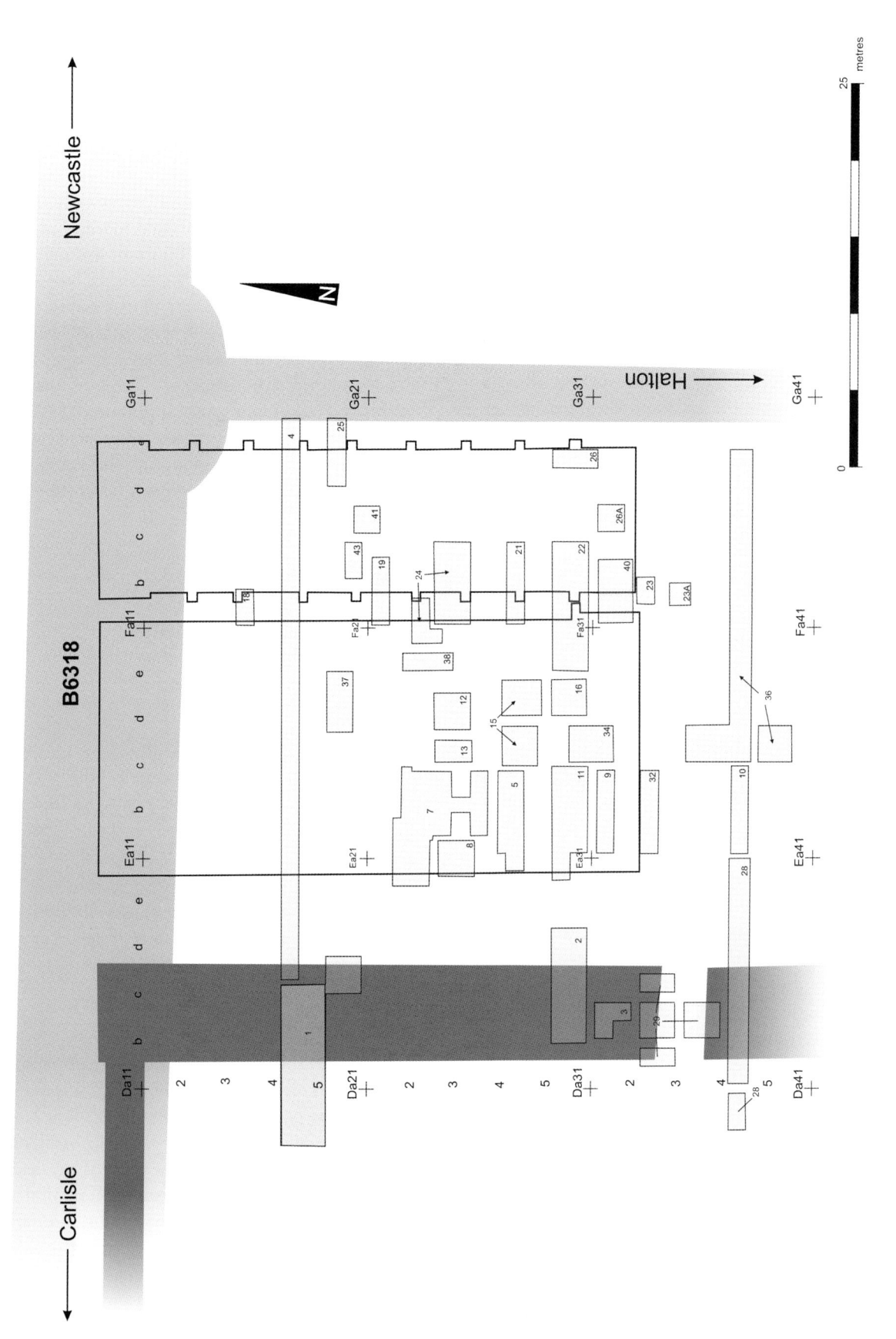

Figure 1.2. The excavations of 1960–61, trench layout in the central area.

This number (prefixed by "C") has been used in this report to reference the slides. For the most part they duplicate the views of the black and white prints.

2) Artefactual
Coins
Pottery
Small Finds *etc.*

Problems inherent in the Primary Archive
Site notebooks, *i.e.* a record of the archaeological contexts, were not used. This was a policy decision by JPG, his view being that all the information which would be written in a Site Notebook could more usefully appear on the plans and in the Finds Book. The way the 'Gillam system' of recording (and JPG did regard it as a planned system rather than a result of happenstance) was intended to work was as a time saving method which cut out the drudgery of the Site Notebook: the plans and sections would clearly show all important structural relationships and would be fully (and from conversations with JPG I clearly remember his emphasis on the word 'fully') annotated with all information which could not be pictorially represented. The Finds Book would contain a record of the artefacts associated with a level or feature, and a fuller description of that level or feature. This was the system used at Corbridge in the years of the Training Excavation between the end of the last war and 1973, and at many of JPG's numerous other excavations in the north-east.

Leaving aside other considerations regarding the advisability of such a system, the one major deficiency is that no method was used of uniquely identifying each archaeological context. Each finds group was uniquely identified, using the double letter code, but the same was not done for the context of the group. The only data linking an entry in the Finds Book to a plan or section were the trench designator and the free text description of the context, but little or no attempt was made to control the terminology used in the textual description so that it could function as a unique identifier. Thus, in most cases the description is not sufficiently unambiguous to enable precise location of the context in relation to other contexts. This is such a fundamental flaw, and it is so obvious with hindsight, that it cannot simply be dismissed as the result of stupidity, but must rather be seen as the product of a belief-system current at the time which is not fully appreciated now. I tend now to think that it stems to a great extent from JPG's preoccupation with pottery. I would hazard a guess that he felt himself to be, metaphorically speaking, working outwards towards the structures, from within the finds, and thus by association, from within the finds recording system. There is a certain amount of internal relatedness about some of the entries in the Finds Book (actually more visible in the Corbridge records than at Haltonchesters) which, I think, tends to confirm this view, and in places (again more in the Corbridge records) JPG had begun to identify, by marginal notes and symbols, collections of related finds groups, but without giving any further clues to the location of individual contexts. The suggestion is that he intended his finished interpretative scheme to be expressed through a finds book 'marked up' with a set of instructions relating important groups within the book, enabling the resulting outline to be overlain, both figuratively and to a certain extent physically, on to the structural plan. Within this kind of thinking, precise location of individual contexts appears less important than identification of groups of artefacts.

Be this as it may, much of the annotation of the plans is not detailed enough, from our point of view now, and JPG never finished 'marking up' the Finds Book; the finished interpretative scheme was never transferred from his memory.

Secondary Excavation Archive
1) The typescript of an interim report of the 1961 season by J. P. Gillam, dated June 1961.
2) The short published interim report in 'Roman Britain in 1960'.
3) The short published interim report in 'Roman Britain in 1961'.
4) References to the excavations in Gillam and Mann's article "The Northern British Frontier from Antoninus Pius to Caracalla" (Gillam and Mann, 1970).
5) References to the excavations in Gillam's article "The Frontier after Hadrian – A History of the Problem" (Gillam 1974).

Since the above form the principal surviving evidence for JPG's interpretation of the results of the excavation, they are reproduced verbatim in Appendix I.

Report Methodology
It is now (2006) forty-five years since the completion of the two seasons of excavations with which this report is concerned. The person who directed the work is dead and the archive, while containing most, if not all, of the primary material, is almost totally devoid of any detailed interpretations or even the most rudimentary drafts for a final report. These circumstances impose limitations on the interpretation which can be wrested from the data and necessitate a clear statement of method and approach before such interpretation can be presented.

For a researcher writing up an excavation directed by persons no longer living, and left with an archive which is flawed or inadequate in some way, perhaps the greatest temptation is to try and supplement the dataset from the memories of people still living, who were connected with the excavation. The problem with this kind of approach is that it takes no account of the memory's lack of accuracy in recording an event in the first place nor of the *post facto* influence of later interpretations, hypotheses and overviews. Thus, it attempts to put together a coherent story out of what usually turns out to be a contradictory set of partial memories, using a methodology which, at best, is not fully supportable, and, at worst is fundamentally flawed. The prime objective of this report is therefore to present what now survives of the primary data in as clear and as comprehensible fashion as possible, together with whatever interpretation can be gleaned from the written record, and to accompany this with an estimation of whether the former will support the latter.

The Presentation of the Primary Archive

The style of presentation most favoured by Richmond was that of the historical narrative based upon a body of archaeological evidence which was more often implied than objectively presented, *i.e.* based upon selections from the body of archaeological evidence which were loosely woven into the historical account rather than being separately presented. Whilst this seamless narrative made for interesting, often compelling reading, it also more often than not prevented the reader from finding his way back to the original data thus making any kind of independent assessment of the evidence impossible. Gillam, as a follower of Richmond, also favoured this approach, regarding the presentation of too much primary data as unsightly scaffolding.

Far removed as we now are from the time of the original excavations, and with an archive of such limited extent, we have little choice but to present all of this 'unsightly scaffolding'. Simply stated, our aim has been to reproduce the primary archive in a rationalised, intelligible and usable way, in order to obviate the need for future researchers to return to it, since it is not of itself in a very user-friendly state, without in any way preventing such a return.

The information in the primary archive is presented as a Structural Synopsis supported by the Plans and Sections and a subset of the context information contained in the Finds Book.

Structural Synopsis (Chapter 7)

This is a description of all the significant archaeological features. It is organised as a series of Trench Blocks which are groupings of one or more related trenches. This system was adopted as a functional solution to the inconsistencies of the original trench reference system (see above under Primary Excavation Archive, Finds Book, Trench Identifier).

Within each Trench Block all the significant archaeological features which can be identified from the plans and sections, or from entries in the Finds Book, are listed. Each feature has been allocated an identifying number. These do not always run in strict sequence within each Trench Block since it was necessary to add and insert numbers after the creation of the main sequence, and a total re-numbering was considered to have greater potential danger (in that it is always difficult after such a re-numbering to track down and correct all the references to the original number system) than a non-linear sequence.

In presenting evidence, the Structural Synopsis confines itself to what can be substantiated from the primary archive. Wherever possible marginal annotations from the plans have been incorporated verbatim. Where an interpretation is given this is the interpretation which was offered or inferred at or soon after the time of excavation.

It is important to emphasise again that the three key reference systems used in this report, that for the archive plans (Pl), for the Trench Blocks and for the significant archaeological features, do not originate from the primary archive but have been grafted on as reference tools during the production of the report.

Plans and sections

These are, by and large, simply tracings from the originals. Detail that is obviously superfluous has been cut out. Phase information, represented on the originals using colour shading, is given in the Structural Synopsis (Chapter 7).

Finds

Chapters 8 – 11 present the coins, decorated and stamped samian, other pottery, and small finds.

Secondary Sources

These are presented in Appendix I.

Finds Group Descriptions

Appendix II presents a subset of the entries from the Finds Book. This includes all the finds groups whose provenance can be more or less established, together with the description of the context as it is given in the Finds Book. For the difficulties of establishing such provenance see above 'Problems inherent in the Primary Archive'.

Finds Locations

Appendix III presents a table (Table III.1) which maps finds appearing in the specialist reports to finds groups.

Interpretation of the Primary Archive

Interpreted summaries of the information presented in the Structural Synopsis (Chapter 7) and organised according to recognisable buildings or building complexes and periods are presented in Chapters 2–5. Conclusions are presented in Chapter 6.

2. The Granary

The remains of the granary lie on the east side of the area excavated in 1960 and 1961, *c.* 28.9m east of the original west wall of the fort (inner face fort wall – outer face granary west wall) and hard up against the field boundary on the west side of the minor road which runs to Halton from the Newcastle to Carlisle road (Fig. 2.1). The northern end of the building was not exposed, since it lies under the Newcastle to Carlisle road. The excavated evidence shows that the building was at least 27.4 metres long (measured on overall plan Pl 3). In his report published in *Roman Britain in 1961* (see Appendix I), John Gillam estimated its length as 135 ft (41.2m) on the basis of the known position of the main west gate. Its width was close to 10m (measured from centre to centre of the east and west wall robber trenches on the detail plan of Block 4 (Pl 17)).

Trenches were cut across the line of the main walls in nine places (Blocks 4 twice, 18, 19, 21, 22, 24, 25, 26). In four of these (Blocks 4 both walls, 18, 24) the walls were completely robbed out. The best preserved length of wall occurred in Block 22 (123: south wall, 124: west wall); here the south wall was *c.* 1.18m wide, the west wall *c.* 0.7m wide; they were well built, faced with a well mortared core, and surviving four courses high in places. In Block 19 the west wall (113) was *c.* 0.89m wide, heavily mortared and survived five courses high in places. In Block 21 the west wall was *c.* 0.77m wide and four courses survived in places (117: west wall); here too the south side of a possible vent was found. In Block 25 the east wall was *c.* 0.77m and survived one or two courses high (146).

Inside the building parts of fourteen sleeper walls were found. In the northern half of the building the sleeper walls were aligned with the longitudinal axis of the building; in the southern half they ran across the building. The two sets were probably contemporary. Block 41 revealed an intersection between three of the north–south walls and one of the transverse walls.

Only short stretches of individual sleeper walls were revealed so it is unclear whether each wall ran uninterruptedly across or along the building, or whether it was divided up into shorter lengths. JPG restored them in the former state.

The walls were roughly faced. The wall in Block 25 is described as "heavily mortared", but apart from this no information is given on the plans of any bonding material. The width varied between a minimum of 0.41m (Block 21) and a maximum of 0.77m (Block 22). Nowhere did they survive more than three courses high.

The foundations for the granary consisted of a massive "raft" (as it is consistently referred to on the plans and in the Finds Book) of broken limestone overlain in turn by a layer of stiff yellow clay and then by a level of large flagstones. This seems to have extended under the whole area covered by the granary and to have been laid as a single operation prior to the erection of either main or sleeper walls. Elements of the foundation were recorded in the following Blocks: 4 (10, 13, 14, 17, 18, 20), 21 (120), 24 (137, 141), 25 (149).

On the west side of the granary, evidence was found of a kerb running from north to south on the line of the outer edge of the buttresses of the main west wall. This feature occurred in the following Blocks: 19 (115), 22 (127), 24 (143). It consisted of a single line of stones faced only on the west side. It was at least two courses high in Block 24. In Block 22 its top was level with the bottom of the lowest visible course of the main west wall (124). In Block 24 it partly underlay the buttress (136) of the main west wall. This clearly indicates that its construction predated that of the buttress and the most likely explanation of its function would seem to be that it was a kerb for the foundation raft. This argument is slightly vitiated by the fact that no foundations are shown in combination with the kerb on any of the plans though this could have been because they were either not exposed or were completely robbed out.

In the trench blocks at the south-west corner of the granary evidence was found for two successive extensions to the building, one extending it *c.* 2.4m further south, the other *c.* 3.96m (Blocks 22 (126), 40 (214, 215, 216, 217) 23 (136)). Only parts of the west and south walls and the south-west corners of these extensions were found. The larger, outer extension abutted the south wall of the granary at the west buttress; the west wall of the smaller, inner extension was situated immediately

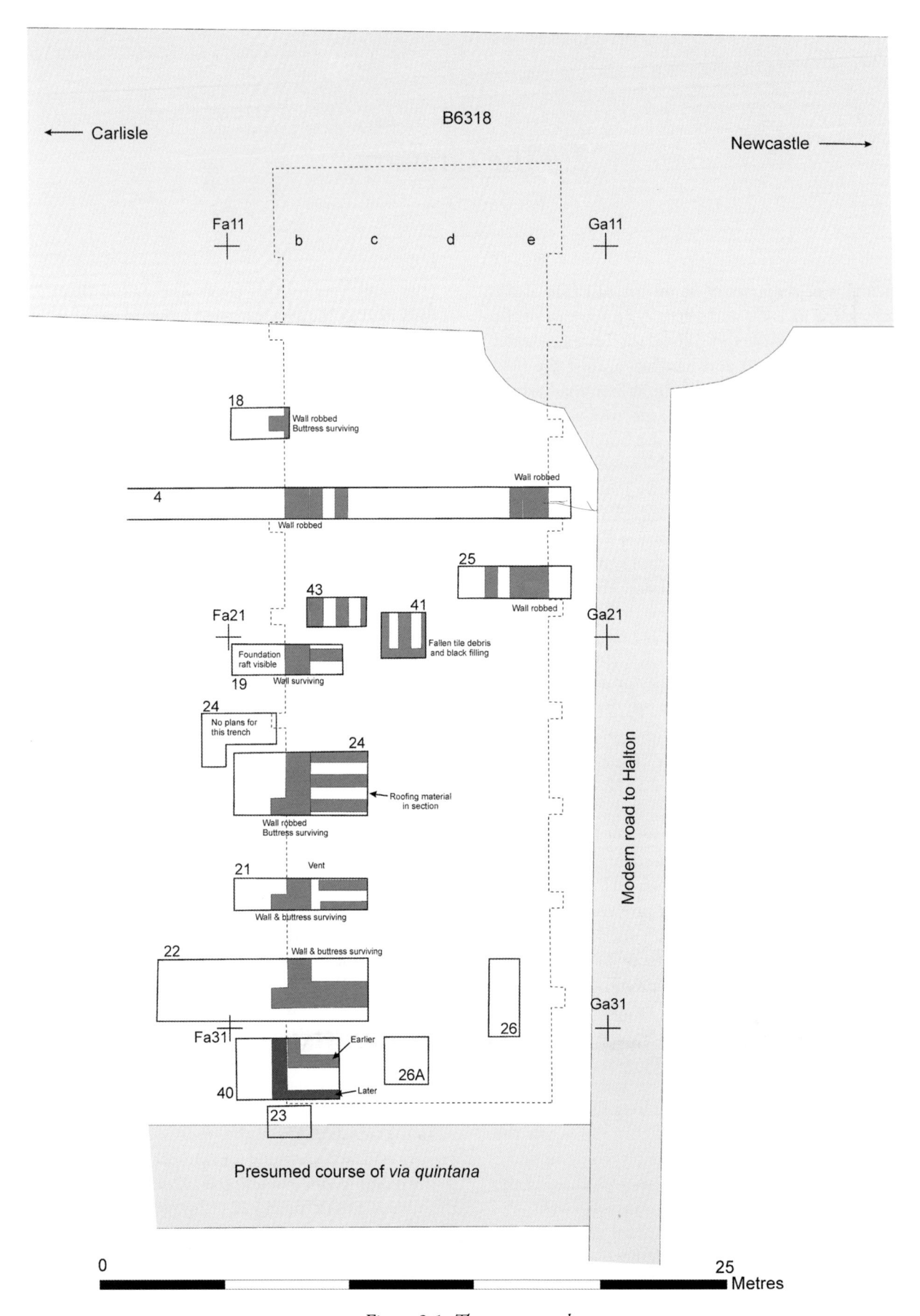

Figure 2.1. The granary: plan.

adjacent to that of the outer. The west wall of the outer was *c.* 0.77m wide and survived three courses high in places. Of the inner two courses survived in places; the west wall was *c.* 0.72m wide and the south wall was *c.* 0.62m wide. It is not clear which was the earlier. On the general plan Pl 3, JPG showed the outer as Period I and the inner as Period II but pottery from packing between the north end of the west wall of the outer, and the buttress suggests that the outer could not have been earlier than the late second century AD (see Block 22, 126 for more detail). They are referred to on the plans and in the Finds Book as Porticoes or Loading Bays, though without knowing more about their superstructure it is difficult to decide which is the correct designation.

There is evidence for two different kinds of roofing material associated with the granary (or at least, recovered from the site of the granary). A layer of stone flags (probably sandstone) is recorded in Block 24 while tile debris is recorded in Block 41 (see entries in the Structural Synopsis (Chapter 7) for the detailed argument as to the identification of the material).

JPG was of the opinion that the building was destroyed by fire:

> It was finally destroyed late in the third century, when its wooden floor and the grain which stood on it were charred, and its sandstone roof collapsed.
> (Typed Interim, June 1961; see Appendix I).

> …destroyed by fire….
> (RB in 1961; see Appendix I).

Figure 2.2. Photograph M12: Labelled 'Haltonchesters 1960. East Granary'; Block 4 Trenches Fb14 Fc14 Fd14 Fe14, looking east, showing granary sleeper walls 11 and 12, and 15 and 16 (foreground), flagging 17 and foundation raft 20.

Figure 2.3. Photograph C241: Block 41 Trench Fc21; view looking south showing the intersection between longitudinal sleeper walls 222–224 and transverse wall 225.

Figure 2.4. Photograph M13: Labelled 'Haltonchesters 1960. East Granary'; Block 21 Trench Fa24 Fb24; the granary from west showing sleeper walls 118 and 119, flagged base 120 and west wall 117 with possible vent.

The extant evidence for this is slight. No evidence of burning below the layer of roofing material can be seen in the east section in Block 24 (see Fig. 7.39 and Fig. 2.5, photograph M14). A Finds Book entry (61EJ) for Block 41 refers to 'black filling above and between granary support walls' (see Structural Synopsis (Chapter 7), Block 41, 227).

Dating

Table 2.1 below sets out the dating evidence for the granary. Entries in italics shown under 'Description' are taken verbatim from the Finds Book. Other entries represent subsequent commentary by Dore.

JPG's opinion on the dating of the granary, derived from his printed and published comments (see Appendix I) can be summarised as follows:

1. The inception of the building is Hadrianic by implication in that it was believed to be the first building on its site.
2. It received minor repairs early in the third century.
3. It was destroyed by fire late in the third century.

Considering first the date of inception of the building, the most promising finds groups are 60GH and 60DX both of which appear to have been sealed in the foundation raft, and 61HM which is less securely sealed. The vessel from 60DX is not particularly diagnostic but the vessels from the other two groups (samian: a Curle 15 and a Dr. 18/31 in Les Martres de Veyre fabric) are quite consistent with a Hadrianic date for the building.

Figure 2.5. Photograph M14: Block 24 Trench Fb23; the granary from the west, with sleeper walls 138, 139 and 140, robbed west wall 136 and flagged base 141 in view. The east section with fallen roofing slates 142 can be seen in the background.

It is not clear whether the 'minor repairs' referred to by JPG encompassed anything more than the renewal of the loading bay at the south end of the building. The presence in 61CT of a BB1 bowl with grooved flange (Other Pottery: 127) provides a *terminus post quem* at the end of the second century AD for this event.

There is no useful dating evidence for the end of the building. There is a finds group from immediately below the fallen roofing slates in Block 24 (61AU) but the only diagnostic vessel known from this is a beaker (probably from Colchester) which is likely to date to the mid–late second century AD.

There is no extant evidence to support JPG's claim that

> fragments of buildings of the character of Period IV (*i.e. fourth century*) were found above its ruins.
>
> (RB in 1961; see Appendix I)

Table 2.1. Dating Evidence for the Granary.

Finds Group	Description	Material
BLOCK 4		
60BG	Black filling of robber trench of earlier N/S stone wall in W part of trench. 26 ins and on down.	Coarseware present; nothing diagnostic.
60GH	Below the "flags". Depth c. 38 ins. These are assumed to be the flags of the foundation raft.	Other pottery: 5: plain samian: 1 wall sherd Curle 15.
BLOCK 19		
60DX	Within the raft.	Other pottery: 101: Large grey-ware jar.
60FA	Cleaning in the structure of the raft. depth 28 ins.	Other pottery: 102: BB2 round rim bowl, and wall sherds of calcite gritted ware. late 3rd C (?) Small finds: 189
60FO	Cleaning raft to top of clay foundation.	
60GI	Inside raft at the E end of the trench.	
60HU	Between raft edge and heavy W wall depth c. 38 ins.	1 small rim sherd of a jar in calcite gritted ware, possibly a Huntcliff type.
60IL	Between edge of raft and the W face of the heavy (granary) wall.	
BLOCK 21		
60HQ	Position of robbed W wall of granary max depth 38 ins.	Samian: Dr 31R and BB2 are present. 2nd half 2nd C AD. Small finds: 66
BLOCK 22		
61HM	Bottom level above yellow clay. It is not clear whether this was sealed by the flags of the raft.	Other pottery: 124: plain samian: 5 rim sherds, 4 wall sherds Dr 18/31 CG (Les Martres de Veyre fabric).
61CT	In packing between buttress and ?portico wall at SW corner of granary, below level of top of Period I wall and above top of raft, or foundations of Period I wall.	Other pottery: 127: BB1 bowl with grooved rim. late 2nd C.
61DE	From black layer immediately above Period I foundations to E of Period III wall. Depth c. 3ft 6 ins.	Other pottery: 128: BB2 jar; 129: LNV CC Beaker. late 2nd C.
61DO	Immediately E of Period III wall, immediately on clay foundation of E/W Period I wall.	
61EA	Immediately E of line of Period III wall near N end in dark soil overlying mortar and clay surface in association with early N/S wall at 48–50 ins.	Plain samian: 1 rim sherd Dr 33 CG; 1 flange frag. Dr 38 ?CG. Decorated Samian: 64: piece by Banuus, AD 160–190. Coarseware: 1 wall sherd jar in BB1 with obtuse angle cross-hatching below scored line. TPQ: mid-3rd C on the basis of the wall sherd of BB1.
61EN	Clay and stones to W of wall of granary below Period III wall to W of buttress.	Decorated Samian: 76: Dr 37, c. AD 155–195.

Table 2.1. continued.

Finds Group	Description	Material
BLOCK 24		
61AU	*Immediately below fallen roofing slates E end of trench.*	Other pottery: 131: beaker in fine buff fabric with orange-brown colour coat. Mid-2nd C.
61AV	*Filling of robber trench, centre of trench.*	Other pottery: small rim sherd calcite gritted ware. late 3rd C+. Plain samian: 1 rim sherd Dr 33 EG, 2 rim sherds Dr 31R CG, 1 rim sherd ?Dr18/31R CG. Stamped samian: 1: Aestivus of Lezoux. AD 160–190. Decorated Samian: 89: *c.* AD 165–200.
61BD	*Immediately E of PI (crossed out, PII inserted, signed JPG 5/6/51 (sic)) wall, between surviving foundation of granary wall or robber trench, and PI (crossed out, PII inserted) wall, below level of surviving top of PI (crossed out, PII inserted) wall, level with or slightly below, surviving top of granary wall, depth of 50 ins from edge of west end of trench. JPG.*	Decorated Samian: 99, 127: *c.* AD 160–200.
61BT	*Stratified in filling low down between granary raft and Period II (JPG) wall* This only provides a TPQ for the filling, not for the Period II wall.	Other pottery: 132: Bowl in sandy grey ware, 133: Jar in BB1, 134: Jar in grey burnished ware, 136: Jar in grey burnished ware, 137: Dish in BB1. TPQ: mid-2nd C.
61LG	*In clay footings between granary foundation and Period II (formerly I) wall.* cf. LD.	Small finds: 152
BLOCK 26		
60JT	*At a depth of between 2 and 4 feet, in material of robber trench.* No plans are known for this trench. Its position makes it likely that the 'robber trench' is that of the main S wall of the granary.	
BLOCK 40		
61CL	*Cobble layer.* This is probably unlocatable.	Other pottery: 199: Bowl in BB1. TPQ: mid-2nd C. Small finds: 179
BLOCK 41		
61EC	*In fallen tile debris.*	1 fragment of *tegula*
61EJ	*Black filling above and between granary support walls.*	Plain samian: 1 base sherd Dr 31R EG; Other pottery: 1 wall sherd in calcite gritted fabric. TPQ: late 3rd C. Small finds: 128

3. The Building Complex to the West of the Granary

This complex of buildings (see Fig. 3.1) presents something of an interpretational challenge since it presents us with the difficulty of substantiating, from the extant records, the interpretation offered by Gillam at or slightly after the time of excavation.

At the end of the 1960 season it was thought that the early (*i.e.* second-century) remains in the area to the west of the granary belonged to three separate buildings (Roman Britain in 1960; see Appendix I):

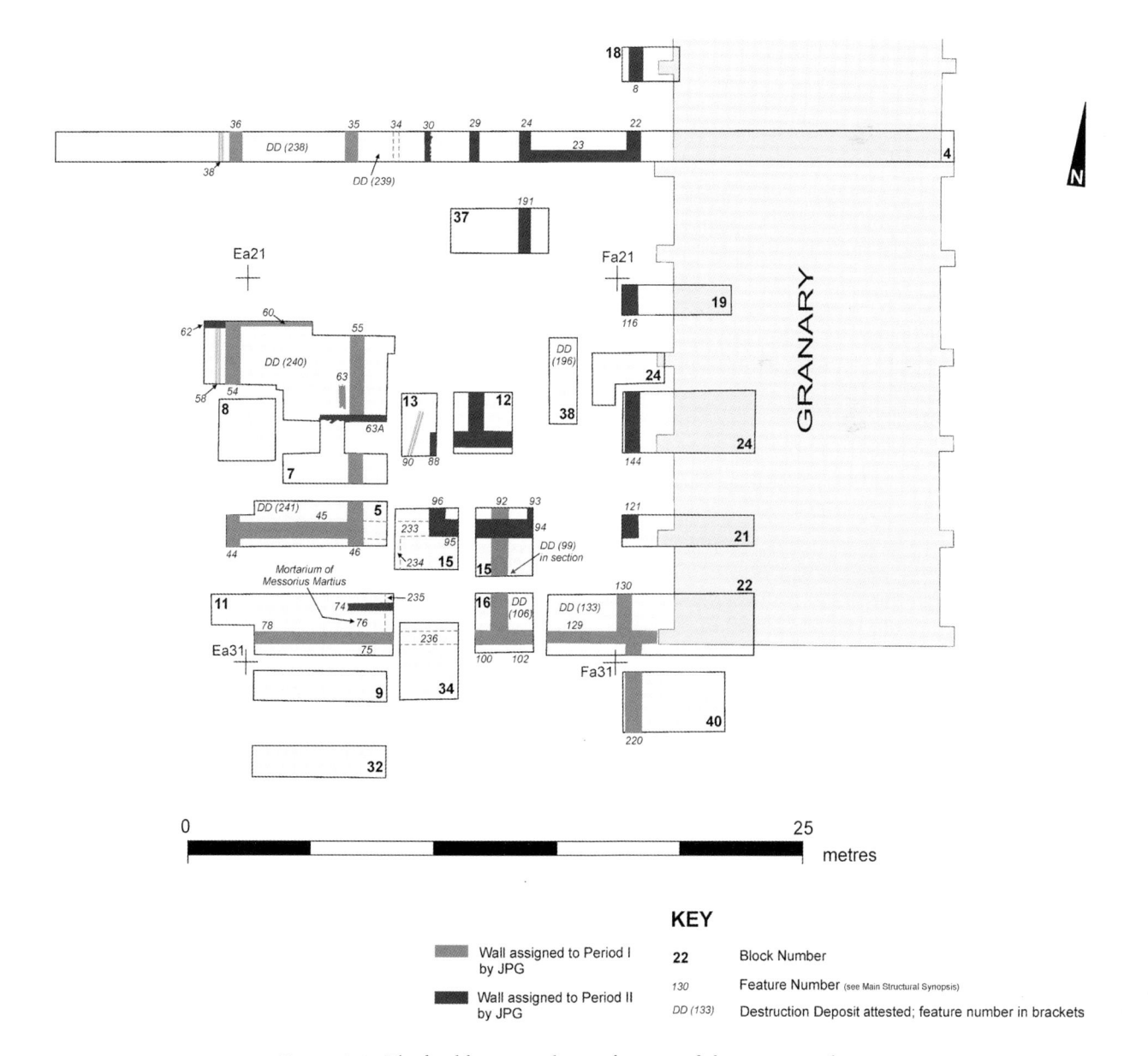

Figure 3.1. The building complex to the west of the granary: plan.

1. A building with a suspended floor but no buttresses, located immediately to the west of the granary. During the 1960 season, it seems to have been known as "the west granary" (from entries in the Finds Book).
2. A building located to the west of 1. Notes on the plans of Block 4 refer to it as a 'forage store'. JPG in *Roman Britain in 1960* (see Appendix I) suggested that it may have been a workshop.
3. A small building of unknown function, located to the south of 1 and 2.

Although it is difficult now to look back and work out the precise configuration of this interpretative scheme, we can surmise that, at the end of the 1960 season few of the remains in the area as a whole had been assigned to Period II, and that most of the remains in the northeast of the area, which were subsequently assigned to Period II, were thought of as belonging to Period I.

By the end of the 1961 season the idea of the three primary buildings had been dropped in favour of a single courtyard building which, it was thought, lasted, with some slight modifications, for most of the second century before being destroyed by fire and substantially replaced by another structure (*Roman Britain in 1961*; see Appendix I). This is the view which is represented on the most complete overall interpretational plan (Pl 3) and which found its way into the synthetic overviews which JPG wrote subsequently (such as Gillam and Mann, 1970).

That the latter interpretational scheme could so easily supercede the former was not simply a consequence of further excavation in the second season; it was also a reflection of the fragmented nature of the remains in this area. While JPG's second scheme is probably closer to the truth than the first, it cannot be regarded as the last word; considerable difficulties remain. The approach which we will adopt here will be to accept broadly the second scheme and then comment on the difficulties and inconsistencies which remain. Figure 3.1 shows the features which can be substantiated from the extant plans and Figure 3.2 represents our best guess now as to the disposition of the two interpretive schemes.

The Period I Building

JPG reckoned the primary building as 54 ft (16.5m) wide by a calculated 98 ft (29.9m) long (*RB in 1961*). The width tallies reasonably closely with measurements from the general overall plan Pl 3 (55 ft). The length was reckoned, as with the granary, on the basis of the known position of the main west gate. The shape of the building was thought to be rectangular having four ranges surrounding a central courtyard or corridor. JPG restored the west, south and east ranges from the available evidence but left the north range since this end of the building lay wholly outside the area available for excavation.

Most is known about the southern end of the building, particularly the south range and the south end of the west range. The west range was *c.* 5.8m wide, the south range somewhat narrower, *c.* 4.9m. The width of the west wall of the west range, the main west wall of the building, (Block 7, 54; Block 5, 44) was *c.* 0.67m, that of the east wall (Block 7, 55; Block 5, 46) slightly narrower, *c.* 0.58m. The main south wall (Block 11, 78; Block 22, 129) and the west wall of the east range (Block 15, 92) were slightly wider at *c.* 0.74m. Generally where they survived, the walls stood only two courses high; the best preserved section of wall occurred in Block 22 where the south wall of the building (129) showed three and four courses.

The proof of evidence for much of the walling from the central section of the south range, on which the argument for making what had been regarded as separate buildings in 1960, into a single building, is generally lacking. Walls appear on the general plan Pl 3 as solid colour which conventionally indicates that they had been substantiated on the ground but the evidence is lacking on the detailed plans. For Block 5 there is no good evidence on plan Pl 20 for wall 45 continuing east of its junction with wall 46, and in Block 15 there is similarly no indication on any of the detailed plans for wall 233 which should, according to Pl 3, run under the Period II wall (95) to a junction with the west wall of the east range (wall 92). The existence of wall 236 in Block 34, and 235 in Block 11 is likewise dependent solely on the general plan Pl 3.

As already mentioned JPG restored the length of the building to the maximum possible before encountering the *via principalis*. A length of at least *c.* 20.3m was regarded as absolutely certain since this was the distance between the south wall of the building in Block 11 and the only lengths of wall assigned to the primary building (west range) in Block 4. However, it must be pointed out that the walls in Block 4 (35 and 36), while they may belong to Period I, need not necessarily belong to the same building which occurs in the blocks to the south. They do appear to continue the line of walls 54 and 55 in Block 7 but this could be mere coincidence; since the west side of the area is up against the *intervallum* road and thus marks the limit of all buildings in the area it seems likely that all the most westerly walls, whether from the same or different buildings, would have been aligned to the same building line anyway. This leaves only wall 35, whose position might be coincidence. Under JPG's second interpretative scheme there are no other walls assigned to Period I in Block 4, nor, in fact, are there any in any of the blocks on the east side of the area north of Block 15, apart from in Block 24 where the wall shown on the general plan Pl 3 cannot

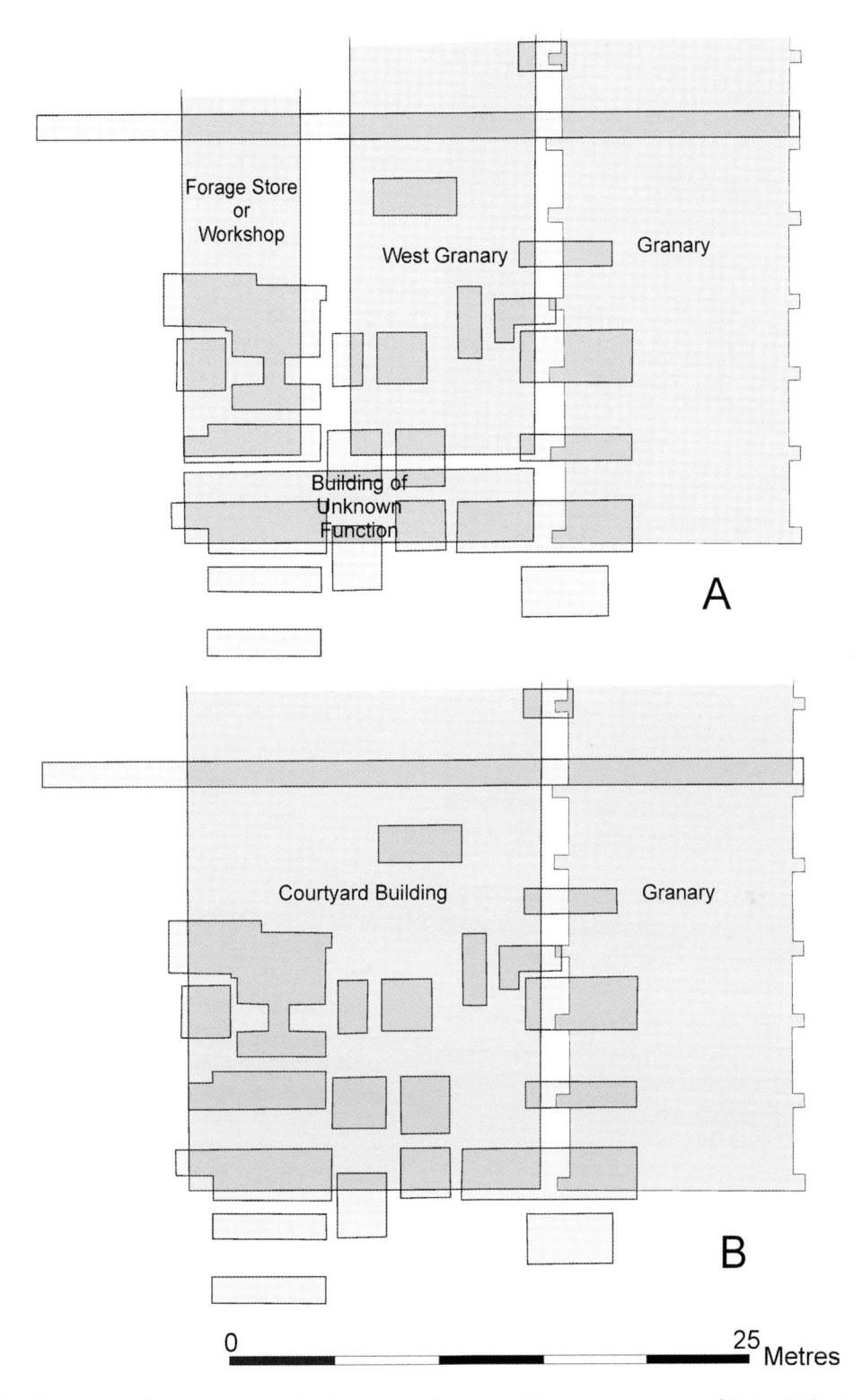

Figure 3.2. Gillam's schemes of interpretation for the area to the west of the granary in period I; A: 1960; B: 1961: plan.

be substantiated from the detailed plans. Thus, one could make a reasonable case for restoring two primary buildings in the area, rather than one. The shape and size of the northern one cannot be guessed at since the only evidence are the short lengths of wall in Block 4, but the southern one could have measured c. 16.5m square.

The alternative is to look again at the evidence for assigning walls on the east side of the area to Period II. The walls shown in Blocks 12, 13 and 15 can be

Figure 3.3. Photograph M17: Block 22 Trenches Ee25 Fa25 Fb25, from west, showing the Period I south wall (129) of the suggested courtyard building abutted by the west wall (130) on the left and the wall of its southern extension (131) to the right; in the rearground the southern end of the granary can be seen with secondary (?) reinforcement 128 and the south-east corner buttress abutted by portico wall 126.

shown to be secondary to the primary structure with a reasonable degree of certainty (see below) but the evidence for walls in Blocks 21, 24, 19, 37 and the central part of 4 is somewhat more equivocal. Those in the central part of 4 were originally assigned either solely to Period I or to Period I or II, and were only later placed in Period II, probably to fit the evidence which emerged from Block 15 in 1961. JPG's idea was that the main east wall of the Period II building (8 in Block 18, 22 in Block 4, 116 in Block 19, 144 in Block 24 and 121 in Block 21) was built immediately alongside the Period I wall ("reconstruction on slightly different lines took place at the beginning of period II": JPG in *Roman Britain in 1961*), and he restored

it as such on the general plan Pl 3. Unfortunately one cannot prove the existence of the Period I wall from the evidence now extant. JPG's general interpretive plane (Pl 3) makes clear all of it to the north of Block 22 was conjecture at the time in any case. Furthermore, if one redraws the features in question, using the trench outlines from Pl 3 but replotting the features from the detailed plans, one finds that the restoration suggested on Pl 3 is somewhat prejudicial to the case. The wall claimed as Period II (8 in Block 18, 22 in Block 4, 116 in Block 19, 144 in Block 24 and 121 in Block 21) is actually much closer to the line of the Period I wall in Block 22 (130) than shown on Pl 3. One could suggest, and none of the presently known evidence goes against this, that the wall was originally Period I and that part or all of it continued to be used in Period II.

Staying with the 1961 interpretational scheme, JPG claimed that the Period I building was enlarged and modified.

"At some time this house, which was of half-timbered construction, was enlarged and modified; at the same time, a wooden floor at a higher level replaced the original flagged floor .... In the packing between the earlier and later floors was found a complete but worn specimen of a mixing bowl (or mortarium) with the stamp of a potter who is known to have worked in the Carlisle region between AD 130 and 160."

JPG in an unpublished interim report.

"Enlargement and modification is dated by Antonine pottery ...."

JPG in *Roman Britain in 1961*.

"At Haltonchesters the building to the west of the west granary, whether hospital or commanding officer's house, was enlarged and re-floored, and the new flooring sealed Hadrianic and early Antonine pottery, including a mortarium stamped by MESSORIUS MARTIUS."

Gillam and Mann, 1970, p. 6.

Enlargement probably refers to what JPG restored as an extension of the building to the south, represented by a wall (220) in Block 40, and possibly to certain pieces of walling in the north-west corner of Block 7 (for details see Structural Synopsis (Chapter 7)). The evidence of the renewal of the floor seems to come from Block 11, but it must be stressed that it was traced to Block 11 only because of the mention in Gillam and Mann, 1970, of the stamped mortarium and not from any specific references on the plans or in the Finds Book, to floor renewal. The stamped vessel is extant (see Other Pottery, no. 75); the vessel gives us the finds group; the corresponding entry in the Finds Book gives us the trench. The finds group is 61PC and the level *may* be number 76 but, again, it must be stressed that there are problems with both identification and interpretation (for the details see Block 11 in the Structural Synopsis (Chapter 7)). There seems to be no evidence, direct or indirect, on any plan or in the Finds Book, for the timber floor whose existence JPG confidently asserted in the interim report.

The Period II Building

There is only one place in the area where the extant records show walls of Period I and II in a clear and close stratigraphic relationship; this is in Block 15. Here the later wall (94), running from east to west and surviving six courses high in places, oversails the earlier wall (92) which runs from north to south. The later wall rests almost directly on top of the earlier; the gap between them is only slight (this can clearly be seen on photograph M18) which strongly suggests that the later wall be assigned to Period II rather than to a later period, since the later structures have a much thicker build-up of material underlying them.

Walls in the surrounding blocks can be associated with wall 94, and thus placed in the same period, on the grounds of aligment, depth and similarity of construction. Thus, in Blocks 12, 13 and 15 we have a fragment of a building which we can confidently place in Period II. We have already discussed the other walls assigned by JPG to Period II (the main east wall and the fragments in Block 37 and the central part of Block 4) and these must be regarded as altogether less certain for the reasons given above and in the Structural Synopsis (Chapter 7).

Dating

Aside from the Destruction Deposit (see below) the dating evidence which can be associated with the inception and use of any of the elements of the building complex described above is very sparse. Table 3.1 sets it out. If it has been correctly identified (see above and Structural Synopsis (Chapter 7), Block 11, Feature 76), the Finds Group 61PC provides a *terminus post quem* for at least one structural change to the Period I building, though in point of fact this is hardly later than its assumed Hadrianic inception.

The Destruction Deposit (Figs 3.5–3.7)

As mentioned in the introduction, one of the key findings of the excavations of 1960 and 1961, which almost immediately became part of the canon of given knowledge about the site, was the presence of a burnt deposit appearing to mark the demise of the modified Period I building. The deposit consisted of a black layer, identified as the remains of carbonised wood, overlain by a thicker orange layer, identified as burnt daub. It was

Figure 3.4. Photograph M18: Block 15 Trench Ed24, from the south, showing Period II wall 94 abutting 93 and directly overlying Period I wall 92 of the courtyard building.

similar in character to deposits excavated at Corbridge in 1945–6 (Richmond and Gillam 1950, 177–201, Bishop and Dore 1989, 248) and was regarded by Gillam as part of the evidence of a widespread and catastrophic breaching of the frontier by enemy forces at some point in the later second century (AD 180, 197 and 207 have, at various times, been suggested as appropriate dates on the basis or literary and epigraphic evidence).

As at Corbridge, though, there is a huge discrepancy between what oral tradition regards as the extent of the deposit and what is represented in the excavation archive (see Bishop and Dore 1989, p. 220). Apart from indirectly in a marginal note by Trench Ea25 (Block 16, Pl 18) the deposit appears only once on any drawing, on the south section of Block 15 (Pl 32). Most of the evidence comes from mentions of the deposit in the Finds Book where its presence is indicated in eight separate locations. Without these entries (some

Table 3.1. Selected finds groups from the Building Complex to the west of the Granary.

Block	Finds Group	Description	Finds
5	60FG	*Base of wall footing protruding from N side of trench. "Hadrianic" level.*	1 base sherd from a bowl in BB1. TPQ: *c.* AD 120.
	60FR	*"Hadrianic level". max depth 60ins.*	1 rim sherd of grey ware jar, 1 wall sherd grey ware jar with rustication.
7	61PZ	*Filling in N end of Period I drain.*	Other pottery: 49: grey ware jar; 50: cooking pot in BB1 with wavy line on neck – early – mid-2nd C.
11	61PA	*Below cobble at E end of trench.*	wall sherd from a jar in BB2 with grouped cross-hatching. TPQ: mid-2nd C.
	61PC	*In and below cobble layer at 38ins below turf, down to 50ins, above clay. N of IA wall below its top.* See Structural Synopsis (Chapter 7), Block 11, Feature 76.	Other pottery: 72: grey ware jar; 73: lid; 74: mortarium – Hadrianic-early Antonine; 75: mortarium stamped by Messorius Martius – *c.* AD 125–55.
24	61PB	*3 ft in core of 2nd Period wall.*	Other pottery: 130: mortarium, first half 2nd C.
	60JN	*In "Hadrianic" level.*	Small finds: 17.

of which are pre-suppositional references embedded in descriptions of other features) one would barely know that the deposit had existed at all.

The blocks in which the deposit is attested are identified on Figure 3.1. The most important of these is in Block 15 since here a section exists which shows the deposit. There are some interpretative problems regarding the section (see the Structural Synopsis (Chapter 7)) but if one allows that a robber trench was missed, then the destruction deposit would originally have lapped up to the Period I wall standing to at least the height of the top of the deposit. The same block would have contained the relationship between the Period II wall and the destruction deposit but we have no record of this.

Finds groups whose descriptions suggest that they come from the deposit or immediately below the deposit are tabulated below (Table 3.2). Entries in italics in the second column (Finds Group) are the verbatim descriptions taken from the Finds Book. The Other Pottery vessels from these groups have been extracted from the main series (Figs 10.1 – 10.7) and are shown in Figure 3.7. The group is small and for this reason one is loath to enter into detailed comparisons with the Corbridge material. However, it is worth remarking that, leaving aside material that is obviously anomalous (nos 164 and 168) and with the exception of the stamped mortarium by Anaus, all the vessel types in the assemblage from the Haltonchesters deposit are also present in that from the Corbridge deposit.

Figure 3.5. Photograph C223: Block 22 Trench Ee25; the north-west corner of the trench with burnt daub deposit present in section.

Figure 3.6. Photograph C206: Block 15 Trench Ed24, north-facing section showing a possible robber trench over Period I wall 92. The destruction deposit of burnt daub (99) is present in the south-east corner.

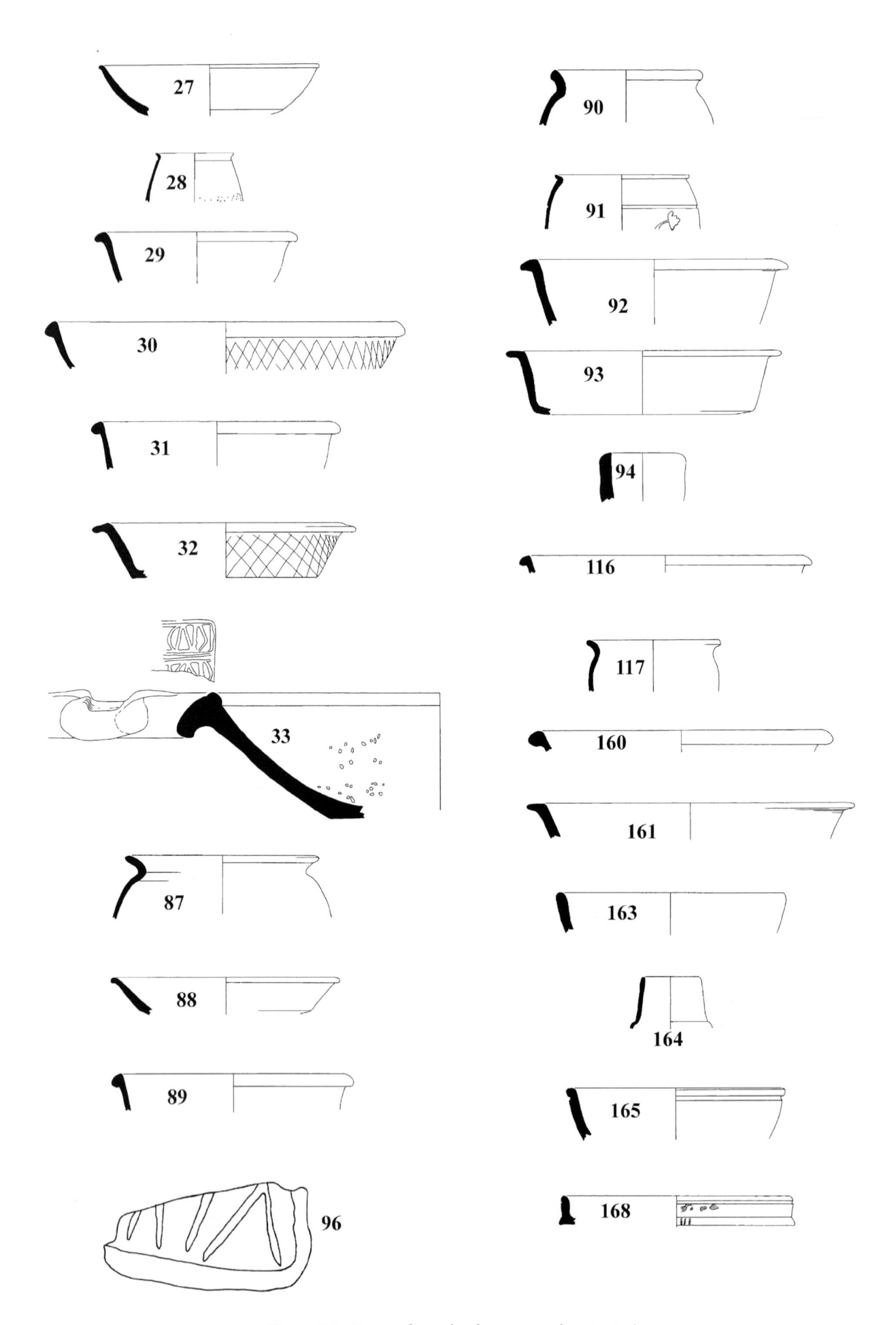

Figure 3.7. Pottery from the destruction deposit; 1:4.

Table 3.2. Dating evidence from the destruction deposit.

Block	Finds Group	Feature	Finds
4	60KB *Burnt wattle and daub below topsoil.*	238	Wall and base sherds from a jar in BB2 with grouped cross hatching. TPQ: mid-2nd C.
	60KG *In dirty orange clay below burnt wattle and daub.*	238	Wall sherd of jar in BB1. Small Finds: 178 (post *c.* AD 250).
	60KU *Burnt material below topsoil.*	239	Wall sherd of bowl in BB1. TPQ: *c.* AD 120.
	60KX *Patch of burnt material below topsoil W of Period IV wall.*	239	Small finds: 16
5	61BF *In and below the destruction layer of yellow clay.*	241	Decorated Samian: 69: Mercator iv. *c.* AD 160–190. Other pottery: 27: Samian Dr 31 CG; 28: Beaker in fine orange rough cast fabric; 29: Bowl in BB2, small round rim; 30: Bowl in BB2, small triangular-section rim; 31: Bowl in BB2, small round rim; 32: Flat rim dish in BB1; 33: Mortarium stamped by Cudrenus. TPQ: mid-2nd C.
7	None.	240 (by implication only).	None.
15	60GO *Destruction level 27–33 ins.*	99	Other pottery: 87: Jar in BB2. TPQ: mid-2nd C. Small finds: 181 (post *c.* AD 160)
	61AS *From immediately under or at corresponding level to the layer of fired daub and charred wattle in SE corner at 2 ft 6 ins.*		Decorated samian: 53: Secundus v, *c.* AD 150–180; 69: Mercator iv *c.* AD 160–180. Other pottery: 88: Samian: Dr 18/31 EG (?); 89: Bowl in BB2, small round rim; 90: Jar in grey ware; 91: Beaker: orange with barbotine decoration. TPQ: late 2nd C.
	61CP *Below destruction level.*	99	Decorated samian: 2: S. Gaulish; 12: Hadrianic/Antonine. Other pottery: 92: Bowl in grey ware; 93: Flat rim dish in BB1, possibly the same vessel as 32. TPQ: mid-2nd C. Other pottery: 94: Crucible.
16	60EU *Below burnt level depth c. 36 ins.*		Other pottery: 96: Mortarium stamped by Anaus, *c.* AD 120–160.
	60LN *In burnt wattle and daub below layer LM.*	106	None.
	60LP *In burnt wattle and daub below layer LM.*	106	None.
	60LT *Grey clay below burnt wattle and daub above Period II (?) wall. below Period III (?) flagging.*		None.
22	61CJ *In burnt level.*		1 wall sherd jar in grey ware.
	61EF *Destruction level depth c. 2 ft 6 ins Dark soil overlying burnt area.*	133	Other pottery: 116: Bowl in BB2, small triangular-section rim. TPQ: mid-2nd C.
	61FV *In burnt layer.*		Decorated samian: 22: Hadrianic/Antonine; 44: Cinnamus ii, *c.* AD 150–180; 90: Doeccus I, *c.* AD 165–190. Other pottery: 117: Jar in BB1.
36	61EG *Cleaning on burnt layer below fallen stones c. 18 ins.*		Other pottery: 168: Bowl in Crambeck Parchment ware. Also 3 wall sherds calcite gritted ware. TPQ: *c.* AD 360.

Table 3.2. continued.

Block	Finds Group	Feature	Finds
36	61JH *Below burnt level.*		Samian: 1 rim sherd Dr 33 CG Other pottery: 1 small rim sherd of a beaker in Lower Nene Valley colour-coated ware (LNV CC). TPQ: late 2nd C.
	61JP *Below burnt level next to E–W wall.*		None.
	61JY *Below burnt level.*		Other pottery: 160: Bowl in BB2; 161: Bowl in BB1. TPQ: mid-2nd C.
	61KG *Below burnt level.*		None
	61LV *Baulk running sout* (sic) *from peg Ec34 Below flat slabs (destruction layer).*	189	Other pottery: 163: plain rim dish in BB1; 164: Beaker in LNV CC; 165: Bowl in grey burnished ware. Also sherds of calcite gritted ware. TPQ: late 3rd C.
38	61CW *In burnt layer. Depth below 3 ft 4 ins.*	196	Other pottery: 176: Jar in BB2. TPQ: mid-2nd C.
	61DC *Cleaning on S side of E/W wall in the burnt layer – 3 ft 6 ins.*	196	Other pottery: 177: Jar in BB2. TPQ: mid-2nd C.
	61FI *Burnt layer.*	196	Decorated samian: 44: Cinnamus ii, *c.* AD 150–180.
	61GY *Below burnt layers* (sic).		None.
	No finds group.	195	

4. The Late Buildings

These are designated Fragments A–G. Fragments B and C may have formed part of the same building. The fragments of late buildings which JPG mentioned (in Roman Britain in 1961 – see Appendix I) over the remains of the granaries cannot now be located on any extant plans.

Figure 4.1 shows the overall plan. Table 4.1 summarises the finds evidence from the various fragments.

Fragment A

This lies in Block 1. Three joining fragments of wall are known, enclosing a space *c.* 1.34m wide, at the east end of the block. The walls were heavily robbed but survived two courses high in places. Where they were exposed across their full width they were *c.* 0.52m wide. The lower course of the east end wall is offset on its east side by *c.* 0.12m from the upper course. One of the stones forming one of the corners of the east end of the fragment (which corner is not specified in the Finds Book) had a 'crude Celtic face' carved on it. It cannot now be located. No trenches were placed in the area immediately to the south of Block 1 so it is impossible to attempt a reconstruction of the building of which the fragment formed part on the basis of the remains found in Block 1. None of the pottery groups recovered from the block in 1960 or 1961 provide any dating for the fragment, but Jarrett's excavations of 1956 (Jarrett 1959, 183) recovered a painted Crambeck mortarium (Gillam Type 290) from a context 'sealed' by the building.

Fragment B

The elements of this fragment extend through Blocks 7, 5 and 11, and appear to form the north-east corner of a building whose length (north–south) was at least 14.4m and whose width was at least 4.4m. The walls are composed of large roughly shaped stones all *c.* 0.5m wide and *c.* 0.3m thick. The longest, which occurs in Block 7, is some 1.44m long. Five stones of the north wall survive in Block 7; seven of the east wall survive (1 in Block 7, 2 in Block 5, 4 in Block 11). All of the stones have holes *c.* 60 mm in diameter and at least 60mm deep in their top surfaces. On most of the stones, the holes are arranged in a single row, longitudinally along the mid line of the face (for precise arrangements of the holes on each stone, see the Structural Synopsis (Chapter 7)). Part of what is thought to be an internal partition was found in Block 7.

Possible surfaces associated with this Building Fragment are known in two places, both in Block 11. A pitched stone or cobbled surface (81) is mentioned in the Finds Book as associated and to the west of the east wall (72). Between the east wall (72) and the west wall of Fragment E (71) was a surface (73) composed of several large flags, a quernstone and a certain amount of smaller stone (see Fig. 4.6). It is described on the plan as 'period IV flagging. Sagged below top of period III wall', the Period III wall being 71, later re-assigned to Period IV. Finds Groups 60IR and 60JL were from below the cobbled surface (81), and Finds Groups 61NQ and 61OB were from below the flagged surface (73). The yield of datable pottery from these finds groups was not high. Neither 60IR nor 60JL contained anything which was necessarily later than the late second century. A *terminus post quem* for 61OB somewhere in the third century was provided by a wall sherd of a Hartshill Mancetter hammer-headed mortarium. 61NQ contained the latest material, a wall sherd of calcite gritted fabric, though this was too small to display any of the diagnostic features of the Huntcliff Type cooking pot and thus could not be dated any later than the late third century.

Other finds groups possibly associated with Fragment B are as follows:

61KJ: Finds Book entry: "Level of period IV stone". It contains a fragment of a Huntcliff Type cooking pot and a sherd of a painted Crambeck mortarium, both of which should date to the second half of the fourth century AD.

61KP: Finds Book entry: "Stony soil below level of period IV", *i.e.*, possibly pre-dating period IV. It contains nothing necessarily later than the second century AD.

61MI: Finds Book entry: "S of N railings from 1ft 6ins depth", *i.e.*, probably in a level pre-dating Period IV.

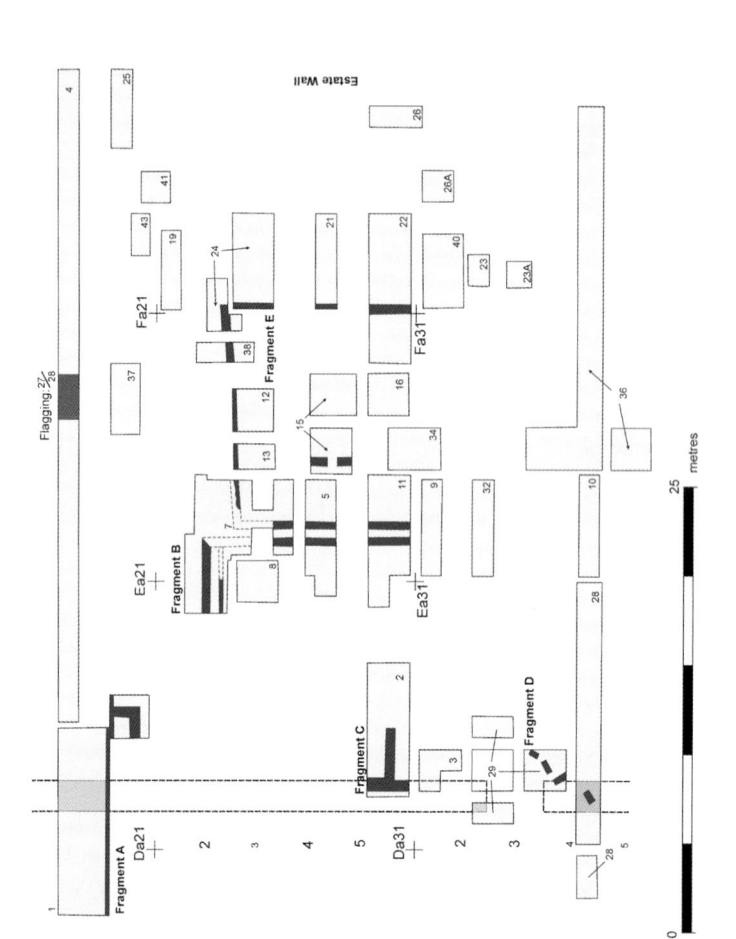

Figure 4.1. The fragments of the late buildings: plan.

Figure 4.2. Photograph M29: Block 7 Trench Ea22, looking east; east end of late wall 49.

It contains nothing necessarily later than the second century AD.

A single, isolated stone (50 in Block 7), of similar size and shape to those composing the walls already mentioned, and bearing the same kind of holes on its upper surface, is shown in the northern half of Block 7, *c.* 1.06m to the east of the eastern end of wall 49, that is to the east of what was restored as the northeast corner of the building. On the general plan Pl 3 it is simply shown as an isolated fragment of walling. The paucity of evidence does not allow any convincing interpretation which incorporates it into Fragment B to be made, particularly if one follows JPG in making Fragments B and E contemporary (see below).

Fragment C

This was contained in Block 2 and consisted of two walls. The first (5), aligned north–south, was located close to the west baulk, and comprised two roughly hewn blocks, the northerly of which measured *c.* 1.1m × 0.3m × 0.3m. The second (6) which ran east from the middle of the first, comprising four roughly hewn blocks whose width and depth appears (from photograph M27) to have been about the same as those of the first. All these stones displayed a row of small, approximately circular holes running longitudinally down the centre of their upper faces. These holes seemed (from the photo) to be about 50mm in diameter and at least 100mm deep. The depth of the stones of Wall 5 below ground level varied between 0.15 and 0.25 metres and the stones of wall 6 were set about 0.23m deeper. From photograph M27

Figure 4.3. Photograph M30: Block 7 Trench Ea22, looking west, 'park-railing' blocks of wall 49 forming part of late Building Fragment B.

Figure 4.4. Photograph M25: Block 2 Trench Db25 Dc25, looking west: footing blocks of walls 5 and 6 and surface(s) 7 associated with late Building Fragment C.

Figure 4.5. Photograph M26: Block 2 Trench Db25 Dc25, looking east; wall bases 5 and 6 and surface of late Building Fragment C.

it appears that wall 5 had no foundations but rested directly on top of a deep layer of fill which in turn overlay the remains of the demolished fort wall; wall 6 appears, however, to have had, at least at its extant eastern end, a foundation course of small, irregularly shaped stone.

There seems to have been a surface (or possibly more than one surface) associated with walls 5 and 6.

Photographs M25 and M26 show, on either side of wall 6 a number of large stone slabs or flags (7) whose tops were at the same level as the tops of the wall stones. Most are irregularly shaped, but at least two are well shaped blocks which could well have been re-used from an earlier period. There is also a sketch plan of this area (on Pl 41) which shows flagstones at different levels, some overlying others, and from the photos, there are certainly suggestions that to the south of 6, these flags formed several surfaces, of different periods, rather than just being tumble. Below this surface, or surfaces, is a mixture of earth and large irregularly shaped stone (8; evidence, again, from photographs M26 and M27). What it represents is not clear, though its confused nature suggests that it is most likely to be demolition or collapse from previous periods.

All of the provenancable finds groups from Block 2 came from 8, the fill below the surface(s) 7. A *terminus post quem* of around AD 360 for Fragment C is provided by Finds Group 61CM, which the Finds Book describes as coming from "Soil below floor level with park railing stones". The latest datable fragment of pottery contained in the group was a Huntcliff type cooking pot. The group also contained a small disc stud (Small Finds: 75) dated post AD 360. The other finds groups are 60HS, 60ID, 60IX and 61CU, and they contained no material later than the second century AD.

It is possible that Fragment C formed part of the same building as Fragment B. How far, if at all, wall 6 extended beyond what is shown on the extant plan (Pl 41) is not clear. On the overall trench plan (Pl 3) JPG showed it as robbed out for *c.* 3m up to the east end of trench Dd25, and then as conjectured for a further 3.7m, *i.e.* as far as the trenches of Block 11. There is no firm evidence on the extant plans for a robbing in either Block 2 or Block 11.

Fragment D

This consists of four large, roughly hewn stone blocks, three of which appear in Block 29 (167), the other in the western end of Block 28 (155). The largest of the stones in Block 29 measured *c.* 1.03m × 0.41m × 0.12m. All of the stones in Block 29 displayed a row of small, approximately circular holes running longitudinally down the centre of their upper faces. No detailed plan of the stone in Block 28 exists. At least three of the stones appear to have been displaced from their original positions; only the most northerly is likely to have been in anything like its original position when found. It appears (from photo M23) to have been resting on or close to the top of a road surface (163) which in turn overlay a considerable depth of road related material (164, 165). The general alignment from which the stones were disturbed seems to have been north–south, rather than east–west.

There were provenancable finds groups associated with Fragment D.

Fragment E

This is situated immediately to the east of Fragment B. A north wall and parts of an east and west wall are known, which enclose a space approximately square, measuring *c.* 12m (E–W) × 9.8m (N–S). Fragments of possibly internal walls were found within this space. The west wall (53 in Block 7, 48 in Block 5, 71 in Block 11) was situated immediately to the east of, and parallel to the east wall of Fragment B. The eastwards turn of the west wall did not survive but was restored in a position approximately 1.8m south of the northeast corner of Fragment B. The most westerly part of the north wall occurs some 1.08m east of the restored corner, in Block 7 (241). It then runs slightly diagonally across the northernmost edges of Blocks 13 and 12 (87 and 83, respectively), through Block 38 (194), and into Block 24 (145) where it returns southwards (the corner is shown as extant on the general plan Pl 3, though no detailed plans survive for the trench in question) through Blocks 24, 21 (122) and 22 (132) on a line parallel to the west wall.

The walls seem, from the visual evidence of plans and photographs, to have been built of small shaped stone facing a core of smaller, irregularly shaped stone, and possibly mortar (though this is nowhere mentioned specifically). The width of the west wall is known in Blocks 11 (*c.* 0.58m) and 5 (*c.* 0.53m). The width of the north wall is known in Block 38 (*c.* 0.63m). The width of the east wall is not known.

In most places the walls survived three or four courses high and quite close to the surface; in Block 11 the top of the west wall was immediately under the turf (see Fig. 4.6).

Two small fragments of wall, on the same line, aligned north–south, occurred in the westernmost trench of Block 15. They were interpreted as being part of the same building as the other walls of Fragment E, mainly, one suspects because of their closeness to the surface.

On the general plan Pl 3 another small fragment is inferred in the space between Blocks 15 and 16, and Block 22. There is no evidence for this fragment.

On the general plan Pl 3 a small isolated fragment of wall, aligned east–west, is shown in the north-east corner of the northernmost trench of Block 24 (a trench for which there are no surviving detail plans), that is outside the north-east corner of Fragment E. It is given the same period shading as Fragment E; there is now no evidence to substantiate this.

There is very little independent dating evidence for Fragment E. In Block 5 a group of finds (60DP) came from below what the Finds Book describes as "fallen stone". This is likely to post-date the buildings of the primary phase but whether it was associated with the collapse or demolition of the primary/secondary buildings or that of Fragment E is not clear. The group contains a BB2 bowl which is more likely to date to the first half of the third century than the later second century.

Block 22 yielded a number of finds groups which could have been associated with some phase of the

Figure 4.6. Photograph M28: Labelled 'Haltonchesters 1960. Late fourth-century "kerbs"'; Block 11, Trench Ea25/Eb25 viewed from the south, with, from left to right, walls 72 and 71 belonging to late Building Fragments B and E respectively, and flagging 73 in the intervening alley.

building's life. A group from a level immediately below the east wall of the building (61EN) contained nothing datable. 61CH which was from in and below tumbled stone which could have predated the building contained nothing necessarily later than the second century AD. 61DZ, from a similar context, contained a triskele openwork stud dated to the late third century (Small Finds: 60). One group (61DM) was recovered from a stone spread close to the surface which suggests that it derived from the collapse or demolition of Fragment E. This group contained an sherd from a Huntcliff Type cooking pot datable to the later fourth century, but this only provides a *terminus post quem* for the end of the building not for its construction.

Area to the North of Fragment E

In the middle section of Block 4 two superimposed levels of flagging were recorded in 1960 (Features 27 and 28). Finds Group 60MB is likely to come from below the lower flagging. It contains an example of a type of jar known from a number of third-century contexts (Bidwell and Speak, 1994, 230 summarises; see also Dore and Wilkes, 1999, Illus. 43, nos 11–14, from Carpow). Its emergence in the north is certainly to be placed in the third century and quite possibly somewhere in its second quarter.

Feature 192 in Block 37 (flagged surface) immediately to the south of Block 4, may represent a continuation of one of the surfaces of Block 4. Finds Group 61OI may have come from below 192; it contained a fragment of Huntcliff type cooking pot.

Fragment F

This consisted of four short lengths of wall located at the east end of Block 39, in the south-western extension of the fort (Block 39, Features 202, 203, 206 and 207). All of the walls were composed of blocks which measured at least 1m in length by 0.5m in width. Each of these blocks displayed a row of small, approximately circular holes running longitudinally down the centre of their upper faces; these holes were spaced at intervals of *c.* 300mm. These four walls could have formed part of a single building *c.* 7.5m wide or two narrower buildings each *c.* 3.3m wide with a narrow passage between. The remains of flagged surfaces were found (Features 204 and 208) which are probably to be associated with the walls.

Fragment G

Immediately to the west of Fragment F are two masonry walls (199 and 200) *c.* 5m apart (centre to centre) and an associated flagged floor (201). Finds Groups 61QM, 61QO and 61QQ are likely to have come from below this surface. Vessel 186 (see Other Pottery) from 61QM provides the best *terminus post quem* for the flagging, somewhere in the latter part of the third century. Also noteworthy is vessel 188 from 61QO and 61QQ which is possibly of north African origin.

4. The Late Buildings

Table 4.1. Finds associated with the late buildings

Block	Finds Group	Description	Finds
Fragment A			
		'sealed' by the building.	Painted Crambeck mortarium (Gillam Type 290). See Jarrett, 1959, 183.
Fragment B			
7	61KJ	*Level of Period IV stone.*	Samian: 1 wall sherd Dr 31R EG; 1 wall sherd Dr 37 ?EG. Other Pottery: 41: Jar, Huntcliff type in calcite gritted ware; 42: Jar; sandy dark grey-brown, black surface; 43: Small mortarium in Crambeck parchment ware (CRA PA); 44: Mortarium in Hartshill-Mancetter white ware (MAH WH). TPQ: *c.* AD 360.
7	61KP	*Stony soil below level of Period IV.*	Decorated Samian: 192: AD 165–200. Samian: 1 rim sherd, 1 base sherd Dr 31 ?EG. Other Pottery: 45: Bowl in BB2 fabric; 46: Bowl in BB2 fabric. TPQ: *c.* AD 160.
7	61MI	*S of N railings from 1 ft 6 ins depth (coin was found 3 ft 6 ins on N-S wall 3 ins from W baulk).*	Coin: 42: AD 211–17. Samian: 1 rim sherd Dr 31R ?CG; 3 wall sherds ?Dr 31R. Other Pottery: 47: Dish in BB1 fabric; 48: Bowl in Crambeck reduced ware (CRA RE). TPQ: late 3rd C.
11	60IR	*W of Period IV wall. In and below layer of rough cobbles.* Below cobbled surface 81.	Samian: 1 rim sherd Dr 37 ?EG. Coarseware: 2 rim sherds from a jar in BB1; 1 small fragment of a mortarium, possibly in a north-western fabric. TPQ: late 2nd C. Small Finds: 27.
11	60JL	*Above long and short wall platform below removed later cobbles.* Below cobbled surface 81.	Samian: 1 wall sherd Dr 31R ?EG. Other Pottery: 66: beaker in Wilderspool fabric, mid-2nd C.
11	61NQ	*Between Period III and Period IV wall sealed by flagging recorded on 22/7/60 and removed 9/6/61.* Below flagged surface 73.	Other pottery: 69: Beaker in soft, sandy pale orange fabric; surface abraded. Coarseware: 1 base sherd from a beaker in orange fabric with an orange brown colour coat; 1 wall sherd from a jar in calcite gritted fabric; 1 wall sherd from a large indented beaker in grey ware. TPQ: late 3rd C. Small Finds: 97 (post late 3rd C), 139.
11	61OB	*Reopened hole between Period III and IV walls, underneath flagging.* Below flagged surface 73.	Decorated Samian: 61: AD 160–90. Plain Samian: 1 rim sherd Dr 33 CG; 1 rim sherd Dr 37 CG; 1 rim sherd Dr 31 EG Other Pottery: 70: Bowl in BB2; 71: Jar in BB1. Coarseware: 1 wall sherd with part of the rim of a hammer-head mortarium in Hartshill-Mancetter fabric. TPQ: 3rd C.
Fragment C			
2	60HS	*In fallen stone to N of late wall (with holes) and at depth 37 ins.*	Samian: 1 sherd, form unidentifiable. Coarseware: 1: Mortarium in Mancetter-Hartshill White ware (MAH WH), late 2nd C.
2	60ID	*Layer of filling above clay (?natural).*	Samian: 1 wall sherd Dr 31 EG.
2	60IX	*Immediately N of Period IV wall. Between the level of the bottom of the Period IV wall at 17 ins and the top of the clay at 42 ins.*	None.

Table 4.1. continued

Block	Finds Group	Description	Finds
2	61CM	*Soil below floor level with park railing stones.*	Decorated Samian: 70: AD 160–90; 113: Mid-Antonine. Plain Samian: 1 rim sherd 3 wall sherds Dr 31 EG. Other Pottery: 138: Jar in hard sandy grey ware; 139: Jar in BB2; 140: Bowl in BB2; 141: Jar in grey burnished ware; 142: Dish in Crambeck Reduced ware; 143: Bowl in BB2; 145: Dish in calcite gritted ware; 146: Huntcliff-type cooking pot in calcite gritted fabric. TPQ: *c.* AD 360. Small Finds: 75: Small disc stud (post *c.* AD 360).
2	61CU	*Layer below the flooring level with park railing stones 18 ins–36 ins down.*	Samian: 1 wall sherd Other pottery: 147: Jar in grey burnished ware; 148: Bowl in BB1; 149: Bowl in BB2; TPQ: *c.* AD 180
Fragment E			
5	60DP	*Below fallen stone to a depth of about 40 ins.*	Samian: 1 rim sherd Dr 31 EG; 1 base sherd Dr 18/31R ?CG. Other Pottery: 33: Bowl in BB2 fabric; 34: Bowl in BB2 fabric; 35: Bowl in BB2 fabric; 61: Beaker in Lower Nene Valley colour-coated ware (LNV CC). TPQ: 3rd C (?).
22	61CH	*Under tumbled stone S of buttress.*	Samian: 2 rim sherds Dr 33 EG; 1 rim sherd Dr 33 EG. Tile: 1 fragment imbrex.
22	61DM	*From stone spread 18 ins below surface.*	Samian: 1 rim sherd Dr 33 CG; 1 wall sherd Dr 30 CG Other Pottery: 103: Bowl in BB2; 104: Jar in a fabric similar to Mucking Black-burnished ware 2 (MUC BB 2). See Bidwell and Speak, 1994, p. 229, fig. 8.7 no. 5; 105: Mortarium in Mancetter-Hartshill White ware (MAH WH); 106: Jar in BB1; 107: Dish in BB2; 108: Huntcliff-type jar in calcite gritted ware; 109: Beaker in fine orange fabric with a red-brown colour-coat. (probably Colchester Colour-coated ware 2 – COL CC 2). TPQ: *c.* AD 360. Small Finds: 83: Large disc stud.
22	61DZ	*Amongst fallen stone down to the burnt level.*	Decorated Samian: 33: *c.* AD 140–70. Samian: 1 wall sherd 1 base sherd Dr 37 CG. Other Pottery: 110: Dish in Crambeck Reduced ware (CRA RE); 111: Bowl in BB2; 112: Jar in sandy grey ware; 113: Bowl in grey burnished ware; 114: Bowl in Crambeck Reduced ware (CRA RE); 115: Dish in BB1. TPQ: late 3rd C. Small Finds: 60: triskele openwork stud (late 3rd C); 173: lead fragment.
22	61EN	*Clay and stones to W of wall of granary below Period III wall to W of buttress.*	Nothing diagnostic.

Table 4.1. continued

Block	Finds Group	Description	Finds
Area to the North of Fragment E			
4	60MB	*Brown soil below Period III flagging.*	Samian: 1 rim sherd Dr 37 EG; 3 other wall sherds unidentifiable forms. Other Pottery: 17: Jar; sandy mid-grey fabric; 18: Jar in BB2 (possibly Mucking BB2: MUC BB 2); 19: Jar in sandy mid-grey fabric with dark grey brown surface; 20: Jar in gritty pale grey fabric with dark grey surface; 21: Jar in BB2. TPQ: 2/4 of 3rd C.
37	61OI	*Huntcliff type rim found at a lower level than the flags which were recorded on June 10 and removed on June 11. 5 ft 6 ins East of West edge of hole. 1ft 6ins South of North edge of hole; 2 ft 9 ins below turf level. IMPORTANT.*	Material from the finds group could not be found.
Fragment G			
39	61QM	*E/W trench across extension. Stratified below flagged floor of building E of field wall. = QO QQ.*	Decorated samian: 58: AD 160–90; 123: AD 160–90. Plain Samian: 1 rim sherd Walters 79 EG; 1 wall sherd Dr 31R CG. Other pottery: 186: Bowl or wide-mouth jar in hard sandy dark grey ware, L (?) 3rd C; 187: Dish in BB1. Small finds: 183: bone needle (post mid-3rd C).
	61QO	*E/W trench across extension. 12 ins below flagged floor of building E of field wall. = QM QQ.*	Plain Samian: 3 rim sherds 2 wall sherds Dr 31R EG. Other pottery: 188: Bowl or cooking casserole in a sandy orange fabric; sherds of this vessel also occurred in 61QQ. 2nd–4th century; 189: Dish in BB1; 190: Jar in BB1. TPQ: late 2nd C. Small finds: 28, 55, 64 (28 and 55 post *c.* AD 250).
	61QQ	*E/W trench across extension. Below flagged floor QM and above burnt level = QM QO.*	Plain Samian: 1 rim sherd 1 wall sherd Dr 31 CG; 1 rim sherd Dr 31R CG. Other pottery: 188: Bowl or cooking casserole. See entry under 61QO. TPQ: *c.* AD 160.

5. The Other Structures

The location of the trench blocks is shown on Figures 1.1 and 1.2. Details of the features can be found under the relevant trench blocks in the Structural Synopsis (Chapter 7). A general plan of what is known of the barracks to the south of the *via quintana* is shown on Figure 5.1.

The Fort Wall and Backing

The west fort wall between the main west gate (*porta principalis sinistra*) and the south-west angle was investigated in Trench Blocks 1, 2, 3, 28 and 29.

Block 1

The westernmost of the two trenches in this block coincided with the trench excavated by Jarrett in 1956 (Jarrett 1959, 178 and figs 2 and 3). No detail plans of this trench are known from the 1960 work; accordingly, the information presented below has been taken from Jarrett, 1959. The remains of the fort wall measured *c.* 2.4m 'over the foundations'. The wall backing was described as 'turfwork'. Jarrett interpreted the section across the fort wall (1959, figs 2 and 3) as demonstrating that the wall had been demolished when the south-western extension of the fort was built and he regarded these two events as having happened in the early third century during the Severan reorganisation of the frontier. His principal evidence was a group of pottery from the 'levelling' associated with the demolition of the fort wall which gave a *terminus post quem* for the demolition in the late second century. He saw the building which was discovered immediately to the west of the fort wall (see Structural Synopsis (Chapter 7),

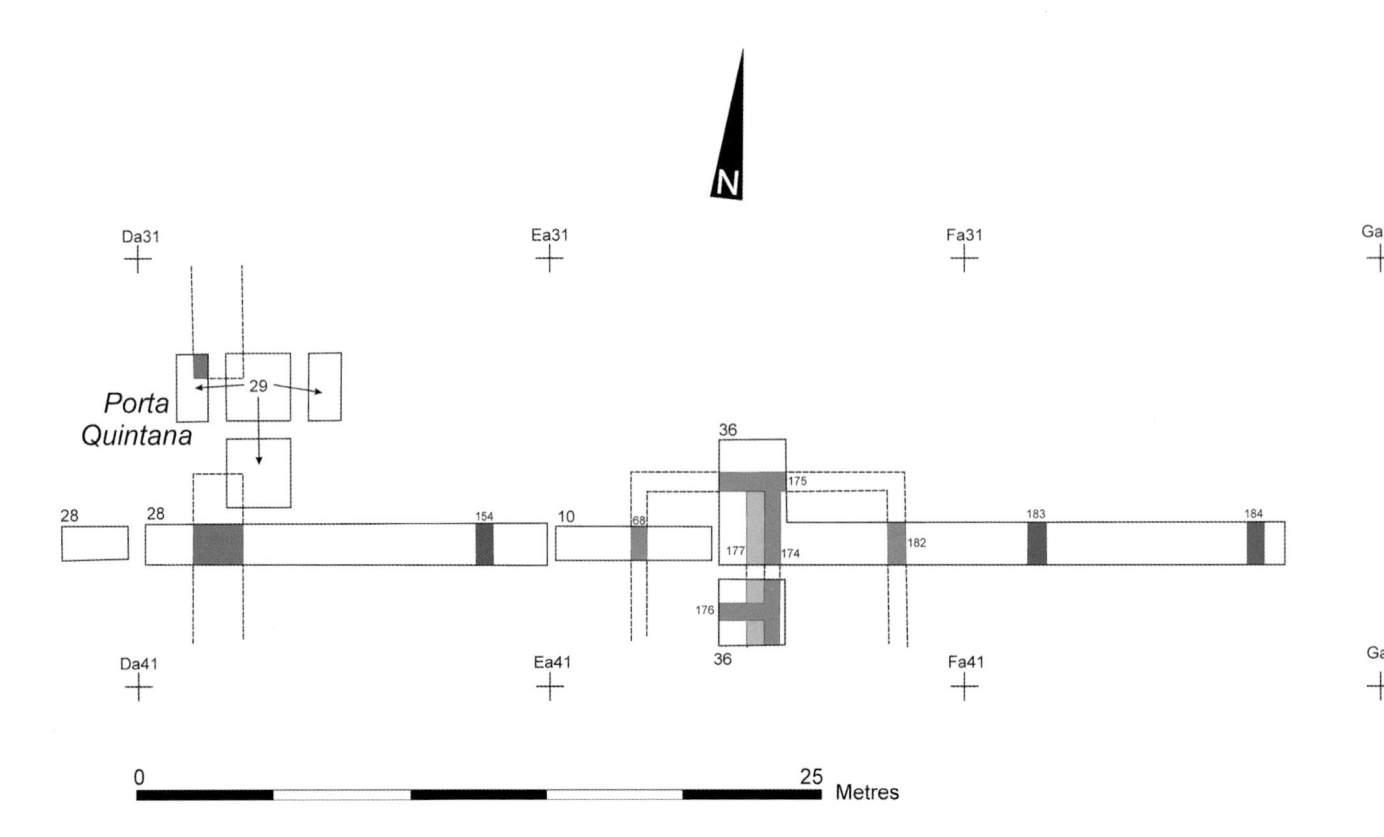

Figure 5.1. The buildings to the south of the via quintana: *plan.*

Block 1, Feature 3) as supporting evidence; he regarded it as having been erected subsequent to the demolition of the fort wall, and reasoned that its close proximity to the fort wall would have robbed the latter of 'all its defensive value if it had still been standing.' While there is no evidence which explicitly contradicts this view of events it is worth bearing in mind that a) the pottery only provides a *terminus post quem*; b) no direct sequential relationship can be established between the fort wall and the building from Jarrett's section.

Block 2

No trace of the fort wall is shown on the plans or is visible in the photographs. Photograph M27 shows what appears to be a clay level at the bottom of the central part of trench (Block 2, Feature 274), below a mixture of earth and irregular stone (Block 2, Feature 8) which in turn underlies a late building surface associated with E–W wall of the late building (Block 2, Feature 7). This could be the remains of the backing but it could equally be natural.

Block 3

There are no known plans of this block.

Block 28

There are no detail plans for this block. The fort wall, backing and *intervallum* road are shown on the general plan (Pl 3) as present rather than inferred. A clay floor recorded in the Finds Book (Block 28, Feature 156) might be the remains of the rampart backing.

Block 29

The four trenches comprising this block were located on the site of the *porta quintana*. Wall 159, running east–west, may represent the remains of a wall revetting the fort-wall backing on the north side of the passageway through the gate. Only the south face of this wall was exposed, in Trench Db32. Flagging 162 may represent the surviving basal flags for the gate threshold.

No detail plans are known for the north-west and north-east trenches of the block so the width of the fort wall and backing are not known at this point.

The *Intervallum* Road

Evidence for the *intervallum* road could have been found in trench Blocks 2, 4, 7, and 28. Of these, it is only for Block 4 that there is any evidence on a detail plan (Pl 17). Here the existence of a surface described as a 'solid mass of stones and chippings' is implicated in the note accompanying wall 41. Another note describes a surface

Figure 5.2. Photograph M27: Block 2 Trench Db25 Dc25 Dd25, from the east; clay level 274 is exposed in the bottom of the trench, below late Building Fragment C walls 5 and 6.

located between walls 40 and 41 as 'Clean orange stone packing at 40 ins' (Feature 42). These two notes may refer to the same surface. The description of the contexts of Finds Groups 60BV, 60CK and 60CZ would seem to imply the existence of at least four superimposed surfaces. No dimensions are available from the detail plan. The width of the road on the general plan (Pl 3) is *c.* 5.5m.

On the general plan (Pl 3) the *intervallum* road is shown in Block 28 as present rather than inferred but no detail plans are known of the block. Two Finds Groups (61QJ and 61QK) are described as coming from the *intervallum* road.

The East Fort Wall

The east curtain wall of the fort was revealed in Block 35. Here the fort wall (243) is *c.* 1.7m wide. There are two offset courses at the base of west (internal) face and one at the base of east (external) face. Its core was composed of undressed stone laid in lime mortar. A gap in the inside face may represent a conduit of some kind through the wall or may only be robbing.

The rampart backing (256) to the west of wall 243 is not represented pictorially on the trench plan (Pl 39), but it is described in a note: "Rampart backing undressed stones set in clay overlying mason's chippings".

Features outside the East Fort Wall

Block 35

A layer of mason's chippings (245) was overlain by cobbles (244) to the east of fort curtain 243. From their depth (3 ft below the surface) the cobbles could be primary whilst the chippings may relate to the initial construction of the fort wall.

Further east, several spreads of flagging (247, 252, 255, 259) and lengths of walling (246, 249, 250) were exposed. There are at least four spreads of flagging located at not less than two different depths which would suggest they cannot all be contemporary. The evidence comes from the area around flags 247. Detail on the plan (Pl 39) which describe the depths (247: 2 ft 5 ins; 259: 5 ft 1 in) makes it clear that 259 underlies 247.

Burnt wattle and daub was associated with flagged area 252 towards the east end of the trench. This is not clearly stratified either above or below the flags but seems to be mixed in with them, which might tend to suggest that it was redeposited from its original site.

A possible edge of the fort's defensive ditch (260) was revealed immediately to the east of flags 259, at a distance of *c.* 5.5m to the east of the fort curtain wall. A note associated with flags (259) states: "Flags at depth of 5 ft 1 ins – This may be a wall on the lip of the ditch".

The interpretation of these features is very uncertain, in particular whether they actually represent buildings outside the fort wall, or just flagged areas and defensive walling. The burnt wattle and daub might suggest real buildings, though, as noted in the Structural Synopsis (Chapter 7), the fact that the wattle and daub occurs both above and below the flagging suggests more that it has been redeposited from somewhere. However it is unclear why the flags would also have been redeposited.

The *Via Quintana*

The trench blocks in which the *via quintana* was recognised or could have occurred are Blocks 23, 29, 32 and 36.

Block 23

No evidence for the road surface was found in this block. The bottom of the trench is simply covered in "buff coloured clay".

Block 29

Feature 163 is described as '*via quintana* road surface'. The proximity of this surface to the turf level and to the stones of a Period IV wall (167), and the depth of the road related material underneath it (clearly visible in photo M23, Fig. 5.3) make it unlikely that it is the Period I road. This is confirmed by pottery from beneath it (Groups 61MA and 61MU) which contains material with a *terminus post quem* of at least the second half of the second century AD (see below Structural Synopsis (Chapter 7)).

Photograph M36 (see Fig. 7.46), shows what may be the north side of the *via quintana*, complete with stone kerb, at the point where it passed through the *porta quintana*. There appeared to be a considerable build-up of metalling above the level of the footings for the gate's north-west pier, which would suggest the surface visible must be later than Period I.

Block 32

A surface described as "Course (sic) orange gravel road surface" extended over the whole of this block at a depth of 35 ins (Feature 168). There is no indication of what period this road surface was assigned to and no finds were recovered from in or below it. What could be interpreted as the kerb for the road surface was located in the north-east corner of the trench (Feature 169). It consisted of a single row of five stones with no trace surviving further to the west or east. The depth to top of the kerb was 27 ins.

Block 36

A road surface and large flags located in Trench Ec33 is mentioned in the Finds Book (Feature 185), but they do not appear on any plans. A small group of pottery (61MJ) found beneath 185 does not contain anything particularly late so the road surface could conceivably represent the Period I *via quintana*.

The *Porta Quintana*

The only features associated with the gate which were recorded were located in Block 29. Feature 159 has been interpreted as the wall revetting the north side of the passage, 162 as flags of a foundation raft for the gateway, 166 perhaps as a foundation block for the gate's south-east pier supporting the inner archway.

Photograph M36 (see Fig. 7.46), which probably relates to the westernmost trench of Block 29–Da 32, shows two large, neatly worked stone blocks, one laid on top of the other, the uppermost being inset, chamfered and in excess of 0.75m long to judge from the 6ft scale. These blocks may conceivably represent the base of the

Figure 5.3. Photograph M23: Block 29 Trench Db33, looking west; the northernmost block of wall 167, associated with late Building Fragment D, rests on via quintana *surface 163; note the substantial depth of road-related material (164, 165) beneath the surface.*

gate's north-west pier. The general plan Pl 3 depicts the north-west corner of the gateway as surviving in a form consistent with the remains recorded by M36 (cf Fig. 5.1).

Barracks south of the *Via Quintana*

Blocks 10, 28 and 36 are the relevant blocks. No detail plans are known for Block 28. JPG interpreted the features encountered in Block 10 and the western end of Block 36 as belonging to a barrack-like building, initially of Period I but replaced or partially rebuilt to almost the same plan in Period II. The building had its longitudinal axis aligned north–south and its north end fronted the *via quintana*. The Period II building was restored with a width of *c.* 10m, and a single longitudinal partition. Its length is not known. No dimensions for the Period I building are known. Walls 68, 174, 175, and 182 were assigned to Period II, Wall 177 to Period I. In Trench Ec35 of Block 36 the relationship between features assigned to the two periods can be seen: Wall 176 oversails wall 177. For the north frontage of the building, no detailed plans are known. JPG restored a barrack with its longitudinal axis aligned north–south. It should be noted, however, that additional north–south aligned walls are recorded on general plan Pl 3 in Blocks 28 and 36, respectively to the west (154) and east (183, 184) of those described above. When the spacing of the combined pattern of walls is considered, 154 and 183, at least, could comfortably be interpreted, along with 68, 174–6 and 182, as belonging to a Period II barrack with its longitudinal axis aligned east–west, parallel with the *via quintana*.

The West Wall of the Extension

The west wall of the extension was excavated in Block 39 (Feature 212). It was *c.* 2.1m wide, and was composed of large ashlar blocks on its west face and small shaped blocks on its east, facing a core of mortared rubble. Five courses of the east face survived. Against the east face was a series of superimposed levels which appear to be the remains of a turf and soil backing (Features 213, 267, 268). Finds Group 61QP is thought to come from the lowest of these (268); it contained two rim sherds of a samian Dr. 31R and an example of a Bellicus-type mortarium (Other Pottery no. 191), which provide a *terminus post quem* of *c.* AD 150.

No measurement of the distance between the west wall of the extension and the original west wall of the fort seems to have been recorded, and although the trench blocks containing the fort wall can be related to the site grid, the same is not possible for Block 39 containing the extension wall. We have, accordingly, resorted to 'dead-reckoning' to calculate an approximate figure for the width of the extension; this is in the order of 48m.

6. Conclusions

The date of erection of fort

The excavations of 1960–61 have little to contribute to this. The fort remains essentially dated by the inscription from the west gate (RIB 1427) to the governorship of Aulus Platorius Nepos (AD 122–c. 126) and those structures identified by the excavations as the first on their site – *i.e.* the granary and the first period of the building complex to the west of the granary are thus, by implication, also Hadrianic. The little stratified datable material we have at our disposal is not at odds with such a date (see Chapter 2, Table 2.1 – Granary; Chapter 3, Table 3.1 – Building Complex to the West of the Granary).

Modifications during the first period

The first building on the site of the complex to the west of the granary seems to have received some modification during its life. JPG claimed (See Appendix I: typescript report) that in one place a wooden floor was replaced by a stone flagged floor. The generally accepted model of the frontier sees the time that the Antonine Wall was in active service as one of reduced occupation on Hadrian's Wall and JPG may have seen this modification as one of the refurbishments of the primary fort as it was brought back into commission in so-called Hadrian's Wall Period Ib, although he nowhere seems to have stated this explicitly. There is no evidence available from the archive to substantiate the character of the floors but we can identify the finds group from between them with a reasonable degree of confidence (for the difficulties that remain see Structural Synopsis, Block 11, Feature 76). The stamped mortarium of Messorius Martius provides a *terminus post quem* of AD 125–155.

Both the report on the coins (Chapter 8) and that on the decorated and stamped samian (Chapter 9) take it as axiomatic that the general model outlined above is the hypothesis to be tested. For the coins it would seem that imperial monetary policy was a factor of such prevailing influence that no evidence of specific site occupancy could be expected to be detected. For the samian, Brenda Dickinson draws attention on the one hand, to the markedly low proportion of pre-Hadrianic and Hadrianic-Antonine material present, and on the other, to the fact that of the Antonine Central Gaulish ware which can be reasonably closely dated, a high proportion was produced by potters who are not likely to have been at work before *c.* AD 160.

Late Second-Century Destruction

Notwithstanding the paucity of pictorial evidence, it is clear from the entries in the Finds Book that an *in situ* burnt deposit was encountered across both the area occupied by the modified Period I building to the west of the granary and the area occupied by buildings (probably barracks) on the south side of the *via quintana*. In the former area JPG was quite clear that the deposit represented the destruction of the modified Period I building and the little direct evidence we can now glean from the archive supports this conclusion. JPG maintained that the character of the deposit was similar to that excavated at Corbridge (Richmond and Gillam 1950). He regarded them both as evidence of destruction resulting from a breaching of the frontier defences by hostile forces from outside the province. Of the various events attested by literary and epigraphic evidence in the later second and early third centuries he came to favour the 'British War' referred to by Cassius Dio (72, 8), against which Commodus sent Ulpius Marcellus. Absolute dating of the deposits has been and remains extremely problematic, and the Haltonchesters material (see Table 3.2) can make no contribution to the solution of this problem. As far as relational matters are concerned, it can be noted that, with the exception of one stamped mortarium, all of the coarseware types in the Haltonchesters deposit occurred in the Corbridge deposit.

Period II

Our knowledge of the succeeding building in the area to the west of the granary is limited to parts of its east range. JPG regarded its inception as Severan. The dating evidence (see Table 3.1) cannot contribute anything to the discussion.

The destruction deposit did not extend across the granary and the inference is that this building was not destroyed at this time. JPG thought that it had received minor repairs in the early third century (the renewal of the loading bay at the south end of the building) and was destroyed by fire at the end of the third century. The deposits linked to this latter event do not offer an entirely straightforward interpretation (see Blocks 24 and 41) and altogether the evidence is somewhat slight. There is no useful dating evidence for the end of the building and there is no extant evidence to support JPG's claim that fragments of late (*i.e.* fourth-century) buildings were found over the ruins of the granary.

The Extension

Both Jarrett and JPG regarded the demolition of the southern section of the west fort wall and the building of the south-western extension as part of the Severan reorganisation of the frontier dating to the early third century, to accommodate a larger cavalry garrison, the *ala Sabiniana* (attested on RIB 1433 and in the *Notitia Dignitatum*). This remains a reasonable interpretation, but while the evidence does not gainsay it, it does not, on the other hand, provide what might be regarded as a comprehensive supporting case. The evidence cited from the trench excavated in the extension (Block 39) only provides a *terminus post quem* for the deposition of the backing found *in situ*, not for the building of the wall. Rampart backings can come and go, as can be seen at Housesteads. The evidence from Jarrett's trench of 1956 is more secure, though it is still difficult to identify clearly on the published section the 'levelling' layer which he associated with the demolition of the fort wall, and no direct sequential relationship can be established between the remains of the fort wall and the building in the extension upon which he bases some of his argument.

Late Third-Century Destruction

JPG's typescript Interim Report of June 1961 (see Appendix I) makes clear that for a while he entertained the notion that the third-century occupation of much, if not all of the fort also ended in destruction:

> While the finer products of the large Roman potteries in Northamptonshire were still on the market, that is not later than the end of the third century, the fort was burnt down a second time. This was doubtless the work of those tribes who were already coming to be referred to as the Picts. Granary, commander's house, barracks and stables were all destroyed, and all by fire.
>
> Typescript Interim

The evidence on which he probably based this assertion can be reconstructed as follows:

1. There was evidence (though we must now regard it as slight; see above) that the granary had been destroyed by fire at the end of the third century.
2. In the area of the barracks south of the *via quintana*, Block 36, Finds Group 61LV (recorded as being 'Below flat slabs (destruction layer))' yielded a beaker in Lower Nene Valley Colour-coated Ware (Other Pottery no. 164); this is certainly one of '*the finer products of the large Roman potteries in Northamptonshire*'.
3. The secondary structures excavated by Richmond in the north-east corner of the fort and dated to the third century contained drains which were '*filled with burnt wattle and daub, attesting the nature of the destroyed and vanished superstructure*' (Simpson and Richmond, 1937, 167)

There is a further piece of evidence which JPG may have been aware of but did not cite explicitly. A finds group (61QE) from Block 39, is recorded as coming from 'a patch of burnt wattle and daub', and contained a fragment of a mortarium with a reeded hammer-head rim in Hartshill-Mancetter fabric whose date, while not now considered to be as late as hitherto, is certainly third century (Other pottery no. 181).

By 1974 JPG had retreated from this view, but his very explicit statement that, '*The burnt wattle and daub, in evidence at both sites at the end of Period I, was absent at the end of Period II*' (Gillam 1974, 13; see Appendix I) is curious and uncharacteristic since he seems to be rejecting the evidence rather than the interpretation. At least two pieces of evidence of burnt wattle and daub containing or sealing pottery which is datable to the third century are known. The interpretation of such small pieces of evidence as a generalised destruction is hardly justified but the evidence, as far as we can tell at this distance, still stands.

The Fourth-Century Buildings

Interpretation of the latest buildings on the site went through two distinct phases. After the end of the 1960 season of work those whose walls were in rough ashlar masonry were assigned to Period III, *i.e.* the Constantian 'Wall Period III' beginning *c.* AD 296, while those whose walls were composed of long slab sills with holes for (timber?) uprights (the so-called 'Park Railing' stones) were assigned to Period IV, *i.e.* the Theodosian 'Wall Period IV' beginning *c.* AD 367–8. By the end of the 1961 season account had been taken of the fact that all the buildings, whatever their constructional type, were at the same general level, that neither type encroached on the other, and that there was dating evidence which placed at least one example of each technique in the later fourth century (Fragments A and D, see Table 4.1), and all the buildings were assigned to Period IV; this is the interpretation that has prevailed to the present. It must, however, be regarded as very much a minimal interpretation and should be seen in the context of the methodological framework of the time in which it was first propounded. Even the small amount of evidence at our disposal in writing this report hints at a much greater level of complexity which was present in the archaeological record but not really addressed.

Abandonment in the late third – early fourth century

One of the consequences of the conflation of the Period III and IV structures was that it left a Period (III) with no assignable structures and it was this which seems to have given further impetus to the idea of an abandonment of the fort in the period *c.* AD 270–367, which had already been taking shape. Evidence which was marshalled in support was mainly the fact that the latest structures were founded on a build-up of material at least 0.6m deep lying over the dilapidated structures of Period II and this was interpreted as an accumulation which had occurred during a long gap in occupation. The evidence at our disposal now does not really allow us to make any kind of independent assessment of the character of this deposit, but, on general grounds alone one might suggest that it could equally well be interpreted as the product of levelling up for new construction rather than soil build-up during a prolonged period of desertion. Neither the coins nor the coarseware can be used to support the case for abandonment either. The, admittedly short, coin list published by Jarrett from 1956–58 excavations (1959, 189–190; 1960, 154–156) includes a significant proportion which fall within the period 268–363 (16 of the 37 identifiable examples) and the full coin assemblage from the site (see Chapter 8) displays broadly the same characteristics as those from the other forts along the Wall. In the coarseware assemblage there are no typological *lacunae* which might be judged significant, and, in any case, the assemblage is neither large enough nor is our dating of a sufficiently fine resolution to enable any statistically valid judgements to be made.

The Phase Plans (Figs 6.1–6.3)

By A. Rushworth

The following three phase plans have been included at the request of English Heritage. JND did not intend to include phase plans of this kind, feeling that their inclusion was more likely to result in confusion than enlightenment given the fragmentary nature of the evidence, and in particular would give the impression that far more was understood regarding the fort's development than was actually the case. The extended captions are an attempt to provide sufficient 'health warnings' to prevent any such confusion or over-confidence arising by making explicit the basis on which each phase plan has been drawn up.

The potential for error when assembling overall plans from diverse published sources, in particular with regard to positioning structures or trenches exactly, is obvious. The results here are intended only to be representational and should not be used as a basis for precise calculations regarding building areas and dimensions or the like.

The allocation of a particular building or phase of building to a specific phase plan is based on the periodisation originally applied to those structures by their excavators. Inevitably this was heavily influenced by the Wall-Period chronology which held unchallenged sway whilst all the three main twentieth-century campaigns of excavation were underway at Haltonchesters (1935–6, 1956–8, 1960–61). The problems inherent in this rigid chronological periodisation are well recognised and need no repetition here.

In general, the aim has been to show exactly where walls were found and, whenever possible, where they were not found within known excavation trenches and plot them in relation to simple building outlines, but not to attempt any speculative, detailed restorations of the internal arrangements of these buildings.

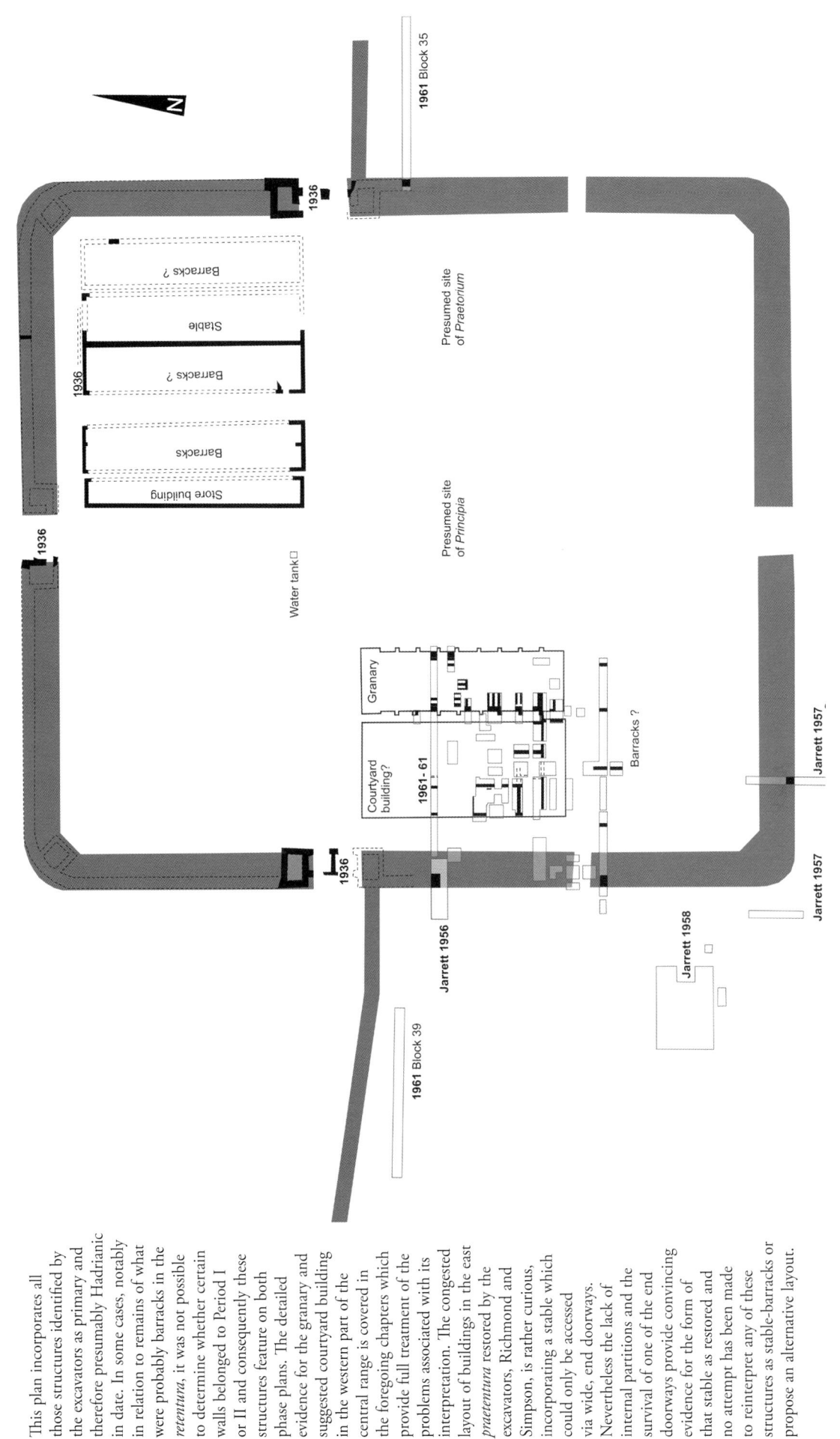

This plan incorporates all those structures identified by the excavators as primary and therefore presumably Hadrianic in date. In some cases, notably in relation to remains of what were probably barracks in the *retentura*, it was not possible to determine whether certain walls belonged to Period I or II and consequently these structures feature on both phase plans. The detailed evidence for the granary and suggested courtyard building in the western part of the central range is covered in the foregoing chapters which provide full treatment of the problems associated with its interpretation. The congested layout of buildings in the east *praetentura* restored by the excavators, Richmond and Simpson, is rather curious, incorporating a stable which could only be accessed via wide, end doorways. Nevertheless the lack of internal partitions and the survival of one of the end doorways provide convincing evidence for the form of that stable as restored and no attempt has been made to reinterpret any of these structures as stable-barracks or propose an alternative layout.

Figure 6.1. Period I Phase Plan.

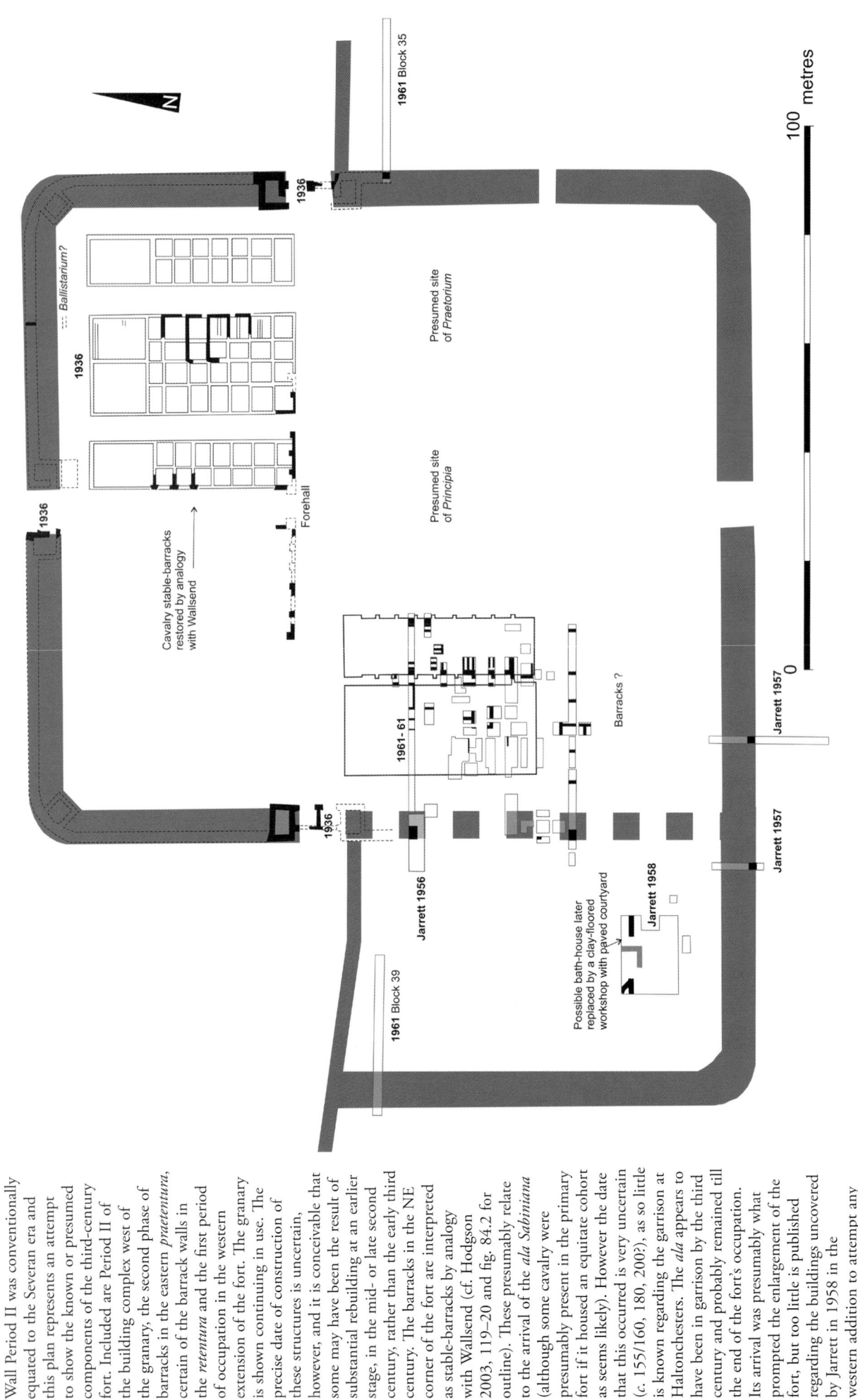

Wall Period II was conventionally equated to the Severan era and this plan represents an attempt to show the known or presumed components of the third-century fort. Included are Period II of the building complex west of the granary, the second phase of barracks in the eastern *praetentura*, certain of the barrack walls in the *retentura* and the first period of occupation in the western extension of the fort. The granary is shown continuing in use. The precise date of construction of these structures is uncertain, however, and it is conceivable that some may have been the result of substantial rebuilding at an earlier stage, in the mid- or late second century, rather than the early third century. The barracks in the NE corner of the fort are interpreted as stable-barracks by analogy with Wallsend (cf. Hodgson 2003, 119–20 and fig. 84.2 for outline). These presumably relate to the arrival of the *ala Sabiniana* (although some cavalry were presumably present in the primary fort if it housed an equitate cohort as seems likely). However the date that this occurred is very uncertain (c. 155/160, 180, 200?), as so little is known regarding the garrison at Haltonchesters. The *ala* appears to have been in garrison by the third century and probably remained till the end of the fort's occupation. Its arrival was presumably what prompted the enlargement of the fort, but too little is published regarding the buildings uncovered by Jarrett in 1958 in the western addition to attempt any reconstruction of their outline.

Figure 6.2. Period II Phase Plan.

This plan incorporates all the late buildings assigned at various stages to Periods III or IV or to the late Roman period more generally. It includes those identified in 1960–61 some of which used the so-called 'park-railing' construction technique, featuring long sill blocks with recessed holes, presumably designed to support a timber-framed superstructure; and also the bathhouse whose discovery and excavation in 1823 and 1827 was described in detail by John Hodgson, which is tentatively positioned in the NE corner of the fort. JPG considered the fort was unoccupied or largely so in Period III, but two phases of structure attributable to the later Roman period appear to have been uncovered by Jarrett in the western extension and there are no evident corresponding lacunae in the coin assemblage from the entire site or 1960–61 coarseware assemblage (see Chapter 6). Moreover the available evidence from the 1960–61 excavations hints that a much greater level of complexity was present in the archaeological record. Accordingly the structures shown on the plan should not be considered as all belonging to a single period of late Roman occupation (IV). Instead they may have been constructed at differing stages during the period stretching from the mid- to late third through the fourth century, whilst those shown as possibly continuing in use from earlier periods (*e.g.* the granary and the NE barracks) may conceivably have gone out of use before some or all of the newer buildings were erected.

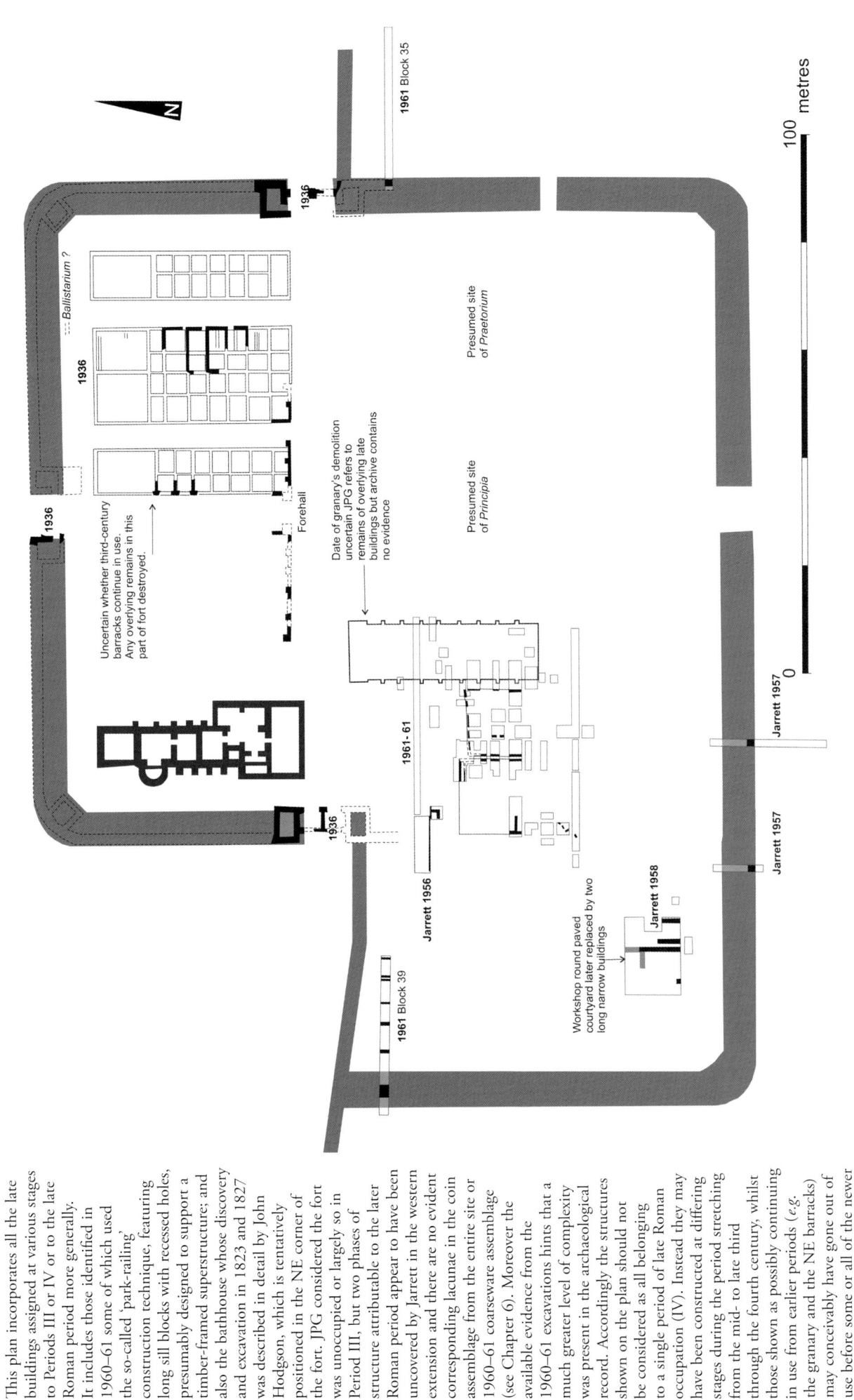

Figure 6.3. Phase Plan Period III/IV Phase Plan.

7. Structural Synopsis

Block 1 (Fig. 7.1).
Trenches: Da14, Db14, Dc15.
Plans: Pl 22.
Photographs: none.
Provenanced Finds Groups: 60DD, 60DZ, 60CJ.

The north-west arm of this trench block (Trenches Da14 and Db14) was a re-excavation of Jarrett's trench of 1956. No detail plans from 1960 are known. One detail plan is known for Trench Dc15 (Pl 22). The position and dimensions of most of the structural elements described below have been taken from Jarrett's plan (Jarrett 1959, Figs 2 and 3).

Structural Elements

1) West fort wall. Jarrett (1959, 178) describes the components of this: a foundation of small squared stones resting on a flagged footing; a basal course of masonry 14 ins. high; a chamfered plinth course; a core of rubble and mortar. He records the width of the wall as seven feet nine inches (*c.* 2.4m) over the foundations. Jarrett's excavation recovered a group of pottery from the 'levelling' associated with the demolition of the wall (Jarrett 1959, 178 and 188, Group A). His report does not include any drawings but references the vessels to Gillam types. The latest type from the group was a Gillam type 313, a round-rim dish in BB2 whose introduction in the north is usually dated to the end of the 2nd century (see Bidwell and Speak, 1994, 227–8).

2) Backing of fort wall. Jarrett (1959, 178 and Figs 2 and 3) simply records this as 'turfwork'. The width shown surviving in the Jarrett trench is *c.* 3.1m; that shown on the 1961 general plan (Pl 3) is *c.* 4.3m.

3) Wall running parallel to, and to the west (*i.e.* outside) of the fort wall. Jarrett's excavations recovered a two pottery vessels of 2nd-century date from below the floor of the building of which this wall formed part (Jarrett 1959, 178 and 188, Group B). On the 1961 general plan (Pl 3), JPG assigned the wall to Period II.

4) The remains of a building whose north wall overlay walls 1 and 3. On the plan of Jarrett's trench (Jarrett 1959, fig. 2) it is shown partially embedded in the south baulk. He described it as 'crudely built' and notes that 'subsidence over the lighter soil of the rampart backing had caused it to break its back across the demolished remains of the fort wall' (Jarrett 1959, 183). The detail plan of trench Dc15 (Pl 22) shows the eastern end of this building. Its internal width is *c.* 1.34m. A maximum of two courses survived, quite heavily robbed. There is no indication of what kind of stone was used. The width of the east wall fragment is 0.52m. The lower course of the east end wall on its east side (*i.e.* outside the building) is offset from the upper course by *c.* 0.12m. Within the walls several large flags are shown; a marginal note says "large flags below

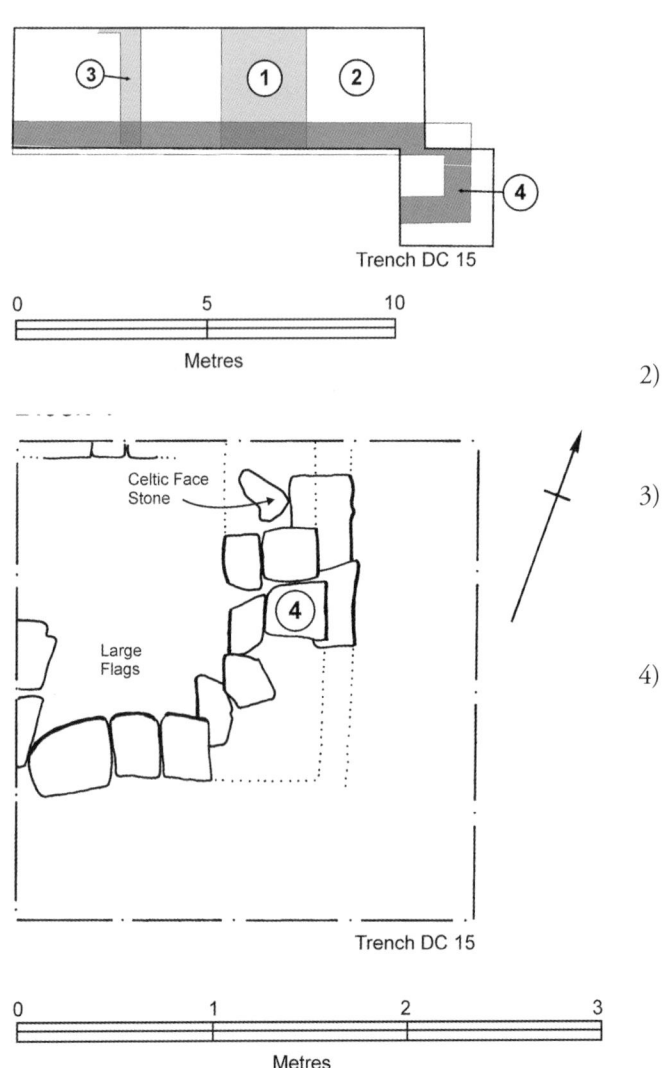

Figure 7.1. Block 1: plan.

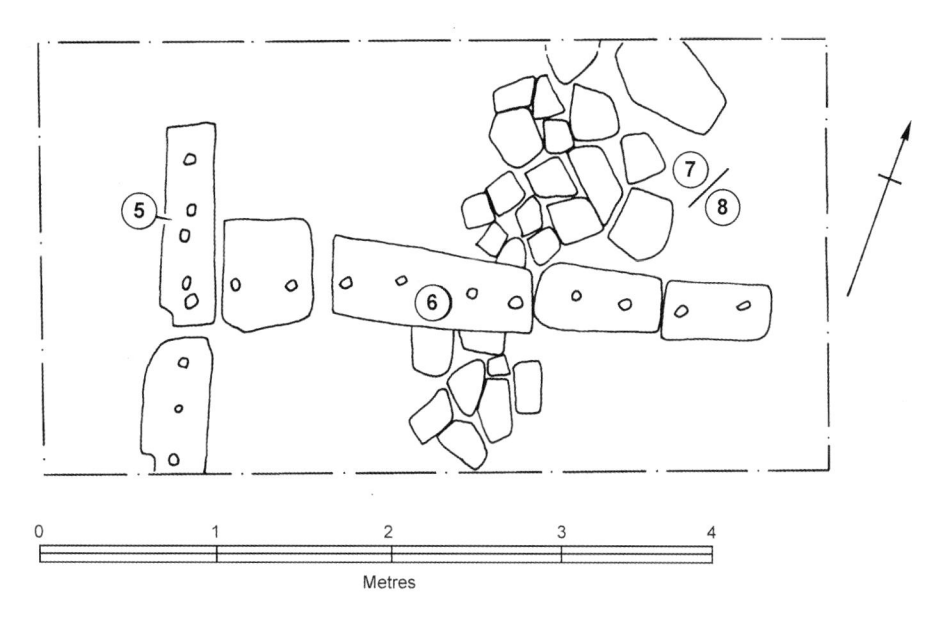

Figure 7.2. Block 2: plan.

level of surviving courses". Outside the building, *i.e.* in the eastern and southern areas of the trench a note indicates "cobbles (broken freestone) over all this area at *c.* 2 1/2 ft". By the fragment of the north wall of the building embedded in the north baulk is a note: "Probably south face of the same wall of which MGJ got N face in 1956". Arrowed to a rounded stone forming part of the north west corner of the building is a note: "Stone with crude 'Celtic' face on SE side". This enables the finds group to be identified as 60DD which has a note: "Rough face engraved on side of large sandstone block". The find is currently missing. Jarrett records that the building 'sealed' a sherd from a painted Crambeck mortarium (Gillam type 290) datable to the late 4th century. JPG assigned the building to Period IV.

Block 2 (Figs 4.4–4.5, 5.2 and 7.2–7.3)

Trenches Db25, Dc25, Dd25
Plans: PI 21, 41
Photographs: M25, M26, M27, M53a, C226, C240
Provenanced Finds Groups: 60HS, 60ID, 60IX, 61CM, 61CU, 61DW (Trench Db25)

Structural Elements

5) North–south wall. This is located close to the west baulk of Db25. It consists of two roughly hewn blocks, the northernmost of which measures *c.* 1.1m × 0.3m × 0.3m. Each stone has a row of small, approximately circular holes running longitudinally down the centre of its upper face. The holes are all about the same size, *c.* 50mm in diameter and at least 100mm deep. There are five holes in the northern stone and three visible in the southern. The vertical stratigraphy is not very clear from the plan. The depth of each stone from ground level is given. This varies from 6 to 10 inches (0.15m–0.25m).

Figure 7.3. Photograph M53a: Block 2 Trench Dc25, north-facing section beneath 'park-railing' sill wall 6 (cf photograph M27 at position of vertical ranging staff), perhaps intended to show a deposit of west rampart clay?

Photo M27 provides some information on what lies below the wall: no foundation courses or cobbling can be seen and the stones appear to rest directly on top of the fill which overlies the demolished/ robbed out fort wall. Assigned to Period IV.

6) East–west wall. This runs at right angles for *c.* 3.1m from 5) above. It consists of four roughly hewn blocks whose width and depth appears (from photo M27) to be about the same as those of wall 5) above. As with 5) each stone has a row of small, approximately circular holes running longitudinally down the centre of its upper face. The dimensions of these appear to be about the same as those of 5) above. From west to east the four blocks have, respectively, two, four, two and two holes. The depths marked on the stones, and the evidence of photo M27 show that wall 6 is set about 0.23m

lower then 5. It also appears (from photo M27) to have, at least at its extant eastern end, a foundation course of small, irregularly shaped stone. How far, if at all, the wall extended beyond what is shown in plan 41 is not clear. On the overall trench plan (Pl 3) Gillam showed it as robbed out for *c*. 3m up to the east end of trench Dd25, and then as conjectured for a further 3.7m. Assigned to Period IV.

7) Surface (?). Photos M25 and M26 give most of the detail of this. On either side of wall 6 were a number of large stone slabs or flags whose tops were at the same level as the tops of the wall stones. Most are irregularly shaped, but at least two are well shaped blocks which could well have been re-used from an earlier period. There is a sketch plan of this area on Pl 41 showing flagstones at different levels, some overlying others. To the south of wall 6 there are certainly suggestions, from the photos, that these flags did form several surfaces, of different periods, rather than just being tumble. All of them could have been associated with wall 5.

8) Mixture of earth and large irregularly shaped stone. Located below 7. What it represents is not clear, though its confused nature suggests that it is most likely to be demolition or collapse from previous periods. Photos M26 and M27 show it most clearly.

274) Clay. This does not appear on any plan but can be seen on photograph M27 below the material (7, 8?) underlying wall 6. It could be the remains of the backing of the west fort wall but as it appears from the photograph to be located quite deep in the trench it could equally be natural. See also M53a for detail of clay in section.

Block 3

Trenches: Db31
Finds Groups: 60JG

There are no extant plans of this trench.

Block 4 (Figs 2.2 and 7.4)

Trenches: Dd14, De14, Ea14, Eb14, Ec14, Ed14, Ee14, Fa14, Fb14, Fc14, Fd14, Fe14
Plans: Pl 17, 23, 25, 26
Pl 23, 25 and 26 show parts of the trench at an early point during excavation. They show mostly small areas of Period III or Period IV flagging. Pl 17 shows the full length of the trench at an advanced state of excavation with main structural elements in coloured pencil.
Photographs: M12 shows the east end of the trench from around the west side of trench Fb14.
Finds Groups: Trench Dd14: 60BV, 60CK, 60CZ
De14: 60GH, 60HF, 60KN
Ea14: 60AK, 60CS, 60FZ, 60KB, 60KG, 60KM
Eb14: 60AS, 60AY
Ec14: 60KU, 60KX, 60LC
Ed14: 60LE, 60LL, 60LQ, 60MB
Fd14: 60BG

Structural Elements (From East–West)

9) Main east wall of granary, running north–south. This is totally robbed out at this point.
10) Foundation for 9. 'Raft' of stone at depth 56 ins.
11) Wall, running north–south. Interpreted as a sleeper wall which originally supported the floor of the building. Only the west face survives. Possibly the east face never existed, and the wall was built up against the inside face of the main east wall. Width *c*. 0.7m. "Top course at 16ins depth".
12) Wall running north–south. Interpreted as a sleeper wall which originally supported the floor of the building. Located *c*. 1.15m to west of 3 (approx centre to centre). Partly robbed. Width *c*. 0.62m. "Top course *c*. 14ins depth".
13) Foundation/footing for 11 and 12. Large flags. "Large flag at 34 ins depth".
14) Yellow clay. Beneath 13.
15) Wall running north–south. Interpreted as a sleeper wall which originally supported the floor of the building. Located *c*. 5.9m west of 12. Partly robbed. Width *c*. 0.53m. "Sleeper wall on flags. Top course 24ins depth."
16) Wall running north–south. Interpreted as a sleeper wall which originally supported the floor of the building. Located *c*. 1.15m west of 15. Partly robbed. Width *c*. 1.9m. "Sleeper wall on flags. White mortar/rubble core. 21 ins depth, top course".
17) Foundation for 15 and 16. Large flags, "25 ins depth".
18) Yellow clay. Below 17. It is not clear if this clay also runs beneath the robber trench for the main west wall of the granary.
19) Robber-trench running north–south. Interpreted as the robber-trench for the main west wall of the granary which appeared to be completely robbed away at this point. "Robber trench; mortar, yellow clay and freestone chips."
20) Raft of irregularly shaped stone. Located in the area between sleeper walls 11 and 12 and 15 and 16. Width *c*. 2.71m. The relationship between this raft and the yellow clay on which the flags and sleeper wall rest is not clear from the plans. Depths written on the plan suggest that the raft and the areas of clay are at about the same level and what can be seen from the photograph tends to confirm this. The point is made clear in the entry in Roman Britain in 1960 (see Appendix I): The Granary "had been founded on a massive stone raft of flagging laid on clay, itself resting on packed broken limestone."
21) Wall running north–south. Located just to west of the robbed-out west wall of granary. Faced on the west side only. Top is 29 ins deep. Called Period III. "Period III wall connecting granary buttresses. One face only". This suggests that JPG associated it with the granaries. This wall does not seem to have been picked up in the other trenches along the west wall of the granary.
22) Wall running north–south. Located just to the west of 21. Width *c*. 0.6m. Five courses survived (there is a note to this effect on Pl 25). Type of stone unknown. "Treat as II" in red biro with a tick next

7. *Structural Synopsis* 47

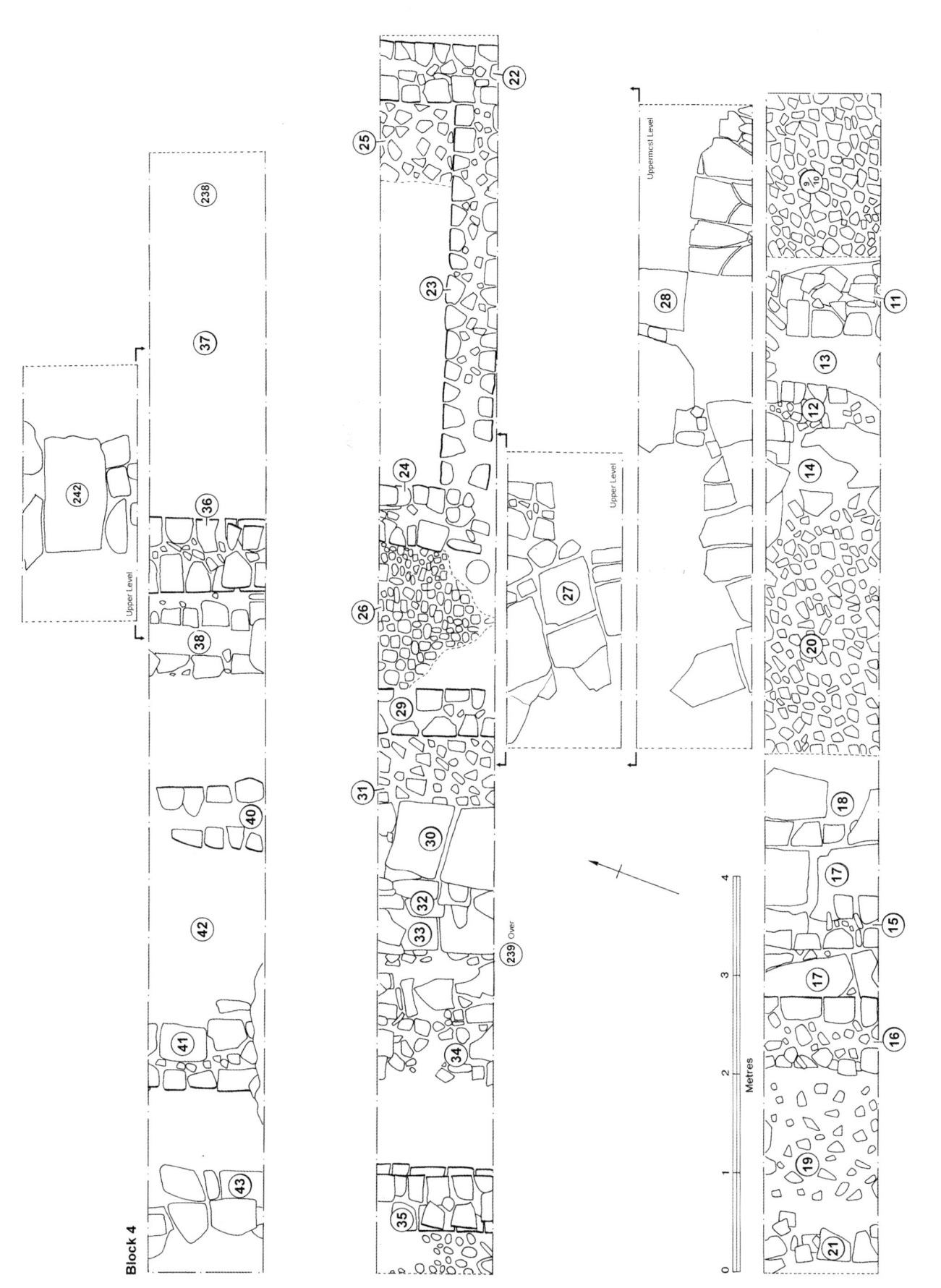

Figure 7.4. Block 4: plan.

to the wall. This has been scribbled through with blue crayon and "II ?" written next to it. "E wall of forage store? Top course at *c*. 13 in depth".
23) Wall running westwards from a straight joint with 22. Similar sized stone, similar width. Number of courses unknown. "Sleeper wall period I *c*. 42 ins depth. It should be 3 ins further north to allow for slope on trench side." "1961 Treat as I" in red biro. This last scribbled through with blue crayon and "II?" written next to it.
24) Wall running north–south parallel to 22. It makes a straight joint with 23. Similar width and size of stone. "28 ins depth". "36 ins depth". "Sleeper wall period III". "1961 Treat as II" in red biro. This last scribbled through in blue crayon and "IV?" written next to it. If elements 22, 23 and 24 are associated, they form a building or a part of a building *c*. 5.23m wide.
25) Robber trench (?) running north–south. Located immediately to the west of 22. This wall is shown restored on the general plan Pl 3. On the detailed plan Pl 17, is a small area of irregular stone marked with "55 ins depth".
26) Robber trench (?) running north–south. Located immediately to the west of 24. This wall is shown restored on the general plan Pl 3. On the detailed plan Pl 17, is a small area of irregular stone marked with "32 ins–36 ins depth".
27) Flagging. Shown on Pl 23 for trench Ed14 (drawn 12.7.60). Located over and to west of 29. Depths given: 13 ins, 19 ins. "Flags of period III (?) below flags of period IV, sloping down to west." Pottery from finds group 60MB underlying the flags provides a *terminus post quem* of *c*. AD 250.
28) Flagging. Shown on Pl 17 and Pl 25. Located over and to west of wall 29 and running eastwards over walls 23, 24 and 29, robber trenches 25 and 26 and flags 27. Pl 17: "Flags of IV 9 ins depth". Pl 25: "Part of great area of ? late C4 flagging at 11 ins".
29) Wall running north–south. Immediately to the west of 26. Width *c*. 0.48m. "30 ins depth". From the different plans and the depths marked, it must underlie flags 27 of period III. In red biro: "1961 treat as I or II". This scribbled out in blue crayon and "II ?" written next to it.
30) Wall (?) running north–south. Located *c*. 1.5m west of 29 (centre to centre). The stretch which is visible in the trench is composed of two large slabs which may be flags rather than elements of a wall. "Period IV wall ? 0–6 ins depth". In red biro: "1961 comment Possibly not wall".
31) Footings/foundations (?). Located between 29 and 30. The representation on the plan suggests irregularly shaped stone. "*c*. 40–45 ins depth".
32) Wall running north–south. Partly underlying the west side of 30. Composed of irregularly shaped stone. At least partly robbed though the east face may survive under 30. "32 ins depth" (top of northernmost stone). "Period II ?". Not shown on general plan Pl 3.
33) Wall or possibly footings for 32). Immediately to west of and partly underlying 32. The stretch visible in the trench is composed of two shaped stones of reasonable size (at least 0.55 × 0.48m) which appear to be aligned north–south. "44 ins depth". Not shown on general plan Pl 3.
34) Footings/foundations (?). Immediately to west of 33. A patch of small irregularly shaped stone extending across the width of the trench and for *c*. 1.4m to the west of 33. "50 ins depth". "Footings of west wall of forage store ?". Not shown on general plan Pl 3.
35) Wall running north–south. Located *c*. 1.2m west of the western edge of 34. Two courses survive. Lower course composed of faced stone (*c*. 0.36 × 0.29m). Upper course composed of faced stone (*c*. 0.24 × 0.26m). Lower course *c*. 0.67m wide. Upper course *c*. 0.53m wide. "Period I wall". "Upper course 33 ins depth. Lower course 42 ins depth". This is probably the east wall of the west range of what was referred to during the 1960 season as the "forage store".
36) Wall running north–south. Located *c*. 4.9m west of 35 (centre to centre). Very similar appearance to 35. Two courses with upper offset from lower. Stone of similar size used in both. "Period I wall". "Upper courses *c*. 36 ins depth". "Lower course *c*. 42 ins depth". This is the west wall of the west range of what was referred to during the 1960 season as the "forage store". The internal width of the range is *c*. 4.18m.
37) Floor (?). The area between walls 35 and 36 is shown on the plan (Pl 17) as covered with cobbles. "Cobbles at 40 ins depth". The relationship between the cobbles and the walls is not made explicit but they do not appear to have extended outside the line of the two walls and therefore should probably be taken as associated with the walls. The finds groups from this area (Ea14) include two (60KB and 60KG) which relate to a layer of burnt wattle and daub (see 238).
38) Drain: stone lining. Located immediately to the west of 36. Composed of faced stone of similar size to that used in walls 35 and 36. Water channel *c*. 0.26m wide. Only one course shown. "48 ins depth". This should probably be seen as the stone lining of a drain of which 39 is also a part. The finds groups from De14: 60GH 60HF and 60KN all seem to be from beneath a flag level in the trench. There is only one flag shown on plan Pl 17 and this is at the south end of the drain and was obviously a drain cover. It is possible therefore that all these groups are from the fill of the drain. The pottery is all probably Hadrianic.
39) Drain: clay sealant (?). Yellow clay shown on either side of the stone lining 38. It fills the gap between the east side of the lining and wall 36 and is shown extending *c*. 0.12m west of the west side of the stone lining 38. No depth given.
40) Wall or drain running north–south. Located *c*. 1.82m west of the drain 38/39 (centre to centre). It is only faintly drawn on the plan (Pl 17). It extends into the south baulk of the trench but not as far as the north baulk. It is not particularly well faced. It is *c*. 0.74m wide. "II?" "40 ins depth". Not shown on general plan Pl 3.
41) Wall running north–south. Located *c*. 2.45m

7. Structural Synopsis

west of wall 40 (centre to centre). Composed of a mixture of more or less shaped stone. "Period ?II walling uncovered by MGJ, recorded by JPG 26/9/60. Depth of *c.* 32 ins. Clean orange well laid stones, like period I lies on solid mass of stones and chippings, which also underlie drain to east, and overly limestone foundation". This last in JPG's handwriting. It is not clear which drain he means: 38/39 or 40 which could be interpreted as a drain.

42) Surface; probably the *intervallum* road. In the area between 40 and 41 on plan PI 17 is a note: "Clean orange stone packing at 40 ins". This is possibly the same level as the "solid mass of stones and chippings" referred to under 41. Finds groups 60BV 60CK 60CZ are associated with this area. The description of their contexts suggests that there were at least four surfaces here, rather than just the one implied by the plan.

43) Wall (?) running north–south. Located *c.* 1.56m west of 41. Several medium to large stones/slabs arranged in two rows aligned north–south. The east edge of the west row overlies the west edge of the east row. Depths: west row: 10 ins, 13 ins, 15 ins; east row: 16 ins, 20 ins. "Period IV wall ???" "1961 comment: Possibly *not* wall". Not shown on general plan PI 3.

238) Destruction Deposit. Mentioned only in Finds Book. In the area between walls 35 and 36 (trench Ea14). Finds Groups 60KB and 60KG. 60KB: "Burnt wattle and daub below topsoil"; KG60: "In dirty orange clay below burnt wattle and daub".

239) Destruction Deposit. Mentioned only in Finds Book. In trench Ec14. Finds Groups: 60KU and 60KX. 60KU: "Burnt material below topsoil"; 60KX: "Patch of burnt material below topsoil W of period IV wall".

242) Small area of flagging shown on plan PI 25. Overlies eastern side of wall 36. Depths given on plan to the tops of various flags range between 29 and 34 ins.

Block 5 (Figs 7.5–7.7)

Trenches: Ea24, Eb24
Plans: PI 20 shows Ea24 and Eb24 in their final state. PI 24 shows Ea 24 at a fairly early stage of excavation. Part of the Hadrianic wall is visible but much of the trench is still covered with tumbled stone at a high level.
Photographs: M32: Eb 24 from east end; M33
Provenanced finds groups: Ea24: 60DA, 60EA, 60EP, 60FJ, 60FP, 60GJ, 61BF
Eb24: 60DP, 60DQ, 60EF, 60FG, 60FR

Main Structural Elements

44) Wall running north–south. This is the main west wall of the Period I courtyard building. JPG shows it running through from north to south, on the general plan PI 3 but it is a little less clear on PI 20. It also seems to have been partly robbed so its shape and dimensions are not well defined. Depths: 36.25 ins, 37 ins, 39.5 ins.

45) Wall running east–west. This runs from a junction with 44 eastwards. As restored by JPG on general plan PI 3 it continues beyond the trench, since it forms the north wall of the south range of the building, but there is no particular evidence for this on plan PI 20, where it stops at its junction with 46. Constructed of faced stone (all *c.* 0.3m long). Wall width *c.* 0.58m. Depths between 37 and 48 ins.

46) Wall running north–south. Located in the east part of the trench. It runs north from a junction with 45. Similar construction and width to 45. Depth of wall top all about 43 ins. All these walls (44, 45 and 46) are designated Period I on both PI 20 and on the general plan PI 3.

47) Floor/foundation (?). Yellow clay layer, shown on PI 20 in all the spaces surrounding the walls 44,

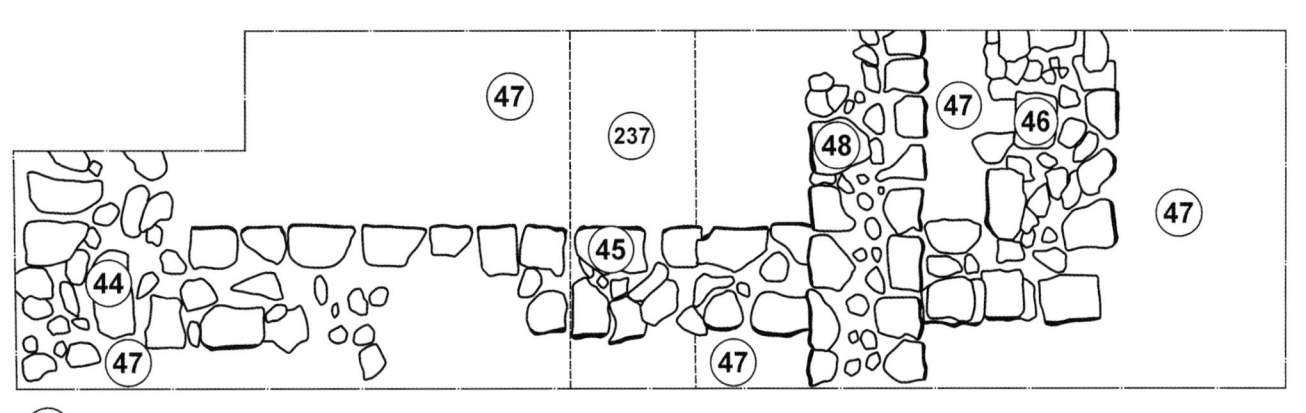

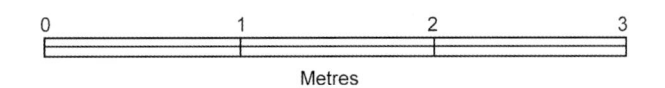

Figure 7.5. Block 5: plan.

Figure 7.6. Photograph M32: Labelled 'Haltonchesters 1960. Corner of second-century building'; Block 5 Trench Eb24 before removal of baulk between it and Ea24; looking west. Shows wall 45 passing beneath 48 and abutting 46.

Figure 7.7. Photograph M33: Labelled 'Haltonchesters 1960. Fourth-century wall above second-century wall'; Block 5 Trench Eb24 before removal of baulk between it and Ea24, looking east. Wall 45 passes beneath 48.

45 and 46. No depths are given for it and thus its relationship to the walls just mentioned is not clear. On analogy with the clay of the granary raft, it is not natural but intended as some kind of foundation or floor base.

48) Wall running north–south. Parallel to and immediately west of wall 46. Runs over wall 45. Photograph M32 shows that there is approx 0.53m between the topmost surviving course of wall 45 and the bottom course of wall 48. Topmost surviving courses are between 2 and 6 ins below ground surface. It is designated Period III on the detailed plan (Pl 20) but Period IV on the general plan Pl 3.

237) Wall running north–south. Parallel to and to the west of 48. Shown only on Pl 3. Continuation of 51 in Block 5 and 72 in block 11. Interpreted as Period IV.

241) Destruction Deposit. Mentioned only in finds book:

Finds Group 61BF, for trench Fa24 (west side of Block 5): "In and below the destruction layer of yellow clay".

Block 6
Trench: Ea15
Finds Group: 60FM

There are no plans of this trench either general or detailed. The only record of its existence is the entry in the Finds Book which associates finds group and trench designator.

Block 7 (Figs 4.2–4.3 and 7.8–7.15)

This block is an amalgamation of a number of trenches dug in 1960 and 61.

Trenches: De22, Ea21, Ea22, Eb22, Eb23
Plans: Pl 19, Pl 23, Pl 42, Pl 43, Pl 51
Provenanced Finds Groups: De22: 61KJ, 61KP, 61MI, 61PZ
Ea21: 61JX 61OC
Ea22: 61DL
Ea23: 60JA
Photographs: M1, M2, M3, C207, C208 and C210 show the early features in trench Ea22 from the east and west.
M29 and M30 show the "Park Railing Stones" of the late levels in trench Ea22, from east.
M34 possibly shows trench Eb22, south-eastern leg, from the east, where the 2nd C and the "late" walls are parallel.
M35 and C211 show walls 55, 63 and 261 (N face) north eastern leg.
M40a and C209 show the possible destruction deposit in Trench Ea22, north facing section (cf. M2 centre left).

Major Structural Elements
Late Structures

49) Wall running east–west. Located in the northern part of the block. It enters the trench through the westernmost baulk of the northern half. It terminates *c.* 4.6m from the west baulk where, according to JPG's interpretative scheme as realised on the general trench plan Pl 3 it turned south. It is composed of five roughly shaped blocks all *c.* 0.5m wide and 0.3m thick. The largest is some 1.44m long. All the stones have holes *c.* 60mm in diameter and at least 60mm deep in their top surfaces. Those in the stone closest to the west baulk and in the stones fourth and fifth from the baulk have holes which are arranged in a single row running longitudinally along the mid-line of the face. Those in the remaining two stones are arranged in a more haphazard fashion. Depths: between 2 and 7 ins below turf level. Nothing can really be said about the foundations of the stones. No comment is made on the plans and the levels below the stones are not visible on the photographs. The photographs do show an area of jumbled stone at the east end of the extant stretch of wall. It seems to be at the same general level as the wall. It could represent: a) something associated with the life of the building; b) something post dating the life of the building, *i.e.* something resulting from a process combining some or all of: demolition, robbing, collapse.

50) Isolated stone. Located *c.* 1.08m east of the easternmost stone of 49. It is of similar dimensions to the stones of 49 and like those it has holes (four somewhat haphazardly arranged) in its upper face. Depth 28 ins. On the interpretative general plan (Pl 3) it is shown as an isolated feature without further comment. As mentioned above, JPG shows wall 49 turning south before it reaches 50.

51) Isolated stone. Located in the south-western part of trench Eb23. It is of similar dimensions to the stones of 49 and has five stone arranged in a roughly linear fashion on its upper face. Depth 14 ins. On the interpretative general plan Pl 3 this is restored as the southward return of 49.

51A) Isolated stone. Located in the north-western part of trench Eb23. Depth 8–18 ins. It may be part of the same feature as 51.

52) Wall running east–west. Located at the west end of the northern part of the block *c.* 1.08m to the south of 49. It runs from the west baulk *c.* 1.44m into the trench. It is composed of four roughly shaped stones all *c.* 0.35m square (in plan). Depths: 9–12 ins. All have holes of roughly similar dimensions to the ones on the stones of 49, on their upper faces. The two westernmost have two, the others one hole apiece. "Period IV partition". Shown on the general interpretative plan Pl 3 as a partition within the building of which 49 and 51 are the north and east walls respectively.

53) Wall running north–south. Located in the middle of the southern half of trench Eb23. A 1.44m length of it is shown on plan Pl 19. It is *c.* 0.71m wide and survives four courses (*c.* 0.48m) high (this can be seen in photograph M34). It comprises roughly shaped stone (average dimensions 0.2 × 0.2 × 0.12m) facing a core which, to judge from plan Pl 19, is of earth and small stone (the core is not visible on the photograph). Depth: 5 ins below turf line. In the interpretation current at the time of the interim report in *Roman Britain in 1960* this was restored as the wall of a Period III (Constantian) building but by the time of *Roman Britain in 1961* JPG had decided that the 'Constantian' buildings were actually contemporary with the "Park Railings" buildings and both were assigned to Period IV (Theodosian).

261) Wall running east–west. Located on east side of northern part of block. The south face only is known and consists of four faced blocks facing some sort of core (*i.e.* the core is represented pictorially but not described on Pl 19). Four courses survived. One height measurement, 26 ins (0.7m), is associated with the wall on plan Pl 19, but it is not clear to

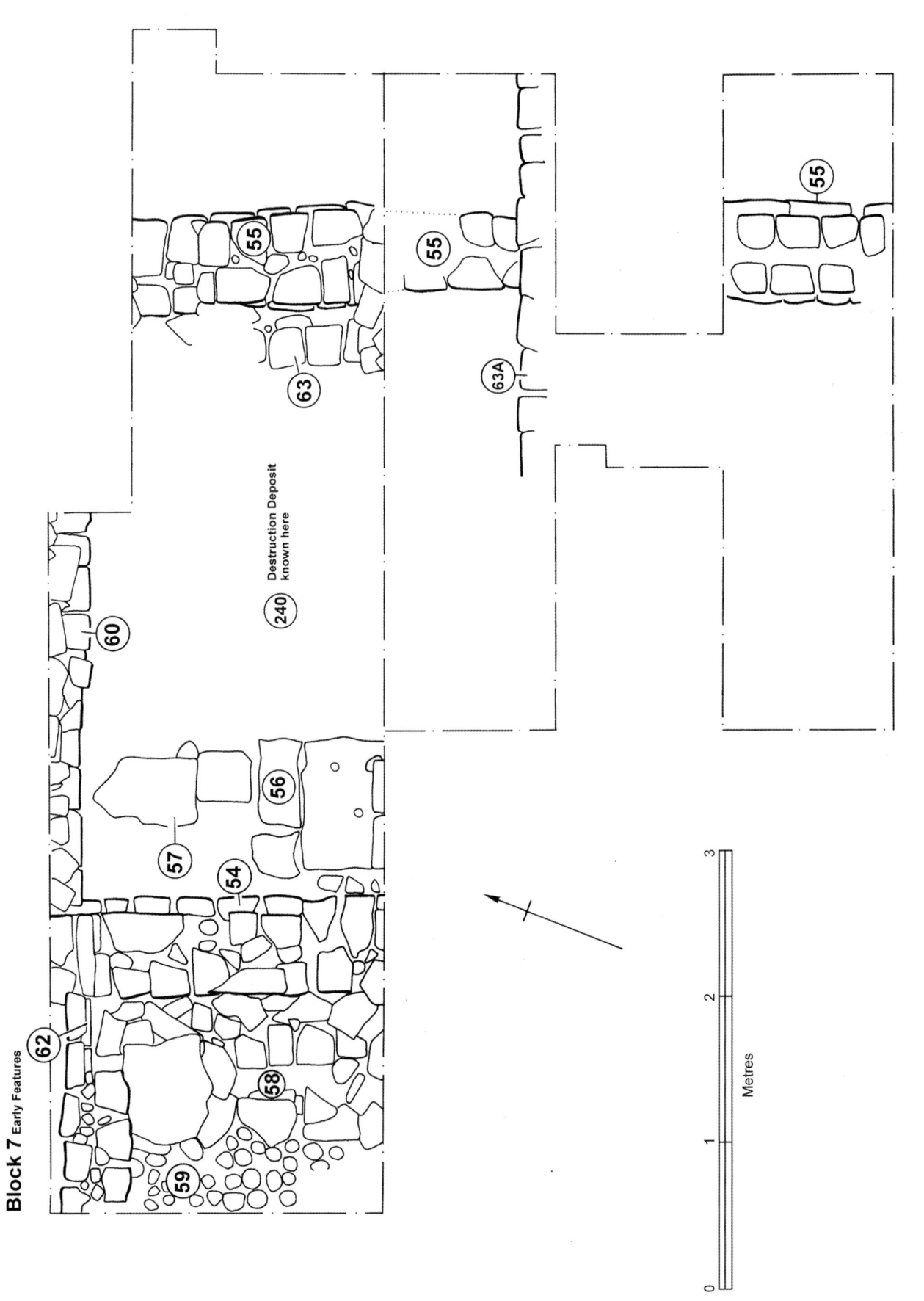

Figure 7.8. Block 7: plan of the early features.

7. *Structural Synopsis* 53

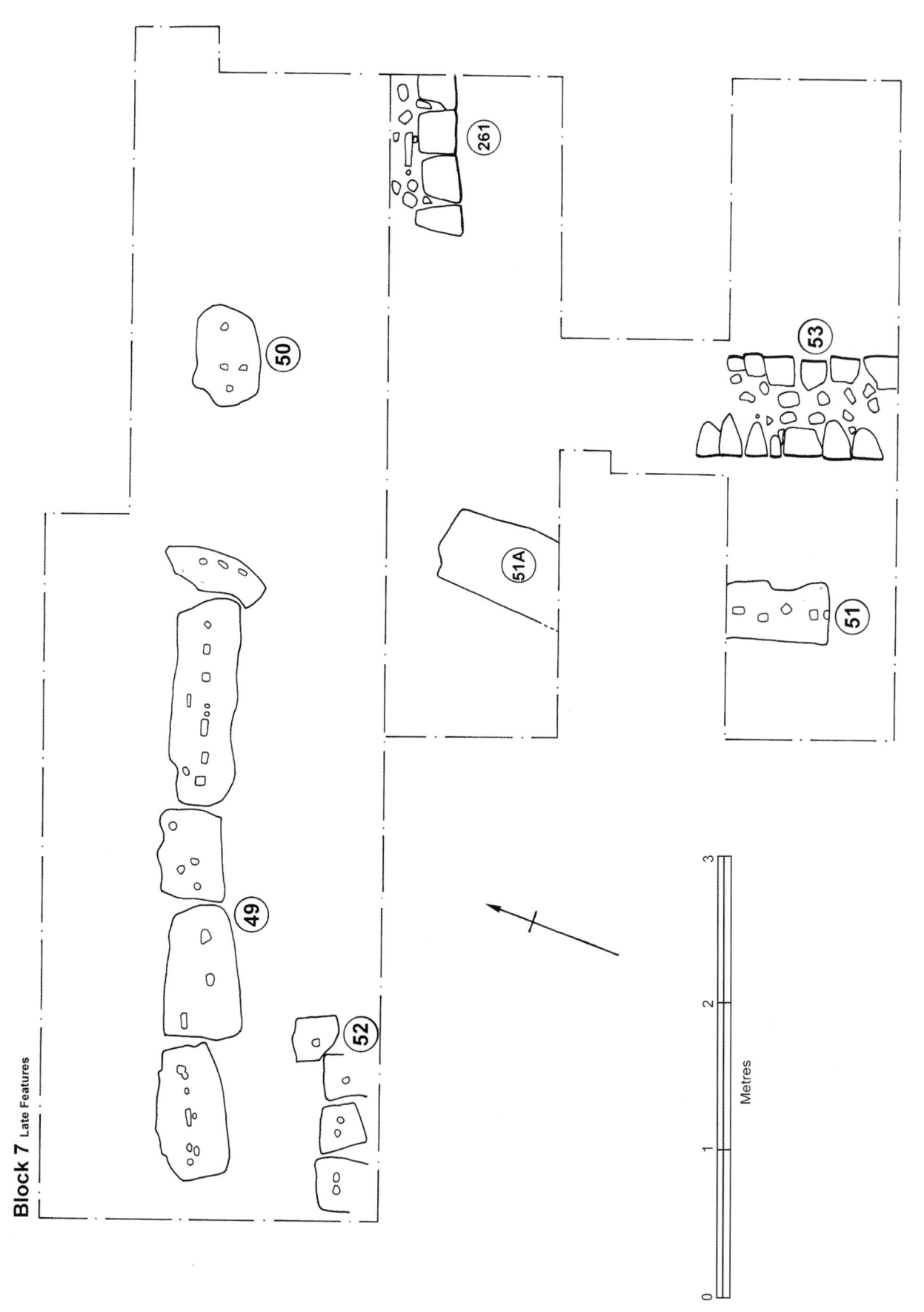

Figure 7.9. Block 7: plan of the later features.

Figure 7.10. Photograph M1: Block 7 Trench Ea22; early structures from the west.

Figure 7.11. Photograph M2: Block 7 Trench Ea22; early structures from the east.

which course it refers. The west end overlay wall 55. It was interpreted as part of the same structure as 53 and as with 53 it was initially assigned to Period III but subsequently moved to Period IV.

Early Structures
54) Wall running north–south. Located on the west side of the north part of block. Width *c.* 0.67m. Faced stone facing. At least two courses with lower course on east side offset. No information on number of courses surviving or foundation. Depth: 37 ins to top of top course. Interpreted as the main west wall of the Hadrianic "forage-store" (the 1960 on-site interpretation) /courtyard house (the 1961, and subsequently published interpretation).
55) Wall running north–south. Located on the east side of the block. Width *c.* 0.58m. At least two courses with lower offset on both sides. Stone facing with mortar core (specifically mentioned on Pl 42). Depth to top of top course *c.* 40 ins. Interpreted as east wall of west range of the Hadrianic "forage-store" (the 1960 on-site interpretation) / courtyard house (the 1961, and subsequently published interpretation).
56) Flagging. Located immediately to east of 54. Depth 46 ins. "IA floor?". Finds groups 61JX and 61OC are possibly to be associated with this flagging.
57) Clay. Shown surrounding 56. Below 56?
58) Drain running north–south. Located immediately to west of 54. Channel faced with stone and covered with slabs. Most of slabs robbed. Width of channel *c.* 0.38m. Should be associated with building of which 54 and 55 are walls. Depth to top of surviving cover slab 33 ins. Finds group 61PZ is probably from the fill of this drain.
59) Road. Located immediately to west of 58. Shown on Pl 51. No depths or other description given. It is likely to have been at least 33 ins below the surface.
60) Wall running east–west. Protruding from north baulk in west of north part of block. Only one face visible. No information on number of courses surviving. The stones which are visible appear very regularly sized. The wall appears to form a butt joint

7. Structural Synopsis

Figure 7.12. Photograph M3: Block 7 Trench Ea22; early flags 56 and wall 54 from the east.

with 54 so was interpreted as an internal partition of the west range of the Hadrianic "forage-store" (the 1960 on-site interpretation) / courtyard house (the 1961, and subsequently published interpretation).

61) Wall running east–west. Located in extreme north-west corner of block. Width *c.* 0.48m. No information on number of courses surviving, or core material. Depth to top is 23 ins. JPG assigned it to Period II. Nothing more is known of the structure of which it formed a part.

62) Small fragment of wall running east–west. Located in extreme north-west corner of the block under the east end of 61. No depth information is given. It appears to butt up to wall 54 and JPG assigned it to Period I on the general plan PI 3.

63) Short length of wall running north–south. Located immediately to west of 55. Three or four stones are shown on plan PI 42 underneath the late wall 50. They appear to be faced on their west side. Depth is between 45 and 50 ins to their tops. The depth and the fact that the wall is faced only on the west side suggests that it relates to 55 and is thus of Period I. At the time of excavation it was interpreted as a sleeper wall for a suspended floor and this gave rise to the designation of the building (during the 1960 season) as a "Forage Store".

63a) Wall. Only north face revealed. Protruding from south baulk of trench Eb23. Length of *c.* 2.78m surviving in trench. Notes appended to wall, approx. at mid point: "2 courses here, 2 further west, 1 over earlier wall and to east". Interpreted on general plan PI 3 as belonging to the Period I "forage-store" (the 1960 on-site interpretation) / courtyard house (the 1961, and subsequently published interpretation).

240) Destruction Deposit. It is mentioned only in the finds book, by implication in the description of

Figure 7.13. Photograph M34: Labelled 'Haltonchesters 1960. Early fourth-century wall above second-century wall'; Block 7 trench Eb23 (?) south east leg from east, showing wall 55 below later wall 53.

Figure 7.14. Photograph M35: Block 7 Ea 22; north facing section at the east end of the block with walls 55 and 63 below and the north face of late wall 261 (not planned) visible in the top left of the section.

Figure 7.15. Photograph C209: Block 7 Trench Ea22, north facing section (cf. M2 centre left) – location of destruction deposit 240?

finds group 61DL, from trench Ea22: "From mixed earth below level of 1st tumble of stones *c.* 2 ft 6 ins down just above the destruction level". Perhaps shown in section in Photograph C209 (south side of Trench Ea22).

Block 8 (Fig. 7.16)
Trench: De23
Plans: Pl 3
Finds Group: 60JA
The trench only appears on the general plan Pl 3. No detailed plans are known.

262) General plan Pl 3 shows a wall, *c.* 0.6m wide, running E–W, located in the southern part of the trench. It is coloured in solid red, the convention used for extant structures of Period IV. It is shown as part of the structure referred to here as Late Building Fragment B.

Block 9 (Fig. 7.17)
Trenches: Ea31, Eb31
Plans: Pl 19
Provenanced Finds Groups: Ea31: None
Eb31: 60DG, 60DO, 60EB, 60GF

Structural Elements

64) Wall running north–south. A single stone of this is located in the north baulk of the trench. "edge of period IV stone in side very near top". No other evidence.
65) Flagged surface. Located in eastern half of trench. "Big flat loose (?) slabs at 24 clay covered". Not assigned to any Period.
66) Surface. Located at west end of trench. "Smooth surface of small broken stones at 24". This surface is at the same level as the flags at the east end of the trench. It is too far east to be the *intervallum* road, or north to be the *via quintana*.
67) Clay level. Over 65. Not explicitly shown on any plan. Its existence is implied by the description of 65, quoted above, and entries in the finds book. Finds groups 60DG and 60EB contain material yielding a *terminus post quem* in the late 2nd century AD.

Block 10 (Fig. 7.17)
Trenches: Ea34, Eb34
Photographs: None
Provenanced Finds Groups: Eb34: 60DY 60GA

Structural Elements

68) Wall running north–south. Located in centre of trench. Width *c.* 0.62m. At least two courses. Faced stone facing a core of smaller stone. Depth to wall top 18 ins. "Period III (?) wall". Restored on the general plan Pl 3 as Period II.
69) Cobbles. Located to east of 68. Depth 27–36 ins. Possibly associated with 68. "Closely packed cobbles".
70) Flagging. Located to west of 68. Depth 8–14 ins. "Heavy flagging period IV (?)."

Block 11 (Figs 4.6 and 7.17)
Trenches: Ea25, Eb25
Plans: Pl 18, 24
Photographs: M28
Provenanced Finds Groups: Ea25: 60IJ, 60IR, 60JL, 61NQ, 61OB, 61PA, 61PC
Eb25: 60EA, 60EG, 60EQ, 60EW, 60FB, 60IG, 60IV, 60JO

Structural Elements

71) Wall running north–south. Located in middle of trench. Width *c.* 0.58m. The wall top is immediately under the turf. At least three courses surviving. The course of the wall across the trench undulates slightly. Composed of small shaped stone (*c.* 0.26m × 0.17m × 0.12m) facing a core of irregularly shaped small stone. "Period III wall".
72) Wall running north–south. Located *c.* 1.54m west of 71. Composed of a line of four large slabs *c.* 0.48m wide and *c.* 0.1m thick (longest is 0.7m long). The most northerly has two holes aligned north–south in its upper surface, the third and fourth from the north both have one hole each. The four holes form an approximately straight line aligned north–south. The tops of walls 71 and 72 are at the same height, immediately below the turf line. "Period IV wall".
73) Flagged surface. Located between walls 71 and 72. Composed of several large flags, a quernstone, and a certain amount of smaller stone. It lies at about the height of the second course from the top of wall

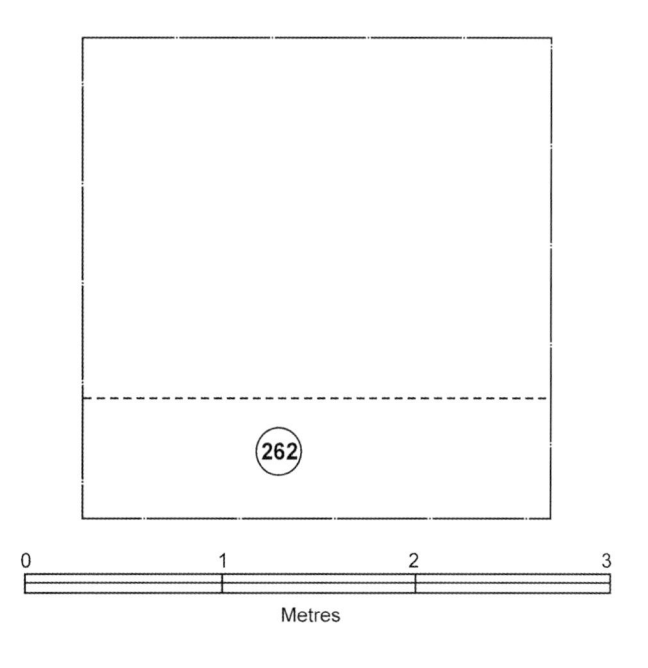

Figure 7.16. Block 8: plan.

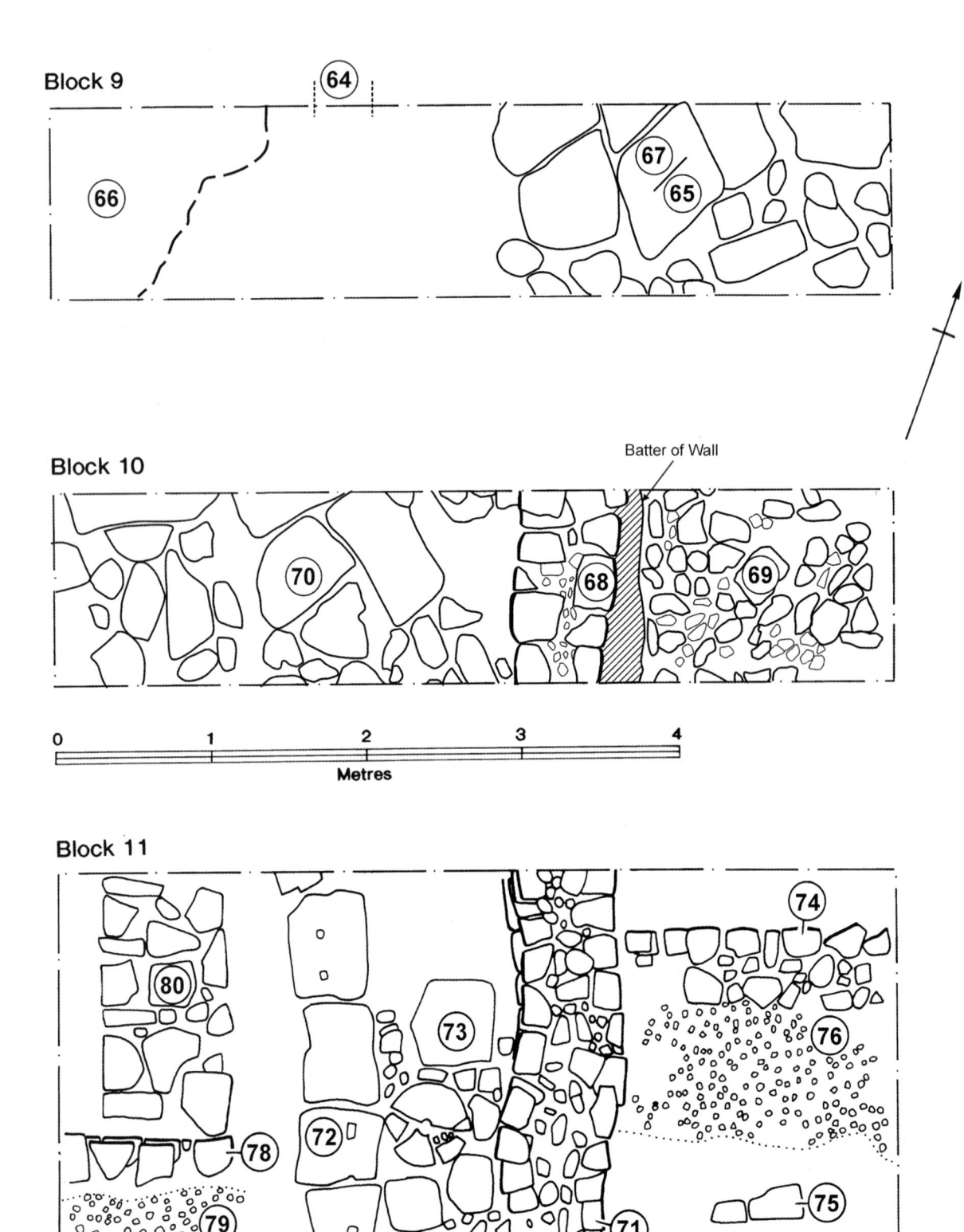

Figure 7.17. Blocks 9, 10 and 11: plans.

71, and the base of the stones of wall 72. "Period IV flagging. Sagged below top of period III wall". Finds groups 61NQ and 61OB came from below this surface.

74) Wall running east–west. Located to east of wall 71, in the north east corner of the trench. Width *c.* 0.48m. Composed of smallish shaped stone (though less shaped, to judge from the plan, than those of wall 71) facing a core of small irregular stone. Depth of wall top 30 ins. Probably earlier than 71. It does not run as far as wall 71. "?Period II wall. Good face on north only." Does not appear on the general interpretative plan Pl 3.

75) Wall running east–west. Small fragment of south face of a wall. Located in south-east corner of trench. Depth of wall top 48 ins. "?south face of period I (or II?) wall beginning to show up." "Not completely excavated" written next to this. It may belong to the same structure as 78.

76) Surface. Located in east half of trench, to east of wall 71, between walls 74 and 75. Composed of small stones or cobbles. "Packed stoney surface partly removed." Depth to top 38 ins. Depths would suggest that it is later than 75, and possibly to be associated with 74. It is possible that finds groups 61PA and 61PC came from this cobble layer. Association of these finds groups with this context is problematic in that the finds book entries give the trench as Ea25 and cobble surface 76 is in Eb25, however, it seems possible that at some time the whole trench could have been referred to as Ea25. If 61PA and 61PC are from 76 then this identifies 76 as "the packing between the earlier and later floors" which JPG mentions in the 1961 interim, since 61PC contains a stamped mortarium by Messorius Martius and a stamp of this potter is referred to by JPG as coming from the packing (only one stamp of this potter is known from the excavations).

77) Layer of clay. This does not appear on any of the plans but it is mentioned in the Finds Book (Finds Groups 60EA, 60EG, 60EQ and 60FB). These entries were entered earlier in the excavation than those relating to cobble surface 76, which would suggest that the clay layer was above the cobble surface. Its other associations are not clear however.

78) Wall running east–west. Located in south western part of trench, to west of wall 72. Only the north face is shown on the plan. It is not clear whether this was all that survived or whether the south face actually lay under the packed stoney surface, 79, shown close to the south baulk. At least three courses of the north face seem to have survived. Depth to wall top 25 ins. The marginal comment on foundation/surface 80 shows that the excavators regarded 78 as Period I or II. The alignment may suggest that it was originally part of the same structure as 75.

79) Surface. Located between 78 and the south baulk. "Packed stoney surface not completely removed". Depth to top 33 ins. The description and the depth suggest that this is part of the same surface as 76. It is not clear whether the surface extended over the south end of wall 78.

80) Area of paving or foundation and associated paving. Located in north west corner of trench, to west of 72 and to north of 78. The west side of these flags is composed of alternate more or less square, and more or less oblong flags which respect a straight edge on their west side. This feature seems to have been referred to during the excavation as the "Long and short" wall or paving. "'Long and short' paving or foundation. Same level as Period I (II?) wall, lowest course, to south". The excavators regarded it as being associated with 78.

81) Rough pitching or cobbles. Not shown on any plan but mentioned in finds book (finds groups 60IJ). The exact location within the trench is not known but the entry suggests that 81 was associated with the Period IV wall 72.

82) Tumbled/fallen stone with clay layer below. Not shown on plan but mentioned in Finds Book (finds group 60EW). Exact location within trench not known. The finds group contained a Huntcliff-type cooking pot.

235) Wall running north–south. This appears only on general plan Pl 3 where it is shown continuing the line of 234 from Block 15 and intersecting with wall 75/78.

Block 12 (Fig. 7.18)

Trench: Ed22 (This trench was called Ec22 in 1960, but another trench Ec22 was later excavated to the west of it in 1961. The original Ec22 actually contains grid peg Ed23. We have called it Ed22 to try and avoid confusion).

Photographs: None

Provenanced Finds Groups: 60LS, 60LV

Structural Elements

83) Wall running east–west. Located in north of trench, partly in north baulk. Depth to wall top 10 ins. "3 course on clay. Sloping upwards from W to E." Interpreted as a wall of Period III (1960), or Period IV (1961).

84) Wall running east–west. Located in south of trench. It runs the full width of the trench. Width *c.* 0.6m. "5 courses well mortared." Depth to wall top 21 ins. Interpreted as Period II on the general interpretation plan Pl 3, but coloured green (usually used for Period I) on Pl 19.

85) Wall running north south. Located in middle of trench. Runs north from straight joint with 84, under 83 and into north baulk. Width *c.* 0.48m. Depth to wall top 42 ins. "2 courses." Interpreted as a sleeper wall forming part of the same structure as 84 (see under 86).

86) Surface. Located to west of 85. Composed of flags. "Flagging level with top course of sleeper wall." Interpreted as part of same structure as 84 and 85.

Block 13 (Figs 7.18–7.20)
Trench: Ec22
Photographs: M41a, M42a
Provenanced Finds Groups: 61CG, 61CR, 61DF

Structural Elements

87) Wall running east–west. Located in north part of trench, partly in north baulk. Depth of wall top 4–8 ins. "PIII wall of 3 courses, above and clear of drain." Interpreted as Period III (1960) Period IV (later 1961).
88) Wall running north–south. In south-eastern part of trench, partly in east baulk. Depth to wall top 17 ins. "Wall corner, 5 courses, deeply founded, date unknown." Pl 46 shows the wall corner returning eastwards into the baulk. Interpreted on the general plan Pl 3 as Period II.
89) Wall (?) running north–south. Located between 87 and 88. Consists of four facing stone arranged in a line. Depth to tops of stones: 29, 32 ins. Overlies drain 91 but its relationship to 88 is not clear.
90) Wall (?) running north–south. Located to west of 88, partly in west baulk. Consists of a very short stretch faced both sides (?). Depth to wall top 11 ins. "Questionable N-S wall, earth and rubble fill, petering out to N with stones at lower level". No interpretation offered. Does not appear on general plan Pl 3.
91) Drain. Located immediately to west of 88. Only the two large cover slabs which occur in the trench are shown on plan Pl 50. Depths 39–41 ins. Underlies wall 89. Presumably associated with wall 88.

Block 14

No plans of this trench are extant.

Block 15 (Figs 3.4, 3.6 and 7.21–7.24)

Trenches: Ec24, Ed24. These trenches are immediately adjacent and do not seem to have been joined at any point during the excavations.
Plans: Pl 32, Pl 42, Pl 47, Pl 49. Pl 32 shows one of the few surviving sections from the excavations.
Photographs: M18, M19, M31, M43a, C206, C213, C214
Finds Groups: Ec24: 61KN
Ed24: 60GO, 61AS, 61CP, 61FK

Structural Elements

92) Wall running north–south. Located in centre of trench Ed24. Surviving two courses high in places, *i.e.* one course with offset foundation/footing course. Width *c.* 0.74m. No information on stone type, core composition or foundation composition. Depth to highest surviving wall top 54 ins. Shown in section (Pl 32) and interpreted as Period I wall.
93) Wall running north–south. Located to east of 92, in trench Ed24. Extends for *c.* 1.22m into trench. Partly concealed in east baulk. Surviving six courses high in places. Interpreted as Period II. Part of same structure as 94, 95, 96.
94) Wall running east–west. Located slightly north of the centre of trench Ed24. Width *c.* 0.74m. Surviving six courses high in places. Its east end makes a butt joint with 93. The lowest courses are founded only very slightly above the remains of the Period I wall 92 (this can clearly be seen on photograph M18). Depth to wall top 18 ins. Interpreted as Period II.
95) Wall running east–west. Located in trench Ec24. Runs from east baulk for *c.* 0.77m before returning northwards as 96. Width *c.* 0.72m. No information on number of courses surviving, or wall or foundation composition. No specific information on depth, but could probably be assumed to have been same depth

Block 12

Block 13

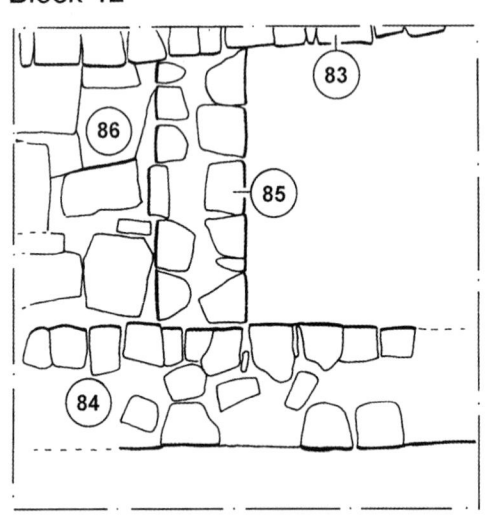

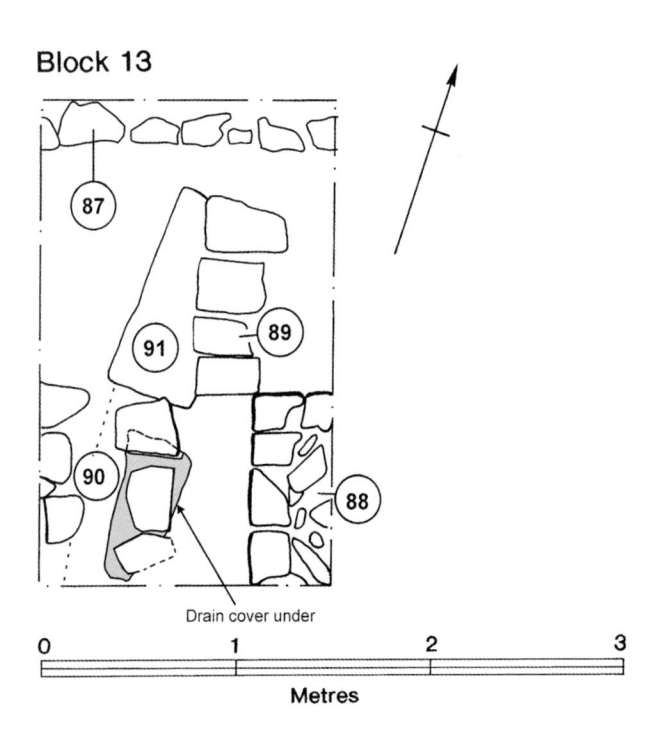

Drain cover under

0 1 2 3
Metres

Figure 7.18. Blocks 12 and 13: plans.

7. Structural Synopsis

Figure 7.19. Photograph M41a: Block 13, looking south.

Figure 7.20. Photograph M42a: Block 13, looking north.

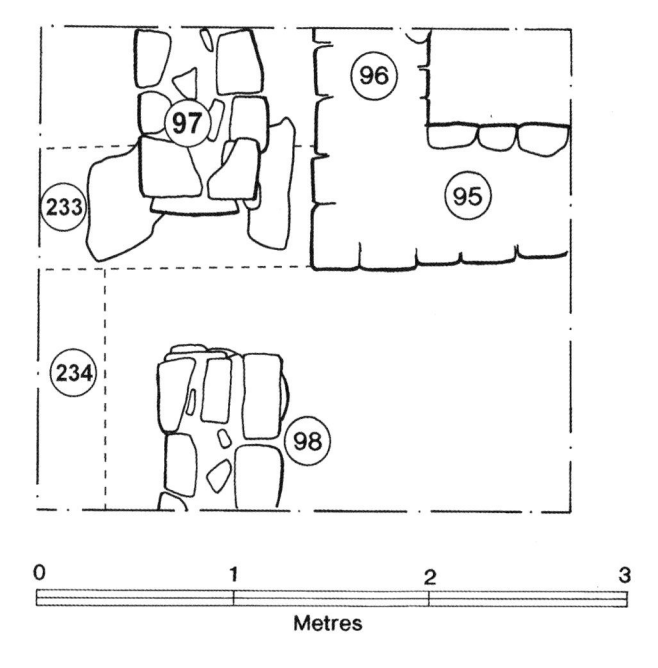

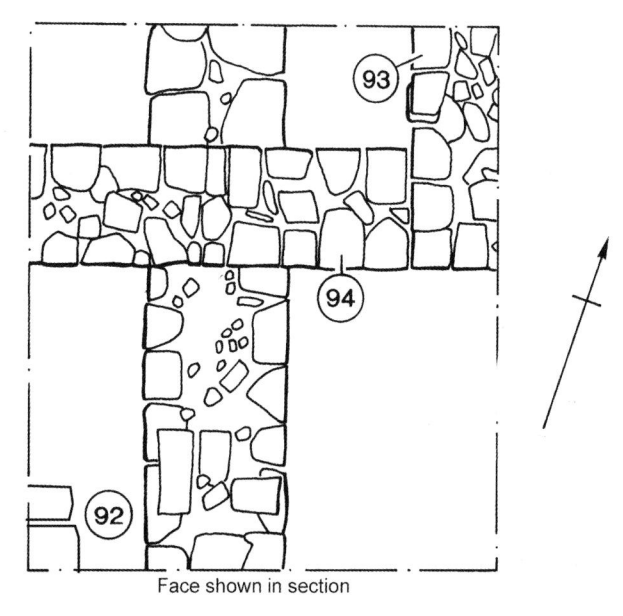

Figure 7.21. Block 15: plan.

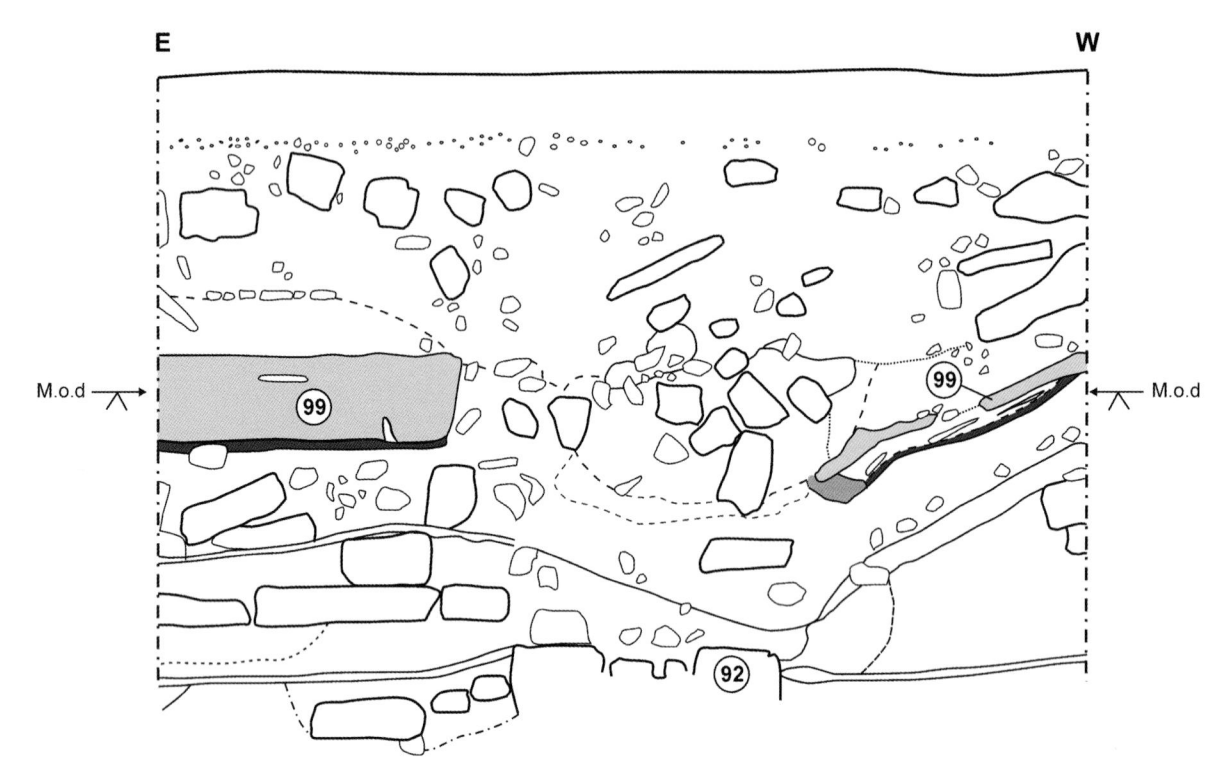

Figure 7.22. Block 15 trench Ed24: section of south face.

Figure 7.23. Photograph M19: Block 15 Trench Ed24; from the east, showing Period II wall 94 overlying Period I wall 92 and abutting 93.

as 96 (18 ins). It continues the line of wall 94 from trench Ed24. Interpreted as Period II.

96) Wall running north–south. Located in north east corner of trench Ec24. This is the northwards return of wall 95. Depth to wall top *c.* 18 ins. Width *c.* 0.6m. Interpreted as Period II.

97) Wall running north–south. Located immediately to the west of 96. A fragment of wall which projects *c.* 1.1m into the trench from the north baulk. Of somewhat rougher construction than wall 96. Width *c.* 0.65m. Depth to wall top 5–7 ins. Interpreted as Period IV.

98) Wall running north–south. Located to the south of, and on the same line as 97. Projects *c.* 0.84m from south baulk. Depth to wall top 7–12 ins. Width *c.* 0.65m. Interpreted as Period IV.

99) Destruction level. This is visible in the south section of trench Ed24 (Pl 32). It actually consists of a layer of what is interpreted as burnt daub, *c.* 0.36m thick, over a very thin black layer which is interpreted as "carbonised wood". As drawn, this section does not permit the association of the destruction deposit with the Period I wall 92, since several of the layers interposed between wall and destruction deposit have been drawn as sealing the wall, implying that the wall had already gone out of use well before the destruction occurred. However, the way that the fragments of destruction deposit, and various other layers terminate on either side of the wall strongly suggests the presence of a robber trench above the remains of the wall, cutting down through the destruction deposit and underlying levels, *i.e.*

Figure 7.24. Photograph C213: Block 15 Trench Ed24 from the north, showing Period II walls 93 and 94 and the destruction deposit (99) and possible robber trench for Period I wall 92.

that the robber trench was cut from at or above the destruction deposit, and that this robber trench was missed by the person drawing the section. This interpretation allows wall and destruction deposit to be associated. The following finds groups came from in or below 99: 60GO, 61AS, 61CP.

233) Wall running east–west. This is shown on the general plan Pl 3, as continuing wall 45, assigned to Period I, in Block 5, on the same line as 95, the Period II wall. On the detailed plan of trench Ec24, Pl 47, two stones are shown in faint outline under wall 97 in a position and at a depth where they could have been part of 233.
234) Wall running north–south. This is shown on the general plan Pl 3 as continuing wall 235 in Block 11, there ascribed to Period I. It is not explicitly identified on the detailed plan, Pl 47 though some of the stone shown protruding from the west and south baulks may have formed part of it.

Block 16 (Figs 7.25–7.26)

Trench: Ed25

Photographs: M44a: *Haltonchesters 1960. Third-century flagging above 2nd century wall*

Plans: Pl 18, 23

Provenanced Finds Groups: 60DU, 60EU, 60FU, 60FV, 60GS, 60HB, 60JU, 60LM, 60LN, 60LP, 60LT, 60LU, 60LY

Structural Elements

100) Wall running east–west. Located in south-eastern corner of trench. Runs from east baulk for *c.* 1.5m. Terminates in a "limestone coin one course higher than those to east, level with those to north". Width *c.* 0.6m. "One course showing, one below ground". No depths given. Core: "solid mortar masking big clean orange stones". Interpreted as Period I.
101) Wall running north–south. Northward return of wall 100. Located in centre and north of trench. "Two courses showing one below ground". Depth to wall top 40 ins. There appears (from the plan) to be a straight joint between 100 and 101.
102) Small fragment of wall running east–west. Located in south-west corner of trench. On the same line as wall 100, it could be the partly robbed westwards continuation of 100. "Thicker stones, possibly start of wall." Interpreted as same Period as 100 and 101
103) Flagged surface. Located in north-west corner of trench, bounded by 101 and 102. Depth to top: 56 ins. "Big flags at level of 2nd and 3rd courses." Presumably this refers to the courses of wall 101.

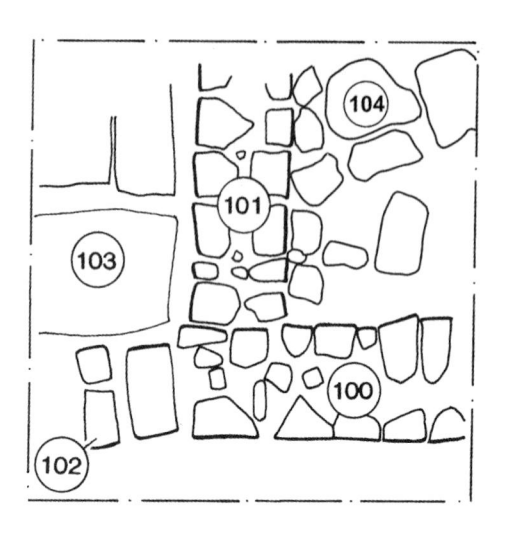

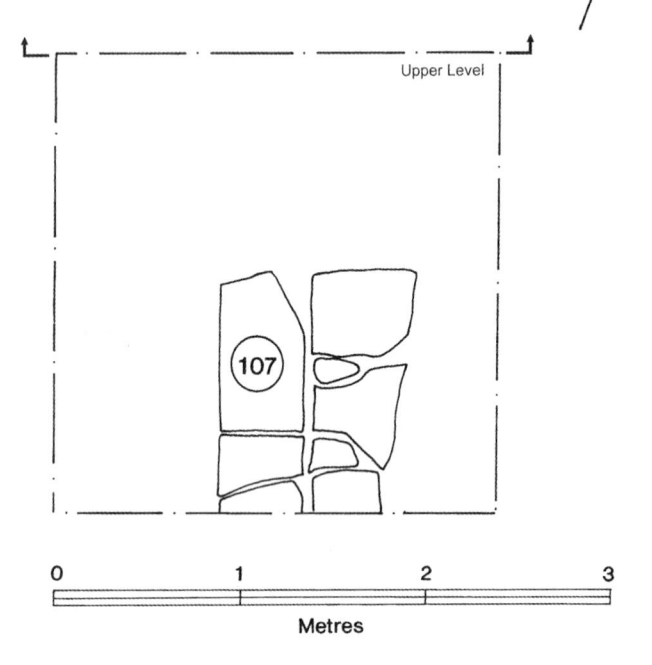

Figure 7.25. Block 16: plan.

Figure 7.26. Photograph M44a: Labelled 'Haltonchesters 1960. Third-century flagging above 2nd century wall'; Block 16, looking north-east, showing flagging 107 over wall 101.

Probably surface associated with walls 100, 101 and 102.

104) Flagged surface. Located in north-east corner of trench, bounded by walls 100 and 101. "Rough flagging at level of bottom of visible course." Probably to be associated with walls 100 and 101.

105) Fallen debris. Located somewhere in the area of the north-east corner of trench bounded by walls 100 and 101. Note close to east baulk: "much fallen debris here." The relationship of this to the flagging is not explicitly stated. Probably at the same level or over.

106) Burnt wattle and daub. Somewhere in the area of the north-east corner of the trench bounded by walls 100 and 101. Next to note on fallen debris (see 105): "Thick layer of burnt wattle and daub over debris.

15 ins from bottom, 9 ins thick, 26 ins from top of hole." Finds groups from in or under 106 are as follows: 60EU, 60FU, 60LN, 60LP, 60LT.

107) Flagging. Located on south side of trench. Taken from plan PI 23. "Plan at depth of *c.* 22 ins. Flags (Period III?) overlying sleeper wall." The sleeper wall is presumably the Period I wall.

108) Flagging (?). Possible further layer of flagging later than 107. Not shown on any plan. Flagging which is later than period one is mentioned in the Finds Book a number of times. Sometimes it is called "Period III flagging" but once (Finds Group 60JU) it is called "late 4th century". At this point (1960) it was considered that there were structures on the site which could be dated to Periods III and IV (that is Wall Periods III and IV, late 3rd century and late 4th century respectively), so it is likely that there was both Period III and Period IV flagging in the trench.

Block 18 (Fig. 7.27)

Trenches: Fa13
Photographs: None
Plans: PI 18
Provenanced Finds Groups: None

Structural Elements

109) Buttress of west wall of east granary. Depth to top 22ins. "Heavily mortared buttress".

110) Robber trench for main west wall of east granary. Located immediately east of 109.

111) Wall running north–south. Located *c.* 0.5m west of 110. Only the east side is visible, the west being covered by 112. Note in pencil by north end: "higher courses visible." Next to this, in ink,: "P I or P II." Note by south end: "lower courses visible. At least 4 courses in all." Shown on the general interpretative plan (PI 3) as Period II.

112) Flagging. Located on west side of trench over 111.

7. Structural Synopsis

Depth to top of largest flag 4ins. "?Per IV flag over wall." Not shown on the general interpretative plan (Pl 3).

Block 19 (Fig. 7.28)

Trenches: Fa21, Fb21
Plans: Pl 18
Photographs: None
Provenanced Finds Groups: 60DX, 60FA, 60FO, 60GI, 60HU, 60IL

Structural Elements

113) Wall running north–south. Located near the centre of the trench. Depth to top of core 18 ins. Near to west face another depth, 46 ins, marked. Width *c.* 0.89m. "Heavily mortared, 5 courses visible." Interpreted as the main west wall of the east granary of Period I.
114) Wall running east–west. Located immediately east of 113, it runs between 113 and the east baulk. Width *c.* 0.65m. No depth given. "Sleeper wall, 2 and 3 courses." At the south joint between 113 and 114 a note: "bonded". Interpreted as a sleeper wall within the Period I granary.
115) Wall running north–south. Located *c.* 0.72m west of 113. Depth to top 21 ins, depth to bottom: 36 ins. "Kerb wall. Faced on W only, leaning E". Interpreted as a kerb surrounding the east granary of Period I.
116) Wall running north–south. Located *c.* 2.28m west of 113 (centre to centre). Width *c.* 0.62m. Depth to top 30 ins. Coloured red. Interpreted on the general interpretative plan as Period II.

Block 20

Trench: Eb44

This trench is known only from a finds book entry for finds group 60EN. No plan either general or detailed is known for such a trench. Its designation places it well to the south of the area of excavation and suggests a mistake in the finds book entry.

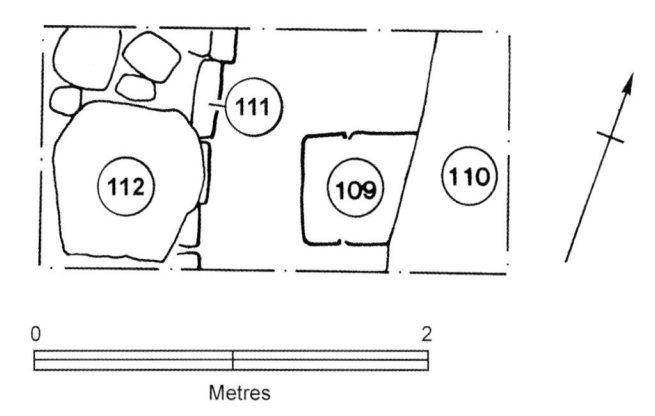

Figure 7.27. Block 18: plan.

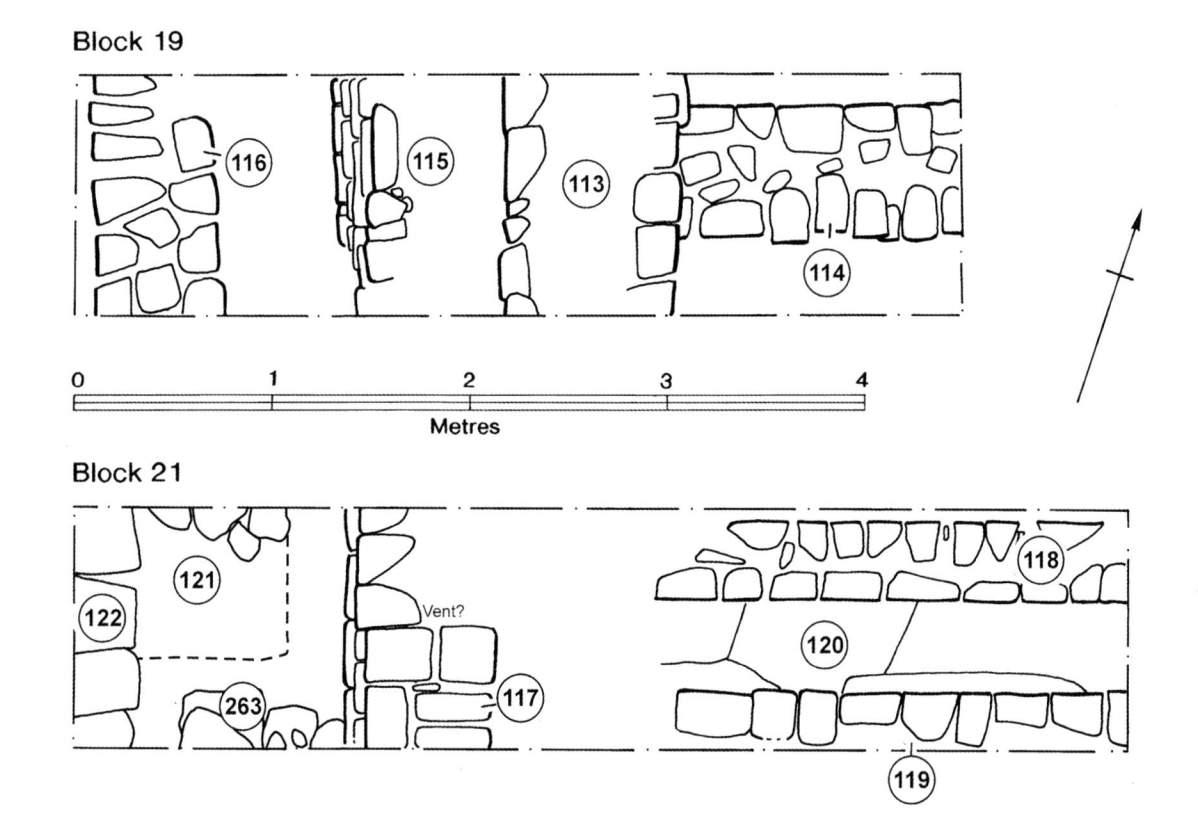

Figure 7.28. Blocks 19 and 21: plans.

Block 21 (Figs 2.4 and 7.28)
Trenches: Fa24, Fb24
Plans: Pl 21
Photographs: M13
Provenanced Finds Groups: 60HQ

Structural Elements

117) Wall running north–south. Located slightly west of the centre of the trench. Width *c.* 0.77m (including offsets). At least four courses surviving. Depths: "5 ft 6 ins to bottom of plinth. 1 ft 6 ins from top of plinth to top of wall". *c.* 0.62m north of the south baulk the top two surviving courses of the wall terminate and there is nothing else between this termination and the north baulk. The end of the wall is so regular and well defined that it suggests that this was how it originally was, rather than the result of selective robbing. Possibly this marks the position of a vent.
118) Wall running east–west. Located at east end of trench close to north baulk. Width *c.* 0.41m. The wall runs from the east baulk for *c.* 2.5m. Only two courses survive anywhere on this wall or on 119 which suggests that this may have been their original height. The photograph appears to show 118 and 119 resting directly on 120. The termination of 118 coincides with that of 119 and with the west edge of 120 which suggests that neither wall originally extended any further than this. "2 ft 3 ins from surface to top of wall". Walls 118 and 119 were interpreted as sleeper walls within the Period I granary.
119) Wall running east–west. Located at east end of trench, partly hidden in south baulk. See also remarks under 118.
120) Paving. Located in east half of trench, directly under walls 118 and 119. "3 ft 6 ins from surface to paving". The west edge of the paving coincides with the west ends of the two walls 118 and 119. It would seem that the walls and flags were not removed in the excavations; at least, there is no record of this. If it follows the pattern of other trenches, the paving will have rested on layers of clay and cobbles.
121) Wall (?). Located *c.* 1.2m west of 117, on north side of trench. It is interpreted as a wall of Period II which enters the trench from the north and immediately turns west. On Pl 21 the area enclosed by the dotted line is labelled "collapsed".
122) Wall running north–south. Located at extreme west end of trench, partly hidden in the west baulk. Width is unknown, details of depth, construction, number of courses surviving, *etc.*, are unrecorded. It is interpreted on the general plan (Pl 3) as a wall of Period IV.
263) Foundation, adjacent to west side of wall 117, partly concealed in the south baulk. Probably the foundation for a buttress.

Block 22 (Figs 3.3, 3.5 and 7.29–7.36)
Trenches: Ee25, Fa25, Fb25
Plans: Pl 31, Pl 33, Pl 45, Pl 46. Of these, Pl 31 is the most useful, though no depths are given on it.

Photographs: M16, M17, M45a–M51a, C219–C221, C223, C236, C237, C242, C243
Provenanced Finds Groups: Ee25: 61CJ, 61DM, 61DZ, 61EF, 61EZ, 61FV, 61GH, 61GR, 61HM, 61MS, 61NG
Fa25: 61CH, 61CT, 61DE, 61DO, 61EA, 61EN

Structural Elements

123) Wall running east–west. Located mostly in Fb25. It runs from the east baulk and terminates *c.* 3.72m west of the baulk. Well built, faced stone facing a well mortared core (to judge from the photographs). At least four courses surviving. Top course offset. The north face between the baulk and the intersection with 124 has, curiously, an extra course of smaller, less regularly shaped stone. It seems possible that this is a piece of later walling reusing the earlier wall. At this point the wall is *c.* 1.18m wide. The western termination of the wall projects beyond the intersection with 124, forming a buttress *c.* 0.67m wide. Three courses of the west face of the buttress are clearly visible in photograph M17 (see Fig. 3.3). Interpreted as the main south wall of Period I granary.
124) Wall running north–south. Runs from north baulk to intersect with 123. Width *c.* 0.7m. Appears to be of similar construction to 123. Three courses are visible in photograph M17. Interpreted as main west wall of Period I granary.
125) Wall running east–west. Located in north-east corner of trench immediately inside angle formed by 123 and 124. Width is *c.* 0.77m wide at widest point (near western end). Wall is roughly faced. Two courses are visible in photograph M17. It survives to about the same height as 123 and 124. Interpreted as a sleeper wall in the interior of the Period I granary.
126) Wall running north–south. A short section of walling running between the buttress at the western end of 123 and the south baulk. Photograph M17 shows at least four courses surviving and that the wall has a straight joint between it and the buttress at the west end of 123. Width is *c.* 0.62m. Interpreted as part of the west wall of a structure of Period I (either a portico or a loading bay) added to the original granary. Mentioned in a number of places (mostly in the Finds Book) as a portico. JPG shows this structure on the general plan Pl 3 as Period I but there is a finds group (61CT), the description of whose context suggests that it comes from the packing between the north end of this fragment of wall and the south face of the buttress. It contains an example of a BB1 grooved rim bowl (*i.e.* what was previously called an incipient flange rim bowl) which is not likely to be earlier than the end of the 2nd century AD. This would suggest that JPG got the porticos/loading bays the wrong way round, *i.e.*, the inner should be Period I and the outer Period II. The text from the finds book is as follows: "in packing between buttress and ?portico wall at S.W. corner of granary, below level of top of P.I. wall, above top of 'raft', on (or possibly 'or') foundations

7. *Structural Synopsis* 67

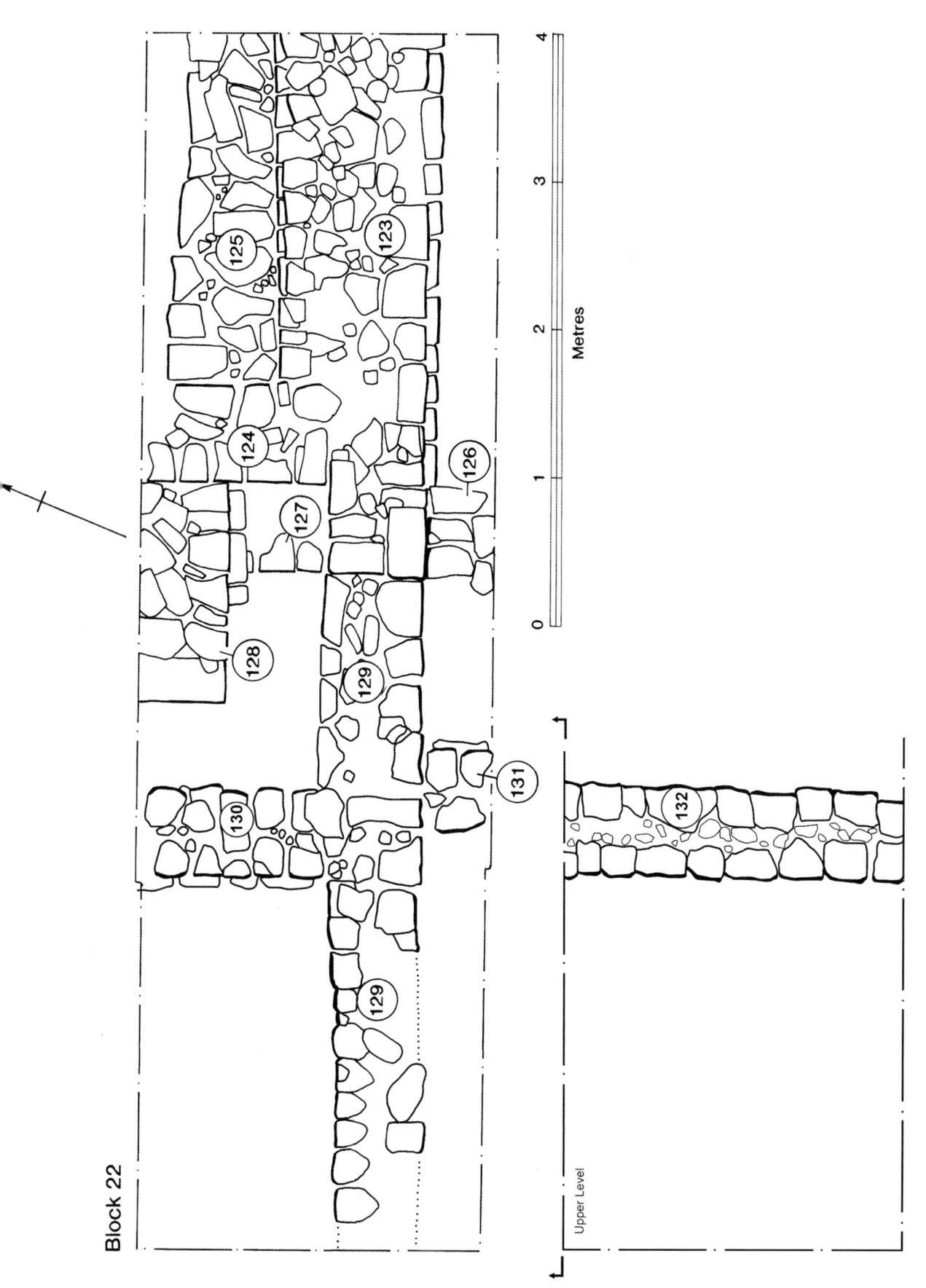

Figure 7.29. Block 22: plan.

Figure 7.30. Photograph M16: Block 22 Trenches Ee25 Fa25 Fb25; from east, showing the south-west corner of the granary and the walls (129, 130, 131) of the suggested Period I courtyard building beyond.

Figure 7.31. Photograph M45a: Block 22; looking south, with wall 129 abutting the west face of granary south-west buttress; whilst granary portico wall 126 abutts the south face of the buttress.

Figure 7.32. Photograph M46a: Block 22 Trenches Ee25 Fa25 Fb25, looking west; showing late north–south wall 132 over the Period I east–west wall 129 and separated from it by a significant depth of deposits.

of Period I wall". The use of the word buttress should unequivocally identify which portico/loading bay was intended since only one of them (the outer) comes into contact with the buttress.

127) Wall running north–south. Located in centre of trench *c.* 0.6m west of 124. Faced on west side only. Composed of a single line of stone. Only one course visible. Wall top is level with bottom of lowest visible course of 124. Interpreted as part of the kerb of the foundation 'raft' of the Period I granary.

128) Wall running east–west. A short length of walling located in the centre of the trench up against the north baulk. Photograph M47a provides a detailed view. Five courses are visible resting on foundations which overlie the kerb 127. At its eastern end the foundations and one, if not two courses above these butt against the west face of 124. *c.* 1.5m west of 124 the wall terminates. Three courses of the face of the termination are clearly visible in the photograph. JPG interpreted it as a wall of Period II, though what structure it related to is not clear. The implication of the relationship between 128 and 124 is that 124

Figure 7.33. Photograph M47a: Block 22; wall 128 overlying kerb 127 and abutting the granary west wall (124) – secondary buttressing for the west wall?

Figure 7.34. Photograph M48a: Block 22, looking north; showing later north–south wall 132 over the east–west wall 129 with granary reinforcement 128 in the top right corner.

Figure 7.35. Photograph M49a: Block 22, looking south; showing north–south wall 132 over the east–west wall 129.

was still standing and functioning when 128 was built.
129) Wall running east–west. Runs from the termination (*i.e.* the buttress) of 123 westwards to the west baulk. Well made, faced stone facing a core of small irregular stone (to judge from photographs M16–M17). Width at widest point (just to west of 123) is *c.* 0.74m. Further westwards it narrows to *c.* 0.62m. Three and in places four courses resting on a foundation are visible in the photographs. Photographs M17 and M45a (detail) clearly show that the east end butts against the west face of the buttress terminating 123. Interpreted as part of the Period I courtyard building to the west of the granary.
130) Wall running north–south. Runs from the north baulk from a point just to the west of 128, to intersect with 129. Of similar construction to 129 but, to judge from the photograph, not as deeply founded. Three courses are visible on photograph M17. The bottom course is offset slightly. The south end of 130 appears to butt against 129. Width, including offset, is *c.* 0.7m.

131) Wall running north–south. A short stretch of wall running between 129 and the south baulk. It is barely visible on the photograph (M16) but does appear to be butted against 129. The line of the wall does not continue that of 130 but is offset slightly to the east. Interpeted as part of the east wall of the southward extension of the Period I courtyard building located to the west of the Period I granary.
132) Wall running north–south. Located over 130. It runs across the full width of the trench. The west face of it is shown on plan Pl 45 and on the general interpretational plan Pl 3. It appears in photographs M46a, M48a, M49a, C237 and C243. Depth to wall top 6–8 ins. Interpreted on the general interpretational plan Pl 3 as a wall of Period IV, though it may have been interpreted, at some stage, as Period III and thus be the same as 135.
133) Destruction Deposit; Mentioned only in finds book. Trench Ee25: "Destruction Level, Depth 2 ft 6 ins": 61EF, "Burnt Level": 61CJ, "Burnt layer": 61FV. Photographs C220, C223, M50a and M51a show what may be the deposit (black and bright reddy-orange layers in the colour slide views) in section in the north-west corner of the trench (cf. M16 for locational reference).
134) "Raft". Foundation of granary (presumably). Mentioned only in Finds Book.
135) "Period III Wall". Mentioned only in Finds Book. This may be equivalent to 132.

Block 23 (Fig. 7.37)
Trench: Fa32
Plan: Pl 51
Photographs: None
Provenanced Finds Groups: None

Structural Elements
136) Wall running east–west. Partly hidden in north baulk. Extends from a point *c.* 0.48m east of the

Figure 7.36. Photograph C220: Block 22 Trench Ee25; south facing section in the north-west corner of the trench with destruction deposit 133 present.

west baulk, to the east baulk. Width unknown. At least two courses surviving. Depth to wall top 29ins. The westward limit of the wall in this trench probably marks a corner where the wall turns north to continue in trench Fa31 (see Block 40). Interpreted on Fa31 (Pl 51) as part of the Period I portico/loading bay for the granary but we have already seen that this structure cannot be earlier than the later 2nd century (see 126).

Block 24 (Figs 2.5 and 7.38–7.42)
Trenches: Fa22, Fa23, Fb23
Plans: Pl 33, 47
Photographs: M14, M37, M39, M52a, C228, C229, C230, C231
Provenanced Finds Groups: Fa22: 61PB
Fa23: 61AU, 61AV, 61BT, 61LG
Fb23: 60JN

No plans exist for trench Fa22, but this is one of the few blocks where a section survives (Pl 33). This shows the relationship of the fallen roof tiles to the granary sleeper walls. It is reproduced here exactly as on Pl 33 (Fig. 7.39). The key below gives the verbatim descriptions.

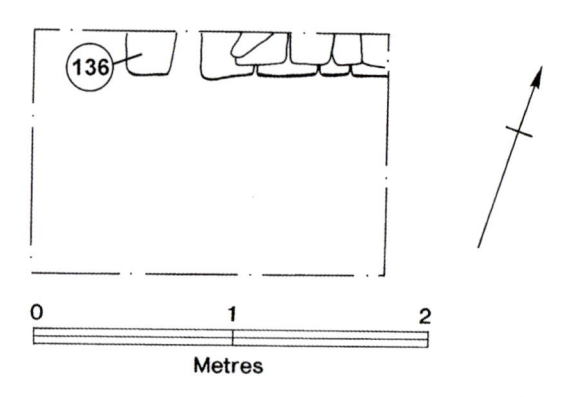

Figure 7.37. Block 23: plan.

Structural Elements

136) Wall running north–south. Located in centre of trench. Almost completely robbed out except for the foundation courses of a single buttress close to the south baulk. Width of robber trench *c.* 0.96m. Part of the buttress is obscured by the batter of the south baulk. Interpreted as the mainwest wall of the granary.
137) Foundation for 136. Mixture of irregularly shaped

7. Structural Synopsis

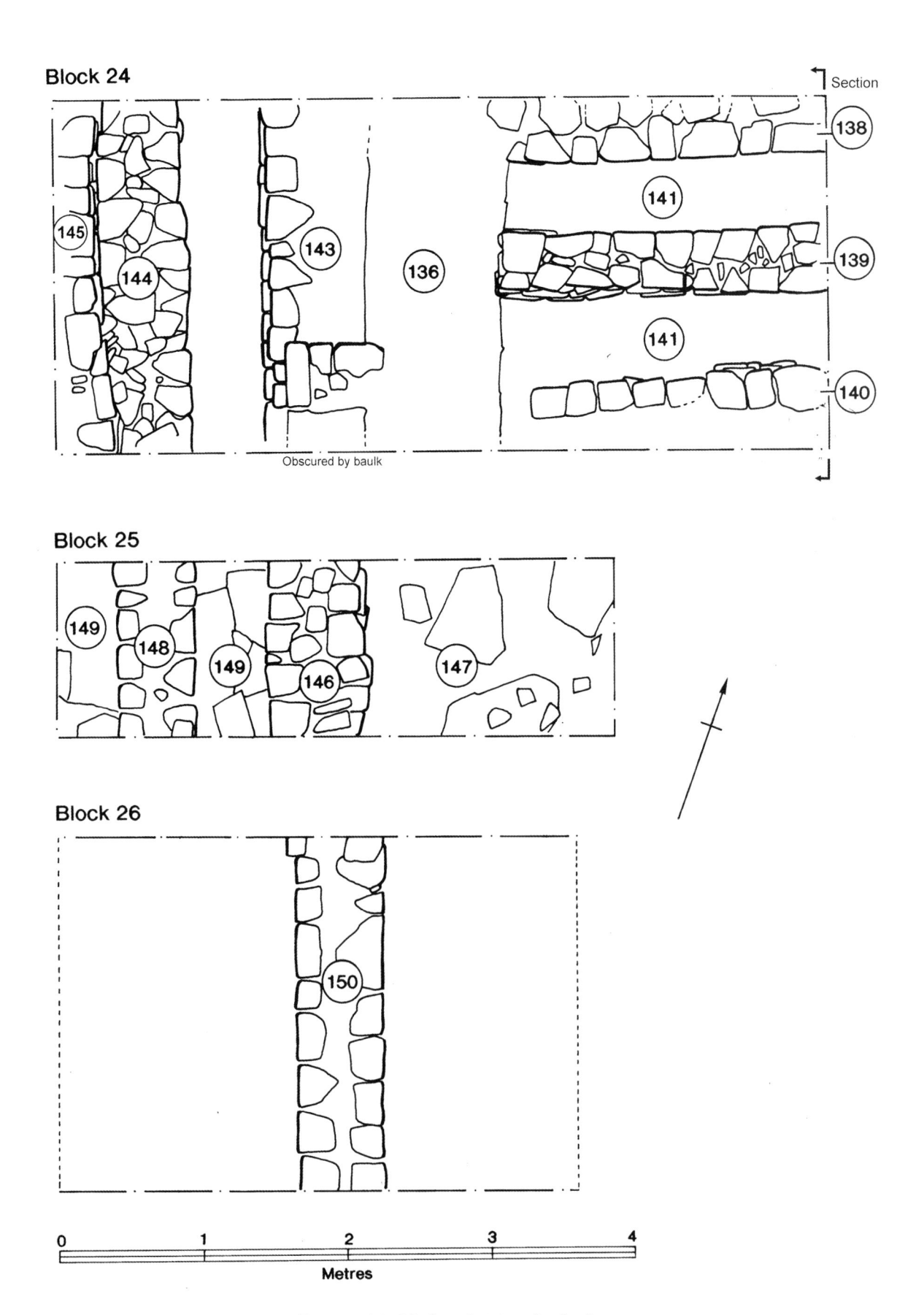

Figure 7.38. Blocks 24, 25 and 26: plans.

stone and stiff yellow clay. The eastern limit of this is the edge of the flagging underlying the sleeper walls, 141. The western limit is the edge of the stone-revetted clay foundation 143. The precise relationship between 137 and 141 and 143 is not known at this location.

138) Wall running east–west. Located in north east corner of block, partly hidden in the north baulk. It extends *c.* 2.28m into the trench from the east baulk. Its western end coincides with the edge of the stone flag "raft" 141 and it seems likely that it never extended any further. Three courses are visible. Depth to wall top is 29–33 ins. Since the surviving height of 138, 139 and 140 is the same it seems likely that this was their original height. Interpreted as a sleeper wall for the floor of the Period I granary.

139) Wall running east–west. Located in the centre of the east end of the trench. It extends *c.* 2.28m into the trench from the east baulk. Its width is *c.* 0.43m. Its western end coincides with the edge of the stone flag "raft" 141 and it seems likely that it never extended any further. Three courses are visible. Depth to wall top is *c.* 30 ins. Since the surviving height of 138, 139 and 140 is the same it seems likely that this was their original height. Interpreted as a sleeper wall for the floor of the Period I granary.

140) Wall running east–west. Located in south east corner of block, partly hidden in the south baulk. It extends *c.* 2.28m into the trench from the east baulk. Its western end coincides with the edge of the stone flag "raft" 141 and it seems likely that it never extended any further. Three courses are visible. Depth to wall top is *c.* 30 ins. Since the surviving height of 138, 139 and 140 is the same it seems likely that this was their original height. Interpreted as a sleeper wall for the floor of the Period I granary.

141) Foundation for 138, 139 and 140. Layer of large flagstones underlying 138, 139 and 140. It extends over the whole area under the sleeper walls. Its relationship to the clay foundation 137 is not clear. Depth to top of flags: 52–53 ins.

142) Layer of fallen roofing material. This appears on the section of the east face of trench Fa23 Fb23 (Pl 33) and is visible in photographs M14 and C229 (see Fig. 2.5). The annotated section drawing refers

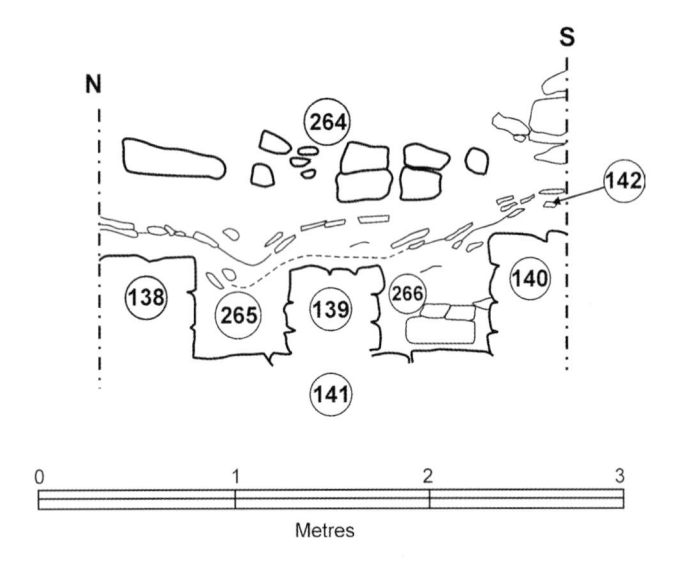

Figure 7.39. Block 24 Trench Fb23: section of east face.

Figure 7.40. Photograph M37: Block 24 Trench Fa23 looking west; foundation (137) revetted platform (143) and buttress for robbed granary west wall 136 in the foreground with 'Period II' wall 144 beyond, below later wall 145.

Figure 7.41. Photograph M39: Block 24 Trench Fa23; stone-revetted clay foundation 143 and buttress for the granary's main west wall (136) with wall 144 to right (west). On the left a distinct edge between west wall foundation 137 and that of the revetment can be seen.

Figure 7.42. Photograph M52a: Block 24 Trench Fa23, showing from left to right, late wall 145, 'Period II' wall 144 and stone-reveted clay foundation 143.

to the material as 'roofing tiles' while the entry for Finds Group 61AU refers to it as 'roofing slates' (the full entry is 'Immediately below fallen roofing slates E end of trench' which would make it highly probable that the entry is indeed referring to the material shown in the section). Its appearance in photograph M14 (Fig. 2.5) is more consistent with it being composed of stone flags than ceramic tiles, and JPG refers to 'its sandstone roof' in his interim of June 1961 (see Appendix I). The material does not lie directly on top of the sleeper walls but *c.* 0.24m above. It is not so obvious in the drawn section but it can be seen in the photograph that the gaps between the sleeper walls are filled with a number of tip or accretion levels and the top ones of these lap over the sleeper walls themselves. There seems to be no surviving evidence of a floor over the sleeper walls. Compare with Block 41, 226.

143) Stone-revetted clay foundation. Located immediately to west of 136/137 and partly underlying the buttress foundations. The revetting has at least two courses, with a slight offset. The fact that 143 is partly overlain by the buttress suggests that it predated the building of at least some of the granary wall, though the precise relationship of 143 to 137 is unclear.

144) Wall running north–south. Located *c.* 0.5m west of 143. Width *c.* 0.62m. Depth to wall top *c.* 29 ins. Photographs M37 and C228 show five courses surviving above and offset foundation course. Interpreted on the general interpretative plan, Pl 3, as a Period II structure.

145) Wall running north–south. Located immediately to the west of 144. Its southern end partly overlies the south end of the west face of 144. Its west face is hidden in the west baulk of the trench. Photographs M37 and C228 show three courses surviving. Interpreted on the general interpretative plan, Pl 3, as a structure of Period IV.

264) 'Topsoil and black soil.' Appears only on the section of the east face of trench Fa23/Fb23 (Pl 33).

265) 'Mortar etc.' Appears only on the section of the east face of trench Fa23/Fb23 (Pl 33).

266) 'Fallen dressed stone.' Appears only on the section of the east face of trench Fa23/Fb23 (Pl 33).

Block 25 (Figs 7.38 and 7.43)
Trenches: Fd15
Plans: Pl 18
Photographs: M15
Provenanced Finds Groups: None

Structural Elements

146) Wall running north–south. Located in centre of trench. "One to two courses above flags". Depth to wall top 26 ins. Width *c.* 0.77m. Interpreted as a sleeper wall for the floor of the Period I granary.

147) Robber trench running north–south. To east of wall 146. "Large flags tumbled debris and robber material." Depth 46 ins. Interpreted as the robbed-out course of the main east wall of the Period I granary.

148) Wall running north–south. Located *c.* 1.13m west of 146. Width *c.* 0.55m. Two courses surviving in places. "Heavily mortared sleeper wall." Depth to wall top 27 ins. Interpreted as a sleeper wall in the interior of the Period I granary.

149) Flags. Located on either side of 148, that is, between 148 and the west baulk and between 148 and 146. They appear to underlie 146 and 148. Depth 35 ins. Almost certainly this is the top level of the flag, clay and stone foundation "raft" for the granary.

Figure 7.43. Photograph M15: Labelled 'Haltonchesters 1960. East Granary'; Block 25 Trench Fd15; the granary looking west showing sleeper walls 146 and 148.

Block 26 (Fig. 7.38)
Trenches: Fd25
Plans: Pl 40
Photographs: None
Provenanced Finds Groups: 60JT

According to the trench designation (Fd25) this trench should be the one shown on Pl 3 located over the south-eastern corner of the granary. However, the shape of the trench shown on the detail plan (Pl 40) does not tally with that shown on Pl 3, but seems more similar to the trench shown on Pl 3 in a position which would have been designated Fc31 (and is here assigned the block number 26a).

Structural Elements

150) Wall running north–south. Width *c.* 0.62m. Depth to wall top 9 ins. "Period III wall, 2 or 3 courses, Turf to 23 ins." "Lowest courses solid but irregular stones, 2nd up, finer, regular." Possibly one of the late structures which Gillam mentioned as being over the remains of the granary.

Block 26a

This trench is shown only on the general plan, Pl 3. See remarks above under Block 26.

Block 27

Trench: Cc34

This trench designator only appears in the Finds Book (finds group: 61HS). No plans of a trench designated Cc34 are known. Perhaps should read Ce34.

Block 28 (Fig. 7.44)

Trenches: Ce34, Da34, Db34, Dc34, Dd34, De34
Plans: Only General Pl 3
Photographs: None
Provenanced Finds Groups: Da34: 61NE
Dc34:   61HO, 61IU
Dd34:   61QJ, 61QK,
De34: 61HZ, 61QA

No detailed plans for this trench exist. The structural elements have therefore been restored from the general plan Pl 3 and the Finds Book.

Structural Elements

151) Fort Wall.
152) Rampart
153) Intervallum
154) Wall running north–south. Located at east end of trench. Interpreted as Period II.
155) Single stone, at west end of trench over Fort Wall. On Pl 3 it is coloured red which convention is used elsewhere on Pl 3 to denote structures of Period IV. Almost certainly a "park railing stone".
157) Clay floor. Three foot down in trench Dc34. Mentioned only in Finds Book (finds group 61HO).
158) Flagged surface at 2 ft 6 ins in trench Dc34. Mentioned only in Finds Book (finds group 61IU).

Block 29 (Figs 5.3 and 7.45–7.47)

Trenches: Da32, Db32, Dc32, Db33
Plans: Pl 34, Pl 35, Pl 42
Photographs: M23, M24 (Db33 only), M36? (Da32?), C212?
Provenanced Finds Groups: Db32: 61MA, 61MU, 61OG
Db33: 61OU

Trenches Db32 and Db33 were the only ones recorded in any detail.

Structural Elements

159) Wall (?) running east–west. Located on north side of Db32. Two, possibly three courses of stone are visible on the plan, the bottom course being offset by some 0.24m. The wall is only roughly faced. Depth to top of top course 13–15 ins. The interpretation is not entirely clear from the general plan Pl 3, but it was probably interpreted as a wall revetting the south termination of the earth mass backing the fort wall, on the north side of the *porta quintana*.
160) Wall running east–west. Only three stones survive. Located near the centre of trench Db32. Only one course survives. "Line of kerb stones". Depth to wall top 37 ins. Interpreted as the kerb on the north side of the *via quintana*.
161) Clay layer. Located on east side of trench Db32 between 159 and 160. No depths given and relationship with surrounding contexts not clear.

Block 28

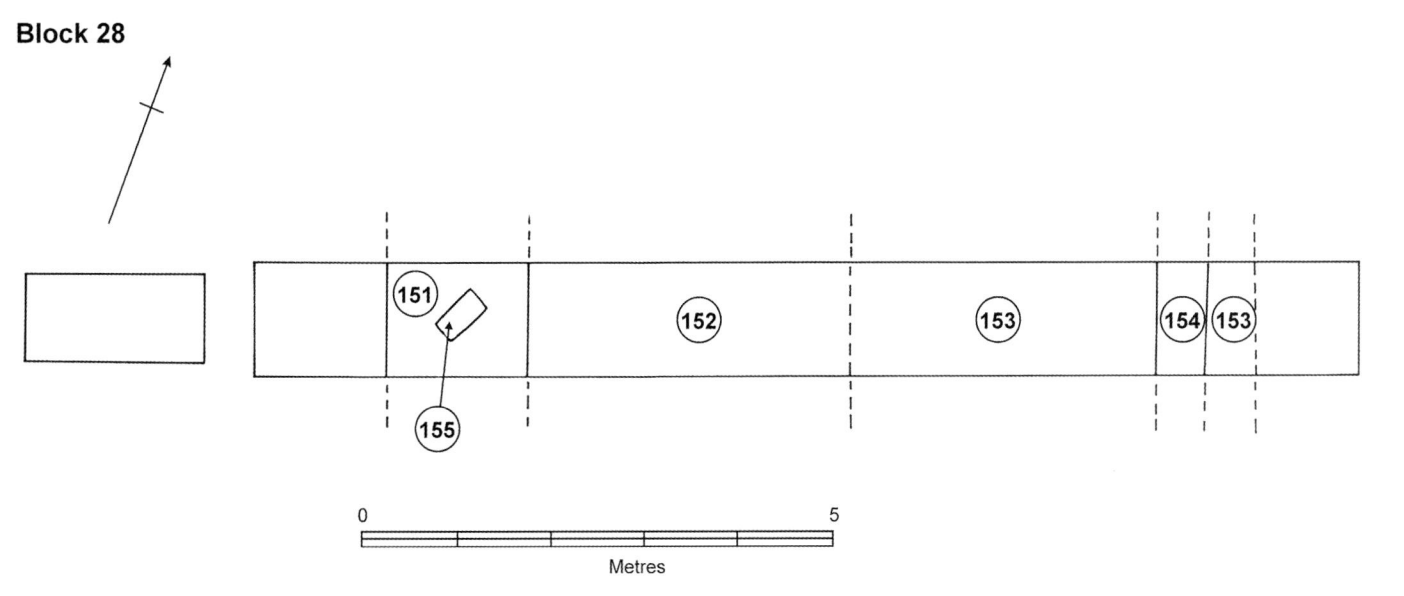

Figure 7.44. Block 28: plan.

Block 29

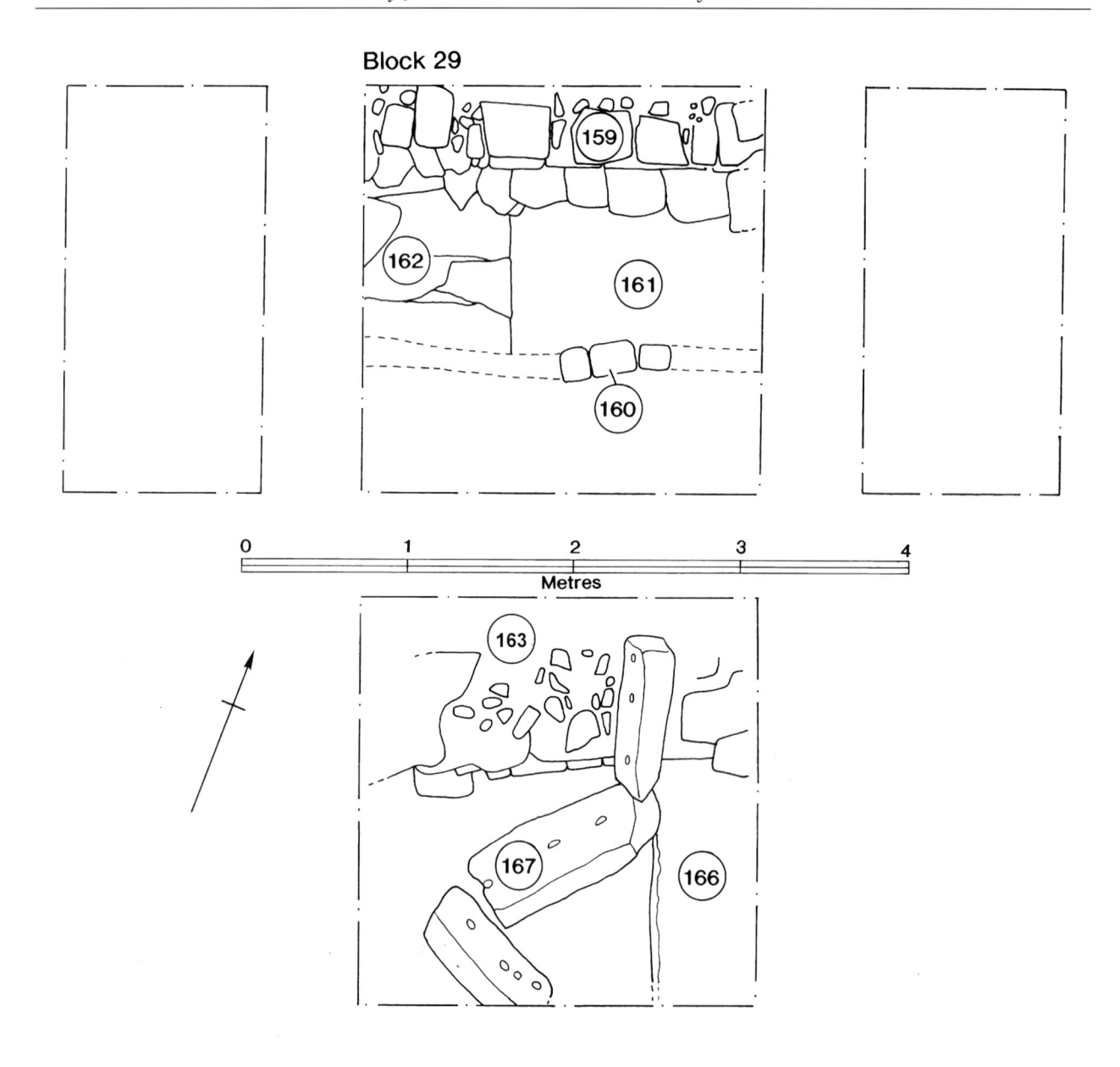

Figure 7.45. Block 29: plan.

162) Flags. Located immediately to west of 161. Depth to top 58 ins. Appears to underlie 159. Relationship to 160 and 161 not clear. Possibly the basal flagging continuing the line of the curtain wall beneath the passageway of the *porta quintana* and forming part of a foundation raft for the gate superstructure.

163) Road surface. Located in northern half of Db33. Presumably it extended into the southern half of trench Db32 though no mention is made of it on plan Pl 42. Depth to top 25 ins. "V course (sic) gravel (Via Quintana road surface)". The proximity of this road surface to the turf level and to the stones of a Period IV wall (167), and the depth of the road related material underneath it (clearly visible in photo M23) make it unlikely that it is the Period I road. This is confirmed by pottery from beneath it (groups 61MA and 61MU) which contains material with a *terminus post quem* of at least the 2nd half of the 2nd century AD.

164) Underpinning for 163 (?). As mentioned above under 163, a considerable depth of this can be seen in photograph M23.

165) Foundations for 163 and 164 (?). In photograph M23, a deep foundation of large stone is visible where it outcrops underneath 163 and 164. This may all relate to 163 and 164 or it may be part of earlier road surfaces.

166) Wall (?). Located in the south east corner of trench Db33 and visible on photo M24. It appears to be a single very large stone (at least 1.44m × 0.62m). It is interpreted on the general plan Pl 3 as a structure of Period I related in some way to the termination

7. Structural Synopsis

of the rampart backing by the *porta quintana*. It was perhaps part of the foundation for the gate's south-east pier, supporting an inner portal.

167) Wall running north–south. Consisting of three large stone blocks (the largest is *c*. 1.03m × 0.41m × 0.12m). These have holes (*c*. 48 mm diameter) along the midline of the top face: the most northerly has 3, the next has 3, and the most southerly has 4. Interpreted as a structure of Period IV. The stones appear to have been displaced from their original positions. Only the most northerly was probably in anything like its original position when found. It appears from photo M23 to have been resting on, or close to, the top surface of 163. It lies across the edge of the surface 163, and it dips down in a southerly direction. The next stone to it continues this dip in both a southerly and a westerly direction. The most southerly stone lies at about the same level as the lower end of its neighbour. It seems likely that the original position of the wall was at or slightly above the level of the road surface 163 and that they either subsided or were dumped into a pit which was either dug around them, possibly in an attempt to remove them, or to the west of them, to remove them or something else.

275) Two large, neatly worked stone blocks, one laid on top of the other, are shown in photograph M36 (see Fig 7.46), which is probably a view of the westernmost trench of Block 29 – Da32. The uppermost stone is inset, chamfered and in excess of 0.75m long to judge from the 6ft scale. The two blocks may represent the base of the gate's north-west pier. On the general plan Pl 3 the north-west corner of the gateway is depicted as surviving in the north-east corner of Trench Da32, which would consistent with the remains shown by M36 (cf Fig 5.1).

Figure 7.46. Photograph M36: Perhaps Block 29, Trench Da32 looking north? No detailed plan of this trench exists, but the two large neatly squared and chamfered blocks (275) in the top right corner might conceivably be associated with the porta quintana *– base of north-west pier?*

Figure 7.47. Photograph M24: Block 29 Trench Db33, looking south: note 'park railing' stones 167 and the massive squared block 166 along the east side of the trench.

Block 30

Trench: Dc22
Plans: None
Photographs: None

This trench designator only appears in the Finds Book (finds groups: 61ES, 61FZ). No plans of a trench designated Dc22 are known.

Block 31

Trench: Dc23
Plans: None
Photographs: None

This trench designator only appears in the Finds Book (finds group: 61JJ). No plans of a trench designated Dc23 are known. Perhaps should read De23.

Block 32 (Figs 7.48–7.49)

Trenches: Ea32
Plans: Pl 30, 42
Photographs: C235
Provenanced Finds Groups: 61AL, 61BM

Structural Elements

168) Road surface. Extending over whole trench at depth 35ins. "Course (sic) orange gravel road surface". No indication on the plans of the period to which the road surface was assigned. There are no finds from in or below the surface.

169) Kerb. Located in north east corner of trench. Consists of a single row of five stones. Not surviving further west or east. Depth to top 27 ins. "Kerb stones".

170) Channel. Runs east–west approximately down the middle of the trench. There is a northerly spur coming off it *c.* 1.51m from the west baulk. Width *c.* 0.12m. Depth to bottom 41 ins, which makes its depth from the top of the road surface *c.* 6 ins (0.15m). "Drain". Possibly it was originally stone lined though this seems unlikely as it is so narrow. More likely it was a channel for a pipe. It is probably Roman since the plan suggests that it was sealed by Roman period rubble.

171) Rubble and earth. Extends over whole trench. Depth to top 8–27 ins. More tightly packed at west end of trench. Appears on plan Pl 30. Must have covered features 168–170. Finds Group 61AL which contains a wall sherd of calcite gritted ware exhibiting the pronounced shoulder which is characteristic of the Huntcliff type (late 4th C.) probably comes from this level.

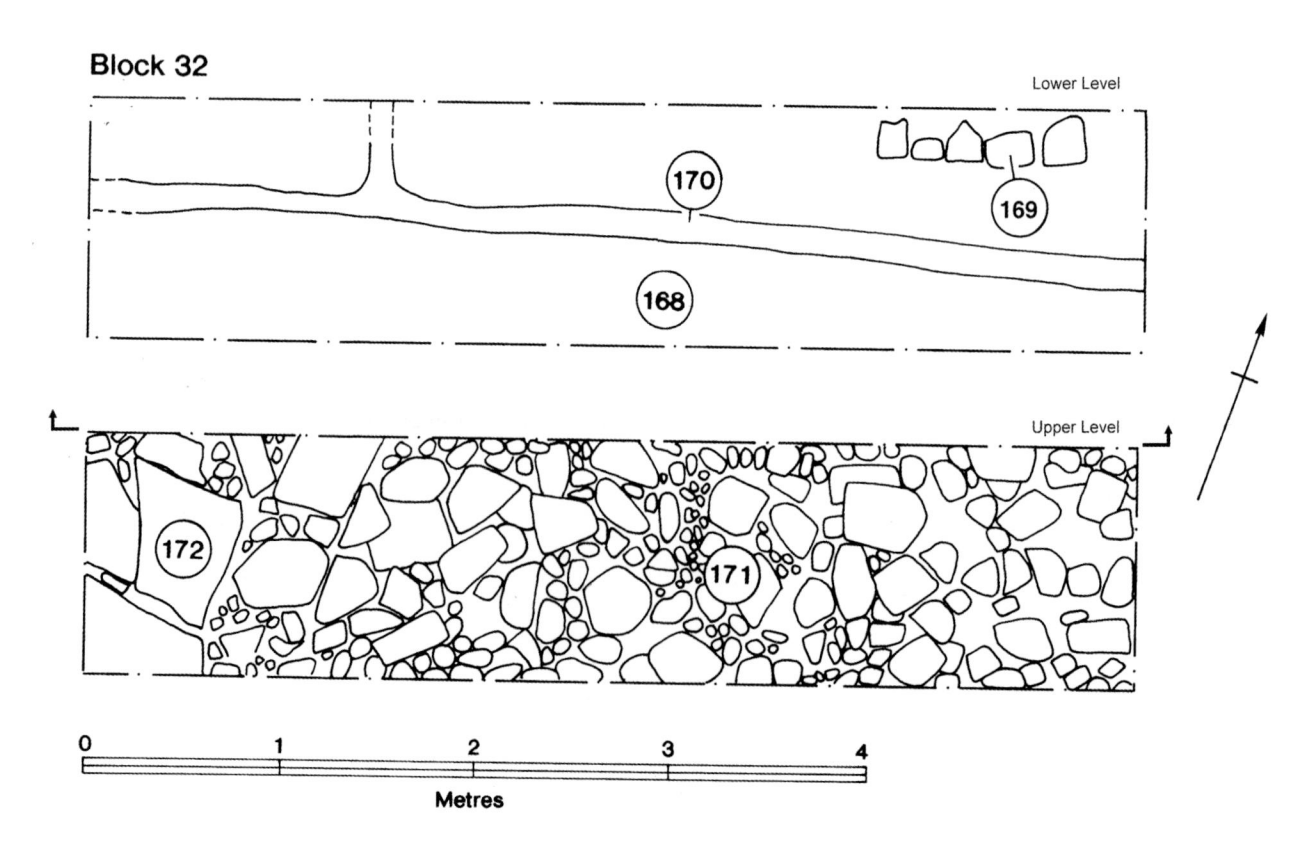

Figure 7.48. Block 32: plan.

7. Structural Synopsis

Figure 7.49. Photograph C235 Block 32 Trench Ea32; view of drain channel 170 and gravel road surface 168, looking east.

172) Flags. Located at west end of trench. Depth to top between 2 and 10 ins. Overlies tightly packed part of 171.

Block 33: Number not used.

Block 34

Trenches: Ec31, Ed31
Plans: Pl 40: this shows the south part of the trench only. Only one feature is shown.
Photographs: None
Provenanced Finds Groups: None

Structural Elements

173) Drain running north–south. Located in roughly the centre of the drawn portion of trench Ec31. "Stones, possibly part of drain at 18 ins down. Other details not shown". The shallowness of its depth probably means that it is later than Period I.
236) Wall running east–west. Shown only on general plan Pl 3. Interpreted as the main south wall of the Period I building.

Block 35 (Fig. 7.50)

Trenches: Trench to east of east fort wall.
Plans: Pl 39. This trench is not located on any of the general plans. The measurements given on plan Pl 39 suggest that it was located close to the Newcastle–Carlisle road, immediately south of the east gate: "4 ft 3 ins to field wall along Military Road" (on drawing at west end of trench); "3 ft to field wall along Military Road" (on drawing at east end of trench). The plan which appears in the Hadrian's Wall Pilgrimage Handbook for 1969 tends to confirm this, since it shows a section across the east fort wall in this position (the plan was drawn by J. Tait who supervised the excavations).
Photographs: None
Provenanced Finds Groups: None

Structural Elements

243) East fort wall. At this point this is 1.75m wide, consisting of small shaped blocks facing a core of undressed stone laid in lime mortar, resting on a foundation of boulders set in clay. Four courses survive in places. The inner (west) face of the wall has two offset courses, the outer one. The surviving wall top was about 0.5m below ground surface.
244) Cobbles. Located to east of 243. "Cobbles overlying mason's chippings, at 3 ft below surface, 1 ft thick". Possibly primary in view of the depth and the relationship to the mason's chippings, assuming these to have resulted from the initial building of the fort wall, and not some subsequent re-build.
245) Mason's chippings. Located beneath 244.
246) Wall. Short length (1.73m) of wall running east–west. Located to east of 243, parallel to the north baulk with its north face hidden in the baulk. Width is at least 0.55m. "Wall at depth of 2 ft 6 ins". Its relationship to cobbles 244 is unclear.
247) Flagged surface. Located to east of 246. One large (0.9m square) and a number of smaller (0.56m × 0.34m average) flags could be seen. "Flags at 2 ft 5 ins below surface at west side sloping to 3 ft 4 ins at east side". The relationship of the surface to wall 246 is not clear but the depths suggest that the surface post-dated the wall.
248) Wall (?). A single line of undressed stone, one course thick. Located at west end of trench above the east edge of the east fort wall 243. "One course of stones lying on dark brown soil. Perhaps Medieval. 3 ins below surface".
249) Wall. Rough wall consisting of both dressed and undressed stone. Runs diagonally across trench from south-west to north-east. Located to east of 247. Width *c.* 0.38m. "2 ft 10 ins below surface". Its relationship to other features is undefined.
250) Wall consisting of dressed stone facing a core. Runs north–south. Located to east of 249. Width is *c.* 0.65m. One course surviving. "Wall one course at 2ft 6ins below surface". Its relationship to other features is undefined.
251) Tumble. Located immediately to east of 250. "Tumbled stones in dark soil at 3 ft 6 ins". Its relationship to other features is undefined.

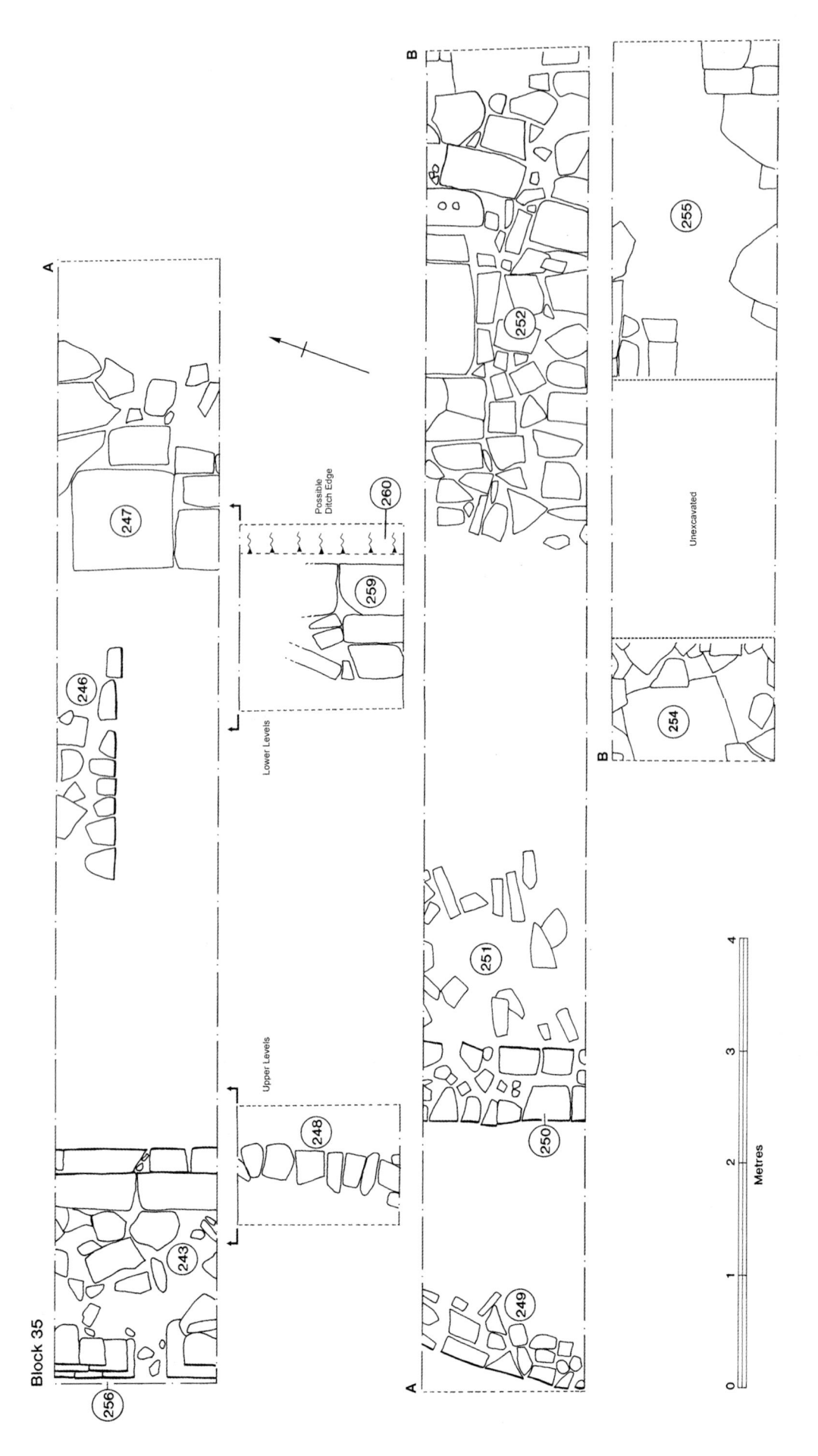

Figure 7.50. Block 35: plan.

252) Flagged surface. Area of flagging located to east of 251. Several large (1m × at least 0.5m) and many smaller (average 0.38m × 0.26m) flags visible. The flags extend for at least 5.6m from east to west. "Flags at 4 ft depth". One stone (whether it is a flag or a stone is not clear) has two holes *c.* 60mm in diameter and *c.* 0.14m apart (measured on the plan) arranged along the mid-line of its upper face. "Socket holes in stone 3 ins deep". It is possible that this stone was one of the 'park railing' stones, though the holes appear somewhat larger on the plan the those in the 'park railing' stones.

253) Burnt material. A small area of burnt wattle and daub located towards the east end of 252. Underlies 252. "Large flag underlying burnt wattle and daub at 5 ft depth. The burnt material continuing under flags" (*i.e.* the flags 252).

254) Large flag located towards the east end of 252. Underlies 253. "Large flag underlying burnt wattle and daub at 5 ft depth. The burnt material continuing under flags".

255) Flagged surface. Area of flags located at east end of trench. "Flags sloping from 1 foot at east end of sq. to 2 ft at W". These flags may be the same as 252 but the depth given suggest that they are a good deal higher.

256) Rampart backing located to west of 243. Not represented pictorially on plan but only mentioned in a note. "Rampart backing undressed stones set in clay overlying mason's chippings".

259) Small area of flagging shown to one side of main trench plan (Pl 39) as a detail of a lower level. Depth given is 5ft 1in which implies that it is well below 246 and 247.

260) Edge of ditch. Note associated with flags 259 says: "Flags at depth of 5 ft 1 in this may be a wall on lip of ditch". This is *c.* 5.5m east of the east face of the fort wall.

Block 36 (Fig. 7.51)

Trenches: Ec33, Ec34, Ec35, Ed34, Ee34, Fa34, Fb34, Fc34, Fc35, Fd34

Plans: Pl 27, Pl 29, Pl 44, Pl 47: The plans do not cover the full extent of the trench. There are no plans of, particularly, the east end. Nothing east of Ee34 survives in detailed plan.

Photographs: None

Provenanced Finds Groups: Ec33: 61JV, 61MJ
Ec34: 61FU, 61JY, 61KG, 61LV
Ec35: 61FL, 61GV, 61JH, 61JP
Ed34: 61EG
Ee34: 61MP

Structural Elements

174) Wall running north–south. Appears in trenches Ec33 Ec34 Ec35. Located towards the east side of these trenches. A little erratic in its course, it appears from the trench plans to undulate gently from side to side as it runs through the trenches. Width at widest *c.* 0.70m. Depth to wall top (only given on plan Pl 44 for trench Ec34) 8–11 ins. Interpreted on the general interpretational plan (Pl 3) as the longitudinal medial wall of a Period II building (barrack or stable to judge from the shape) on the south side of the *via quintana*.

175) Wall running east–west. Located in trench Ec33. Shown only on the general plan Pl 3. Wall 174 is shown intersecting with it. It is interpreted as the main north wall of a Period II building (barrack or stable to judge from the shape) on the south side of the *via quintana*. It is interpreted as occupying the same position as a wall of Period I.

176) Wall running east–west. Located in trench Ec35. Width *c.* 0.55m. No information on coursing or depth below turf. Intersects with 174 (a straight joint is shown at the level of the top courses, on plan Pl 27). Interpreted as an internal partition in the structure of which 174 and 175 form part.

177) Wall (?) running north–south. Located in trench Ec35, to west of 174. Two lines of stone are shown, one above the other, with an offset of *c.* 200mm, faced only on their west sides. No east face for the wall is shown. It is interpreted as a wall of Period I on the general plan Pl 3. It is shown running through trench Ec34 on Pl 3 though it does not appear on the detailed plan of Ec34.

178) Wall running east–west. Located in trench Ec33. It is shown only on the general plan Pl 3, not on any of the detailed plans. It is shown as occupying the same position as wall 175 of Period II. Presumably it underlay it, or possibly 175 reused it in Period II. It is not clear. 177 is shown intersecting with it.

179) Cobble surface. Located in trench Ec34 to west of wall 174. "Orange cobbled surface average depth 30ins". The surface stops short of wall 174 so the relationship between the two is not clear. Not shown in trenches further to north or south.

180) Two blocks, or possibly flags, shown in trench Ec34, (plan Pl 44), partly hidden in the north baulk and overlying surface 179. Depth to top *c.* 14 ins. There are indication that they dipped down towards the south.

181) Flagstones. Located in trenches Ed34 and Ee34. Depth to top *c.* 10ins. Presumably Period III or IV.

182) Wall running north–south. Shown only on general plan (Pl 3) of trench Ee34. It is interpreted as the main east wall of a Period II building (barrack or stable to judge from the shape) on the south side of the *via quintana*.

183) Wall running north–south. Shown only on general plan (Pl 3) of trench Fa34. Period not interpreted.

184) Wall running north–south. Shown only on general plan (Pl 3) of trench Fd34. Period not interpreted.

185) Road surface and large flags. Trench Ec33. Mentioned only in finds book. Not shown on any plans. Presumably the road is the *via quintana*. There is a small group of pottery (61MJ) from under the road surface and large flags. There seems to be nothing particularly late in it so the road could be the Period I *via quintana*.

186) Flags. Located in baulk between Ed34 and Ee34. Shown on Pl 47. Depth to top 13–18 ins. "Large thick slabs. Period IV flooring".

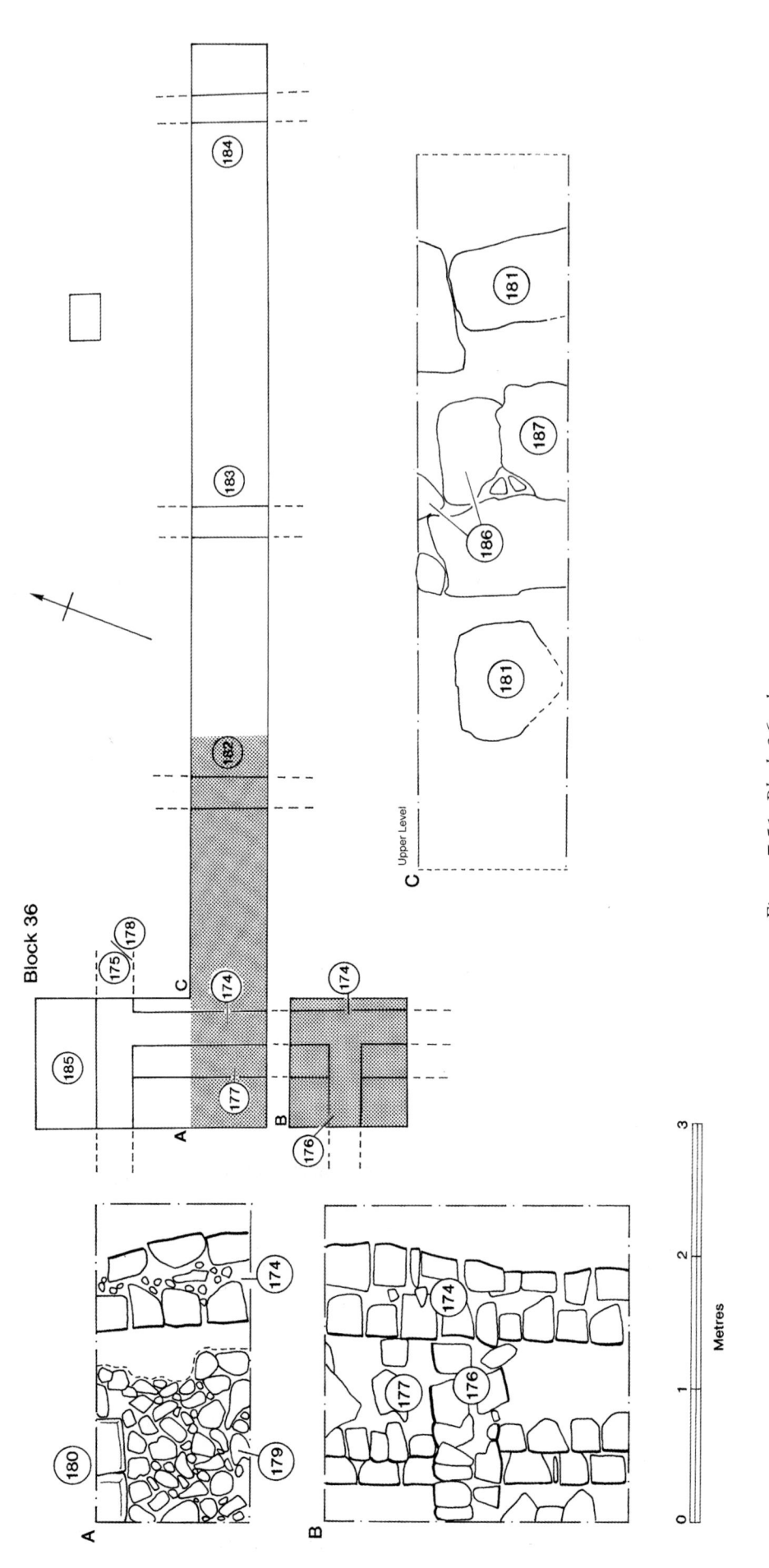

Figure 7.51. Block 36: plan.

187) Single flagstone. Located in baulk between trenches Ed34 and Ee34. Shown on Pl 47. Appears to overlie 186. Depth to top 4 ins. "Thick slab at higher level".
188) Sandstone floor. Trench Ec34. Mentioned in finds book. Not shown on any plan.
189) "Burnt level"/"Destruction layer". Mentioned in finds book. Not shown on any plan. Finds groups: 61JY, 61KG, 61LV, 61JH, 61JP, 61EG. 61LV is somewhat suspect. Description in finds book says: "Baulk running south from peg Ec34, below flat slabs(destruction layer)". The group contains a few sherds of calcite gritted ware and also a sherd from an indented beaker with a plain rimmed funnel neck which should be later than the late 2nd C. 61EG is also suspect since the group contains painted Crambeck and sherds of calcite gritted ware.
190) Hearth and flagstones. Trench Ee34. Mentioned only in Finds Book. Does not appear on any plan. Finds Group 61MX.

Block 37 (Fig. 7.52)

Trenches: Ed15
Plans: Pl 28
Photographs: None
Provenanced Finds Groups: 61NY, 61OI, 61OP

Structural Elements

191) Wall running north–south. Shown on general plan Pl 3 only. Shown on general plan as period unknown, but it aligns with 24 in Block 4 which was interpreted as Period II.
192) Flagged surface. Over most of trench. Shown on Pl 28. Depth to top *c.* 14 ins. Finds Group 61OI may have come from below this surface; it contained a fragment of Huntcliff type cooking pot.
193) Cobble surface. Mentioned in finds book; not shown on any plan. Finds Groups 61OP says: "between flags at 1ft depth and cobble layer at 3 ft".

Block 38 (Fig. 7.52)

Trenches: Ee22, Ee23
Plans: Pl 50
Photographs: None
Provenanced Finds Groups: Ee22: 61CW, 61CZ, 61DC, 61EE, 61GY
Ee23: 61FI

Structural Elements

194) Wall running east–west. Located in approx centre of trench. Width 0.63m. Slight offset on north side. Depth to top *c.* 12 ins. "P.III wall of 2 to 3 courses". Interpreted on general plan Pl 3 as wall of Period IV.
195) A marginal comment, "Thin black layer", on the detail plan is arrowed to the area immediately south of 194. The colouring of the plan suggests that this layer covered the whole of the area either side of of 194. Depths given are 44 and 48 ins.
196) "Burnt layer"/"Burnt level". Mentioned only in Finds Book. Not shown on plan. Depths: "below 3 ft 4 ins" (61CW), 3 ft 6 ins (61DC).
197) Clay layer. Located above burnt layer 196. Mentioned only in Finds Book. Not shown on plan. Depths: 3 ft 3 ins (61CZ), 3 ft 3 ins (61DD).

Block 39 (Figs 7.53–7.54)

Trenches: Annexe trench, located in north-west corner of the annexe close to the road.
Plans: Pl 36 (section), Pl 37, Pl 38
Photographs: None
Provenanced Finds Groups: 61QE, 61QF, 61QH, 61QM, 61QO, 61QP, 61QQ, 61RE, 61RF

Structural Elements

198) Wall running north–south across trench. "Wall two courses, 1 ft 9 ins below topsoil, resting on cobble foundation". Width *c.* 0.91m.
199) Wall running north–south across trench. Immediately east of 198. "Ashlar wall 4 courses high, 3 ins below surface". Width *c.* 0.6m. Shown on the plan published in the 1969 Pilgrimage Handbook and interpreted as part of same structure as 200.
200) Wall running north–south across trench. Located *c.* 5.16m east of 199. "Ashlar wall 5 courses high plus large offset course on east side and an offset 2nd course from top on west side". Width at widest *c.* 0.84m, at narrowest *c.* 0.55m. Depth to top 9 ins. Shown on the plan published in the 1969 Pilgrimage Handbook and interpreted as part of same structure as 199.
201) Flagged surface. Covers the area west of wall 200 up to a point *c.* 0.84m east of wall 199. "Flags at a depth of between 1 ft 6 ins and 2 ins (*sic*, probably to be read 2ft) underlying topsoil". The good edge at the east side of the flags should mean that they were associated with wall 200 and thus formed part of the same structure as wall 199 and 200. Finds Groups 61QM, 61QO and 61QQ can be identified as having a high degree of probability of having come from beneath 201 and suggest a *terminus post quem* of *c.* AD 250.
202) Wall. Only two stones surviving, protruding from the north and south baulks respectively. Each has one hole visible in its upper surface. "Period IV wall". Shown on the plan published in the 1969 Pilgrimage Handbook as part of the same structure as 203, dating to the late 4th century AD.
203) Wall. Consisting of a line of two stones running across the trench from north–south. Located *c.* 3.6m east of 202. Each stone has a number of holes along the longitudinal midline of its upper surface. There are two on the northern stone and four on the southern one. "Wall period IV, 9 ins below topsoil on north 2 ft at south". Shown on the plan published in the 1969 Pilgrimage Handbook as part of the same structure as 202, dating to the late 4th century AD.

Block 37

Block 38

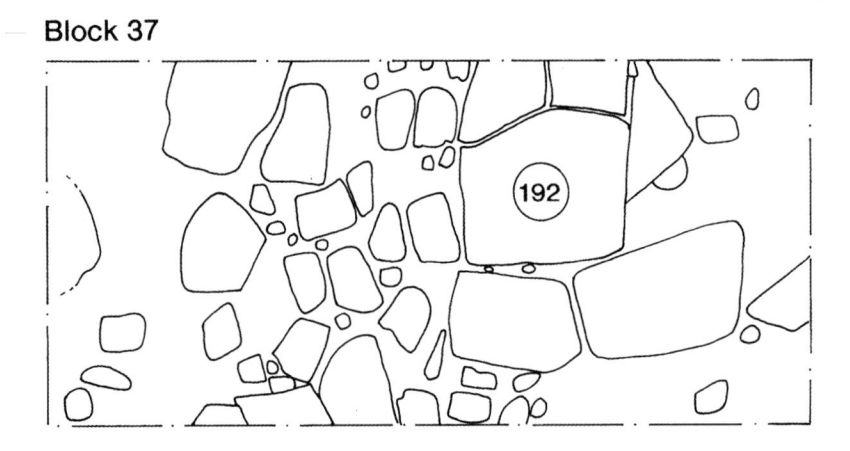

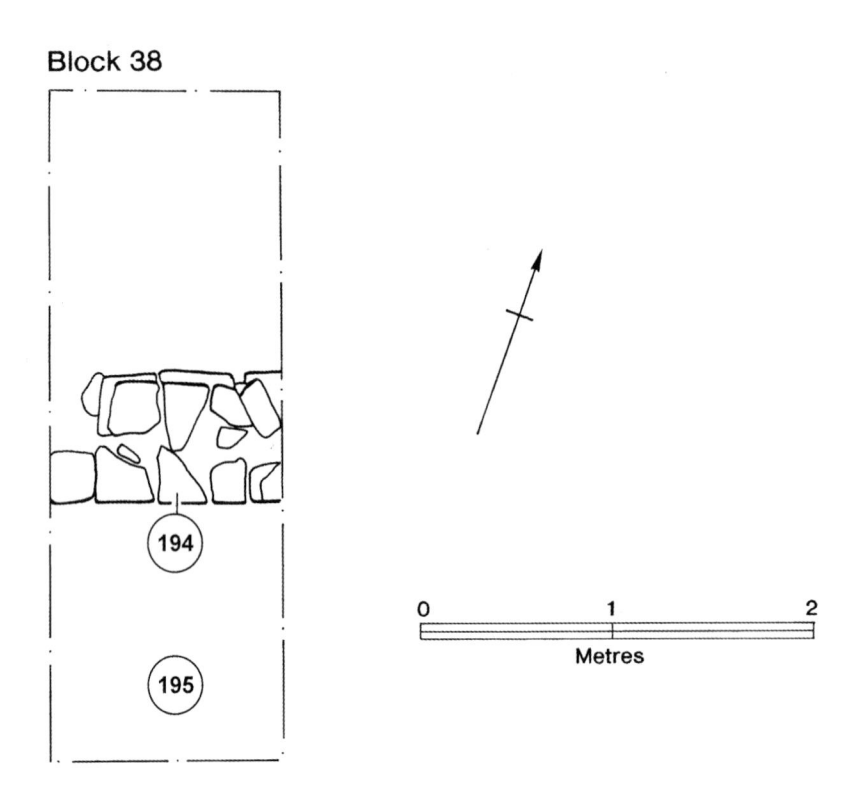

Figure 7.52. Blocks 37 and 38: plans.

204) Flagged surface. Three flagstones situated immediately west of 203. "Flags at 1 ft 5 ins below topsoil". Probably to be associated with walls 202 and 203.
205) Wall running north–south across trench. Located underneath flags 204. Only west face survived. "Remains of wall at 3 ft 1 ins below topsoil under flags". Probably 2nd century.
206) Wall. Consisting of a line of two stones running across the trench from north–south. Located immediately east of 203. Each stone has a number of holes along the longitudinal midline of its upper surface. There are two on the northern stone and three on the southern one. Shown on the plan published in the 1969 Pilgrimage Handbook as part of the same structure as 207, dating to the late 4th century AD.
207) Wall. Consisting of a single stone running across the trench from north–south. Located c. 3.41m east of 206. It has three holes along the longitudinal midline of its upper surface. Top surface, north end: "6 ins below topsoil", south end "16 ins below topsoil". Shown on the plan published in the 1969 Pilgrimage Handbook as part of the same structure as 206, dating to the late 4th century AD.
208) Flags. Two flagstones located immediately west of 207. "Flags at 1 ft 4 ins depth". Probably to be associated with the same structure as 206 and 207.
209) Patch of burnt wattle and daub. Located "to E of

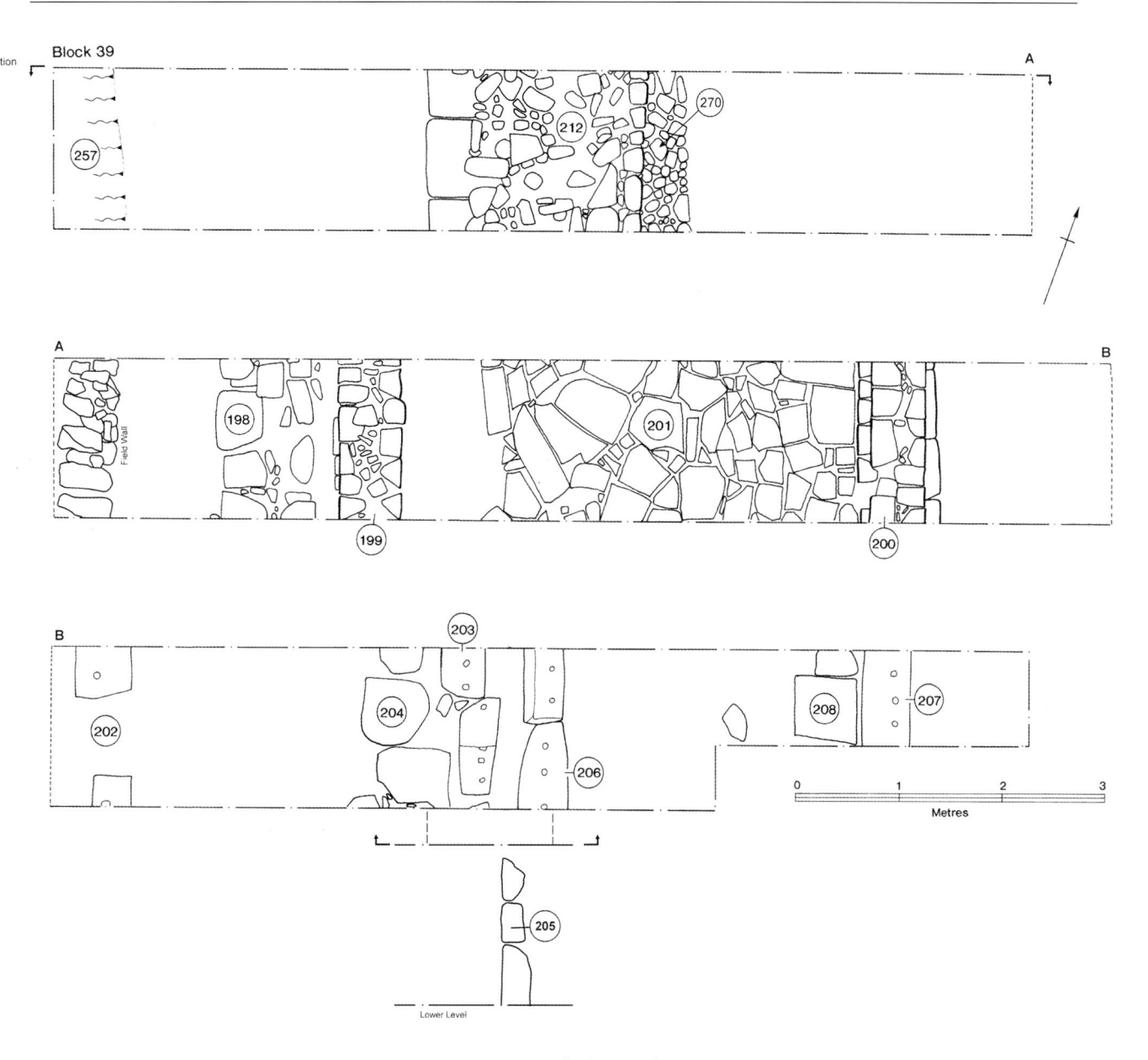

Figure 7.53. Block 39: plan.

N/S wall" (?). "Below topsoil". Mentioned in Finds Book but not shown on any plan. The Finds Group (61QE) contains a Hartshill-Mancetter mortarium with reeded hammer-head rim.

210) Cobble layer. "to E of burnt wattle and daub (61QE) at 3 ft 6 ins below topsoil". Mentioned in Finds Book (Finds Group 61QH) only. Does not appear on any plan.

211) "Burnt level". Mentioned in Finds Book only. Not shown on any plan. Below Finds Group 61QQ and below flags (probably the flags 201).

212) Wall running north–south. Width *c.* 2.06m. Large ashlar blocks on west face, small shaped blocks on east face. The core is mortared rubble. The east face is standing five courses high. The east side rests on a cobble foundation (270). Interpreted as the west wall of the extension/annexe.

213) Uppermost level of material backing the east side of wall 212. The description from the section key is 'grey clay with charcoal.'

257) Cut of ditch. Filled by 272 and 273. The lip of a ditch lies *c.* 3m to the west of the west face of wall 212. It appears to have been cut from approximately the same level as that on which wall 212 sits. Presumably this was the defensive ditch for the extension/annexe.

258) Layer of loose stone shown in section covering the area to the west of wall 212. It overlies 271 and the fill of the ditch 272. It appears to derive from the collapse or demolition of wall 212.

267) Layer of material backing the east side of wall 212. The description from the section key is 'stiff brown clay.' Below 213.

268) Layer of material backing the east side of wall 212.

The description from the section key is 'Stiff dark grey brown clay.' Below 267. The original drawing (Pl 36) indicates that a fragment of samian was recovered from this context. The only finds groups which references the 'rampart backing' is 61QP which contained two rim sherds of a Dr. 31R and an example of a Bellicus type mortarium, which provide a *terminus post quem* for the context of *c.* AD 150.

269) Layer of material at the base of the backing material 213, 267 and 268, sealing the foundations 270 of wall 212. The description from the section key is 'stiff pale brown clay.'
270) Cobble foundation of wall 212.
271) Layer of material overlying the natural ground surface to the west of wall 212. At its east side it laps up to the basal course of 212; At its west end it grades into the material filling ditch 257. The description from the section key is 'stiff brown clay with charcoal frags.'
272) Uppermost fill of ditch 257. The description from the section key is 'black ditch silt.'
273) Lower fill of ditch 257. Below 272. The description from the section key is 'stiff grey ditch silt.'

Block 40 (Figs 7.55–7.58)

Trenches: Fa31 Fb31
Plans: Pl 51
Photographs: M20, M21, M22, C238, C239
Provenanced Finds Groups: 61CL

Structural Elements

214) Wall running north–south. Located in centre of trench. At least three courses surviving. Faced blocks facing a rubble and mortar core. Width (max) *c.* 0.77m. Depth to top 25–26 ins. Interpreted as the west wall of the Period I loading bay of the east granary.
215) Wall running east–west. Runs from an intersection with 214 into the east baulk. Mostly buried in south baulk. Interpreted as the south wall of the Period I loading bay of the east granary.
216) Wall running north–south. Located immediately east of 214. Runs for *c.* 1.3m from north baulk before turning east to become 217. Does not appear to have been found on E (inner) side to judge from photographs M21–22. Width *c.* 0.72m. At least two courses survived. Depth to top 12 ins. Interpreted as the west wall of the Period II loading bay of the east granary.
217) Wall running east–west. Runs eastwards from corner with 216, into east baulk. Width *c.* 0.62m. At least two courses surviving. Does not appear to be faced on N (inner) side. Depth to top *c.* 17 ins. Interpreted as the south wall of the Period II loading bay of the east granary.
218) Stone packing between 214, 215 and 217. Depth to top 27–31 ins. "Packing between period I and II loading bay walls".
219) Clay. In north-east corner of trench bounded by 216 and 217. "Stony buff clay (revealed by removal of parts of loose rubble fill of P.II loading platform)".

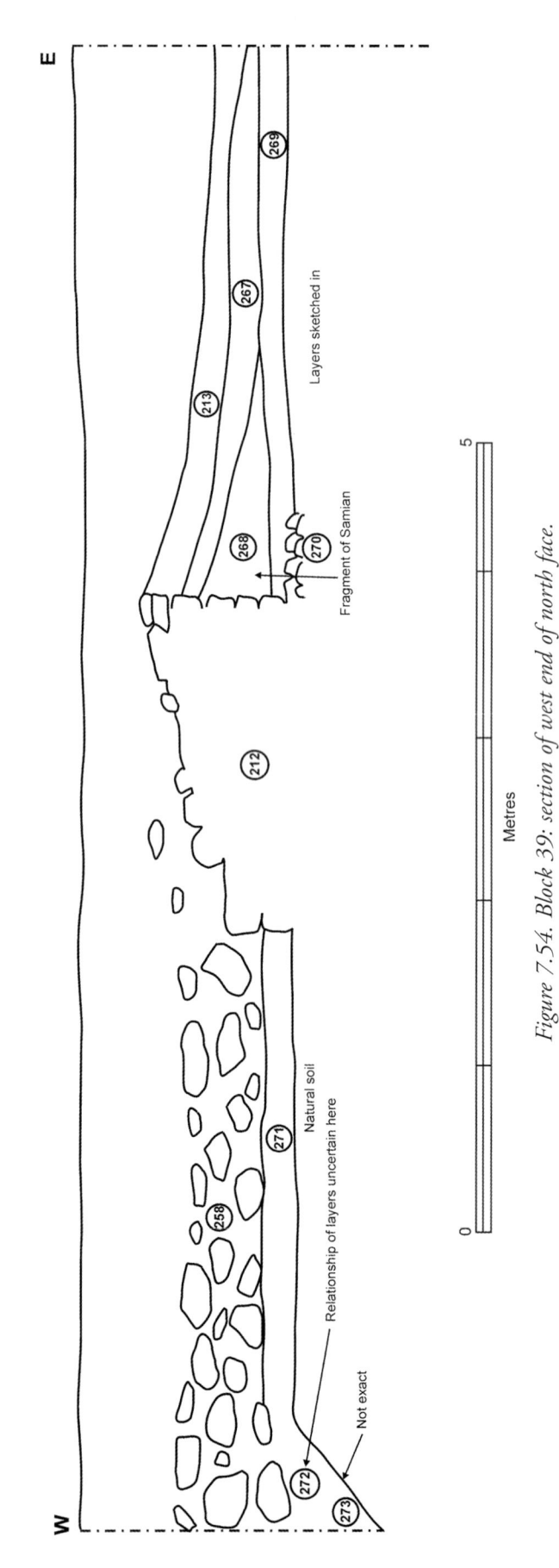

Figure 7.54. Block 39: section of west end of north face.

7. *Structural Synopsis* 87

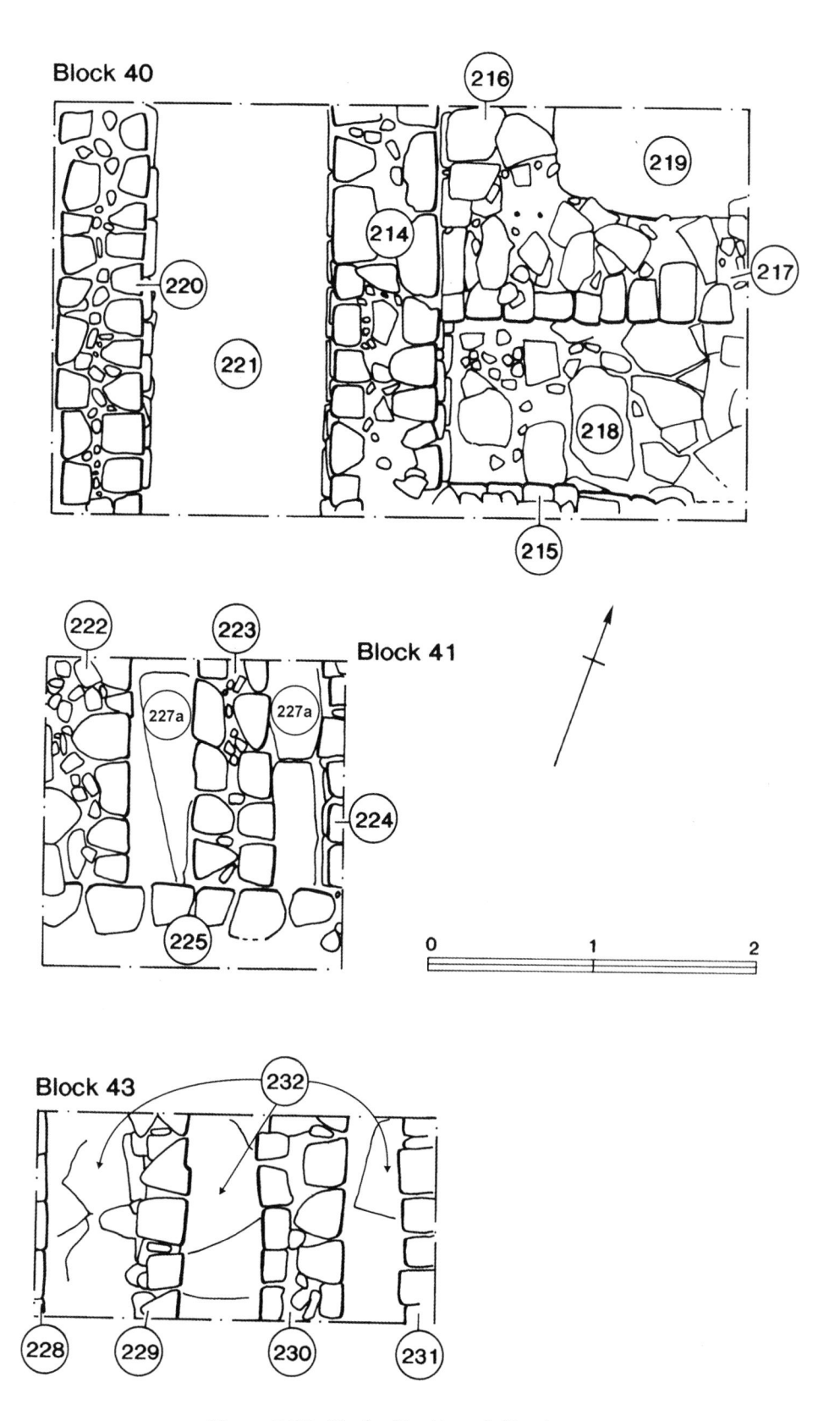

Figure 7.55. Blocks 40, 41 and 43: plans.

Figure 7.56. Photograph M20: Block 40 Trench Fa31 Fb31; from the west, showing the two phases of granary portico/loading bay.

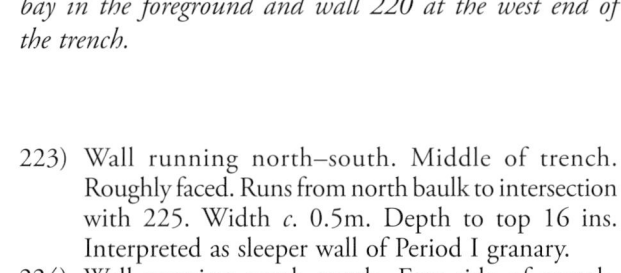

Figure 7.57. Photograph M21: Block 40 Trench Fa31 Fb31; from the east, with the granary portico/loading bay in the foreground and wall 220 at the west end of the trench.

220) Wall running north–south. Located *c.* 1.8m to west of 214 (centre to centre). At least two courses surviving. Offset on east side. Max width *c.* 0.58m. Depth to top 34–37 ins. Interpreted as the east wall of a southwards extension to the Period I courtyard building.
221) Clay. Between 214 and 220. "Buff stony clay". No depth given.

Block 41 (Figs 2.3 and 7.55)
Trenches: Fc21
Plans: Pl 40
Photographs: C241
Provenanced Finds Groups: 61EC 61EJ

Structural Elements
222) Wall running north–south. West side of trench. Only east face properly visible. Roughly faced. Runs from north baulk to intersection with 225. Interpreted as sleeper wall of Period I granary.
223) Wall running north–south. Middle of trench. Roughly faced. Runs from north baulk to intersection with 225. Width *c.* 0.5m. Depth to top 16 ins. Interpreted as sleeper wall of Period I granary.
224) Wall running north–south. East side of trench. Roughly faced. At least two courses surviving. Only the west side is visible. The east side is buried in the east baulk. Runs from north baulk to intersection with 225. Depth to top 13 ins. Interpreted as a sleeper wall of the Period I granary.
225) Wall running east west across south side of trench. Only the north face is visible, the south face being buried in the south baulk. Intersects with 222, 223 and 224. Depth to top 26 ins. Interpreted as a sleeper wall of the Period I granary. The southern ends of the three sleeper walls which are aligned north–south make simple straight joints with the north face of the single transverse wall. Their tops are also at the same level. JPG regarded the two sets as contemporary, saying in Roman Britain in 1960, that "they appeared nevertheless to be contemporary".

Figure 7.58. Photograph M22: Block 40 Trench Fa31 Fb31; from the south, with, from left to right, walls 220, 214, and 216/217 and packing 218 visible.

Figure 7.59. Photograph M38: Block 43, Trench Fb15; looking north, with, from left to right granary sleeper walls 229, 230 and 231 in view, overlying flagging 232.

226) "Fallen tile debris". Mentioned only in the Finds Book (61EC). Not shown on any plan. Finds Group 61EC contained a fragment of ceramic *tegula*. Compare with Block 24, 142.

227) "Black filling above and between granary support walls". Mentioned only in Finds Book (61EJ). Not shown on any plan.

227a) Large flags. Foundation for the three sleeper walls running north–south (222, 223, 224). Depth to top of flags 22".

Block 42

Trenches: Fc24
Plans: None
Photographs: None

This trench designator only appears in the Finds Book (Finds Group: 61JS). No plans of a trench designated Fc24 are known.

Block 43 (Figs 7.55 and 7.59)

Trenches: Fb15
Plans: Pl 29 Pl 40
Photographs: M38, C232
Provenanced Finds Groups: None

Structural Elements

228) Wall running north–south. Most of it is buried in the west baulk of the trench. Only the very edge of the east face is visible. "Granary west wall 3 courses". Depth to top 23 ins. Interpreted as the main west wall of the granary.
229) Wall running north–south. One face only (the east) located *c.* 0.74m east of 228. "Wall face 3 courses". Interpreted as a sleeper wall of the Period I granary.
230) Wall running north–south. Located in centre of trench. At least three courses surviving. Depth to top 14ins. Width *c.* 0.48m. Interpreted as a sleeper wall of the Period I granary.
231) Wall running north–south. At least half of it is buried in the east baulk. At least two courses surviving. Interpreted as a sleeper wall of the Period I granary.
232) Flagging. Visible in the gaps between 228, 229, 230 and 231. Probably underlies the sleeper walls. Depth to top 28–40 ins. Probably forms part of the massive foundation raft for the granary.

8. The Coins

P. J. Casey and R. J. Brickstock

The surviving record of coinage from Haltonchesters consists of 134 items derived from excavation, site collection or literary reference. Of these, 105 are identifiable to date and/or issuer. In the following study the coins, from whatever source, have been conflated into a single catalogue and presented as a consolidated histogram, using a now standard formula:

$$\frac{\text{Coins per period}}{\text{Length of period}} \times \frac{1000 \text{ (a notional multiplier)}}{\text{site total}}$$

Five collections are represented in this manner:

1) Coins, now missing, from excavations by M. Jarrett in 1956–1958 (Jarrett 1959, 1960); see List 1.
2) Excavations by J. P. Gillam in 1960–1961; List 2.
3) Coins in the Hedley Collection (PSAN 4 ser; 2 (1927). 38); List 3.
4) Donations to Newcastle Museum of Antiquities by unnamed benefactor, "from ploughed field on the north side of the Military Road"; List 4.
5) Miscellaneous literary references to finds.

That this is but a poor residue of the money circulating on the site in the Roman period can be judged by references to the site extending back to the 18th century, and by the use of local toponyms, Silver Hill and Brunt (*i.e.* Burnt) Ha'penny Field to describe parts of the site which appear to have been particularly rich in coin finds:

"Very few other Roman remains have been recorded from Hunnum. Occasional pieces of pottery and coins have doubtless come to light. Indeed, the southern half was in Horsley's time called Silver Hill, doubtless from finds of coins. But nothing seems to have been put specifically on record, except copper coins of Constantine, Magnentius and Decentius."

(Craster 1914, 468–73).

Note, in passing, the reference to coins of Magnentius and Decentius (coin period 24) not otherwise found in extant site finds.

"Considerable quantities of Roman copper coin are still occasionally found in the northern part of the station, now a field called Burnt Halfpenny Field; so plentifully, indeed, formerly that, as was remarked 'they were hard fash'd to pass them for a farthing'."

(Abbatt 1849, 20).

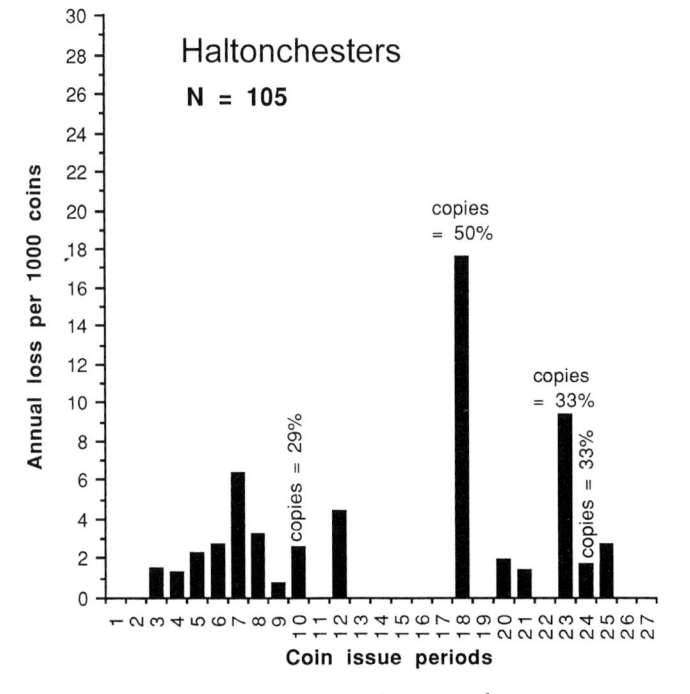

Figure 8.1. Coins graph

Figure 8.1 period divisions are as follows:

1	AD	43–54	15		244–9
2		54–68	16		249–53
3		68–81	17		253–60
4		81–96	18		260–73
5		96–117	19		273–86
6		117–38	20		286–96
7		138–61	21		296–317
8		161–80	22		317–30
9		180–92	23		330–48
10		193–217	24		348–64
11		218–22	25		364–78
12		222–35	26		378–88
13		235–8	27		388–402
14		238–44			

No coins from the excavations by F. G. Simpson and I. A. Richmond (1937) are recorded or can be traced.

As far as can be ascertained from the poor records, the various collections can be located within, or adjacent to, the fort, as follows.

1) The excavations by M. Jarrett examined the '3rd-century' extension on the south-west of the fort, and the defences of the main fort which comprised the east wall of the extension. In the main it is now impossible to differentiate between coin deposits associated with the extension itself and those associated with the defences.
2) The excavations by J. P. Gillam examined the western range of the administrative buildings in the central and southwestern sector of the *retentura* of the fort. It has likewise proved difficult, if not in most cases impossible, to locate coins from these excavations to specific contexts.
3) The Hedley Collection derives from the so-called Brunt Ha'penny Field, *i.e.* the *praetentura* of the fort.
4) The Museum donations derive from the same location as 3.

Catalogue conventions

Mints (followed, where appropriate, by *officina* letter, *e.g.* P,I,a, denoting Primo, 1st or Alpha):

AN	Antioch	RM	Rome
LN	London	TR	Trier

Denominations

ANT	Antoninianus	DP	Dupondius
AS	As	FOLL	'Follis'
AUREL	Aurelianus	SEST	Sestertius
AE	illegible bronze		
DEN	Denarius (pl = plated counterfeit)		

A copy or counterfeit of a particular ruler or issuer is denoted by single quotation marks, and by the use of a lower case 'c' in the catalogue reference, *e.g.* c. of 261 = a copy of RIC 261. The use of the word 'of' indicates that a precise catalogue reference has been obtained; for official issues and copies 'as' is used to denote an incompletely catalogued coin.

Catalogue references are to RIC unless otherwise stated

RIC	The Roman Imperial Coinage, volumes 1–10, H. Mattingly, E. A. Sydenham, C. H. V. Sutherland, R. A. G. Carson, J. P. C. Kent, A. M. Burnett eds, London, 1926–1994.
CK	Late Roman Bronze Coinage, part II by R. A. G. Carson and J. P. C. Kent, London, 1960.
CRAW	Roman Republican Coinage, M. Crawford, London, 1974.
HK	Late Roman Bronze Coinage, part 1, by P. V. Hill and J. P. C. Kent, London, 1960.

Where recorded, flan diameter is given in millimetres (mm), and weight in grams (g).

Condition of the obverse and reverse is denoted by the following abbreviations:

UW	Unworn	VW	Very worn
SW	Slightly worn	EW	Extremely worn
W	Worn	C	Corroded

Discussion

The overall coin pattern for Haltonchesters closely follows that dictated by the currency policies of successive emperors or dynasties, reflecting the decline of the traditional silver and *aes* coinage system, set up by Augustus, to its demise in the 3rd century during, or shortly after, the establishment of the Gallic Empire (AD 258–73). These trends have been discussed in a number works (*e.g.* Casey 1994). The pattern, irrespective of specific site occupancy, may be interpreted as showing the supply of an abundance of copper and brass currency in the military area, especially well represented by issues of Trajan, Hadrian and Antoninus Pius. Coins of these reigns (Periods 6–8) remain in circulation until the third quarter of the 3rd century, though with a rapidly diminishing purchasing power. This factor accounts for the high incidence of Antonine coins (Period 7) from a period when the fort might be assumed to be unoccupied.

An analysis of the wear pattern (where recorded) of the pre-Severan coins indicates that they had been, for the most part, in heavy use before loss or discard:

condition	UW	SW	W	VW	EW
pre-Hadrian		1			5
Hadrian	1	1			2
Antoninus Pius	1	2		2	2
M. Aurelius	1	2			2

From the later 2nd century increasing emphasis is placed on silver issues, especially after the debasement of the *denarius* by Marcus Aurelius. Coins from Period 10 (AD 193–217) onwards are exclusively *denarii* or *antoniniani* (*i.e.* double *denarii*), with the exception of a single *dupondius* of Severus Alexander (cat. no. 49). As is usual, a number of the Severan silver coins are plated counterfeits (cat. nos. 43, 46) probably produced at a time when Severan *denarii* were of sufficient intrinsic value to command a premium, possibly as late as the reign of Trajan Decius (AD 249–51). As is usual in the assemblages from the military area, though hitherto not commented upon in print, there is a distinct upswing in coin deposits of the reign of Severus Alexander (Period 12, AD 222–35). The possibility of imperial intervention of some sort in the wall area in this period may be advanced. Epigraphically, Alexander is represented at South Shields fort where the water supply is credited to this reign (RIB 1060), whilst recent coin finds, including counterfeit Severan *denarii*, from the bridge abutments at Chesters, also appear to provide a peak for the second quarter of the 3rd century (Brickstock, forthcoming; Brickstock and Dungworth, forthcoming).

As is normal, activity (if any) in Periods 13–17 (AD 235–60) cannot be judged by the absence of coins of these periods. Even allowing for the small total sample from Haltonchesters, the hiatus at this period is normal in all histograms for British sites, a function of the rapid debasement of the silver currency, which prompted the equally rapid disappearance from circulation (through withdrawal or hoarding) of earlier, intrinsically more valuable, issues.

The pronounced peak for Period 18 (AD 260–73) is, once again, entirely as expected, corresponding to the ultimate collapse of the silver currency, which reached its nadir of 2.5% silver during the reign of Claudius Gothicus (AD 268–70), resulting in the circulation of huge quantities of intrinsically near-worthless coin. In line with most Romano-British sites, 50% of the coins of Period 18 are copies of issues of Tetricus I and II (AD 270–73) and were undoubtedly produced to compensate for the dearth of Aurelian's reformed coinage in Britain in Period 19, and may be regarded as a component of coinage of this latter period.

Following the currency collapse of Period 18, a pattern is observable that is well-established in Hadrian's Wall and associated forts. As is usual in the north the coinage of Carausius (Period 20) is under-represented, which may indicate garrison changes at this time perhaps associated with the manning of coastal defences in the south, or the need for the movement of forces to campaign in Gaul (Casey 1994b).

The contrast between coin deposits of Periods 3–12 and Periods 22–27 has been commented upon on a number of occasions (*e.g.* Casey 1994a). As compared to urban sites in southern Britain, military sites in the north present an under-representation of 4th-century coins. An explanation for this has been sought in the operation of the *annona militaris*, which substituted payment to the army in kind for payment in cash. No conclusion as to density of occupation or size of garrison can be drawn from coins in this period without independent confirmation such as might be obtained from quantitative pottery studies.

On present evidence, in particular given the relatively small sample available for Haltonchesters, there is no reason to suppose that the absence of coins of Periods 26 and 27 (AD 378–402) has any significance in establishing whether or not occupation extends into the 5th century. The appearance of Hunnum in the *Notitia Dignitatum* may be taken as acceptable evidence of occupation despite the lack of coins.

Contexts and site distribution

Despite the poor recording of find spots, a certain pattern emerges when the coins are viewed in broad context. It is notable that the overall distribution of both issuers and denominations is similar in the three main areas excavated, the extension/annexe, the south-west *retentura*, and the *praetentura*: recorded ploughing within the fort may account for the general mixing of finds. In contrast to this general statement it may be noted that all of the coins of Period 12 were recovered from the south western quadrant of the fort by Jarrett and Gillam in separate campaigns of excavation, perhaps suggestive of specific site activity in this area in the second quarter of the 3rd century. Since the coins are of a relatively high value, the presence of a prestige building, such as a centurion's quarters, may be evidenced.

Listings

List 1: 1956–58 excavations (Jarrett, 1960)
Catalogue nos.

    2, 4, 5, 10, 16, 17, 18, 24, 27, 28, 30, 31, 38, 39, 43, 45, 46, 47, 48, 56, 64, 67, 69, 70, 71, 74, 78, 81, 93, 99, 100, 101 102, 106, 107, 114, 115, 116, 130, 131.

List 2: 1960–61 Excavations
Catalogue nos.

    1, 3, 6, 7, 12, 15, 19, 20, 21, 23, 25, 26, 33, 35, 37, 40, 41, 42, 50 51, 52, 53, 54, 57, 59, 62, 65, 66, 68, 73, 75, 76, 77, 79, 82, 84, 87, 89, 91, 92, 95, 96, 97, 98, 108, 110, 112, 113, 117, 118, 119, 120, 121, 122, 123, 124, 126, 127, 128, 129, 132, 133, 134.

List 3: coins in the Hedley Collection
Catalogue nos.

    8, 13, 55, 58, 60, 63, 83, 86, 88, 94, 103, 104, 105, 109, 111, 125

List 4: Museum Donations
Catalogue nos.

    9, 11, 14, 22, 29, 32, 34, 36, 61, 72, 80, 85, 90.

Catalogue

1   M.ANTONIUS   denom: DEN   Obv   ANT AVG III RPC
      date: 32–31BC   mint: -   cat: CRAW 544   Rev   LEG...
      wear: EW/EW   diam: 16.0   wt: 2.4
   Year: 1960   Sf no   28   Status: PRESENT   Ref: -
   Context: H60KI, Ec14, S. side of trench at depth of 22" (opposite peg Ec14), 30.6.60.

2   TITUS   denom.   DEN   Obv   [IMP TIT]VS CAES VESP[ASIAN AVG PM]
      date: 80   mint: RM   cat: 22a   Rev   Elephant
      wear: diam: wt: -
   Year: 1958   Sf no   25   Status: MISSING   Ref: AA1960
   Context: Unstratified

3   TITUS   denom.   DEN   Obv   DIVVS AVGVSTVS VESPASIANVS
      date: 80–81   mint: RM   cat: 62   Rev   EX SC
      wear: W/C   diam: 20.0   wt: 1.9
   Year: 1961   Sf no   57   Status: PRESENT   Ref: -
   Context: HOLE Ea22. Mixed soil below 1st tumble of Period IV stone. Depth *c.* 2'6", 27.5.61.

4   DOMITIAN   denom.   AS   Obv   -
      date: 81–96   mint: RM   cat: -   Rev   -
      wear: diam: -   wt: -
   Year: 1958   Sf no   20   Status: MISSING   Ref: AA1960
   Context: "Above the clay floor of 296 and below a later re-laying of it, assignable to some date before 367."

5   DOMITIAN   denom.   SEST   Obv   ...VG GERM....
      date: 81–96   mint: RM   cat: -   Rev   -
      wear: diam: -   wt: -
   Year: 1956/7   Sf no   1   Status: MISSING   Ref: AA1959
   Context: "In the material used to fill in the Hadrianic ditch in the early years of the third century"

6   TRAJAN   denom.   SEST   Obv   -
      date: 98–117   mint: RM   cat: -   Rev   -
      wear: EW/EW   diam: 33.0   wt: 22.5
   Year: 1961   Sf no   40   Status: PRESENT   Ref: -
   Context: HOLE De22, N. of park railings 18" below

7   TRAJAN   denom.   AS   Obv   -
      date: 98–117   mint: RM   cat: -   Rev   -
      wear: EW/C   diam: 26.0   wt: 5.6
   Year: 1960   Sf no   6   Status: PRESENT   Ref: -
   Context: Ea14, HAL.ES.60, in fallen stone, 2.6.60.

8   TRAJAN   denom.   DP   Obv   -
      date: 98–117   mint: RM   cat: -   Rev   -
      wear: EW/EW   diam: 27.0   wt: 9.9
   Year: 1925.4   Sf no   1   Status: NMA, BOX 1134   Ref: PSAN4, 2, 1927, 38
   Context: Brunt Ha'penny field

9   TRAJAN   denom.   SEST   Obv   -
      date: 98–117   mint: RM   cat: -   Rev   -
      wear: EW/EW   diam: 33.0   wt: 18.9
   Year: 1978.8   Sf no   6   Status: NMA, BOX 1230   Ref: -
   Context: North side of military road, collected over four years from ploughed field.

8. The Coins

10   TRAJAN   denom.   SEST   Obv   ...RVAE TRAIANO AVG
       date: 103–114   mint: RM   cat: -   Rev   -
       wear: diam: -   wt: -
   Year: 1956/7   Sf no   2   Status: MISSING   Ref: AA1959
   Context: -

11   HADRIAN   denom.   SEST   Obv   -
       date: 117–25   mint: RM   cat: -   Rev   -
       wear: VW/EW   diam: 33.0   wt: 23.3
   Year: 1978.8   Sf no   7   Status: NMA, BOX 1230   Ref: -
   Context: North side of military road, collected over four years from ploughed field.

12   HADRIAN   denom.   AS   Obv   -
       date: 117–38   mint: RM   cat: -   Rev   -
       wear: C/C   diam: 26.0   wt: 6.1
   Year: 1960   Sf no   7   Status: PRESENT   Ref: -
   Context: H60LX, Fa32, in or below 2nd cobble layer, 18.7.60.

13   HADRIAN   denom.   AS   Obv   [IMP CAESAR TRAIANVS
                                                                                               HADRIANVS AVG]
       date: 119   mint: RM   cat: 577a/b   Rev   [PONT MAX TR POT COS III SC
                                                                                               BRITANNIA]
       wear: W/W   diam: 25.0   wt: 7.3
   Year: 1925.4   Sf no   2   Status: NMA, BOX 1134   Ref: PSAN4, 2, 1927, 38
   Context: Brunt Ha'penny field

14   HADRIAN   denom.   SEST   Obv   [HADRIANVS AVGVSTVS]
       date: 125–38   mint: RM   cat: as 745   Rev   -
       wear: EW/EW   diam: 32.0   wt: 20.2
   Year: 1978.8   Sf no   5   Status: NMA, BOX 1230   Ref: -
   Context: North side of military road, collected over four years from ploughed field.

15   HADRIAN   denom.   DP   Obv   HADRIANVS AVGVSTVS PP
       date: 134–38   mint: RM   cat: 974   Rev   HILARITAS PR COS III SC
       wear: SW/SW   diam: 28.0   wt: 11.5
   Year: 1961   Sf no   55   Status: PRESENT   Ref: -
   Context: IM, HOLE Ea22, orange mixed stoney clay. Depth 4'. W. end of trench, 29.6.61.

16   HADRIAN   denom.   DEN   Obv   HADRIANVS [AVGV]STVS PP
       date: 134–38   mint: RM   cat: 367   Rev   TRANQVILLITAS AVG COS III
       wear: diam: -   wt: -
   Year: 1958   Sf no   16   Status: MISSING   Ref: AA1960
   Context: "In material used to fill in the Hadrianic ditch in the early years of the third century"

17   ANTONINUS PIUS   denom.   AS   Obv   -
       date: 138–61   mint: RM   cat: -   Rev   -
       wear: diam: -   wt: -
   Year: 1958   Sf no   26   Status: MISSING   Ref: AA1960
   Context: Unstratified

18   ANTONINUS PIUS   denom.   DP   Obv   ....AVG....
       date: 138–61   mint: RM   cat: -   Rev   .....NIA... SC
       wear: diam: -   wt: -
   Year: 1958   Sf no   27   Status: MISSING   Ref: AA1960
   Context: Unstratified

19   ANTONINUS PIUS   denom.   DEN   Obv   -
       date: 138–61   mint: RM   cat: -   Rev   -
       wear: diam: 18.0   wt: 2.0
   Year: 1961   Sf no   44   Status: PRESENT   Ref: -
   Context: HOLE De22, N. of park railings, depth 2', 7.6.61.

20 ANTONINUS PIUS   denom. SEST   Obv -
    date: 138–61   mint: RM   cat: -   Rev -
    wear: W/W   diam: 33.0 wt: 22.3
    Year: 1960   Sf no 2   Status: PRESENT   Ref: -
    Context: HAL.AN.60.

21 ANTONINUS PIUS   denom. DEN   Obv -
    date: 138–61   mint: RM   cat: as 177   Rev -
    wear: SW/SW   diam: 15.0 wt: 2.1
    Year: 1961   Sf no 48   Status: PRESENT   Ref: -
    Context: H61DS, 10" from N. wall 28" from E. wall, 3' depth, 21.5.1961.

22 ANTONINUS PIUS   denom. SEST   Obv -
    date: 138–61   mint: RM   cat: -   Rev -
    wear: VW/VW   diam: 30.0 wt: 20.2
    Year: 1978.8   Sf no 1   Status: NMA, BOX 1230   Ref: -
    Context: North side of military road, collected over four years from ploughed field.

23 ANTONINUS PIUS   denom. AS   Obv -
    date: 138–61   mint: RM   cat: as 562a   Rev -
    wear: SW/W   diam: 15.0 wt: 11.7
    Year: 1961   Sf no 49   Status: PRESENT   Ref: -
    Context: H61DL, Ea22. About 2'6" down, below level of Period IV stone at W. end of N. side, 20.5.61

24 ANTONINUS PIUS   denom. SEST   Obv ANTONINVS AVG PIVS PP TRP COS III
    date: 140–44   mint: RM   cat: 635   Rev SALVS AVG SC
    wear: diam: -   wt: -
    Year: 1958   Sf no 17   Status: MISSING   Ref: AA1960
    Context: "In the make-up below a clay floor dated by pottery to the reconstruction of AD 296"

25 ANTONINUS PIUS   denom. AS   Obv [ANTONINVS AVG PIVS PP TRP XVIII]
    date: 154–55   mint: RM   cat: 934   Rev BRITANNIA COS IIII SC
    wear: C/C   diam: 25.0 wt: 7.6
    Year: 1961   Sf no 36   Status: PRESENT   Ref: -
    Context: BB, Ed24

26 probably ANTONINUS PIUS   denom. AS   Obv -
    date: 138–61?   mint: RM   cat: -   Rev -
    wear: C/C   diam: 25.0 wt: 4.5
    Year: 1960   Sf no 9   Status: PRESENT   Ref: -
    Context: H60LR, 14.7.60

27 ANTONINUS PIUS, POSTH.   denom. DEN   Obv DIVVS ANTONINVS
    date: 161+   mint: RM   cat: M.Aurelius 422   Rev DIVO PIO
    wear: diam: -   wt: -
    Year: 1958   Sf no 21   Status: MISSING   Ref: AA1960
    Context: "Above the clay floor of 296 and below a later re-laying of it, assignable to some date before 367"

28 FAUSTINA I   denom. SEST   Obv -
    date: 138+   mint: RM   cat: -   Rev -
    wear: diam: -   wt: -
    Year: 1958   Sf no 28   Status: MISSING   Ref: AA1960
    Context: Unstratified

29 FAUSTINA I, POSTH.   denom. SEST   Obv -
    date: 141+   mint: RM   cat: -   Rev -
    wear: EW/EW   diam: 29.0 wt: 13.8
    Year: 1978.8   Sf no 8   Status: NMA, BOX 1230   Ref: -
    Context: North side of military road, collected over four years from ploughed field.

8. The Coins

30   FAUSTINA I, POSTH.   denom.   DP   Obv   [D]IVA [FAVSTINA]
     date: 141+   mint: RM   cat: -   Rev   - S[C]
     wear: diam: -   wt: -
   Year: 1958   Sf no   18   Status: MISSING   Ref: AA1960
   Context: "In the make-up below a clay floor dated by pottery to the reconstruction of AD 296"

31   FAUSTINA I, POSTH.   denom.   DEN   Obv   DIVA FAVSTINA
     date: 141+   mint: RM   cat: 344   Rev   AETERNITAS Juno stdg. l.
     wear: diam: -   wt: -
   Year: 1956/7   Sf no   8   Status: MISSING   Ref: AA1959
   Context: "In the make-up below a clay floor dated by pottery to the reconstruction of AD 296"

32   FAUSTINA I, POSTH.   denom.   SEST   Obv   [DIVA FAVSTINA]
     date: 141+   mint: RM   cat: -   Rev   -
     wear: EW/EW   diam: 30.0   wt: 19.3
   Year: 1978.8   Sf no   4   Status: NMA, BOX 1230   Ref: -
   Context: North side of military road, collected over four years from ploughed field.

33   FAUSTINA II   denom.   AS/DP   Obv   -
     date: 145–75   mint: RM   cat: -   Rev   -
     wear: EW/EW   diam: 23.0   wt: 4.8
   Year: 1961   Sf no   31   Status: PRESENT   Ref: -
   Context: HOLE Ec14, topsoil, AM, 10.5.

34   MARCUS AURELIUS   denom.   SEST   Obv   [M AVREL ANTONINVS AVG ARMENIACVS PM]
     date: 164–65   mint: RM   cat: 909   Rev   [TR POT XIX IMP II COS III – SC]
     wear: EW/EW   diam: 31.0   wt: 19.3
   Year: 1978.8   Sf no   2   Status: NMA, BOX 1230   Ref: -
   Context: North side of military road, collected over four years from ploughed field.

35   MARCUS AURELIUS   denom.   SEST   Obv   IMP M ANTONINVS AVG TRP XXV
     date: 170–71   mint: RM   cat: 1017   Rev   VOTA SVSCEP DECENN II COS III SC
     wear: SW/SW   diam: 30.0   wt: 17.8
   Year: 1960   Sf no   12   Status: PRESENT   Ref: -
   Context: HOLE Db31, HAL.IB.60, 9.6.60.

36   MARCUS AURELIUS   denom.   SEST   Obv   IMP M ANTONINVS AVG TRP XXV
     date: 170–71   mint: RM   cat: 998   Rev   FIDES EXERCITVVM COS III – SC]
     wear: W/W   diam: 30.0   wt: 25.0
   Year: 1978.8   Sf no   3   Status: NMA, BOX 1230   Ref: -
   Context: North side of military road, collected over four years from ploughed field.

37   MARCUS AURELIUS? fragment   denom.   DEN?   Obv   -
     date: 161–80?   mint: RM   cat: -   Rev   -
     wear: C/C   diam: 17.0   wt: 0.4
   Year: 1960   Sf no   17   Status: PRESENT   Ref: -
   Context: HAL.60.AO.

38   FAUSTINA II, POSTH.   denom.   SEST   Obv   [DIVA] FAVSTINA PIA
     date: 175+   mint: RM   cat: M.Aur. 1715   Rev   SIDERIBVS RECEPTA SC
     wear: diam: -   wt: -
   Year: 1956/7   Sf no   9   Status: MISSING   Ref: AA1959
   Context: "In the make-up below a clay floor dated by pottery to the reconstruction of AD 296"

39   LATE ANTONINE (COMMODUS?)   denom.   SEST   Obv   -
     date: 180–92?   mint: RM   cat: -   Rev   -
     wear: diam: -   wt: -
   Year: 1956/7   Sf no   3   Status: MISSING   Ref: AA1959
   Context: -

40	SEPTIMIUS SEVERUS		denom.	DEN	Obv	-
	date: 193–211	mint: -	cat: -		Rev	-
	wear: C/C	diam: 17.0	wt: 1.3			
	Year: 1961	Sf no 24	Status:	PRESENT	Ref:	-
	Context: Spoil heap, 12.5.61.					

41	CARACALLA		denom.	DEN	Obv	-
	date: 198–217	mint: -	cat: -		Rev	-
	wear: C/C	diam: 14.0	wt: 0.7			
	Year: 1960	Sf no 11	Status:	PRESENT	Ref:	-
	Context: H60LR, 14.7.60					

42	CARACALLA		denom.	DEN	Obv	ANTONINVS AVGVSTVS
	date: 198–217	mint: -	cat: -		Rev	-
	wear: SW/-	diam: 18.0	wt: 1.1			
	Year: 1961	Sf no 53	Status:	PRESENT	Ref:	-
	Context: De22, MI, 3'6" on N.S wall from W. bank, 5.6.61.					

43	'CARACALLA'		denom.	DENpl	Obv	ANTONINVS PIVS AVG B[RIT]
	date: 211–17	mint: -	cat: -		Rev	VOTA SVSCEPTA ....
	wear:	diam: -	wt: -			
	Year: 1958	Sf no 22	Status:	MISSING	Ref:	AA1960
	Context: "Above the clay floor of 296 and below a later re-laying of it, assignable to some date before 367"					

44	GETA CAESAR		denom.	DEN	Obv	P SEPT GETA CAES PONT
	date: 200–02	mint: -	cat: 99		Rev	PIETAS
	wear: UW/UW	diam: 18.0	wt: 1.4			
	Year: 1961	Sf no 43	Status:	PRESENT	Ref:	-
	Context: HOLE Ea32, topsoil, 8.5.61.					

45	GETA CAESAR		denom.	DEN	Obv	P SEPT GETA CAES PONT
	date: 200–02	mint: -	cat: 9a		Rev	FELICITAS PVBLICA
	wear:	diam: -	wt: -			
	Year: 1956	Sf no -	Status:	MISSING	Ref:	E.Birley archive
	Context: Brunt Ha'penny field, 26.7.56					

46	'GETA'		denom.	DENpl	Obv	[...SEP]T GETA ....
	date: 209–12	mint: -	cat: -		Rev	.....COS II....
	wear:	diam: -	wt: -			
	Year: 1958	Sf no 19	Status:	MISSING	Ref:	AA1960
	Context: "In the make-up below a clay floor dated by pottery to the reconstruction of AD 296"					

47	SEVERUS ALEXANDER		denom.	DEN	Obv	IMP SEV ALEXAND AVG
	date: 222	mint: AN	cat: 266 var.		Rev	PM TRP COS PP Mars stdg. l.
	wear:	diam: -	wt: -			
	Year: 1956/7	Sf no 10	Status:	MISSING	Ref:	AA1959
	Context: -					

48	SEVERUS ALEXANDER		denom.	DEN	Obv	-
	date: 222–35	mint: -	cat: -		Rev	-
	wear:	diam: -	wt: -			
	Year: 1958	Sf no 29	Status:	MISSING	Ref:	AA1960
	Context: Unstratified					

49	SEVERUS ALEXANDER		denom.	DP	Obv	M...EV....
	date: 222–35	mint: -	cat: -		Rev	.....AVG...
	wear:	diam: -	wt: -			
	Year: 1958	Sf no 23	Status:	MISSING	Ref:	AA1960
	Context: "Above the clay floor of 296 and below a later re-laying of it, assignable to some date before 367"					

8. The Coins

50   SEVERUS ALEXANDER   denom. DEN   Obv IMP ALEXANDER PIVS AVG
         date: 222–35   mint: -   cat: -   Rev   -
         wear: UW/C   diam: 18.0   wt: 1.7
     Year: 1961   Sf no   50   Status: PRESENT   Ref: -
     Context: H61PT, 5.7.61

51   JULIA MAMAEA   denom. DEN   Obv IVLIA MAMAEA AVG
         date: 222–35   mint: -   cat: 343   Rev   IVNO CONSERVATRIX
         wear: C/C   diam: 28.0   wt: 1.7
     Year: 1961   Sf no   47   Status: PRESENT   Ref: -
     Context: HOLE Ec14. AM. Topsoil, 11.5.61.

52   JULIA MAMAEA   denom. DEN   Obv IVLIA MAMAEA AVG
         date: 222–35   mint: -   cat: 343   Rev   IVNO CONSERVATRIX
         wear: VW/W   diam: 18.0   wt: 1.9
     Year: 1961   Sf no   56   Status: PRESENT   Ref: -
     Context: De22, PD, Topsoil, 1.6.61

53   GALLIENUS   denom. ANT   Obv -
         date: 260–68   mint: -   cat: -   Rev   -
         wear: W/W   diam: 20.0   wt: 2.0
     Year: 1960   Sf no   14   Status: PRESENT   Ref: -
     Context: Fb24, HAL EV.60, in black earth, 2.6.60.

54   GALLIENUS   denom. ANT   Obv IMP GALLIENVS AVG
         date: 260–68   mint: -   cat: 176   Rev   DIANAE CONS AVG
         wear: SW/SW   diam: 18.0   wt: 1.6
     Year: 1961   Sf no   38   Status: PRESENT   Ref: -
     Context: Fa31, on top of the level of the wall, *c.* 30", 24.5.61.

55   GALLIENUS   denom. ANT   Obv [GALLIENVS AVG]
         date: 260–68   mint: RM   cat: 157   Rev   [ABVND]ANTIA AV[G]
         wear: C/SW   diam: 17.0   wt: 1.9
     Year: 1925.4   Sf no   4   Status: NMA, BOX 1134   Ref: PSAN4, 2, 1927, 38
     Context: Brunt Ha'penny field

56   CLAUDIUS II   denom. ANT   Obv -
         date: 268–70   mint: -   cat: -   Rev   -
         wear: diam: -   wt: -
     Year: 1958   Sf no   31   Status: MISSING   Ref: AA1960
     Context: Unstratified

57   CLAUDIUS II?   denom. ANT   Obv -
         date: 268–70?   mint: -   cat: -   Rev   -
         wear: C/C   diam: 18.0   wt: 1.1
     Year: 1960   Sf no   22   Status: PRESENT   Ref: -
     Context: H60LC

58   'CLAUDIUS II'?   denom. ANT   Obv -
         date: 270+   mint: -   cat: c.as -   Rev   -
         wear: VW/W   diam: 12.0   wt: 1.1
     Year: 1925.4   Sf no   15   Status: NMA, BOX 1134   Ref: PSAN4, 2, 1927, 38
     Context: Brunt Ha'penny field

59   CLAUDIUS II, POSTH.   denom. ANT   Obv DIVO CLAVDIO
         date: 270   mint: -   cat: 266   Rev   CONSECRATIO Eagle
         wear: C/C   diam: 15.0   wt: 1.1
     Year: 1961   Sf no   42   Status: PRESENT   Ref: -
     Context: Db34, N.W. corner, 3', 28.5.61.

60	'CLAUDIUS II, POSTH.'		denom.	ANT	Obv	[DIVO CLAVDIO
	date: 270+	mint: -	cat: c.as 261/6		Rev	[CONSECRATIO]
	wear: W/C	diam: 16.0	wt: 1.4			
	Year: 1925.4 Sf no 5	Status: NMA, BOX 1134	Ref: PSAN4, 2, 1927, 38
	Context: Brunt Ha'penny field

61 VICTORINUS denom. ANT Obv [IMPC VICT]ORINVS PFAVG
  date: 268–70   mint: -   cat: 78   Rev VIRTVS AVG
  wear: SW/W   diam: 19.0   wt: 2.3
  Year: 1978.8   Sf no 10   Status: NMA, BOX 1230   Ref: -
  Context: North side of military road, collected over four years from ploughed field.

62 VICTORINUS, POSTH. denom. ANT Obv [DIVO VICT]ORINO P[IO]
  date: 270   mint: -   cat: 83   Rev ?[CONSECRATIO]
  wear: SW/C   diam: 20.0   wt: 1.7
  Year: 1961   Sf no 60   Status: PRESENT   Ref: -
  Context: FY, HOLE Ec35, Topsoil. 23.5.61.

63 TETRICUS I denom. ANT Obv IMP..TETRICVS PFAVG]
  date: 270–73   mint: -   cat: 87/88   Rev [LAETITI]A AVGG
  wear: W/SW   diam: 19.0   wt: 2.4
  Year: 1925.4   Sf no 3   Status: NMA, BOX 1134   Ref: PSAN4, 2, 1927, 38
  Context: Brunt Ha'penny field

64 TETRICUS II, CAESAR denom. ANT Obv -
  date: 270–73   mint: -   cat: -   Rev -
  wear: diam: -   wt: -
  Year: 1958   Sf no 32   Status: MISSING   Ref: AA1960
  Context: Unstratified

65 'TETRICUS II, CAESAR' denom. ANT Obv -
  date: 273+   mint: -   cat: c.as -   Rev ?Aequitas
  wear: SW/SW   diam: 15.0   wt: 1.7
  Year: 1961   Sf no 64   Status: PRESENT   Ref: -
  Context: H61PK

66 'TETRICUS II, CAESAR' denom. ANT Obv -
  date: 273+   mint: -   cat: c.as -   Rev -
  wear: C/C   diam: 15.0   wt: 1.8
  Year: 1961   Sf no 59   Status: PRESENT   Ref: -
  Context: Db32, Topsoil, LA. 3.6.61.

67 RADIATE denom. ANT Obv -
  date: 260–73   mint: -   cat: -   Rev -
  wear: diam: -   wt: -
  Year: 1958   Sf no 33   Status: MISSING   Ref: AA1960
  Context: Unstratified

68 RADIATE denom. ANT Obv -
  date: 260–73+   mint: -   cat: -   Rev -
  wear: C/C   diam: 14.0   wt: 0.5
  Year: 1960   Sf no 4   Status: PRESENT   Ref: -
  Context: AH.60

69 RADIATE COPY denom. ANT Obv -
  date: 273+   mint: -   cat: -   Rev -
  wear: diam: -   wt: -
  Year: 1958   Sf no 34   Status: MISSING   Ref: AA1960
  Context: Unstratified

8. The Coins

70 RADIATE COPY   denom. ANT   Obv -
    date: 273+   mint: -   cat: -   Rev -
    wear: diam: -   wt: -
    Year: 1958   Sf no 37   Status: MISSING   Ref: AA1960
    Context: Unstratified

71 RADIATE COPY   denom. ANT   Obv -
    date: 273+   mint: -   cat: -   Rev -
    wear: diam: -   wt: -
    Year: 1958   Sf no 36   Status: MISSING   Ref: AA1960
    Context: Unstratified

72 RADIATE COPY   denom. ANT   Obv -
    date: 273+   mint: -   cat: c.of -   Rev -
    wear: C/C   diam: 15.0 wt: 0.6
    Year: 1978.8   Sf no 13   Status: NMA, BOX 1230   Ref: -
    Context: North side of military road, collected over four years from ploughed field.

73 RADIATE COPY   denom. ANT   Obv -
    date: 273+   mint: -   cat: -   Rev -
    wear: W/W   diam: 14.0 wt: 0.9
    Year: 1961   Sf no 37   Status: PRESENT   Ref: -
    Context: (ET), Dc34, Topsoil. 22.5.61.

74 RADIATE COPY   denom. ANT   Obv -
    date: 273+   mint: -   cat: -   Rev -
    wear: diam: -   wt: -
    Year: 1958   Sf no 35   Status: MISSING   Ref: AA1960
    Context: Unstratified

75 RADIATE COPY?   denom. ANT   Obv -
    date: 273+?   mint: -   cat: -   Rev -
    wear: C/C   diam: 7.0   wt: 0.3
    Year: 1960   Sf no 13   Status: PRESENT   Ref: -
    Context: HAL.CC.60, Fa13N, 15", 25.5.60.

76 probable RADIATE COPY   denom. ANT   Obv -
    date: 273+   mint: -   cat: -   Rev -
    wear: C/C   diam: 15.0 wt: 1.6
    Year: 1960   Sf no 45   Status: PRESENT   Ref: -
    Context: HOLE Dc15, CB, 25.5.

77 CARAUSIUS   denom. AUREL   Obv IMPC DIOCLETIANVS PFAVG
    date: 293   mint: -   cat: Car.Dio.Max. Rev PAX AVGGG
                                         5
    wear: SW/SW   diam: 21.0 wt: 1.8
    Year: 1960   Sf no 27   Status: PRESENT   Ref: -
    Context: HAL.CC.60, Fa13N, 15", 25.5.60.

78 ALLECTUS   denom. AUREL   Obv [IMP C A]LLECTVS PFAV[G]
    date: 293–96   mint: LN   cat: 26   Rev ORIE[N]S AV[G] S/P/ML
    wear: diam: -   wt: -
    Year: 1958   Sf no 24   Status: MISSING   Ref: AA1960
    Context: "Above the clay floor of 296 and below a later re-laying of it, assignable to some date before 367"

79 DIOCLETIAN   denom. FOLL   Obv IMP DIOCLETIANVS AVG
    date: c.303   mint: LN   cat: 6LN28a   Rev GENIO POPVLI ROMANI
    wear: UW/UW   diam: 28.0 wt: 7.2
    Year: 1960   Sf no 30   Status: PRESENT   Ref: -
    Context: HAL.HI.60, HOLE Ea23, 7.6.60.

80	CONSTANTINE I		denom.	FOLL	Obv	[IMP CONSTANTINVS P AVG]
	date: c.307–10	mint: LNP	cat: 6LN104		Rev	[GENIO POP ROM]
	wear: SW/SW	diam: 26.0	wt: 4.6			
	Year: 1978.8	Sf no 9	Status: NMA, BOX 1230		Ref: -
	Context: North side of military road, collected over four years from ploughed field.

81	CONSTANTINE I		denom. -		Obv -
	date: 308–37	mint: -	cat: -		Rev -
	wear:	diam: -	wt: -		
	Year: 1958	Sf no 38	Status: MISSING		Ref: AA1960
	Context: Unstratified

82	CONSTANTINE I		denom. -		Obv IMP CONSTANTINVS PFAVG
	date: 310	mint: -	cat: 6LN121a		Rev SOLI INVICTO COMITI
	wear: C/C	diam: 22.0	wt: 1.6		
	Year: 1961	Sf no 25	Status: PRESENT		Ref: -
	Context: EX. Ee34 at 3' in black soil at S.E. corner, 23.5.61.

83	CONSTANTINE I		denom. -		Obv [VRBS ROMA]
	date: 330–35	mint: -	cat: as 7TR522		Rev Wolf and Twins
	wear: C/C	diam: 17.0	wt: 2.1		
	Year: 1925.4	Sf no 16	Status: NMA, BOX 1134		Ref: PSAN4, 2, 1927, 38
	Context: Brunt Ha'penny field

84	CONSTANTINE I		denom. -		Obv VRBS ROMA
	date: 330–35	mint: -	cat: 7TR529, HK58		Rev Wolf and Twins
	wear: C/C	diam: 14.0	wt: 1.0		
	Year: 1961	Sf no 33	Status: PRESENT		Ref: -
	Context: EM, Fa34, in fallen stone above flag floor, 22.5.61.

85	CONSTANTINE I		denom. -		Obv CONSTAN-TINOPOLIS
	date: 332–33	mint: TRS	cat: 7TR548		Rev Victory on prow
	wear: W/W	diam: 16.0	wt: 2.3		
	Year: 1978.8	Sf no 11	Status: NMA, BOX 1230		Ref: -
	Context: North side of military road, collected over four years from ploughed field.

86	'CONSTANTINE I'		denom. -		Obv [CONSTAN-TINOPOLIS]
	date: 341–46	mint: -	cat: c.as 7TR523		Rev Victory on prow
	wear: C/W	diam: 13.0	wt: 1.1		
	Year: 1925.4	Sf no 13	Status: NMA, BOX 1134		Ref: PSAN4, 2, 1927, 38
	Context: Brunt Ha'penny field

87	'CONSTANTINE I'		denom. -		Obv [CONSTANTINOPOLIS]
	date: 341–46	mint: -	cat: c.of 7TR523		Rev Victory on prow
	wear: C/C	diam: 8.0	wt: 0.4		
	Year: 1961	Sf no 5	Status: PRESENT		Ref: -
	Context: H61PT

88	'CONSTANTINE I'		denom. -		Obv [CONSTANTINOPOLIS]
	date: 341–46	mint: -	cat: c.as 7LG246		Rev Victory on prow
	wear: SW/SW	diam: 10.0	wt: 0.9		
	Year: 1925.4	Sf no 12	Status: NMA, BOX 1134		Ref: PSAN4, 2, 1927, 38
	Context: Brunt Ha'penny field

89	CONSTANTINE II, CAESAR		denom. -		Obv CONSTANTINVS IVN NOBC
	date: 330–35	mint: TR	cat: 7TR520, HK49		Rev GLORIA EXERCITVS 2 stds.
	wear: W/W	diam: 14.0	wt: 1.2		
	Year: 1960	Sf no 19	Status: PRESENT		Ref: -
	Context: HAL.BM.60.

90   'CONSTANTIUS II, CAESAR'   denom.   -   Obv   [FL IVL CONSTANT]IVS NOBC
       date: 341–46   mint: 'TR'   cat: c.of 7TR546   Rev   GLOR-IA EXERCITVS NOBC
                                      'S'
       wear: W/W   diam: 13.0   wt: 1.1
    Year: 1978.8   Sf no   12   Status: NMA, BOX 1230   Ref: -
    Context: North side of military road, collected over four years from ploughed field.

91   CONSTANS   denom.   -   Obv   CONSTAN-S PFAVG
       date: 346–48   mint: -   cat: 8TR195,   Rev   VICTORIAE DDAVGGQNN
                                                   HK148
       wear: C/C   diam: 15.0   wt: 1.4
    Year: 1961   Sf no   1   Status: PRESENT   Ref: -
    Context: HOLE Dc34, LE, in tumble of stones at 2'6" depth.

92   CONSTANS   denom.   -   Obv   DN CONSTA-NS PFAVG
       date: 348–50   mint: -   cat: as CK33   Rev   FEL TEMP REPARATIO
       wear: W/C   diam: 15.0   wt: 1.0
    Year: 1961   Sf no   41   Status: PRESENT   Ref: -
    Context: HOLE Dc34, IV, at depth of 2'6" in dark soil and tumble, 30.5.61.

93   CONSTANTIUS II   denom.   -   Obv   -
       date: 348–58   mint: -   cat: -   Rev   FEL TEMP REPARATIO Falling
                                                                      horseman
       wear: diam: -   wt: -
    Year: 1956/7   Sf no   13   Status: MISSING   Ref: AA1959
    Context: -

94   'CONSTANTIUS II'   denom.   -   Obv   [DN CONSTAN-TIVS PFAVG]
       date: 353+   mint: -   cat: c.as 8TR359   Rev   [FEL TEMP REPARATIO] FH3
       wear: SW/C   diam: 15.0   wt: 1.2
    Year: 1925.4   Sf no   10   Status: NMA, BOX 1134   Ref: PSAN4, 2, 1927, 38
    Context: Brunt Ha'penny field

95   CONSTANTIUS II/CONSTANS   denom.   -   Obv   -
       date: 346–48   mint: -   cat: -   Rev   VICTORIAE DDAVGGQNN
       wear: C/C   diam: 13.0   wt: 0.9
    Year: 1961   Sf no   35   Status: PRESENT   Ref: -
    Context: H61PN

96   CONSTANTIUS II/CONSTANS   denom.   -   Obv   -
       date: 346–48   mint: -   cat: -   Rev   VICTORIAE DDAVGGQNN
       wear: C/C   diam: 10.0   wt: 0.2
    Year: 1961   Sf no   3   Status: PRESENT   Ref: -
    Context: HOLE Fc23, Topsoil, 9.5.61.

97   CONSTANTIUS II/CONSTANS   denom.   -   Obv   -
       date: 346–48   mint: -   cat: -   Rev   VICTORIAE DDAVGGQNN
       wear: C/C   diam: 14.0   wt: 1.0
    Year: 1960   Sf no   21   Status: PRESENT   Ref: -
    Context: H60KQ

98   CONSTANTIUS II/CONSTANS   denom.   -   Obv   -
       date: 346–48   mint: -   cat: -   Rev   VICTORIAE DDAVGGQNN
       wear: C/C   diam: 12.0   wt: 1.0
    Year: 1961   Sf no   16   Status: PRESENT   Ref:
    Context: IV. N.E. Corner, topsoil. Dc34, 30.5.61

99   HOUSE OF CONSTANTINE   denom.   -   Obv   -
       date: 306–64   mint: -   cat: -   Rev   -
       wear: diam: -   wt: -
    Year: 1956/7   Sf no   6   Status: MISSING   Ref: AA1959
    Context: -

100	HOUSE OF CONSTANTINE			denom.	-		Obv	-		
	date:	306–64	mint:	-	cat:	-	Rev	-		
	wear:		diam:	-	wt:	-				
	Year:	1956/7	Sf no	4	Status:	MISSING			Ref:	AA1959
	Context:	-								

101	HOUSE OF CONSTANTINE			denom.	-		Obv	-		
	date:	306–64	mint:	-	cat:	-	Rev	-		
	wear:		diam:	-	wt:	-				
	Year:	1956/7	Sf no	12	Status:	MISSING			Ref:	AA1959
	Context:	-								

102	HOUSE OF CONSTANTINE			denom.	-		Obv	-		
	date:	306–64	mint:	-	cat:	-	Rev	-		
	wear:		diam:	-	wt:	-				
	Year:	1956/7	Sf no	5	Status:	MISSING			Ref:	AA1959
	Context:	-								

103	HOUSE OF CONSTANTINE			denom.	-		Obv	-		
	date:	330–35	mint:	-	cat:	as 7TR520	Rev	[GLOR-IA EXERC-ITVS] 2 stds		
	wear:	C/SW	diam:	20.0	wt:	1.6				
	Year:	1925.4	Sf no	6	Status:	NMA, BOX 1134			Ref:	PSAN4, 2, 1927, 38
	Context:	Brunt Ha'penny field								

104	HOUSE OF CONSTANTINE			denom.	-		Obv	-		
	date:	330–35	mint:	-	cat:	as 7TR518	Rev	[GLOR-IA EXERC-ITVS] 2 stds		
	wear:	C/SW	diam:	17.0	wt:	1.0				
	Year:	1925.4	Sf no	8	Status:	NMA, BOX 1134			Ref:	PSAN4, 2, 1927, 38
	Context:	Brunt Ha'penny field								

105	HOUSE OF CONSTANTINE			denom.	-		Obv	-		
	date:	330–35	mint:	-	cat:	as 7TR518	Rev	[GLOR-IA EXERC-ITVS] 2 stds		
	wear:	C/UW	diam:	16.0	wt:	0.9				
	Year:	1925.4	Sf no	7	Status:	NMA, BOX 1134			Ref:	PSAN4, 2, 1927, 38
	Context:	Brunt Ha'penny field								

106	HOUSE OF CONSTANTINE			denom.	-		Obv	-		
	date:	330–64	mint:	-	cat:	-	Rev	-		
	wear:		diam:	-	wt:	-				
	Year:	1958	Sf no	39	Status:	MISSING			Ref:	AA1960
	Context:	Unstratified								

107	HOUSE OF CONSTANTINE			denom.	-		Obv	-		
	date:	330–64	mint:	-	cat:	-	Rev	-		
	wear:		diam:	-	wt:	-				
	Year:	1958	Sf no	40	Status:	MISSING			Ref:	AA1960
	Context:	Unstratified								

108	HOUSE OF CONSTANTINE			denom.	-		Obv	-		
	date:	341–46	mint:	-	cat:	-	Rev	GLORIA EXERCITVS 2 stds.		
	wear:	W/W	diam:	15.0	wt:	1.1				
	Year:	1961	Sf no	54	Status:	PRESENT			Ref:	-
	Context:	EO, 1, Eb34, topsoil above cobbles, 22.5.61.								

109	HOUSE OF CONSTANTINE			denom.	-		Obv	-		
	date:	341–46	mint:	-	cat:	as 8TR39	Rev	[GLOR-IA EXERC-ITVS] 1 std.		
	wear:	SW/SW	diam:	15.0	wt:	1.1				
	Year:	1925.4	Sf no	9	Status:	NMA, BOX 1134			Ref:	PSAN4, 2, 1927, 38
	Context:	Brunt Ha'penny field								

8. The Coins

110 VALENTINIAN I   denom. -   Obv DN VALENTINI-ANVS PFAVG
      date: 364–75   mint: -   cat: as CK481   Rev SECVRITAS REIPVBLICAE
      wear: SW/SW   diam: 17.0   wt: 1.8
  Year: 1961   Sf no 32   Status: PRESENT   Ref: -
  Context: H61PL

111 VALENTINIAN I   denom. -   Obv [DN VALE]NTINI-[ANVS PFAVG]
      date: 364–75   mint: -   cat: as CK96   Rev [SECVRITAS – REIPVBLICAE]
      wear: C/C   diam: 17.0   wt: 1.5
  Year: 1925.4   Sf no 11   Status: NMA, BOX 1134   Ref: PSAN4, 2, 1927, 38
  Context: Brunt Ha'penny field

112 VALENTINIAN I?   denom. -   Obv -
      date: 364–78   mint: -   cat: -   Rev [GLORIA ROMANORVM]
      wear: C/C   diam: 14.0   wt: 0.9
  Year: 1961   Sf no 62   Status: PRESENT   Ref: -
  Context: AN, HOLE Ed24, found at 2' level, 11.5.

113 HOUSE OF VALENTINIAN   denom. -   Obv -
      date: 364–78   mint: -   cat: -   Rev SECVRITAS REIPVBLICAE
      wear: C/C   diam: 18.0   wt: 1.6
  Year: 1961   Sf no 46   Status: PRESENT   Ref: -
  Context: Dc34, KB, 2'6", 2.6.

114 ILLEGIBLE   denom. -   Obv -
      date: -   mint: -   cat: -   Rev -
      wear: diam: -   wt: -
  Year: 1956/7   Sf no 15   Status: MISSING   Ref: AA1959
  Context: -

115 ILLEGIBLE   denom. -   Obv -
      date: -   mint: -   cat: -   Rev -
      wear: diam: -   wt: -
  Year: 1956/7   Sf no 14   Status: MISSING   Ref: AA1959
  Context: -

116 ILLEGIBLE   denom. -   Obv -
      date: -   mint: -   cat: -   Rev -
      wear: diam: -   wt: -
  Year: 1956/7   Sf no 7   Status: MISSING   Ref: AA1959
  Context: -

117 ILLEGIBLE   denom. AS   Obv -
      date: C1/2nd   mint: RM   cat: -   Rev -
      wear: C/C   diam: 23.0   wt: 9.0
  Year: 1960   Sf no 10   Status: PRESENT   Ref: -
  Context: Fa13N, 15", HAL.CC.60, 25.5.60

118 ILLEGIBLE fragments   denom. DEN   Obv -
      date: C1st   mint: -   cat: -   Rev -
      wear: C/C   diam: -   wt: -
  Year: 1961   Sf no 34   Status: PRESENT   Ref: -
  Context: EL25, Western extension, from latrine drain, 18.6.61.

119 ILLEGIBLE   denom. AS   Obv -
      date: C2nd   mint: RM   cat: -   Rev -
      wear: C/C   diam: 26.0   wt: 7.1
  Year: 1960   Sf no 18   Status: PRESENT   Ref: -
  Context: HAL.AZ.60.

120	ILLEGIBLE		denom.	AE	Obv	-
	date: C3/4th	mint: -	cat: -		Rev	-
	wear: C/C	diam: 14.0	wt: 0.5			
	Year: 1961	Sf no 51	Status:	PRESENT	Ref:	-
	Context: EO, 2, Eb34, topsoil above cobbles, 22.5.61.					

121	ILLEGIBLE		denom.	AE	Obv	-
	date: C3/4th	mint: -	cat: -		Rev	-
	wear: C/C	diam: 14.0	wt: 0.5			
	Year: 1960	Sf no 8	Status:	PRESENT	Ref:	-
	Context: HAL.EJ.60, 1.6.60.					

122	ILLEGIBLE fragments		denom.	AE	Obv	-
	date: C3/4th	mint: -	cat: -		Rev	-
	wear: C/C	diam: -	wt: -			
	Year: 1961	Sf no 63	Status:	PRESENT	Ref:	-
	Context: H61CF, HOLE Ea22,					

123	ILLEGIBLE fragment		denom.	AE	Obv	-
	date: C3/4th	mint: -	cat: -		Rev	-
	wear: C/C	diam: 10.0	wt: 0.4			
	Year: 1961	Sf no 39	Status:	PRESENT	Ref:	-
	Context: H61PT, 26.6.61.					

124	ILLEGIBLE fragments		denom.	AE	Obv	-
	date: C3/4th	mint: -	cat: -		Rev	-
	wear: C/C	diam: -	wt: -			
	Year: 1961	Sf no 15	Status:	PRESENT	Ref:	-
	Context: CU. Db25. Layer below flooring 18"–36" down, 5.19.61.					

125	ILLEGIBLE		denom.	-	Obv	-
	date: C3/4th	mint: -	cat: -		Rev	-
	wear: C/C	diam: 14.0	wt: 1.3			
	Year: 1925.4	Sf no 14	Status:	NMA, BOX 1134	Ref:	PSAN4, 2, 1927, 38
	Context: Brunt Ha'penny field					

126	ILLEGIBLE fragment		denom.	AE	Obv	-
	date: C3/4th	mint: -	cat: -		Rev	-
	wear: C/C	diam: 16.0	wt: 0.6			
	Year: 1960	Sf no 20	Status:	PRESENT	Ref:	-
	Context: HAL.AY.60.					

127	ILLEGIBLE fragment		denom.	AE	Obv	-
	date: C3/4th	mint: -	cat: -		Rev	-
	wear: C/C	diam: 12.0	wt: 0.4			
	Year: 1961?	Sf no 23	Status:	PRESENT	Ref:	-
	Context: Db34					

128	ILLEGIBLE fragment		denom.	AE	Obv	-
	date: C3/4th	mint: -	cat: -		Rev	-
	wear: C/C	diam: 10.0	wt: 0.4			
	Year: 1960	Sf no 26	Status:	PRESENT	Ref:	-
	Context: HAL.EL.60, 36", 1.6.60.					

129	ILLEGIBLE		denom.	AE	Obv	-
	date: C3/4th	mint: -	cat: -		Rev	-
	wear: C/C	diam: 8.0	wt: 0.8			
	Year: 1960	Sf no 29	Status:	PRESENT	Ref:	-
	Context: HAL CM.60, Baulk Ee14/Fa14, c.12" deep, in disturbed humus, 26.5.60.					

130   ILLEGIBLE   denom. DENpl   Obv -
          date: C3rd   mint: -   cat: -   Rev Pax?
          wear: diam: -   wt: -
      Year: 1958   Sf no 30   Status: MISSING   Ref: AA1960
      Context: Unstratified

131   ILLEGIBLE   denom. ANT   Obv -
          date: C3rd   mint: -   cat: -   Rev -
          wear: diam: -   wt: -
      Year: 1956/7 Sf no 11   Status: MISSING   Ref: AA1959
      Context: -

132   ILLEGIBLE   denom. AE   Obv -
          date: C4th   mint: -   cat: -   Rev -
          wear: C/C   diam: 13.0   wt: 1.2
      Year: 1961   Sf no 52   Status: PRESENT   Ref: -
      Context: HOLE Fb34, SW corner 2' deep in sandy soil, 29.5.61.

133   ILLEGIBLE fragments   denom. AE   Obv -
          date: C4th   mint: -   cat: -   Rev -
          wear: C/C   diam: -   wt: -
      Year: 1960   Sf no 61   Status: PRESENT   Ref: -
      Context: HOLE Dc15, CB, 25.5.

134   ILLEGIBLE fragment   denom. AE   Obv -
          date: C4th   mint: -   cat: -   Rev -
          wear: C/C   diam: 11.0   wt: 0.4
      Year: 1961   Sf no 58   Status: PRESENT   Ref: -
      Context: H61PT. 5.7.61.

9. The Decorated Samian and Potters' Stamps

Brian Hartley and Brenda Dickinson

Report submitted in 1977

Abbreviations
BM   British Museum
CAJ   *Chester Archaeological Journal*
D.   Déchelette, 1904
JRS   *Journal of Roman Studies*
MAN   Musée des Antiquités Nationales, St-Germain-en-Laye.
O.   Oswald, 1964
Rogers   Rogers, 1974
S. and S.   Stanfield and Simpson, 1958

The assemblage examined here shows a markedly low proportion of pre-Hadrianic and Hadrianic to Antonine material. The same is apparently true of those sites connected with Hadrian's frontier which have produced similar, or greater, quantities of samian, with the exception of Birdoswald and Maryport.

The material which is assumed to belong to the Hadrianic occupation consists of five decorated bowls from La Graufesenque, one from Les Martres-de-Veyre, five from Lezoux and two from East Gaul. There are also two potters' stamps which are more likely to have reached the site before, rather than after, AD 140.

The Antonine Central Gaulish ware which can be reasonably closely dated consists of the work of twelve Lezoux potters or, in some cases, groups of potters. Of these, nine can scarcely have been at work before *c*. AD 160. The rest probably worked until AD 170 or so. Most, if not all, of this material seems to point to a reoccupation of the fort around AD 160.

It is interesting to note, in passing, that of the potters assumed to have started work *c*. AD 160 or later none, with the exception of Casurius ii, is represented at any Scottish site with a normal Antonine occupation. Similarly, although a third of the stamps on plain ware belong to potters whose work turns up in Scotland only two (Beliniccus iii 2a and Muxtullus 1b) are from dies represented in Scotland.

All the Lezoux potters to whom the decorated ware has been attributed are represented elsewhere on Hadrian's Wall or at forts in the Hinterland, as are all the makers of plain ware, with one exception (Aper ii).

The East Gaulish ware is dominated by Rheinzabern, as might be expected.

The samian as a whole does not support the probability of an early-Antonine occupation, though some individual pieces could, of course, be of that date.

The Decorated Ware

South Gaulish

1. 61BP. Form 37, with a blurred basal wreath of small leaves. Flavian-Trajanic. Not illustrated.
2. 61CP. Form 37, with a fragment of ovolo. Flavian. Not illustrated.
3. 61DF. Two fragments from a bowl of form 37, with small, looped leaves and a stag (unidentified). The leaf appears on bowls from Catterick and the Bregenz Cellar (Jacobs 1913, Taf. IV, 23). *c*. AD 90–110. Not illustrated.
4. Probably IJ. Form 37, with two satyrs, side-by-side (both Hermet 1934, pl. 19, 80 or 81). *c*. AD 90–110. Not illustrated.
5. 61JZ. Form 30, with a trident-tongued ovolo and a triangular leaf. Both were used by Patricius i, the ovolo on form 37 from Chester (*CAJ* 33 (1939), p.98, 7), the leaf (Knorr 1919, Taf. 65, 4) on form 29 (unprovenanced) in Strasbourg Museum. *c*. AD 75–95. Not illustrated.

Central Gaulish

A. Les Martres-de-Veyre
6. 61AG. Form 37, with tendrils and a panther (D.792), both used on a bowl from London in the style of X-2 (S. and S. 1958, pl. 3, 30). *c*. AD 100–120. Not found.

B. Lezoux
Hadrianic or early-Antonine
7. 60HT. Form 37, with an ovolo (Rogers B76) and zig-zag border used by Geminus iv, whose latest work appears in the Castleford shop group of *c*. AD 140–150.

Only one sherd of this potter is recorded from Antonine Scotland. *c.* AD 120–145. Not found.

8. 61MG. Two joining fragments of form 37, with panels: 1) A woman on a pedestal (O.578). 2) a medallion with widely-spaced double borders, over a bear (O.1626). 3) = 1. 4A) A double festoon or medallion; 4B) an acanthus. Probably by a member of the Quintilianus i group, and similar in execution to 60FP, with the same blobby junction-masks. *c.* AD 125–145. Fig. 9.1

9. 60FP. Form 37, with a cursive signature Quintilian[retrograde, from a mould signed, before firing, below the decoration. Panelled decoration, with: 1) A captive (D.642). 2) A Venus (D.181). 3A) A double festoon or medallion; 3B) a bear (O.1626). Only the captive seems to be known for Quintilianus. *c.* AD 125–145. Fig. 9.1

10. 61DU. Form 37, worn, with a small vine-scroll (Rogers M7) used by X-6. His bowls are relatively common on Hadrian's Wall and in Antonine Scotland (Hartley 1972, p. 32). *c.* AD 125–150. Not illustrated.

11. 61MK. Form 37, slightly burnt, probably with the ovolo Rogers B3. This is on a bowl in the Oswald-Plicque Collection (presumably from Lezoux) with a cursive signature of Sissus ii; the coarse, wavyline borders also suggest his work. Comparatively little is known about his repertoire of figure-types and the lion (D.794) and bear (D.827) are not known for him, but occur on stamped moulds of Anunus from Lezoux. *c.* AD 130–160. Fig. 9.1

Hadrianic or Antonine

12. 61CP. A fragment from a thick-walled bowl of form 37, with a saltire incorporating an acanthus, over a chevron wreath. *c.* AD 125–145. Not illustrated.

13. 61CG. Form 37, with an unusual scheme of decoration, involving a lion (O.1425), over a row of rosettes with central bosses and beaded borders. Diagonally-striated borders are impressed (vertically) over the lion's tail and (diagonally) across the zone of rosettes. The adjacent panel contains a large leaf of the variety normally used in scrolls. The lion was used by Quintilianus i, but there is no other obvious connection with him. The fabric and glaze suggest Hadrianic-Antonine date. Fig. 9.1

14. 60CB. Form 37, with an ovolo used mainly by Cinnamus ii (Rogers B231), but also by Sacer i and Pugnus ii. Not closely datable. Not illustrated.

15. 60CL. Form 37, with a double festoon in one panel and a (double?) medallion in the next. Not found.

16. 60IJ. Form 37, with panelled decoration but no recognisable detail. Not illustrated.

17. 60IQ. A fragment from a small bowl of form 37, with a double medallion perhaps containing an eagle. Not illustrated.

18. 60IQ. Form 37, with Apollo and chariot (D.58), used by both Hadrianic and Antonine potters, but here rather more likely to be Antonine. Not illustrated.

19. 61AO. Form 37, probably with the T-tongued ovolo (Rogers B206) used by the Quintilianus i and Paternus v groups of potters. The fabric and glaze are very orange, due to underfiring. Not illustrated.

20. 61EI. Form 37, with a double festoon containing a hare (D.950A), used in both the Hadrianic and Antonine periods. A hint of rhomboidal beads suggests Antonine date. Not illustrated.

21. 61EL or FL. Form 30, burnt, with a panel containing an eight-petalled rosette in a small, double medallion. Not found for illustration.

22. 61FV. Form 37, with a fragment of (unidentified) ovolo. Not illustrated.

23. 61HS. Form 37, without recognizable decoration. Not illustrated.

24. 61JL. Form 37, with scroll decoration. The leaf (Rogers J5) was used by Docilis i and Casurius ii, but the bowl cannot be firmly assigned to one or the other. Not illustrated.

25. 61LQ. Form 37, without recognisable decoration. Not illustrated.

26. 61ME. Form 37, perhaps with a rosette-tongued ovolo. Probably scroll decoration, perhaps with a striated or chevron medallion in the lower concavity and a bird (D.1019?) in the upper. Not illustrated.

27. 61PY. Form 37, with a sphinx (O.856), with the tail altered to make it fit into a double medallion (cf. O.856A). Not illustrated.

28. 61QT. A tiny scrap of form 37, with part of a large leaf of the type used in scrolls (Rogers H1–62). Not illustrated.

Early to mid-Antonine

29. 61MK. Form 37, in the style of Criciro v, with a narrow panel of circles and another with trilobed motifs (S. and S. 1958, fig. 33, 6) impressed back-to back. Both details are on a signed bowl from Cardurnock (*ibid.*, pl. 117, 2), together with his beaded junction masks, as here. *c.* AD 140–170. Fig. 9.1.

30. 61LK. Form 37, with a double-cogged festoon containing a hare (O.2120). The ovolo is an unusual, narrow one, with a tongue ending in a ring incomplete on the left-hand side. This is probably due to a blockage of the mould with clay, since a complete version is known. A bowl from Baylham Mill, Suffolk, which may be from the same mould as the Haltonchesters piece, has in addition the large rosette junction-masks of Pugnus ii (cf. S. and S. 1958, pl. 155, 20, which really has seven petals). The straight line below the ovolo suggests a possible connection with either Pugnus or Secundus v. *c.* AD 140–180. Fig. 9.1

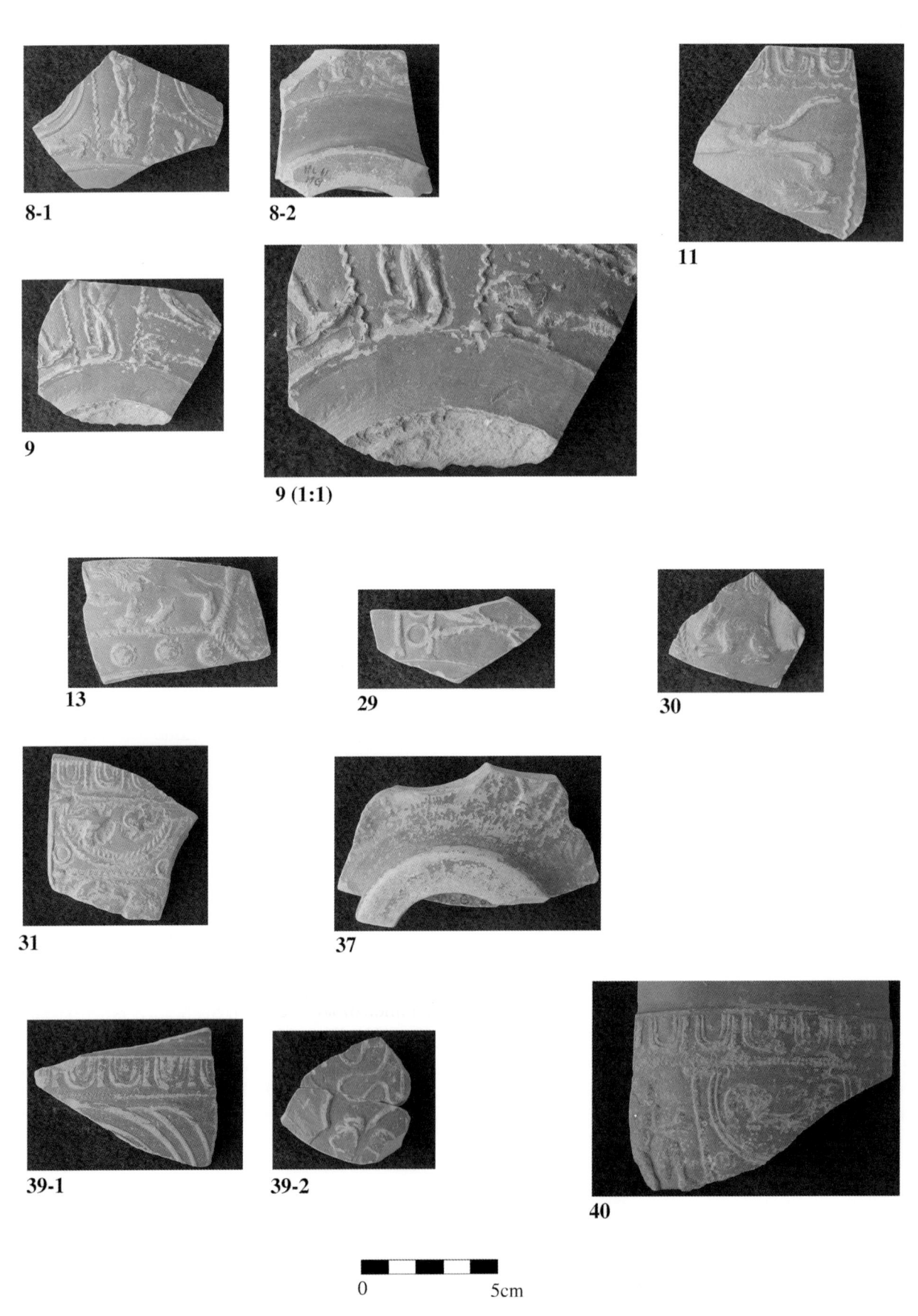

Figure 9.1. Decorated samain 8–40, 1:2.

THE CERIALIS II-CINNAMUS II GROUP

All the bowls in this section, with the exception of nos. 34 and 36, have the ovolo most commonly associated with this group of potters (Rogers B144).

31. 60IX. Form 37, with a panel with a double-cogged festoon (Rogers F41) in the upper half, containing a crane (O.2214A) and pygmy (O.696A). The lower half contains a bear (D.817). Cf. Simpson and Rogers 1969, Fig. 3, 19 for an almost identical panel. The fabric of the Haltonchesters bowl is underfired, and a dull orange colour. c. AD 140–170. Fig. 9.1.

32. 60JM. Form 37, burnt. Only the ovolo is identifiable. c. AD 140–170. Not illustrated.

33. 61DZ. Form 37, with freestyle decoration, including a bear (O.1633H) and a partly-impressed leaf-tip. c. AD 140–170. Not illustrated.

34. 61DJ. Form 37, with a bird (D.1038) in a small, double medallion with widely-spaced borders. The medallion is particularly characteristic of this group of potters, several of whom also used the bird. c. AD 140–170. Not illustrated.

35. 61EH. A small fragment of form 37, with the ovolo and, perhaps, a leaf-tip in the background of the decoration. c. AD 140–170. Not illustrated.

36. 61KQ. Form 37, with freestyle decoration, including a lioness (D.795) and, possibly, the lion D.766, The leafiness in the background suggests the work of this group. c. AD 140–170. Not illustrated.

CINNAMUS II

37. 60BY. Form 37, a badly-made small bowl, probably with three repeated panels: 1) A mask (D.675). 2) A medallion, perhaps a blurred version of the double-cogged medallion of which Rogers F40 is a partial impression. 3) A composite motif (Rogers Q43). All the details are on bowls either stamped by, or in the style of, Cinnamus, but the workmanship suggests that this was made by an inexperienced apprentice in his factory. The footring is very worn and the lack of clarity in the details suggests that the bowl comes from an old mould. c. AD 150–180 or possibly later. Fig. 9.1.

38. 60EW. Form 37, with scroll decoration. The leaf (Rogers H13) is on stamped bowl from Newstead. The large ring and the astragalus binding are not common for Cinnamus, but are attested on stamped bowls. c. AD 150–180. Not illustrated.

39. 60GP, 61GB, QA. Three joining fragments of form 37, with ovolo 4 (Rogers B145). Scroll decoration, with leaves Rogers H72, J1. The leaves are on a stamped bowl from Segontium (Wheeler 1923, fig. 73, 48). c. AD 150–180. Fig. 9.1.

40. 60GQ. Form 37, with his ovolo 1 (Rogers B223). Panelled decoration, with: 1) Neptune (D.14). 2A) A double festoon containing a cockerel (O.2346A). Both the figure-types are on stamped bowls from Wels (Karnitsch 1959, taf. 65, 7; 68, 4). c. AD 150–180. Fig. 9.1.

41. 60GX. Form 37, with freestyle decoration, including a dog (D.915) and stag (D.852). Both were used separately by several Antonine potters, but Cinnamus is perhaps the only one to have used them both. c. AD 150–180. Not illustrated.

42. 60IP. Form 37, with freestyle decoration, including a horse and rider (D.156) and dog (D.934). The leaf is probably a partial impression of one used in scrolls (cf. Rogers H13). All the details occur on his stamped bowls. c. AD 150–180. Not illustrated.

43. 61AL, BM (4). Five small fragments, two joining, of form 37, with his ovolo 1 (Rogers B223). A freestyle scene includes a horse and rider (D.156), stag (D.852), boar (D.834) and corn stook (Rogers N15). Three of the details are on a stamped bowl from Wels (Karnitsch 1959, taf. 77, 2). The stag is on a stamped bowl from London (S.and S. 1958, pl. 163, 66). c. AD 150–180. Not illustrated.

44. 61FI, FV (3). Four small fragments from a panelled bowl of form 37, with his ovolo 4 (Rogers B145), and a double-cogged festoon (Rogers F40). c. AD 150–180. Not illustrated.

45. 61GH (2, and perhaps BP). Form 37, two joining fragments and one other which perhaps comes from the same bowl. Panelled decoration, with: 1) An acanthus (Rogers K12). 2) A plant (Rogers H113). 3) A double medallion with a Venus (D.184) and bird (probably the Venus and bird. not showing). 61BP shows the Venus and bird. Most of the details are on stamped Cinnamus bowls, the acanthus from London (S. and S. 1958, pl. 159, 25), the plant from Wroxeter (*ibid.*, pl. 160, 38), the Venus from Corbridge (*ibid.*, pl. 160, 39) and also, with the cornucopia in panel 3 (Rogers U245), from Chester. c. AD 150–180. Fig. 9.2.

46. 61BP. Form 37, perhaps from the same bowl as the last, with the same medallion, Venus and bird, but with the bird outside the medallion. c. AD 150–180. Not found.

47. 61GZ. Form 37, with one of Cinnamus's less-common ovolos (Rogers B182). c. AD 150–180. Fig. 9.2.

48. 61HI. Form 37, probably with the same ovolo as the last. c. AD 150–180 (?). Not found.

49. 61HY (4), IQ. Five fragments only 4 found, some joining, of form 37, with his ovolo 1 (Rogers B223). Scroll decoration, with leaves Rogers H72 and J58, as on a stamped Cinnamus bowl from Segontium (Wheeler 1923; Fig. 73, 48). The bird (the reverse of O.2298) occurs frequently on his scroll bowls. c. AD 150–180. Fig. 9.2.

50. 61IS. Form 37, with his ovolo 4 (Rogers B145). Scroll decoration, with the polygonal leaf Rogers J1, as on the Segontium bowl, above. The bird (not in Déchelette or Oswald) has apparently not been recorded for Cinnamus. c. AD 150–180. Fig. 9.2.

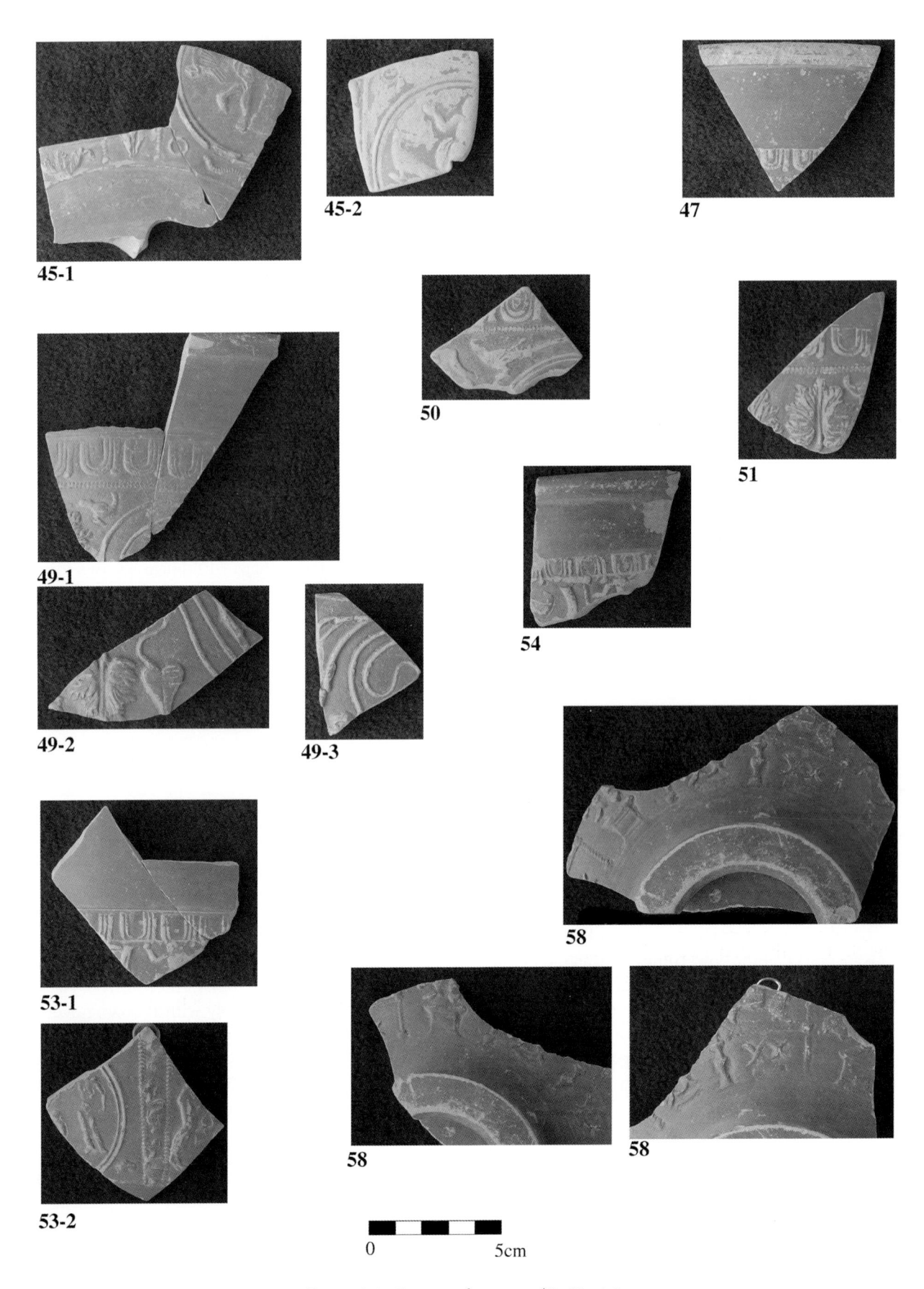

Figure 9.2. Decorated samain 45–58, 1:2.

51. 61JL. Form 37, perhaps from the same mould as no.49, with the same bird and one of the leaves (Rogers H72) impressed twice, side-by-side. *c.* AD 150–180. Fig. 9.2.
52. 61PL. Form 37, with a tapering gadroon with concave top (Rogers U121), as on an unstamped bowl in the style of Cinnamus in Roanne Museum. The gadroons are impressed at different levels, perhaps forming a large, stylised leaf. *c.* AD 150–180. Not illustrated.

SECUNDUS V
53. 61AS (3). Three fragments, two joining, of form 37. The decoration consists of at least three panels: 1) A double medallion, containing two or more figures, one of them the naked man O.570. The bottom, right-hand corner of this panel has a dolphin (a partial impression of the one in panel 2). 2) A narrow panel of dolphins (D.1057), impressed vertically. 3) A Vulcan (D.14). 4) A double festoon, containing an Amazon (D.154). This may be from the upper part of panel 1 or 3. The ovolo, based on Cinnamus's no. 1 (Rogers B223), but never used by him with a straight line below, occurs on bowls in the style of Secundus v. The Amazon and dolphins (in both impressions) are on a stamped bowl from Great Chesterford and the man is on another, from York. Both bowls have straight lines below their ovolos. For bowls in this potter's style, see S. and S. 1958, pl. 154, 14–16; 155, 23–8 (assigned to Pugnus but, in view of recent discoveries, more likely to be by Secundus). The Vulcan is on two of these (pl. 154, 14, 16). One of Secundus's other ovolos also derives from one of Cinnamus's, and this and the number of figure-types they share suggest that they were contemporaries. *c.* AD 150–180. Fig. 9.2.
54. 61MI. Form 37, with the ovolo (Rogers B233) impressed over a straight line. The ovolo occurs on a stamped bowl of Pugnus ii (S. and S. 1958, pl. 154, 13), but is often found on bowls in the style of Secundus. The detached festoon is a feature of Secundus's style, as are the bird (the reverse of O.2298) and composite motif in the adjacent panel (Rogers Q43). *c.* AD 150–180. Fig. 9.2.

ADVOCISUS
55. 61FE. Form 37, with a panel with a Minerva (D.77) and Apollo (D.55, without the stand). The neat beads suggest the work of Advocisus, who used both figure-types. *c.* AD 160–190. Not illustrated.
56. 61HP. Form 37, with the less-common of his ovolos (Rogers B102). The stag (O.1822 0) has not been recorded for him. *c.* AD 160–190. Not illustrated.
57. 61MI, DL. Two joining fragments of form 37, with panels: 1) Trilobed motifs (Rogers G71?), impressed back-to-back. 2) A draped figure. The motifs are on a stamped bowl from Silchester (S. and S. 1958, pl. 112, 6). The figure-type (not in Déchelette or Oswald) is on a bowl in his style from Corbridge (*ibid.*, pl. 113, 17). *c.* AD 160–190. Not illustrated.
58. 61QM. Form 37, with repeated panels: 1) A Minerva (D.77, commonly used by Advocisus) on a pedestal (Rogers Q62). 2) His common motif (Rogers U103), on either side of a tier of cups. The upper part of this panel has a kneeling Cupid (D. 282) on the right-hand side. The pedestal and tier of cups (Rogers Q49), though not common in his work, have both been recorded on stamped bowls. *c.* AD 160–190. Fig. 9.2.

IULLINUS II
59. 60EP. Form 37, with panelled decoration and his ovolo 1 (Rogers B156). *c.* AD 160–190. Not illustrated.
60. 60LW. Form 37, with the same ovolo as the last and with a panel containing a double festoon. *c.* AD 160–190. Not illustrated.
61. 61OB. Form 37, with the smaller of his common ovolos (Rogers B164) and a kneeling stag (O.1704A) in a double festoon. The stag is not known for Iullinus, but the general style is certainly his. *c.* AD 160–190. Fig. 9.3.
62. 61PT. Form 37, with scroll decoration. The ovolo (Rogers B153), similarly blurred examples of which are known) and the smaller leaf (Rogers H70) are on a stamped bowl from Rouen. The larger leaf (Rogers H75) is on a bowl in his style from Corbridge (S. and S. 1958, pl. 127, 29). The bird (D.1041) does not seem to be known for him. *c.* AD 160–190. Fig. 9.3.

BANUUS
63. 61AX. Form 37, with ovolo S. and S. 1958, Fig. 41, 3. The rosette at the top of the panel border was often used by Banuus. *c.* AD 160–190. Not illustrated.
64. 61EA. Form 37, very worn, with the same ovolo as the last, and with a panel containing a single festoon. *c.* AD 160–190. Not illustrated.

SERVUS IV, OR ONE OF HIS ASSOCIATES
65. 61IA, LE. Five joining fragments and a flake from a freestyle bowl of form 37. The ovolo (Rogers B153) and sea-horse (D.35) are on bowls from Lezoux (signed and stamped, respectively). The urn (Rogers T20) and stag (D.847 variant) are on bowls in his style from Lezoux and Colchester (S. and S. 1958, pl. 138, 5), respectively. The bird (D.1009) has not been recorded for him. *c.* AD 160–190. Fig. 9.3.
66. 61KQ. Form 37, with a small, straight-tongued ovolo. The zig-zag borders suggest the work of Servus or one of his associates, and the shell-shaped plant in a double festoon appears on one of his signed bowls, from Lezoux. The ovolo is possibly the same as one on

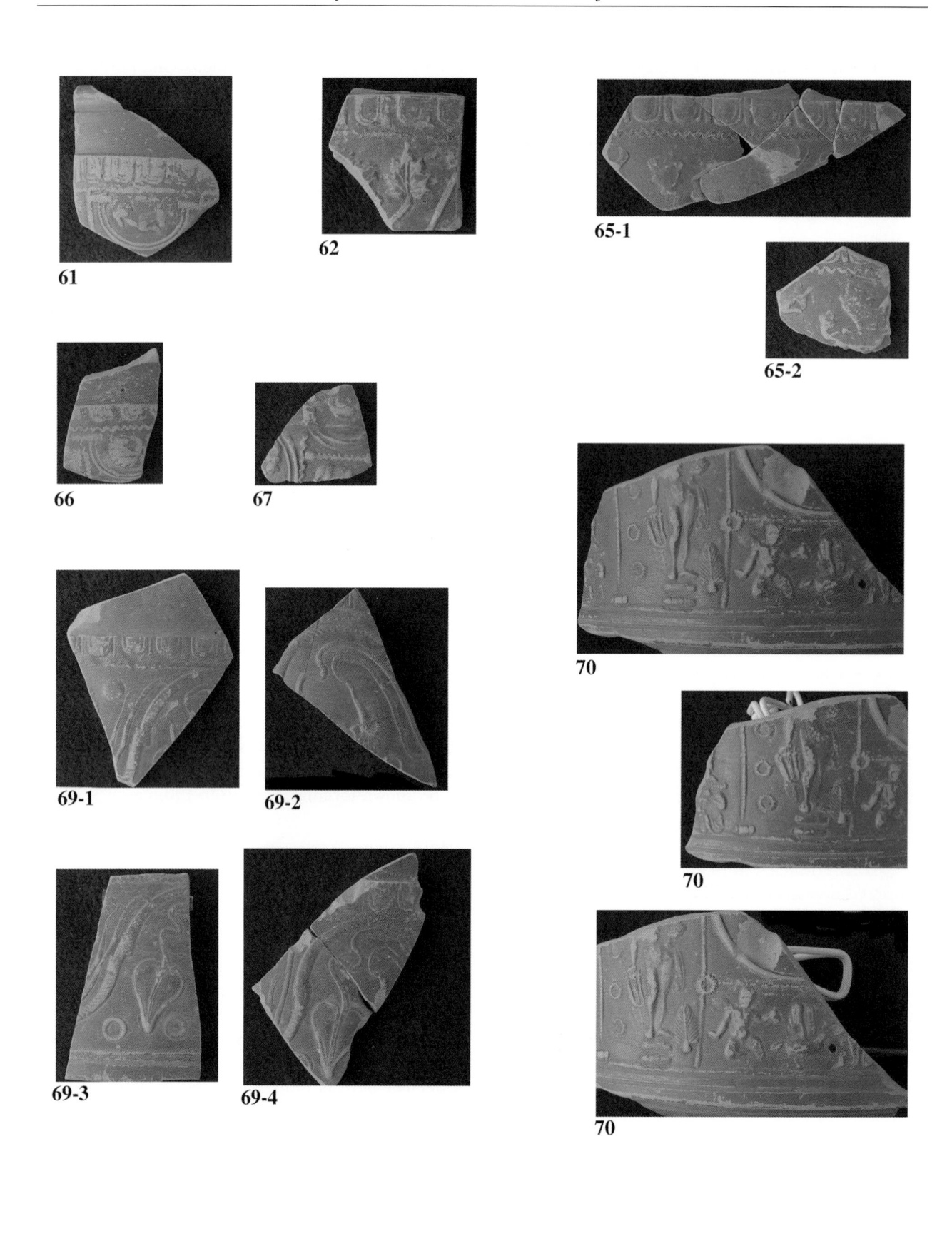

114 *Excavations Directed by J. P. Gillam at the Roman Fort of Haltonchesters, 1960–61*

Figure 9.3. Decorated samain 61–70, 1:2.

a mould from Lezoux signed by a potter whose name begins in Ca... *c.* AD 160–190. Fig. 9.3.

IUSTUS II
67. 60CB. A fragment from a carelessly-moulded bowl of form 37, with panels: 1) A double medallion, probably containing a mask. 2A) A double festoon or medallion, containing a bird (not closely identifiable); 2B) a mask (?). The details are all blurred, but the types of zig-zag border used suggest Iustus. The festoon or medallion and bird are on stamped bowls from Lezoux and London (S. and S. 1958, pl. 110, 10), respectively. *c.* AD 160–190. Fig. 9.3.
68. 61AN. Form 37, with coarse, zig-zag borders. The upper half of one panel contains a double festoon. The lower part has a lozenge (Rogers U7), as on a stamped Iustus bowl from Lezoux (MAN). *c.* AD 160–190. Not illustrated.

MERCATOR IV
69. 61AS, AY, BF, BO, CD. Five fragments of form 30, two joining, with scroll decoration. The small leaf (Rogers H129) and rosette (Rogers C171) are on a stamped Mercator bowl from Corbridge (S. and S. 1958, pl. 146, 12) and the ovolo (Rogers B25) is on bowls from South Shields and Corbridge (*ibid.*, pl. 145, 3, 4). The heart-shaped leaf (Rogers J51) is on a bowl from Little Chester. The scroll, formed by impressing a festoon stamp (Rogers F2) first one way up and then the other, is on a mould from Lezoux with his style of decoration. *c.* AD 160–190. Fig. 9.3.
70. 61CM. Form 30, with panels: 1) A figure (unidentified), over a mask (D.675). 2) An Apollo (D.46), flanked by toothed circles (Rogers E57) and a leaf (Rogers J119). 3A) A single festoon; 3B) a bird (D.1010) between Cupids (D.264, 261, respectively). The Apollo, circles, leaf and Cupids are all on a stamped bowl from Wilten (Karnitsch 1960, taf. 2, 3). The bird is on a stamped bowl from Corbridge (S. and S. 1958, pl. 145, 2). The mask does not seem to be known for Mercator. Most of the details were used by Paternus v, too, but he does not seem to have used the circles as junction-masks, as here. *c.* AD 160–190. Fig. 9.3.
71. 61HJ. Form 30, with ovolo as on no. 69, and a horizontal border of rhomboidal beads, as used on many of Mercator's bowls. *c.* AD 160–190. Not illustrated.
72. 61IN. Form 30, with ovolo as on no. 69. Panelled decoration, with a rosette, arcade or medallion and a spindle. The last is on a bowl in Mercator's style from the Wroxeter Gutter (Atkinson 1942, pl. 35, G8). *c.* AD 160–190. Fig. 9.4.
73. 61PT. Form 37, with a double medallion containing a leaf (Rogers H78?) and perhaps a similar adjoining medallion. The rosettes below the medallion (Rogers C171) were used by Mercator (cf. no. 69), but the leaf does not seem to be known for him. It was used by Paternus v, however, and the bowl may be by him, though if a series of medallions is involved, it is more likely to be by Mercator. Cf. S. and S. 1958, pl. 145, 2. *c.* AD 160–190. Not illustrated.

PATERNUS V AND HIS ASSOCIATES
74. 60JG. Form 37, with freestyle scene, incorporating one of Paternus's spindles, as on 61IH. *c.* AD 160–190. Not illustrated.
75. 61AB, AR (2), HL. Form 37, burnt, with one of Paternus's less-common ovolos (Rogers B178). Freestyle decoration, with a horse and rider (D.157), horse (D.906), bears (D.807, 810), dog (O.2007A) and spindle, which are all on a stamped bowl from Wingham, Kent (S. and S. 1958, pl. 106, 22) and a lioness (D.794 variant), also used by him. *c.* AD 160–195. Fig. 9.4.
76. 61EN. A worn fragment from a freestyle bowl of form 37, perhaps with the ovolo Rogers B224. The stag (D.883) was used by Paternus and some of his associates, but the ovolo is not attested for any of these potters. *c.* AD 155–195. Not found.
77. 61FL, HZ. Two joining fragments of form 37, one grooved for a rivet. The ovolo (S. and S. 1958, fig. 30, 4) tends to appear on Paternus's smaller bowls, usually with either scroll decoration or, as here, a freestyle scene. The horse (D.906), goat (D.968) and stag (D.860) are all on a bowl from Wingham (S. and S. 1958, pl. 106, 22). The lioness to right and the leaf (Rogers J146) are on bowls from Clermont-Ferrand (BM) and Carrawburgh (S. and S. 1958, pl, 106, 21; 105, 12, respectively). The lioness to left (D.794 variant) is on a bowl from Albens. All these bowls carry Paternus's familiar label-stamp. There is also perhaps a boar (D.835?), which he used. *c.* AD 160–195. Fig. 9.4.
78. 61IH. Form 37, with freestyle decoration. The horse and rider (D.157, here with the horse's tail impressed twice), dog (O.2007A) and striated spindles all appear frequently on Paternus's freestyle bowls. *c.* AD 160–195. Not found.
79. 61IQ. Form 30, with a large winding scroll. The use of a striated spindle as a junction on the scroll suggests Paternus (cf. S. and S. 1958, pl. 108, 37). The rest of the decoration is very abraded. *c.* AD 160–195. Not found.
80. 61IS. Form 37 rim, burnt, probably with one of the ring-tongued ovolos used by this group of potters. *c.* AD 150–195. Not illustrated.
81. 61JS, JL. Two joining fragments of form 37, with scroll decoration and a ring-tongued ovolo (Rogers B105). *c.* AD 150–l95. Not illustrated.
82. 61OZ. Form 37, burnt, with scroll decoration. The leaf (Rogers H28) is on stamped Paternus bowls from Chesters and Mainz (S. and S. 1958, pl. 107,

31; 104, 8). The ovolo is similar to Rogers B135. *c.* AD 160–195. Fig. 9.4.

83. 61QL. Form 37, with a border of rhomboidal beads and a scroll with a detached tendril, both suggesting Paternus or one of his associates. *c.* AD 150–195. Not illustrated.

84. 61QR. Form 37, with a plant (Rogers G55) used by Paternus on a bowl from Watercrook (S. and S. 1958, pl. 109, 16). The ovolo, one of his less-common ones (perhaps Rogers B135) is on a stamped bowl from Richborough and on one in his style from Catterick. The Haltonchesters piece has a border of rhomboidal beads below the ovolo, instead of his more usual squarish-beaded one. *c.* AD 160–195. Fig. 9.4.

Casurius ii

85. 60KO. Form 37, with an ovolo used by both Casurius ii and Docilis (Rogers B20). The bowl is by Casurius, to judge by the type of beaded border below the ovolo. *c.* AD 160–190. Not illustrated.

86. 60KF. Form 37, with panels: 1A) A single festoon containing an acanthus (Stanfield 1935, pl. IX, 7A); 1B) a saltire incorporating the same acanthus. 2) A larger acanthus (*ibid.*, 21) separated from a stylised plant (*ibid.*, 15). The ovolo (*ibid.*, 5) is similar to, but probably not the same as, Cinnamus's ovolo 1. The smaller acanthus and plant are on a stamped Casurius bowl from Corbridge (*ibid.*, pl. II, 9). The larger acanthus is on a stamped bowl from Wels (Karnitsch 1959, taf. 63, 1). The horizontal motif in panel 2) is on a bowl in his style from Corbridge (S. and S. 1958, pl. 134, 29). The particular type of saltire, with both beaded and wavyline diagonals, is a feature of several bowls in his style (*ibid.*, pl. 135, 35, 38, for instance). *c.* AD 160–190. Fig. 9.4.

87. 61BT. Form 37, with the same ovolo as the last. Probably panelled decoration, with a medallion with a plain inner border and toothed outer one (Rogers E25), containing a sea-horse (D.33). Both occur on stamped Casurius bowls (S. and S. 1958, pl. 133, 17; 134, 20, respectively). *c.* AD 160–190. Fig. 9.4.

Do(v)eccus i

88. 60LB. Form 37, with panels: IB) A double medallion with a plain inner, and corded outer, border (Rogers E28). 2) A double medallion containing a mask (D.675), over a double festoon depending from rosettes (Rogers C167) and containing an acanthus (Rogers K22). All the details in panel 2) are attested on his stamped bowls, and he occasionally used detached festoons, as here (cf. S. and S. 1958, pl. 151, 57). The smaller medallion is on form 30 in his style from London (*ibid.*, pl. 151, 62). *c.* AD 165–200 Fig. 9.4.

89. 61AV. Form 37, with intersecting beaded diagonals between double festoons. This unusual kind of arrangement seems to be peculiar to Do(v)eccus (cf. S. and S. 1958, pl. 149, 33). He also used the rosette (Rogers C167) and leaf (Rogers H134) in the upper and lower parts of the saltire. The ovolo (Rogers B160) resembles his ovolo 2, but has narrower borders and a shorter tongue. *c.* AD 165–200. Fig. 9.4.

90. 61FV, IK. Two fragments of form 37, with panels: lA) A small, double festoon; lB) a heart-shaped leaf (?). 2) A double medallion containing a Cupid (D.264), and Do(v)eccus's double-D motif in one corner of the panel. The Cupid is on a stamped bowl from Silchester (S. and S. 1958, pl. 148, 14). The ovolo, one of his least common ones (Rogers B235), is on a stamped, unprovenanced bowl in Clermont Ferrand Museum. *c.* AD 165–200. Fig. 9.4.

91. 61KB. A small fragment from a panelled bowl of form 37, with the rosette Rogers C167 (as on no. 88) and a triton (smaller than D.16), as on a stamped Do(v)eccus bowl from London (S. and S. 1958, pl. 149, 35. *c.* AD 165–200. Not illustrated.

92. 61KP. Form 37, with a double festoon in one panel and a double medallion in the next. The kneeling stag in the festoon (D.879) is on a stamped Do(v)eccus bowl from Silchester (S. and S. 1958, pl. 148, 14) and the panel border consists of his large, square beads. *c.* AD 165–200. Not illustrated.

93. 61LQ. Form 37, heavily burnt, with an elongated leaf in one panel (Rogers U161) and a double festoon in the other. The festoon is suspended from Do(v)eccus's familiar D-motif. *c.* AD 165–200. Not found.

94. 61NO. Form 37, with Do(v)eccus's square-beaded borders, on a panelled bowl with a double festoon containing a sea-horse (D.33), also used by him. The ovolo (common on his bowls, but with no equivalent in S. and S. or Rogers) is smaller than Rogers B161, but approximately the same shape. *c.* AD 165–200. Not illustrated.

95. 61OQ. Form 37, slightly burnt, with panelled decoration. Do(v)eccus used the double medallion, leaf (Rogers J16) and Cupid (D.282, but with a wing showing). *c.* AD 165–200. Not illustrated.

96. 61PT. Form 37, probably with the same ovolo as no.94. For the stamp, DO[IICCVS], impressed on the rim after moulding, see stamp no. 14. Fig. 9.4.

Antonine

97. 60BW. Form 37, with panels: 1) Bacchus (D.534). 2) Eagle (D.981). Not illustrated.

98. 60EH. Form 37, with traces of a polygonal leaf. Not illustrated.

99. 61BD. Form 37, with the Apollo D.56, used by several potters in the mid- to late Antonine period. Not illustrated.

100. 61BM. A small fragment of form 30, with an astragalus border (Rogers A10), with a human figure

9. *The Decorated Samian and Potters' Stamps*   117

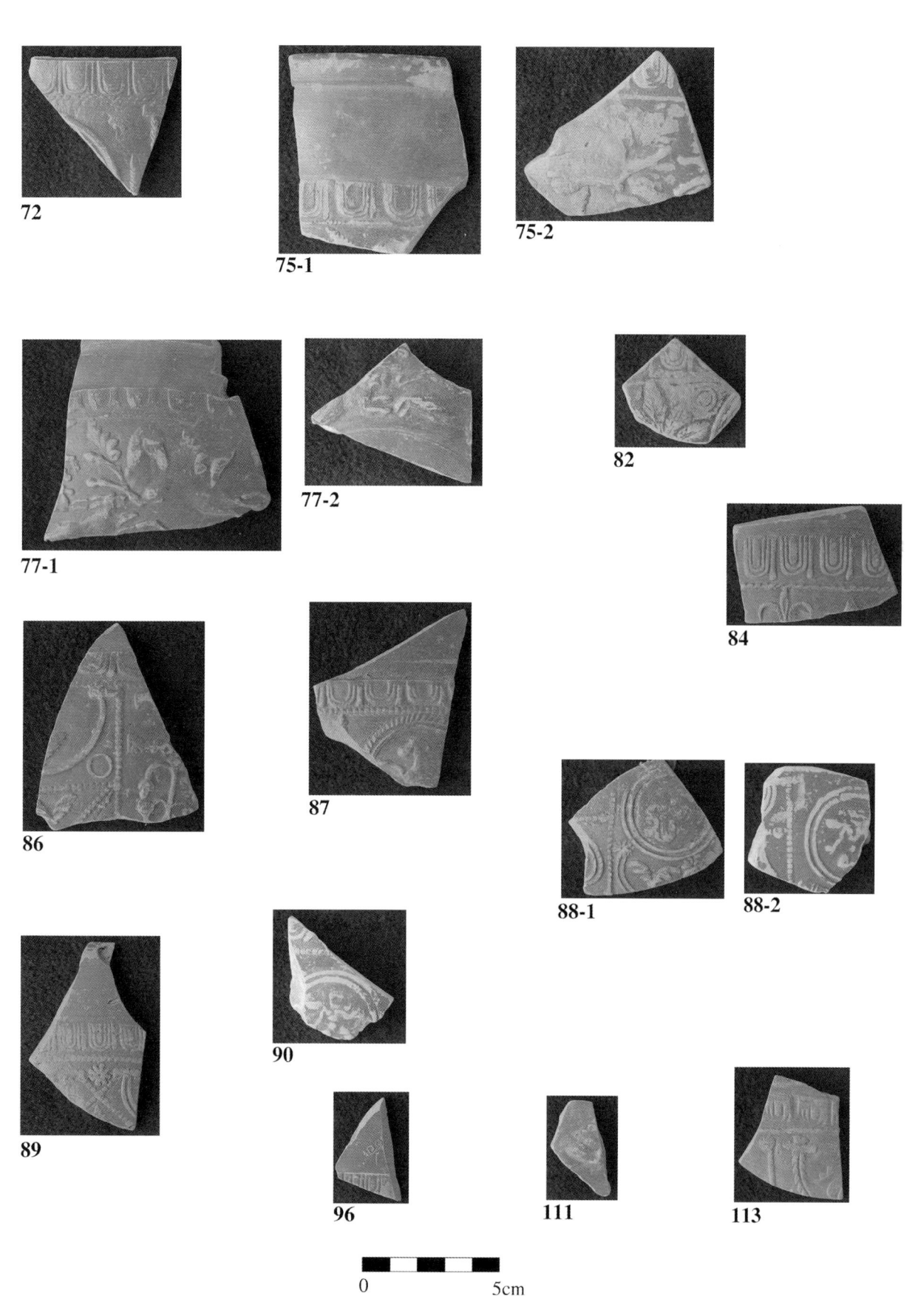

Figure 9.4. Decorated samain 72–113, 1:2.

above it and a spiral enclosing a seven-petalled rosette, below. Perhaps by Illixo, though too little is known of his style to be certain. Not illustrated.

101. 61DL. Form 37, with a double festoon possibly containing the sea-centaur D.36. This was used by such potters as Catussa, Cinnamus ii and Secundus v. Mid- to late Antonine. Not illustrated.

102. 61EK. Form 37, with an ovolo not unlike Cinnamus's ovolo 3 (Rogers B143), but narrower. The single festoon in the decoration makes this unlikely to be by him. Not illustrated.

103. 61EV or EY. Form 37, with a figure-type (perhaps the sea-centaur D36) cut through by the basal groove. Not illustrated.

104. 61FZ. Form 37, perhaps with zonal decoration. The bear (O.1626) was used in the mid- to late Antonine period. Not illustrated.

105. 61IB. Form 37, with a fragment of unidentified ovolo. Not illustrated.

106. 61IQ. Form 37, probably with leaves in both surviving panels. Mid- to late Antonine. Not illustrated.

107. 61JQ. Form 37, with only a zig-zag border recognisable. Perhaps from bowl no. 68.

108. 61PT. Form 37, with freestyle decoration, including a panther (O.1512) and, probably, a lioness (D.793). Not illustrated.

109. 61PT. Form 37, with a panel containing a Pudicitia (D.540), perhaps with a lozenge below. The dotted border may suggest Paternus v or an associate. Not illustrated.

Central or East Gaulish

110. 61FR. Form 37, with a fragment of ovolo. Probably Central Gaulish, though the fabric is not very informative. Not closely datable. Not illustrated.

East Gaulish

Blickweiller

111. 61GA. Form 37, with a bear (Knorr and Sprater 1927, taf. 78, 9). Blickweiler ware is uncommon in Britain. Hadrianic or early Antonine. Fig. 9.4.

La Madeleine

112. HAL*. Form 37, with a chevron festoon (Fölzer 1913, taf. XXV, 111) containing a bird (*ibid.*, 61). *c.* AD 130–160. Not illustrated.

113. 60IX, 61CM (2). Three fragments of form 37, with bright orange fabric and glaze. There is no clear impression of the ovolo, since both it and the tongue fade out at the bottom. Panelled decoration, with a double-cogged festoon containing the merman O.23A, which appears on late La Madeleine ware (cf. Ricken 1934, taf. VIII, 15). Below the festoon is a dog (not closely identifiable). On the whole, the piece is rather more likely to come from La Madeleine than from the Argonne, in spite of the fabric and glaze, since beaded borders below ovolos are not common in the Argonne. Mid-Antonine. Fig. 9.4.

Argonne

114. 61EK. Form 37, with a panel containing a medallion with a striated outer and plain inner border; (Fölzer 1913, taf. XXVIII, 447), a rosette (*ibid.*, 435?) and a spiral (*ibid.*, 424). The spiral is also impressed over a beaded vertical border. Second half of the second century. Fig. 9.5.

115. 61IN, NS. Five fragments, some joining, of form 37, in orange fabric with very little glaze surviving. The panels are separated by lengths of double-cogged border joined by rosettes and contain: 1) A saltire, consisting of beaded diagonals and a central, vertical bead row. 2) A leaping figure (Ricken 1934, taf. XIII, 42) and Hercules (O.748A), separated by an unidentified motif. 3) Bacchus (Oswald 1945, fig. 7, 7). Another panel has a different leaping figure. Simple saltires, like the one here and the same, and similar divisions of panels are typical of Lavoye ware (*ibid.*, fig. 8, 28 and 9, 41; 8, 15. Second half of the second century. Fig. 9.5.

Heiligenberg

116. 61LE. Form 37, with a squarish ovolo with tongue turned to the right, used by Ianus ii at Heiligenberg but not, apparently, at Rheinzabern. *c.* AD 140–160. Not found.

Rheinzabern

117. 61DR or OR. Form 37, with a panel probably containing a bear. The striated border and large rosette (Ricken-Fischer 1963, O41) are typical of Ianus ii and Cerialis v. *c.* AD 160–190. Not illustrated.

118. 61PT. Form 37, with a panel containing a medallion (Ricken-Fischer 1963, K48), used by Ianus ii and Cerialis v. *c.* AD 160–190. Not illustrated.

119. 61CF. Form 37, with ovolo Ricken-Fischer 1963, E19, used by Ianus ii and Mammilianus. *c.* AD 160–200. Not illustrated.

120. 61BL. Form 37, with a basal wreath (Ricken-Fischer 1963, R34) and striated festoon (*ibid.*, KB116, used upside-down). Both were used by Cerialis v. *c.* AD 160–190. Not illustrated.

121. 60JW. Form 37, with freestyle decoration. The tree with the leaf Ricken-Fischer 1963, P47, griffin (*ibid.*, T180) and goblet (*ibid.*, 021) were all used separately by several second-century potters, but the general arrangement suggests either Ianus ii or Cerialis v (Ricken 1948, taf. 7, 10; 65, 3). *c.* AD 160–190. Fig. 9.5.

122. 61QU. Form 37, with an arcade (Ricken-Fischer 1963, KB87) supported by a column (*ibid.*, 0228) and containing a Vulcan (*ibid.*, M80a). To the right is

9. *The Decorated Samian and Potters' Stamps* 119

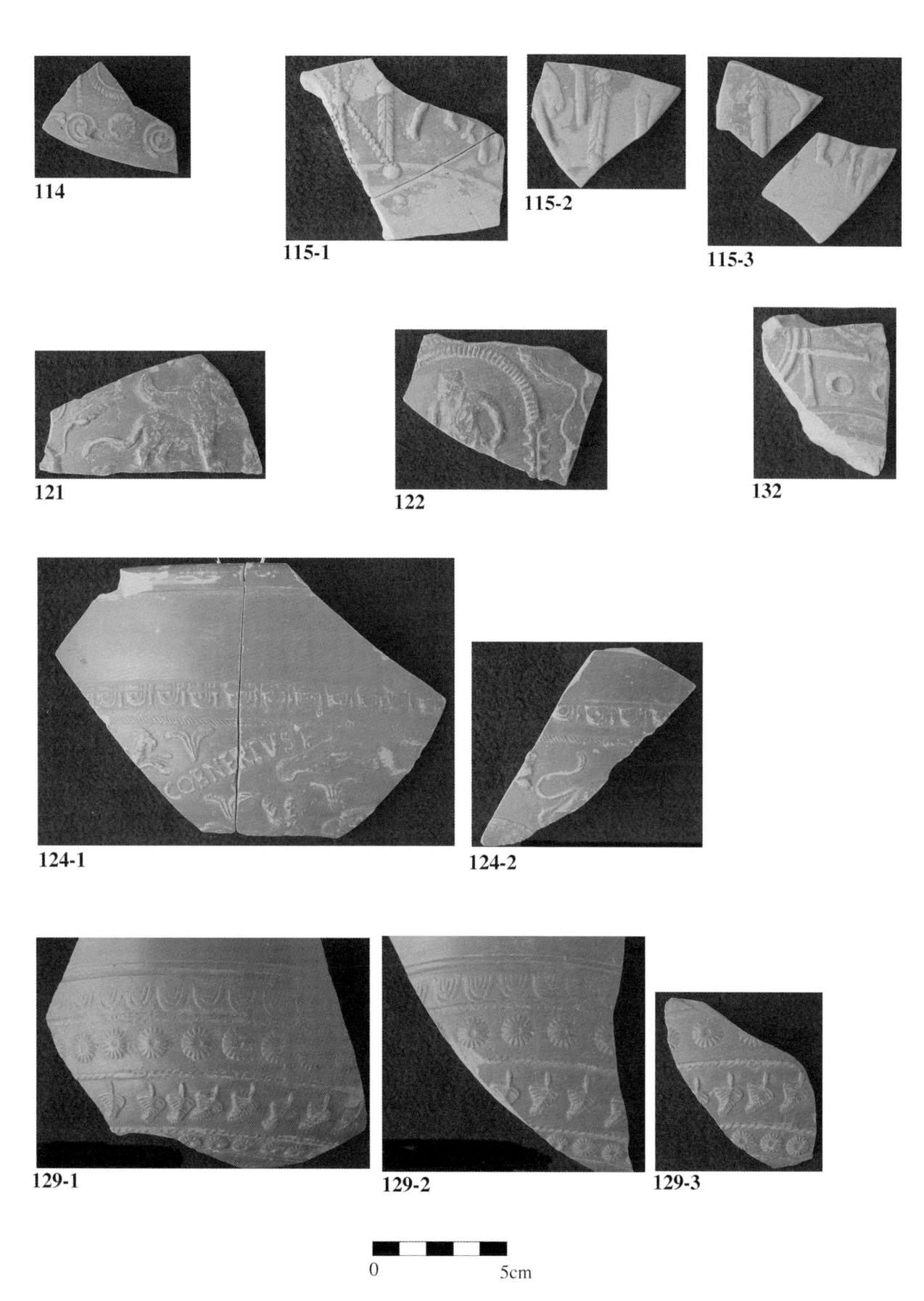

Figure 9.5. Decorated samian 114–132, 1:2

a tree, with the same leaf as on no.121, above. Almost certainly by Ianus ii, in view of the striated border below the ovolo. Cf. Ricken 1948, taf. 3, 11a, b for a bowl with the same decoration and an ovolo used by Ianus. *c.* AD 160–190. Fig. 9.5.

123. 61QM. Two joining fragments of form 37 with a large, tongueless ovolo (Ricken-Fischer 1963, E67) and leopard (*ibid.*, T41a), both used by Reginus vi. *c.* AD 160–190. Not illustrated.

124. 60GX, IX. Several large fragments, some joining, of form 37, with the label-stamp COBNERTVSF (Cobnertus iv 4a). Freestyle decoration, with ovolo Ricken-Fischer 1963, E44), goat (*ibid.*, T127), bear (*ibid.*, T57), stag (*ibid.*, T99), lion (*ibid.*, T4), lioness (*ibid.*, T32) and double leaf (*ibid.*, P150) are all known for him. A bowl with this stamp occurs in the Aquincum Hoard. *c.* AD 155–180. Fig. 9.5.

125. 61AR. Form 37, with an inverted festoon (Ricken-Fischer 1963, KB116) in the upper zone and a dog (*ibid.*, T140) in the lower. *c.* AD 160–200. Not found.

126. 60GD. Form 37 with ovolo with tongues alternating with two eggs (Ricken-Fischer 1963, E1), used by several potters in the period *c.* AD 160–200. Not illustrated.

127. 61BD. Form 37, with a basal wreath (Ricken-Fischer 1963, R34), used by several potters in the period *c.* AD 160–200. Not illustrated.

128. 61QT. Form 37, with freestyle decoration. Late second- or early third-century. Not illustrated.

Trier
129. 61LD. Six fragments, some joining, giving the greater part of a bowl of form 37, with three zones of decoration. The ovolo (Fölzer 1913, taf. XXXII, 956?), rosette in the upper zone (*ibid.*, 851?) and leaf in the middle zone (*ibid.*, taf. XXXI, 770) are all known for Trier, but the rosette in the basal zone is not, apparently. For general parallels for the style of decoration see Werkstatt I (Huld-Zetsche 1972, taf. 22). A thin, delicate bowl, with a good glaze. Antonine. Fig. 9.5.

130. 61NZ. Form 37, with a band of ovolos (Fölzer 1913, taf. XXXII, 956) below the decoration. This device appears occasionally on Trier ware (*ibid.*, taf. XX, 23, for instance). Late second- or early third-century. Not illustrated.

131. 61LZ. Form 37 with a panel (?), probably containing a saltire. Probably third-century. Not illustrated.

132. 61ET. Form 37, with panels: 1) A double medallion. 2A) A double medallion or festoon; 2B) a row of rings. No parallel has been found on signed or stamped bowls. The fabric, clumsiness of the moulding and thickness of the wall suggest that this bowl is either late Trier ware or was made at Lezoux at a time when export had virtually ceased. It is likely to be early third-century, in any case. Fig. 9.5.

East Gaulish, unassigned
133. 61LA. Form 37, perhaps with a panel containing a single festoon. Late second- or early third-century. Not illustrated.

134. 61LB. Form 37, with a horizontal border of rhomboidal beads and a vertical border of rectangular beads. One panel has a double medallion with plain outer and corded inner border, containing a six (?)-petalled rosette. Late second- or early third-century. Not found.

135. 61BJ. A small flake of form 37, with the top of the ovolo. Late second- or early third-century. Not illustrated.

The Potters' Stamps
Superscript a, b, c indicate:

a A stamp attested at the pottery in question.
b Not attested at the pottery in question, but other stamps of the same potter known from there.
c Attributed to the pottery on the evidence of fabric, distribution, etc.

The entries run: finds group, potter (i, ii, etc.), die, form, reading, pottery of origin.

1. 61AV Aestivus 3c 31 AESTIVIM (Initial A missing bar; VI touching) Lezoux.[a]
This appears mainly on form 31R and, occasionally, on form 79. Most of Aestivus's output is probably late Antonine and one of his stamps occurs on vessels from Pudding Pan Rock, but he made a few examples of form 27 and so must have started work by AD 160, at the latest. This particular stamp is probably to be dated *c.* AD 160–190. Fig. 9.6.

2. 61QU Albinus iv 6c 31 (slightly burnt) ALB[INIW] (A missing bar; B reversed; N mirrored) Lezoux.[b]
Albinus iv's wares occur in the Rhineland, suggesting activity before *c.* AD 150. They also come from Antonine Scotland, Binchester (2) and Chesterholm. His forms include 18/31, 18/31R and 27. There is no independent dating evidence for this particular stamp. *c.* AD 130–155. Fig. 9.6.

3. 61JL Albucianus 6c 33 ALBVCIANI Lezoux.[a]
This is found mainly on the later Antonine forms (including 31R, 79 and 80), but there is one example on form 27. The stamp occurs at several Hinterland forts, including Catterick and Chesterholm. *c.* AD 160–190. Fig. 9.6.

4. 60LV Albucius ii 4c 38 ALBVCI·M Lezoux.[b]
This occurs on forms 31R, 79, 80 and Ludowici Tg. It is therefore likely to be from one of his later dies, since he used several others on form 27. *c.* AD 160–180. Fig. 9.6.

5. 61CR Aper ii 1a 33 APRI·M (A missing bar) Lezoux.[a] Aper ii seems to have used only one die. His forms include 79, 80 and Ludovici Tx. *c.* AD 160–200. Fig. 9.6.

6. 61JM Beliniccus iii 2a 18/31 BELINICIM retrograde, with a graffito VOGDI inscribed, after firing, under the base.

Although Beliniccus used some of his dies successively at both Les Martres-de-Veyre and Lezoux, all the stamps noted from this particular die are in Lezoux fabric and examples are known from there. It occurs on forms 15/31, 18/31R and 80. The site record includes Camelon (2), Catterick (2) and Wroxeter (the forum destruction). *c.* AD 135–165. Fig. 9.6.

7. 61OU Belsa Arve(rnicus?) 1a 31R BELSA·ARVEF (V and E ligatured) Lezoux.[a]

This is also recorded from South Shields and Pudding Pan Rock. It occurs on forms 79 and 79R. Belsa's decorated ware shows that he was an associate of Paternus v. *c.* AD 165–200. Fig. 9.6.

8. 60KH Capellianus 1a 33 [CAPEL]LIANI Lezoux.[c]
This cup has two grooves on the upper side of the base, instead of the usual one. The stamp is known so far only on form 33. It occurs at South Shields and again at Haltonchesters (1927 excavations). Mid- to late Antonine, on the fabrics and forms. Fig. 9.6.

9. 60CW Catullus ii 4a (probably) 33 (?) [C]AT[VLLIM] Lezoux.[c] Graffito FLA inscribed, after firing, on the underside of the base.
This occurs at Catterick, Chesterholm and South Shields. Catullus's most common form is 33, but this particular stamp was also used on forms 31 and 31R. *c.* AD 150–190. Fig. 9.7.

10. 61GV Cavannus 1a 33 CAVANNI Argonne.[c]
Cavannus's range includes forms 18/31 and 18/31–31. This particular stamp occurs on form 27 and has been noted from Benwell. Antonine. Fig. 9.7.

11. 60GX Cobnertus iv 4a 37 COBNERTVSF Rheinzabern.[a]
Cobnertus iv was one of the earlier makers of decorated ware at Rheinzabern. This, his commoner mould-stamp, occurs at Benwell, Ebchester and Stanwix and in the Aquincum Hoard. See also no. 124 in the decorated ware. *c.* AD 155–180. Fig. 9.5.

12. 61JS Cuccillus i 2a 33 [CVC]ILL. IM Lezoux.[b]
Cuccillus's stamps occur in Antonine Scotland, in the Wroxeter Gutter and at Chesterholm and Malton. His forms include 18/31, 18/31R, 27 and 31, the last predominating. *c.* AD 140–170. Fig. 9.7.

13. 61LK Do(v)eccus i 13a 31 DOIICC[VS] Lezoux.[a]
A stamp used on plain ware, decorated moulds and the rims of decorated bowls (including one from a mould with the same stamp). It occurs in the predominantly late-Antonine material from the Brougham cemetery and at Benwell and South Shields. *c.* AD 165–200. Fig. 9.7.

14. 61PT Do(v)eccus i 13c 37 rim DO[IICCVS] Lezoux.[a]
This was also used on plain forms, including 31R and 79/80. It occurs at Catterick and Chester-le-Street. *c.* AD 165–200.
Editor's Note: there are added characters at the end of this die which are difficult to represent

15. 61BB Iullinus ii 7c 31 IVLLINI Lezoux.[b]
There are eight examples of this from the Wroxeter Gutter. Iullinus's stamps occur at Pudding Pan Rock and there are a few examples from Hadrian's Wall and the Hinterland forts. His plain forms include 31R, 79 and 80. His decorated ware is mid- to late Antonine. *c.* AD 160–190. Fig. 9.7.

16. 61KL Maior i 11a 38 MAIOR. I Lezoux.[a]
Maior's stamps occur elsewhere on Hadrian's Wall, at several of the Hinterland forts and at Pudding Pan Rock. His range includes forms 3lR and 79 but also, occasionally, 27. This particular stamp, known from Malton and South Shields, was used on forms 31R and 79R. *c.* AD 160–185. Fig. 9.7.

17. 61LD Malluro i 5a 18/31]MALLVRo (retrograde); as the stamp is broken at its left side it would be possible to read in either of two ways: initial MA ligatured or broken M, A. Lezoux.[b]
No other example of this stamp has been noted. Malluro's site record includes Chesters, Bar Hill and forts in the Rhineland. He made forms 27, 42, 79, 80 and Ludovici Tg, among others. *c.* AD 140–170 should cover his range, with AD 140–160 for this particular stamp. Fig. 9.7.

18. 61JZ Mammius 2a 33 MAMM. OF Lezoux.[b]
This has been noted elsewhere on Hadrian's Wall and at several Hinterland forts. His stamps occur also in Antonine Scotland, at Chester-le-Street and in a group of burnt samian of *c.* AD 170 at Tác (Hungary). His output includes occasional examples of forms 27 and 80. *c.* AD 155–185. Fig. 9.7.

19. 61FO Mansuetus ii 2a[l] 31 [MA. SV.] ETIc Lezoux.[b]
The end of the die was shortened, through fracture or wear, so that the final letter eventually registered as c, instead of small o. A stamp from the full die occurs on form 80, but both versions appear on form 27. Examples from the shortened die come from Malton and Benwell. *c.* AD 160–180. Fig. 9.7.

20. 61OA Muxtullus 1b (probably) 31 [MVXTVLLI]M Lezoux.[b]

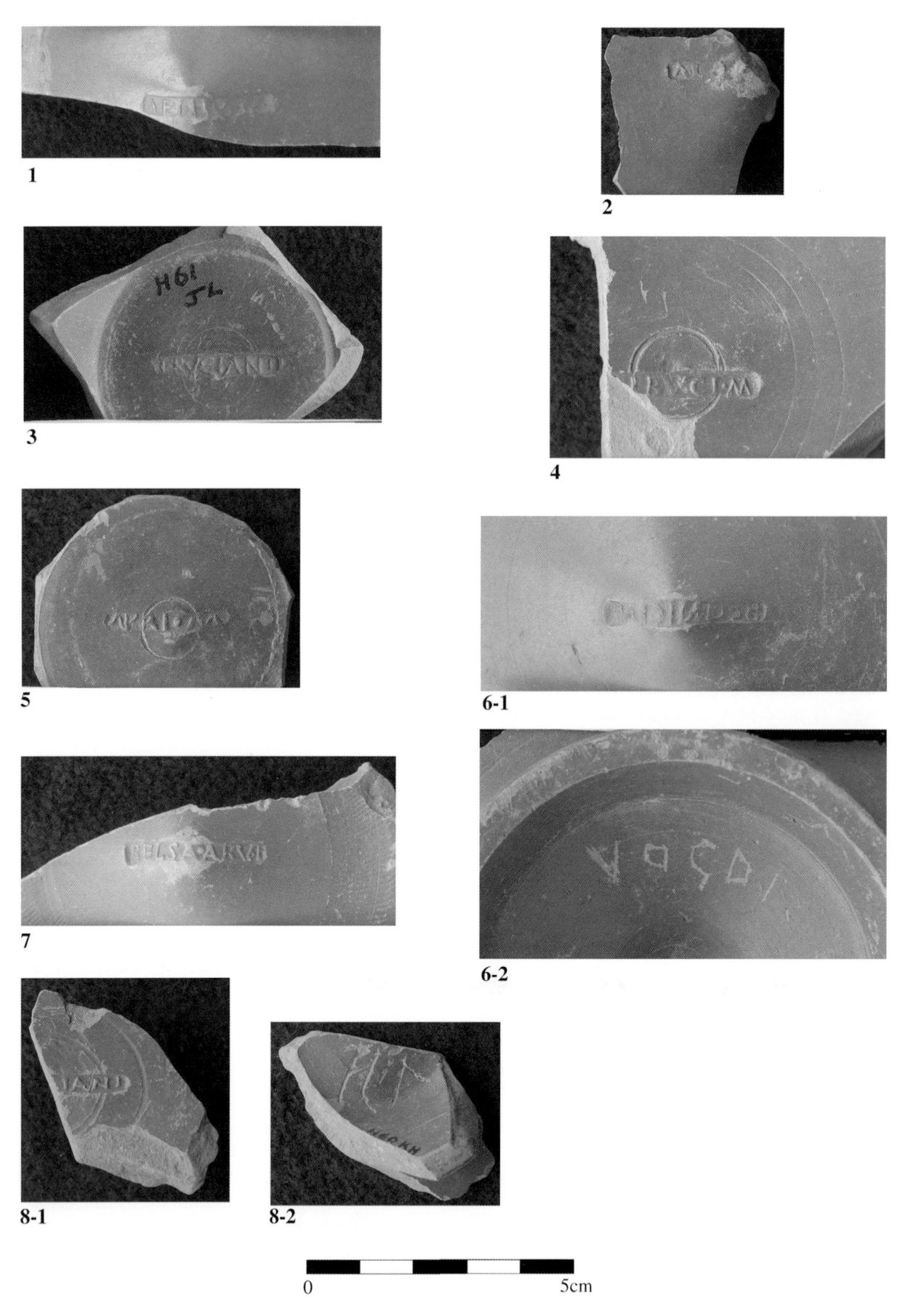

Figure 9.6. Samian potters' stamps 1–8, 1:1.

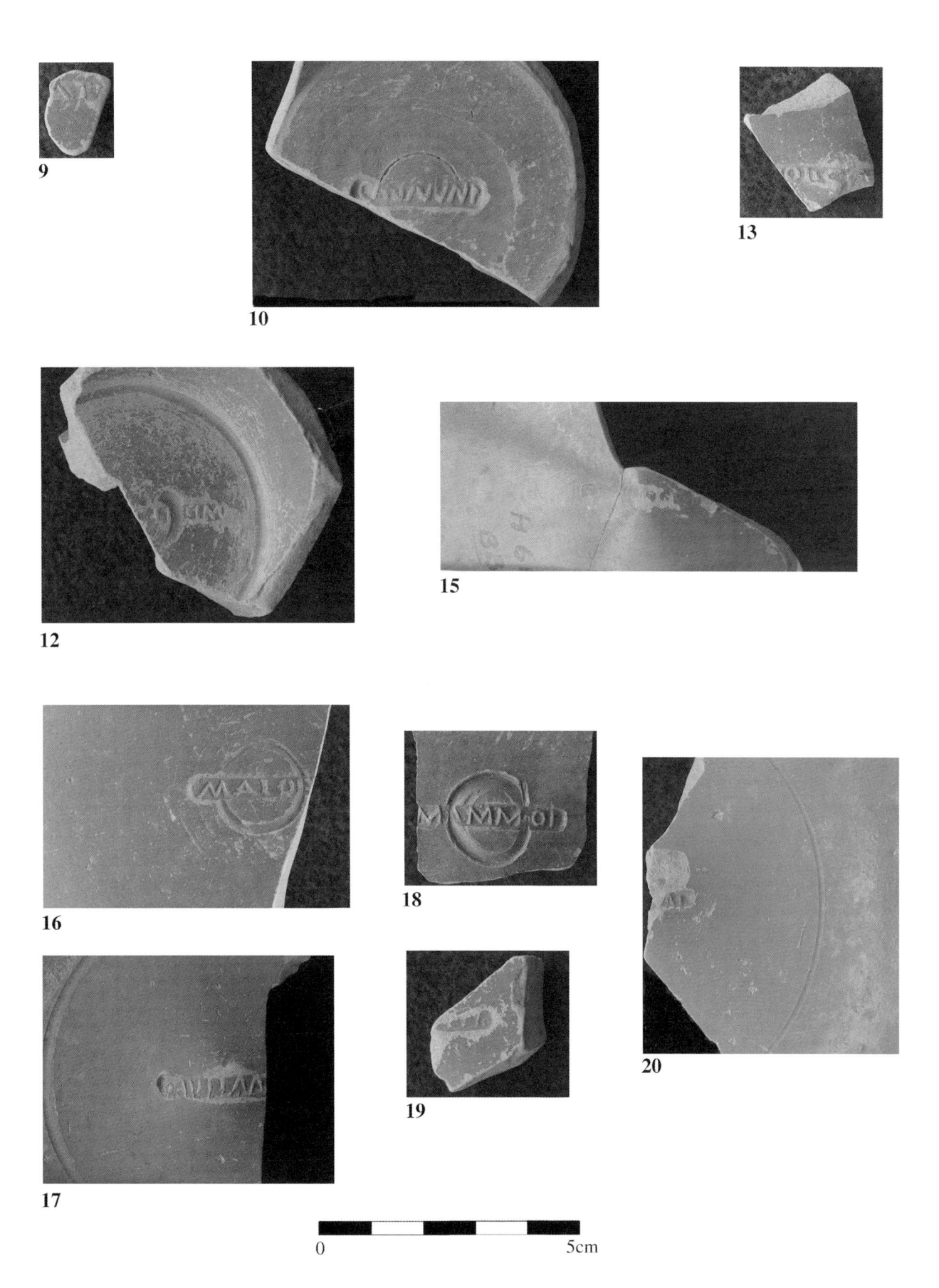

Figure 9.7. Samian potters' stamps 9–20, 1:1.

One of Muxtullus's earlier stamps, noted in Scotland and in early Antonine groups at Alcester and Castleford. It occurs on forms 18/31, 18/31R and 27. His work is relatively common on Hadrian's Wall and at some of the Hinterland forts, but there are no other examples from this particular die there. *c.* AD 140–160. Fig. 9.7.

21. 61JB Paullus v 8b/ 31 [PAV]I·L·I· Lezoux.[b]
This is from a modified, or damaged, die which originally gave PAV·L·L·I. Stamps from both versions of the die come from Hadrian's Wall. His wares occur also at Pudding Pan Rock and include forms 79 and Ludowici Tg. *c.* AD 165–200. Fig. 9.8.
Editor's Note: problems with representing die

22. 61MC Pottacus 3a 31R [POT·]TACVS Lezoux.[b]
This was also used on form 80. Pottacus's stamps occur at Chesterholm and South Shields, and in the Wroxeter Gutter. *c.* AD 160–200. Fig. 9.8.

23. 60FP Quintilianus i cursive 37 Quintilian[retrograde.
See no. 9 in the decorated ware. *c.* AD 125–145.

24. HAL * Quintus v 5a 31R QVINTIM Lezoux.[a]
There are many examples of this stamp from Hadrian's Wall and the Hinterland forts, and six from Pudding Pan Rock. It was used on forms 31R, 79 and 79R. *c.* AD 160–200. Fig. 9.8.

25. 61JD Rufianus 2a 33 (burnt) RVFIANI Lezoux.[c]
There are nine examples of this from the Wroxeter Gutter and one from Chesterholm. His small output consists mainly of forms 31 and 33, but one form 80 (stamped with a different die) has been noted. Second half of the second century. Fig. 9.8.

26. 61BG Secundus v 3a 33 SIICVNDI Lezoux.[c]
No other examples of this particular stamp have been noted. Secundus v's plain forms include 18/31, 18/31R, 27, 42 and 80 and some occur in early-Antonine groups at Alcester and Castleford. His decorated ware may be slightly later (cf. nos. 53–4 from Haltonchesters). *c.* AD 145–175. Fig. 9.8.

27. 60GU Senilis iii 3b 31 [S.EI·I:IL·IS]E Lezoux.[a]
This occurs on forms 31R and 79, but Senilis is known to have used another die on forms 18/31 and 27. A range *c.* AD 150–180 is likely, therefore, with 160–180 for the stamp in question. Fig. 9.8.

28. 61HG Senilis iii Incomplete 1 31 SENILI·M[Lezoux.[b]
No other examples of this stamp have been noted. See no. 27 for dating. Fig. 9.8.

29. 61LK T[, I[or]I on form 31, Central Gaulish, with a graffito -]TIN inscribed, after firing, under the base. Antonine. Fig. 9.8.

30. 60HP A A I C[on form 31R, Central Gaulish. Mid- to late Antonine. Fig. 9.8.
Editor's Note: problems representing die

9. The Decorated Samian and Potters' Stamps

Figure 9.8. Samian potters' stamps 21–30, 1:1.

10. The Other Pottery (Figs 10.1–10.7)

John Dore

This chapter is based on an examination by JND in 1994 of all the finds groups that could be located at that time. It is largely composed of coarseware but there is a residue of plain samian which remained in the groups after the decorated and stamped material had been extracted and sent to Brian Hartley and Brenda Dickinson; hence the title 'Other Pottery' rather than simply 'Coarseware'.

The featured vessels described below were given a catalogue number (a Featured Vessel number) at the time of cataloguing and this number was written on the sherds in question. This number has been retained in the report so that any individuals misguided enough to want to view the archive sherds will be able to identify them unequivocally. One of the results of this is that the numbers in the report below are not always sequential; though regrettable this was unavoidable. Fabric codes (for example MOS BS) are taken from Tomber and Dore 1998.

The catalogue is arranged by block, and within each block by finds group.

Block 1

60CJ
Total sherds: 6
Samian:
1 base sherd Dr 18/31R EG.
Coarseware:
   2) Beaker in Moselkeramik Blackslipped ware (MOS BS).
Also:
Small rim sherd of a bowl in BB1, as Gillam, 1976, no. 42.
TPQ*: somewhere round about the turn of the 2nd and 3rd C.

60DZ
Total sherds: 3
Samian:
1 wall sherd Dr 31R CG.
Coarseware:
1 wall sherd probable BB2.
1 wall sherd grey ware.
TPQ: *c.* AD 160.

Block 2

60HS
Total sherds: 7
Samian: 1 sherd, form unidentifiable.
Coarseware:
   1) Mortarium in Mancetter-Hartshill White ware (MAH WH). Late 2nd C.
TPQ: late 2nd C.

60ID
Total sherds: 4
Samian:
1 wall sherd Dr 31 EG.
TPQ: *c.* AD 150.

61CM
Samian:
1 rim sherd 3 wall sherds Dr 31 EG.
6 other wall sherds samian.
Coarseware:
138) Jar in hard sandy grey ware.
139) Jar in BB2.
140) Bowl in BB2.
141) Jar in grey burnished ware.
142) Dish in Crambeck Reduced ware.
143) Bowl in BB2.
145) Dish in calcite gritted ware.
146) Huntcliff-type cooking pot in calcite gritted fabric.
TPQ: *c.* AD 360.

61CU
Total sherds: 20
Samian:
1 wall sherd samian.
Coarseware:
147) Jar in grey burnished ware.
148) Bowl in BB1.
149) Bowl in BB2.
TPQ: *c.* AD 180.

Block 3

60JG
Total sherds: 4
Samian:
1 rim sherd Dr 33 ?CG.

*terminus post quem

Coarseware:
1 wall sherd beaker in orange pink fabric with black-colour coat; vegetable decoration *en barbotine*.
TPQ: mid-late 2nd C.

Block 4

60AK
Total sherds: 5
Samian:
1 wall sherd Dr 33 CG.
Coarseware:
  8) Wall sherd of a jar in BB2.
  9) Jar; fabric allied to BB2; sandy dull orange brown, dark grey brown surface.
  10) Bowl in Crambeck Parchment ware (CRA PA).
TPQ: *c.* AD 360.

60AS
Total sherds: 5
  14) Bowl; BB2.
TPQ: mid-2nd C.

60BG
Total sherds: 2

60CK
Total sherds: 4
Samian:
1 rim sherd Dr 31R CG.
Coarseware:
  4) Wide mouth jar or bowl in sandy grey fabric.
TPQ: 3rd C.

60CS
Total sherds: 1 wall sherd from a beaker in fine white fabric with black colour coat.
TPQ: Late 2nd C?

60FZ
Total sherds: 4
2 wall sherds of a jar in grey ware; 2 wall sherds of a jar in BB1.
TPQ: *c.* AD 120.

60GH
Total sherds: 6
Samian:
  5) 1 wall sherd Curle 15; Central Gaulish; Hadrianic
TPQ: Hadrianic.

60HF
Total sherds: 5
Coarseware:
  6) Mortarium; very pale yellow, traces of orange-brown paint on surface; abundant quartz mainly 0.1–0.2mm, some up to 0.5mm, occasional red ferrous grains 0.2–0.5mm; trituration grits quartz 4.0–8.0mm.
  7) Bowl; sandy orange brown with dark grey core; surface probably once slipped; possibly Wilderspool ware (WIL RS?).
TPQ: second half of 2nd C.

60KB
Total sherds: 8, including several wall and base sherds from a jar in BB2.
TPQ: mid-2nd C.

60KG
Total sherds: 1
1 wall sherd from a jar in BB1.

60KM
Total sherds: 3
Samian:
1 rim sherd Dr 37 ?EG.
Coarseware:
1 wall sherd from a jar in BB2.
TPQ: mid-2nd C.

60KN
Total sherds: 3
Samian:
1 rim sherd Dr 18/31, Central Gaulish.
TPQ: First half of the 2nd C.

60KU
Total sherds: 2
1 wall sherd from a bowl in BB1.
TPQ: *c.* AD 120.

60KX
Total sherds: 1
Samian:
1 tiny fragment, form unidentifiable.

60LC
Total sherds: 1
1 wall sherd from a bowl in BB1.
TPQ: *c.* AD 120.

60LQ
Total sherds: 3
Coarseware:
  15) Jar; sandy mid grey, burnished fabric.
TPQ: mid-2nd C?

60MB
Total sherds: 25
Samian:
1 rim sherd Dr 37 EG.
3 other wall sherds unidentifiable forms.
Coarseware:
  17) Jar; sandy mid grey fabric.
  18) Jar in BB2 (possibly Mucking BB2: MUC BB 2).
  19) Jar in sandy mid grey fabric with dark grey brown surface.
  20) Jar in gritty pale grey fabric with dark grey surface.
  21) Jar in BB2.
TPQ: probably somewhere in the 2/4 3rd C on the basis of FV 18.

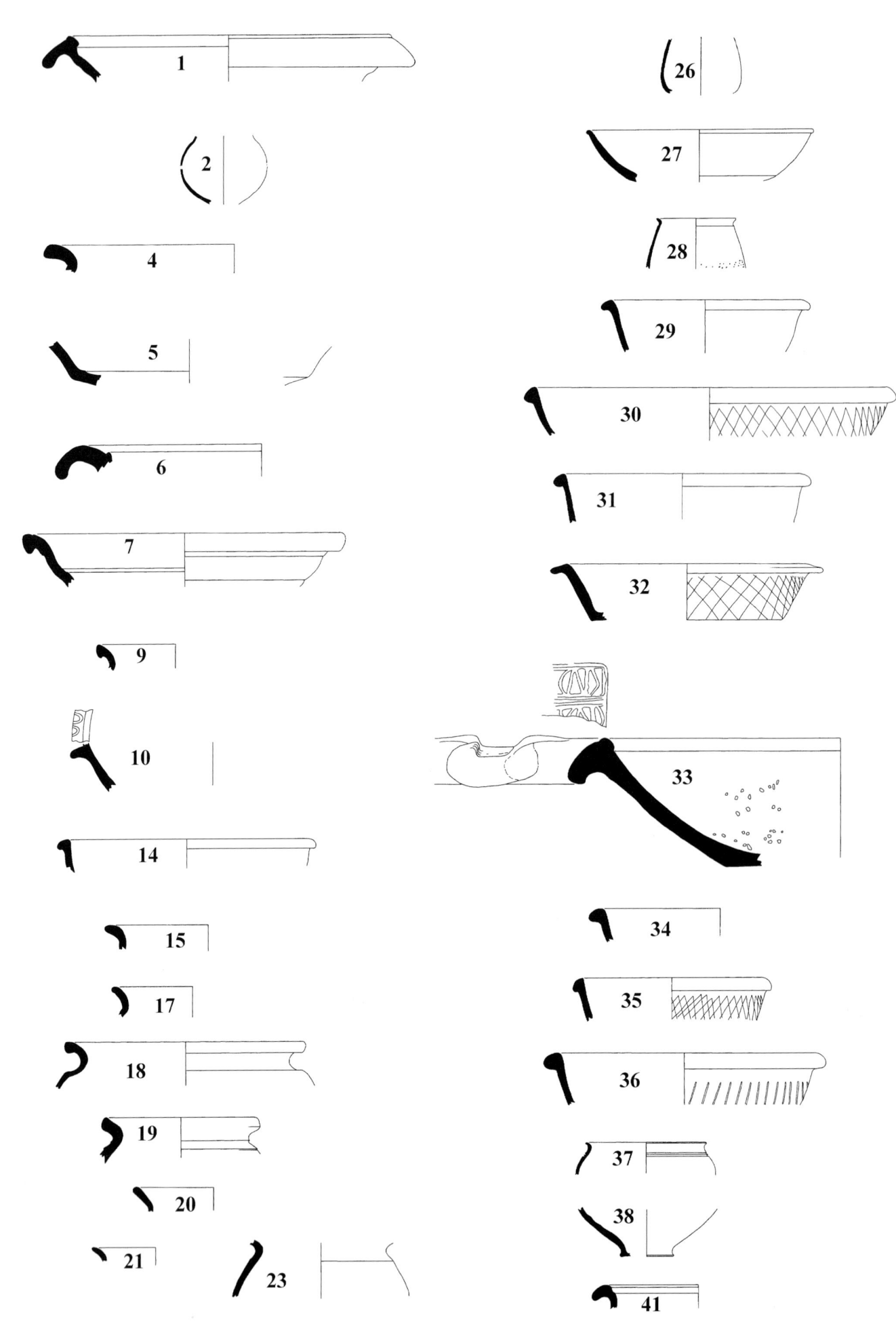

Figure 10.1. Other pottery: nos 1–41, 1:4.

Block 5

60DP
Total sherds: 105
Samian:
1 base sherd Dr 18/31R ?CG.
1 rim sherd Dr 31 EG.
Coarseware:
- 34) Bowl in BB2 fabric.
- 35) Bowl in BB2 fabric.
- 36) Bowl in BB2 fabric.
- 61) Beaker in Lower Nene Valley colour-coated ware (LNV CC).

TPQ: 3rd C (?)

60DQ
Total sherds: 15
Coarseware:
- 37) Beaker; sandy orange with orange-brown micaceous slip.
- 38) Base of a large beaker or jar; sandy dull red-brown with pale core; pinkish-brown micaceous surface.

TPQ: mid-late 2nd C.

60EF
Total sherds: 17
Samian:
1 rim sherd Dr 18/31 CG.
Coarseware:
- 62) Bowl; gritty mid grey with orange-brown core; dark grey surface.

Also a small rim sherd of a jar in BB2.
TPQ: mid-2nd C.

60EP
Total sherds: 20
Coarseware:
- 23) Jar in BB1 fabric.
- 26) Bag shaped beaker in Lower Nene Valley colour-coated ware (LNV CC).

Also:
1 base sherd from a bowl in BB2.
1 base sherd from a jar in calcite gritted fabric.
TPQ: late 3rd C on the basis of the calcite gritted jar.

60FG
Total sherds: 8
1 base sherd from a bowl in BB1.
TPQ: *c.* AD 120.

60FR
Total sherds: 3
1 small rim sherd of grey ware jar.
1 wall sherd grey ware jar with rustication.

61BF
Total sherds: 33
Samian:
- 27) 1 rim sherd Dr 31 CG.

1 wall sherd closed form EG.
1 other sherd samian.

Coarseware
- 28) Beaker in Wilderspool Red Slip ware (WIL RS).
- 29) Bowl in BB2 fabric.
- 30) Bowl in BB2 fabric.
- 31) Bowl in BB2 fabric.
- 32) Bowl in BB1 fabric.
- 33) Mortarium; pale yellow; orange-brown slip over the stamp; inclusions: common, rounded red iron-rich grains mostly 0.2–0.5mm, occasionally up to 2mm; rounded limestone mostly 0.2–0.5mm occasionally up to 1.0mm; quartz 0.2–0.5mm; also some fine-grained rock fragments and clay pellets; trituration grits are sub-rounded quartz and quartz sandstone up to 8.0 mm in diameter. (COR WH). Stamped by the potter Cudrenus. A Corbridge product.

TPQ: mid-2nd C.

Block 7

61KJ
Total sherds: 20
Samian:
1 wall sherd Dr 31R EG.
1 wall sherd Dr 37 ?EG.
Coarseware:
- 41) Jar; Huntcliff type in calcite gritted ware.
- 42) Jar; sandy dark grey-brown, black surface.
- 43) Small mortarium in Crambeck parchment ware (CRA PA).
- 44) Mortarium in Hartshill-Mancetter white ware (MAH WH).

TPQ: *c.* AD 360 on the basis of 41 and 43.

61KP
Total sherds: 52
Samian:
1 rim sherd, 1 base sherd Dr 31 ?EG.
2 other wall sherds samian.
Coarseware:
- 45) Bowl in BB2 fabric.
- 46) Bowl in BB2 fabric.

TPQ: *c.* AD 160.

61MI
Total sherds: 32
Samian:
1 rim sherd Dr 31R ?CG.
3 wall sherds ?Dr 31R.
Coarseware:
- 47) Dish in BB1 fabric,
- 48) Bowl in Crambeck reduced ware (CRA RE).

TPQ: late 3rd C.

61PZ
Total sherds: 3
Coarseware:
- 49) Large jar; sandy dark grey.
- 50) Jar in BB1 fabric.

TPQ: *c.* AD 120.

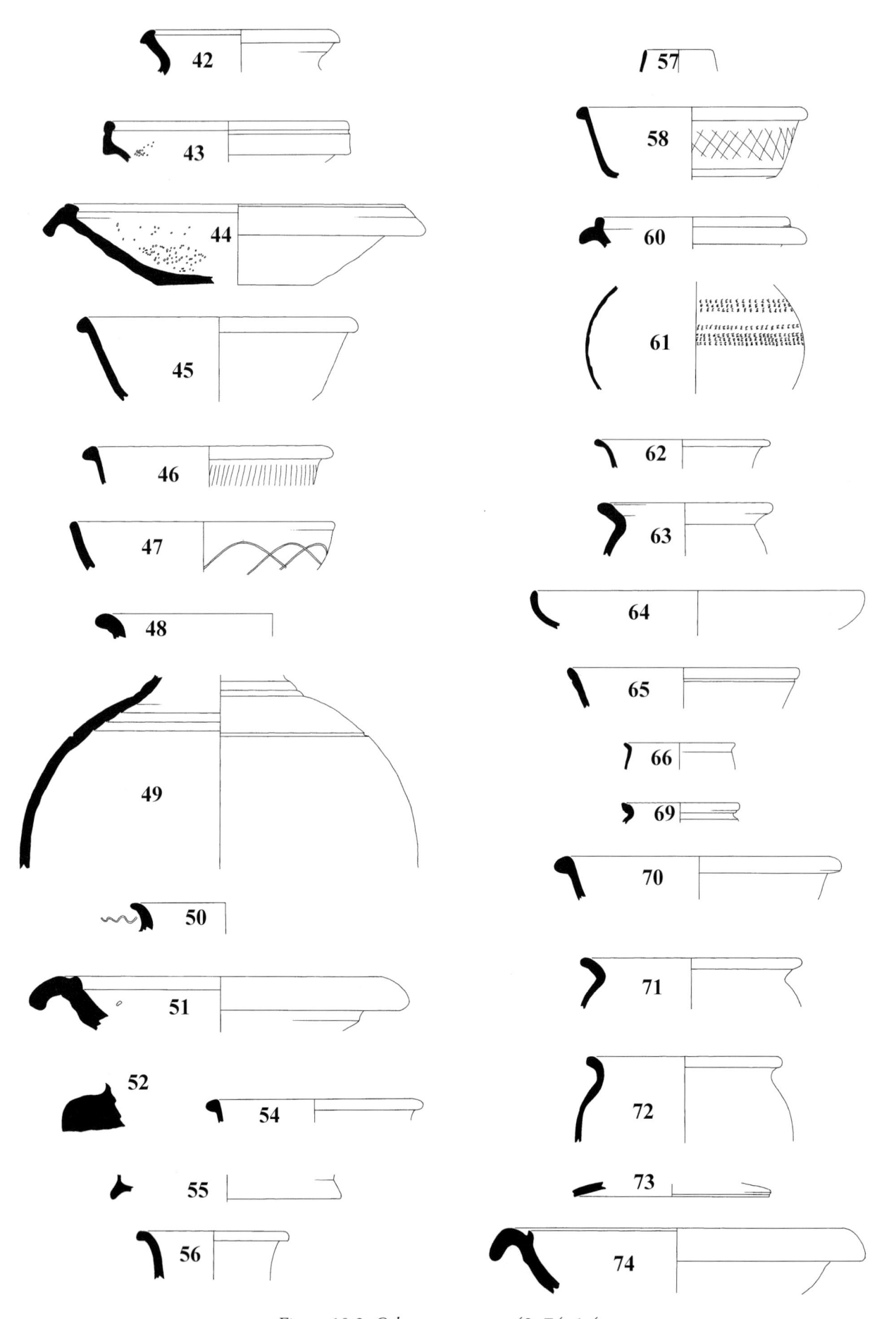

Figure 10.2. Other pottery: nos 42–74, 1:4.

61JX

Total sherds: 6
Coarseware:
51) Mortarium; very pale yellow with slightly darker surface; compact slightly micaceous clay matrix; inclusions: common, quartz *c.* 0.5mm, some red iron-rich grains up to 1.0mm.
52) Fragment of tegula.
TPQ: mid-2nd C.

61OC

Total sherds: 36
Coarseware:
2 wall sherds BB1 jar showing acute angle cross-hatching.
26 wall sherds of Dressel 20 amphora.

61DL

Total sherds: 15
Samian:
2 rim sherds Dr 31R CG.
1 rim sherd Dr 33 CG.
4 other wall sherds samian.
Coarseware:
54) Bowl; sandy black with thin orange-brown surface margins and burnished black surface.
55) Bowl in Crambeck reduced ware (CRA RE).
56) Jar; micaceous dark grey, burnished surface.
TPQ: late 3rd C.

Block 9

60DG

Total sherds: 3
Coarseware:
57) Beaker in Lower Nene Valley colour-coated ware (LNV CC).
Also 1 large wall sherd AM Dr 20.
TPQ: late 2nd C.

60DO

Total sherds: 1
Coarseware:
58) Bowl in BB2 fabric (sherds of this vessel also in 60GF).
TPQ: *c.* AD 160.

60EB

Total sherds: 4
Samian:
1 wall sherd Dr 31R CG.
Coarseware:
1 small rim sherd of a jar in BB2.
1 tiny fragment of a colour-coated beaker (probably LNV CC).
TPQ: *c.* AD 160.

60GF

Total sherds: 6
Coarseware:
58) Bowl in BB2 fabric. (sherds of this vessel also in 60DO).
TPQ: *c.* AD 160.

Block 10

60GA

Total sherds: 1
Coarseware:
63) Jar; gritty pale grey with darker surface.
TPQ: Certainly 3rd C, probably late 3rd C.

Block 11

60EQ

Total sherds: 3

60EA

Total sherds: 4
Coarseware:
60) Bowl, originally in Crambeck Parchment ware (CRA PA), now burnt.
TPQ: *c.* AD 360.

60EG

Total sherds: 7

60EW

Total sherds: 4
Coarseware:
76) Bowl in BB2.
77) Jar: Huntcliff type cooking pot in calcite gritted fabric (HUN CG).
TPQ: *c.* AD 360.

60FB

Total sherds: 7
Samian:
1 wall sherd, unidentifiable form. ?EG.
Coarseware:
78) Bowl in Crambeck reduced ware (CRA RE).
Also:
2 wall sherds calcite gritted jar.
1 wall sherd from a beaker in Lower Nene Valley ware (LNV CC).
TPQ: late 3rd C.

60IG

Total sherds: 11

60IJ

Total sherds: 24
Samian:
64) 1 rim sherd Dr 32 EG.
Coarseware:
65) Bowl in BB2.
Also:
1 wall sherd and 1 base sherd from a jar in calcite gritted fabric.
TPQ: late 3rd C.

60IR

Total sherds: 42
Samian:
1 rim sherd Dr 37 ?EG.
Coarseware:
2 rim sherds from a jar in BB1.

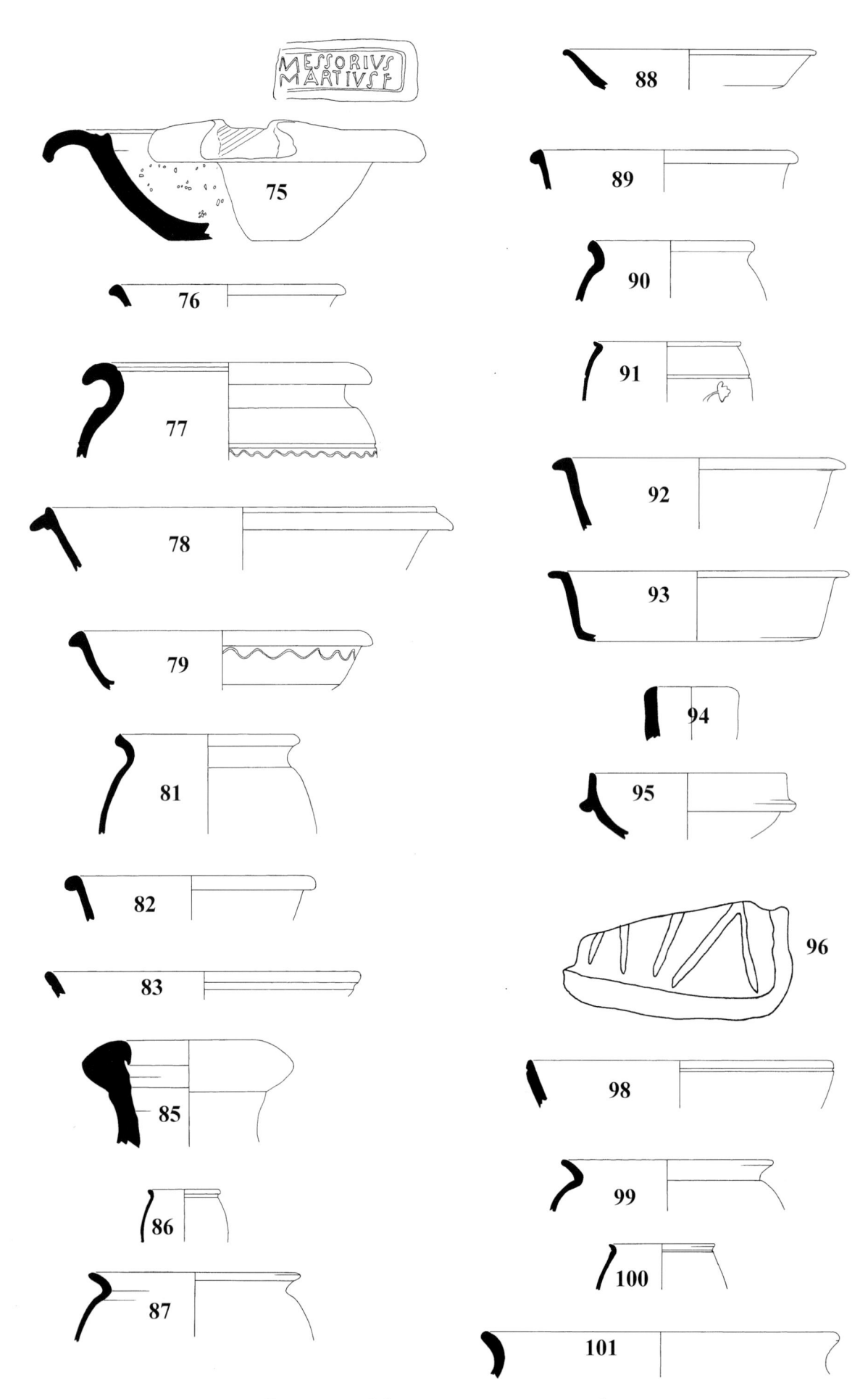

Figure 10.3. Other pottery: nos 75–101, 1:4.

1 small fragment of a mortarium, possibly in a north-western fabric.
TPQ: 2nd C.

60JL
Total sherds: 26
Samian:
1 wall sherd Dr 31R ?EG.
Coarseware:
66) Beaker in Wilderspool fabric (WIL OX).
Also:
1 small rim sherd of grey ware beaker.
1 handle stump and 4 wall sherds from a Dressel 20 amphora.
TPQ: c. AD 160.

60JO
Total sherds: 22
Samian:
1 small incomplete wall sherd from an inkwell, probably EG.
Coarseware:
201) Bowl in BB1.
202) Jar in BB2.
Also:
2 small rim sherds of a jar in BB1.
TPQ: mid-2nd C.

61NQ
Total sherds: 12
Coarseware:
69) Beaker in soft, sandy pale orange fabric; surface abraded.
Also:
1 base sherd from a beaker in orange fabric with an orange brown colour coat.
1 wall sherd from a jar in calcite gritted fabric.
1 wall sherd from a large indented beaker in grey ware.
TPQ: late 3rd C on the basis of the calcite gritted wall sherd.

61OB
Total sherds: 62
Samian:
1 rim sherd Dr 33 CG.
1 rim sherd Dr 37 CG.
1 rim sherd Dr 31 EG.
3 other wall sherds samian.
Coarseware:
70) Bowl in BB2.
71) Jar in BB1.
Also:
1 wall sherd with part of the rim of a hammer-head mortarium in Hartshill-Mancetter fabric.
TPQ: 3rd C.

61PA
Total sherds: 10
1 wall sherd from a jar in BB2 with grouped cross-hatching.
TPQ: mid-2nd C.

61PC
Total sherds: 22
Coarseware:
72) Jar in sandy grey fabric.
73) Lid; hard sandy orange with grey core; dark brown upper surface.
74) Mortarium; sandy orange-brown fabric with grey core; thin cream coloured wash on surface; only a few trituration grits are visible: quartz c. 3.0mm, dark coloured rock fragments c. 3.0–4.0mm and one possible clay pellet 6.00mm.
75) Virtually complete mortarium; sandy orange-brown with a thin cream wash over the rim and external surface (this may originally have extended over the interior as well); trituration grits: angular white quartzite 2.0–7.0mm. Two stamps survive from either side of the spout. One is complete, the other almost so. Both read: MESSORIVS MARTIVS. Hartley (2002a, 342) has recently commented on this potter in her report on material from Catterick. She suggests that he worked in north-east England, perhaps at Corbridge, in the period AD 125–55.
TPQ: c. AD 125.

Block 12

60LS
Total sherds: 2
Coarseware:
79) Bowl in BB2
TPQ: mid-2nd C.

60LV
Total sherds: 19
Samian:
1 rim sherd Dr 33 CG
2 rim sherds, 1 wall sherd Dr 31 CG.
Coarseware:
81) Jar in Derbyshire coarse ware (DER CO).
82) Bowl in BB2.
83) Bowl in BB2.
85) Rim of amphora: south Spanish Dressel 20 (fragments of this vessel also occurred in 60CR).
100) Beaker in Lower Nene Valley Colour-coated fabric (LNV CC).
TPQ: probably mid-3rd C.

Block 13

61CG
Total sherds: 6
Coarseware:
1 small rim sherd from a Jar in BB1, probably 3rd-century AD or later.
TPQ: 3rd C.

61CR
Total sherds: 21
Samian:
1 rim sherd Dr 33.

Coarseware:
- 85) Rim of amphora: south Spanish Dressel 2 (fragments of this vessel also occurred in 60LV).
- 86) Beaker in Lower Nene Valley Colour-coated fabric (LNV CC).

TPQ: late 2nd C.

61DF

Total sherds: 5
Samian:
1 rim sherd, 1 wall sherd Dr 33 CG Hadrianic.
1 wall sherd ?Dr 18/31 CG Hadrianic.
TPQ: Hadrianic.

Block 15

60GO

Total sherds: 14
Coarseware:
- 87) Jar in BB2.

TPQ: mid-2nd C.

61AS

Total sherds: 58
Samian:
- 88) Dr. 18/31 EG.

Also:
2 rim sherds Dr 31 CG.
1 wall sherd Dr 33 CG.
1 wall sherd Dr 37 CG.
Coarseware:
- 89) Bowl in BB2.
- 90) Jar in sandy grey fabric with darker surface.
- 91) Beaker in soft sandy orange fabric. The heavily abraded surface may once have been colour-coated.

Also
1 wall sherd from an indented beaker in Lower Nene Valley Colour-coated fabric (LNV CC).
1 wall sherd from a beaker of form Gillam 70 or 71 in Upchurch Fine Reduced Ware (UPC FR).
TPQ: late 2nd C.

61CP

Total sherds: 44
Samian:
1 wall sherd Dr 18/31 CG.
Coarseware:
- 92) Bowl in fine grey burnished fabric.
- 93) Bowl in BB1.
- 94) Crucible in gritty grey-brown fabric.

Also:
3 fragments tegula.
1 wall sherd from a bag-shaped beaker in orange fabric with a dark brown colour-coat.
TPQ: mid-2nd C.

Block 16

60DU

Total sherds: 1

60EU

Total sherds: 5
Coarseware:
- 96) Small fragment of mortarium rim bearing part of a stamp of ANAVS. Hartley (2002b, 467–8) has recently commented on this potter in her report on material from Catterick. She suggests that he worked in north-east England, probably at Corbridge, and also in the area of Binchester and Catterick, in the period AD 120–60.

Also:
1 large fragment of amphora, form Dressel 20.
TPQ: *c.* AD 120.

60FV

Total sherds: 1
1 small rim sherd of a jar in BB2.
TPQ: Mid 2nd C.

60GS

Total sherds: 2
Coarseware:
1 base sherd from a small bag-shaped beaker in Lower Nene Valley colour-coated ware (LNV CC).
TPQ: late 2nd C.

60HB

Total sherds: 1
Coarseware:
- 98) Dish in BB1.

TPQ: 2nd C.

60LM

Total sherds: 5
Coarseware:
- 99) Jar in BB2.

Also:
1 fragment tegula.
TPQ: mid-2nd C.

Block 19

60DX

Total sherds: 1
Coarseware:
101) Large jar in sandy grey ware.

60FA

Total sherds: 6
Coarseware:
102) Bowl in BB2.
Also:
1 wall sherd from a jar in calcite gritted fabric.
TPQ: late 3rd C on the basis of the calcite gritted ware.

60FO

Total sherds: 2
Samian:
1 wall sherd, form unidentifiable, CG.

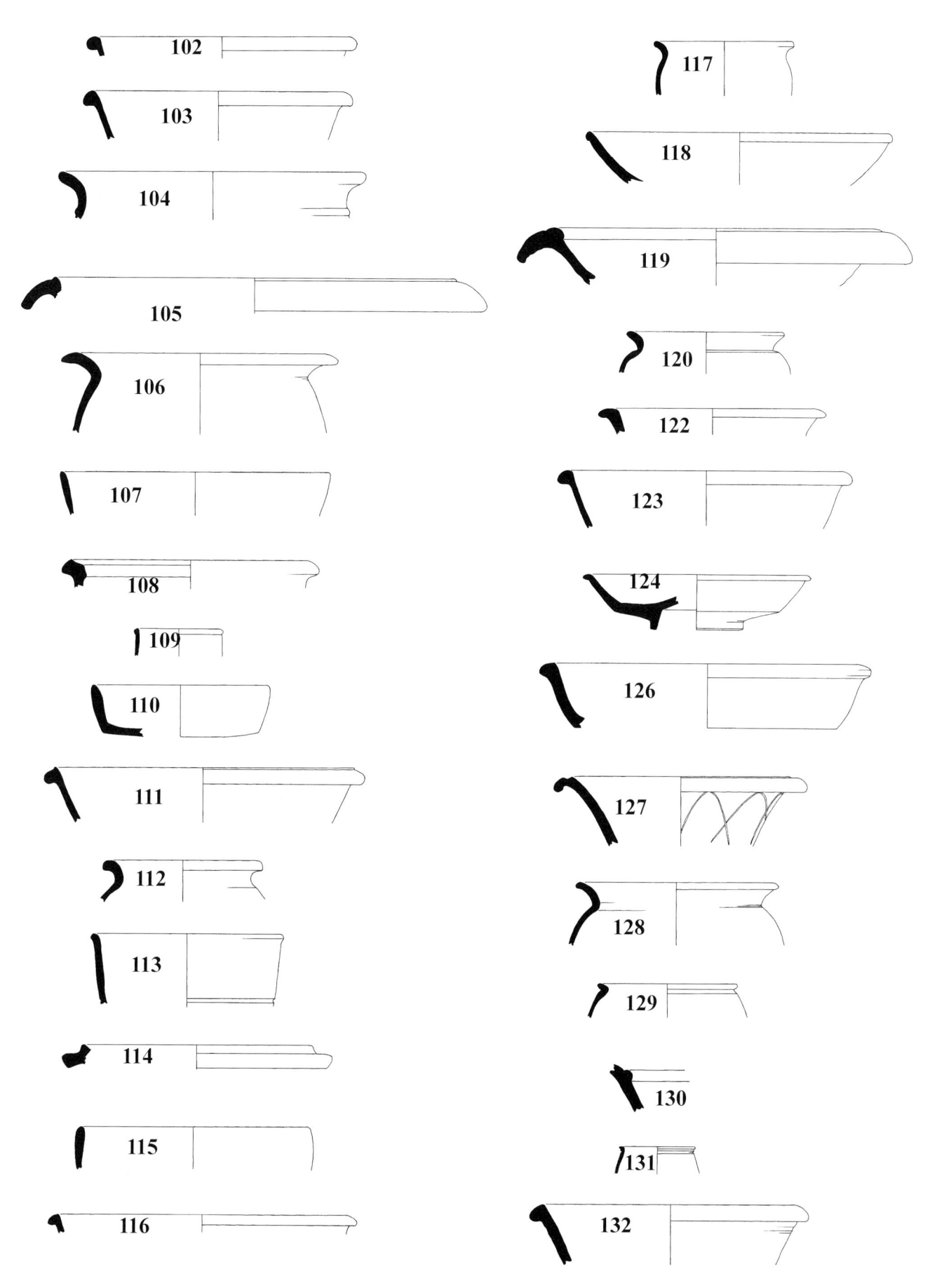

Figure 10.4. Other pottery: nos 102–132, 1:4.

60HU

Total sherds: 1
Coarseware:
1 small rim sherd from a jar in calcite gritted fabric.
TPQ: late 3rd C.

Block 21

60HQ

Total sherds: 25
Samian:
1 rim sherd Dr 31 CG.
1 rim sherd 1 wall sherd Dr 31R CG.
1 rim sherd Dr 18/31R CG.
Coarseware:
1 small rim sherd from a jar in BB2.
TPQ: *c.* AD 160.

Block 22

61CH

Total sherds: 20
Samian:
2 rim sherds Dr 33 EG.
1 rim sherd Dr 33 EG.
Also:
1 fragment imbrex tile.

61CJ

Total sherds: 1
Coarseware:
1 wall sherd from a jar in grey ware.

61CT

Total sherds: 4
Coarseware:
127) Bowl in BB1.
TPQ: late 2nd C on the basis of FV 127.

61DE

Total sherds: 5
Coarseware:
128) Jar in BB2
129) Beaker in Lower Nene Valley colour-coated ware (LNV CC).
TPQ: late 2nd C.

61DM

Total sherds: 36
Samian:
1 rim sherd Dr 33 CG.
1 wall sherd Dr 30 CG.
Coarseware:
103) Bowl in BB2.
104) Jar in a fabric similar to Mucking Black-burnished ware 2 (MUC BB 2). See Bidwell and Speak, 1994, p. 229, fig. 8.7 no. 5.
105) Mortarium in Mancetter-Hartshill White ware (MAH WH).
106) Jar in BB1.
107) Dish in BB2.
108) Huntcliff-type jar in calcite gritted ware.
109) Beaker in fine orange fabric with a red-brown colour-coat (probably Colchester Colour-coated ware 2 – COL CC 2).
TPQ: *c.* AD 360 on the basis of FV 108.

61DO

Total sherds: 1
Samian: 1 wall sherd CG samian.

61DZ

Total sherds: 37
Samian:
1 wall sherd 1 base sherd Dr 37 CG.
Coarseware:
110) Dish in Crambeck Reduced ware (CRA RE).
111) Bowl in BB2.
112) Jar in sandy grey ware.
113) Bowl in grey burnished ware.
114) Bowl in Crambeck Reduced ware (CRA RE).
115) Dish in BB1.
TPQ: late 3rd C on the basis of 110 and 114.

61EA

Total sherds: 27
Samian:
1 rim sherd Dr 33 CG.
1 flange frag Dr 38 ?CG.
Coarseware:
1 wall sherd of a jar in BB1 with obtuse angle cross hatching below a scored line.
TPQ: mid-3rd C on the basis of the wall sherd of BB1.

61EF

Total sherds: 8
Coarseware:
116) Bowl in BB2.
Also:
1 wall sherd amphora, form Dressel 20.
1 fragment of square flat tile.
TPQ: mid-2nd C.

61EN

Total sherds: 13

61EZ

Total sherds: 18

61FV

Total sherds: 5
Coarseware:
117) Jar in BB1.
TPQ: 2nd C.

61GH

Total sherds: 92
Samian:
118) Dr 31, CG
124) Dr 18/31, CG (Les Martres de Veyre fabric – (LMV SA). Sherds from this vessel also in 61HM.
Coarseware:
119) Mortarium; hard, fine pale orange with paler core; thin orange slip on surface. probably Mancetter-Hartshill White ware (MAH WH).

120) Jar in BB2.
122) Bowl in BB1.
123) Bowl in BB2.
TPQ: *c.* AD 180.

61GR
Total sherds: 18

61HM
Total sherds: 10
Samian:
124) Dr 18/31, CG (Les Martres de Veyre fabric – (LMV SA). Sherds from this vessel also in 61GH.
TPQ: *c.* AD 100.

61MS
Total sherds: 3
Coarseware:
126) Bowl in grey burnished ware.

61NG
Total sherds: 20

Block 24

61AU
Total sherds: 3
Coarseware:
131) Beaker in fine buff fabric with orange-brown colour-coat.
TPQ: mid-2nd C.

61AV
Total sherds: 14
Samian:
1 rim sherd Dr 33 EG.
2 rim sherds Dr 31R CG.
1 rim sherd ?Dr18/31R CG.
Coarseware:
1 small rim sherd from a jar in calcite gritted fabric (not a Huntcliff type).
TPQ: late 3rd C on the basis of the calcite gritted rim sherd.

61BT
Total sherds: 26
Samian: 1 rim sherd Dr 31 CG.
Coarseware:
132) Bowl in sandy grey ware.
133) Jar in BB1.
134) Jar in grey burnished ware.
136) Jar in grey burnished ware.
137) Dish in BB1.
TPQ: mid-2nd C.

61LG
Total sherds: 1

61PB
Total sherds: 2
Samian:
1 rim sherd Dr 18/31 CG.

Coarseware:
130) Mortarium in soft, sandy white fabric.
TPQ: *c.* AD 120.

Block 26

60JT
Total sherds: 2
No Featured Vessels.

Block 28

61HO
Total sherds: 2

61HZ
Total sherds: 5
Samian:
1 rim sherd Dr 31R CG.
Coarseware:
1 wall sherd bowl in BB2.
TPQ: *c.* AD 160.

61IU
Total sherds: 6
Samian:
1 wall sherd ?Dr 18/31R CG.

61QA
Total sherds: 6
Samian: 1 wall sherd Dr 31 EG.
Coarseware:
1 rim sherd bowl in BB2.
TPQ: mid-2nd C.

61QJ
Total sherds: 2
Samian:
150) Walters 79, CG.
TPQ: *c.* AD 160.

61QK
Total sherds: 2
Samian:
Dr 18/31 CG.
Coarseware:
1 wall sherd jar in BB2.
TPQ: mid-2nd C.

Block 29

61MA
Total sherds: 42
Samian:
152) Small bowl (Dr 37?) with rouletted decoration, EG.
1 rim sherd 1 wall sherd Dr 31R CG.
Coarseware:
153) Jar in BB2.
154) Beaker in Lower Nene Valley colour-coated ware (LNV CC).
TPQ: 3rd C (?).

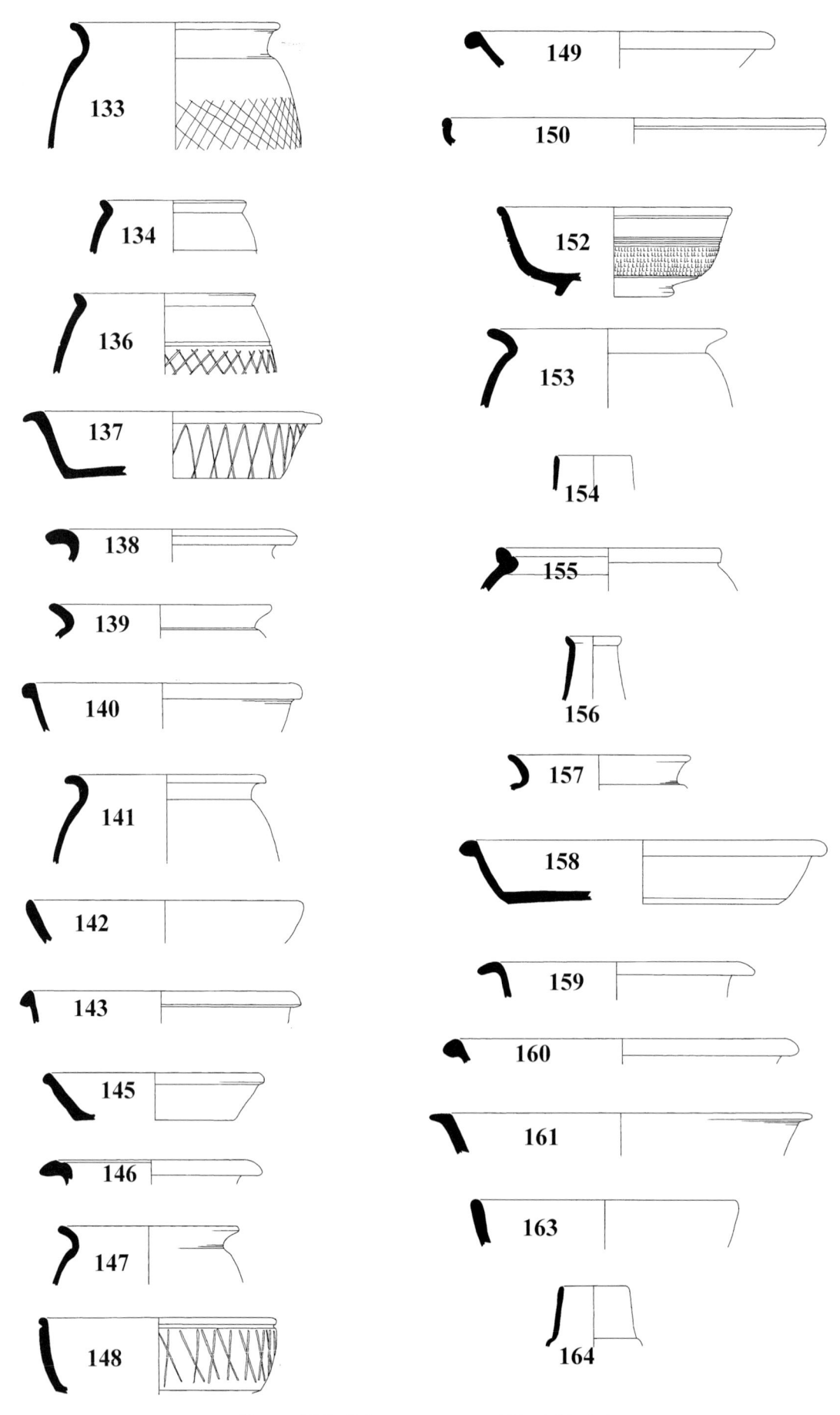

Figure 10.5. Other pottery: nos 133–164, 1:4.

61MU
Total sherds: 5
Samian:
1 wall sherd probably Dr 31R CG.
TPQ: *c.* AD 160 if the samian vessel is a Dr 31R.

Block 32

61AL
Total sherds: 7
Coarseware:
1 wall sherd of a jar in calcite gritted fabric. The sherd shows the pronounced shoulder which is characteristic of the Huntcliff type, but not enough survives to show any of the other characteristics.
TPQ: *c.* AD 360 if the calcite gritted vessel is a Huntcliff type.

61BM
Total sherds: 32
Samian:
1 rim sherd Dr 37 CG.
3 other wall sherds samian.
Coarseware:
155) Jar in the gritty fabric related to Mucking BB2.
156) Beaker in sandy pale yellow fabric with a black colour-coat.
157) Jar in grey burnished fabric.
Also:
1 wall of a jar in calcite gritted fabric.
TPQ: late 3rd C.

Block 36

61EG
Total sherds: 26
Coarseware:
168) Bowl in Crambeck Parchment ware (CRA PA).
Also:
3 wall sherds calcite gritted.
TPQ: *c.* AD 360.

61FL
Total sherds: 1

61FU
Total sherds: 1

61GV
Total sherds: 4
Samian: 1 rim sherd Dr 33 EG with graffito: BIT[---.
Coarseware:
166) Bowl in sandy orange ware.
Also:
1 wall sherd calcite gritted ware.
TPQ: late 3rd C.

61JH
Total sherds: 4
Samian:
1 rim sherd Dr 33 CG.
Coarseware:
1 small rim sherd of a beaker in Lower Nene Valley colour-coated ware (LNV CC).
TPQ: late 2nd C.

61JV
Total sherds: 13
Coarseware:
158) Dish in BB2.
TPQ: *c.* AD 180.

61JY
Total sherds: 10
Coarseware:
160) Bowl in BB2.
161) Bowl in BB1.
TPQ: mid-2nd C.

61KG
Total sherds: 3

61LV
Total sherds: 31
Coarseware:
163) Bowl in BB1.
164) Beaker in Lower Nene Valley colour-coated ware (LNV CC).
165) Bowl in grey burnished ware.
Also:
2 wall sherds calcite gritted ware.
TPQ: late 3rd C.

61MJ
Total sherds: 10
Samian:
1 rim sherd Dr 18/31 or 18/31R CG.
Coarseware:
159) Bowl in sandy grey ware.
Also 1 wall sherd from a jar in BB1.
TQP: *c.* AD 120.

61MP
Total sherds: 11
Samian:
1 rim sherd Dr 31 or 31R CG
TPQ: *c.* AD 150

61MX
Total sherds: 20
Coarseware:
169) Bowl in BB1.
Also:
1 small rim sherd from a flat rimmed bowl in BB1.
1 small rim sherd from a jar in grey burnished ware.
1 wall sherd from a jar in BB2.
TPQ: mid-2nd C.

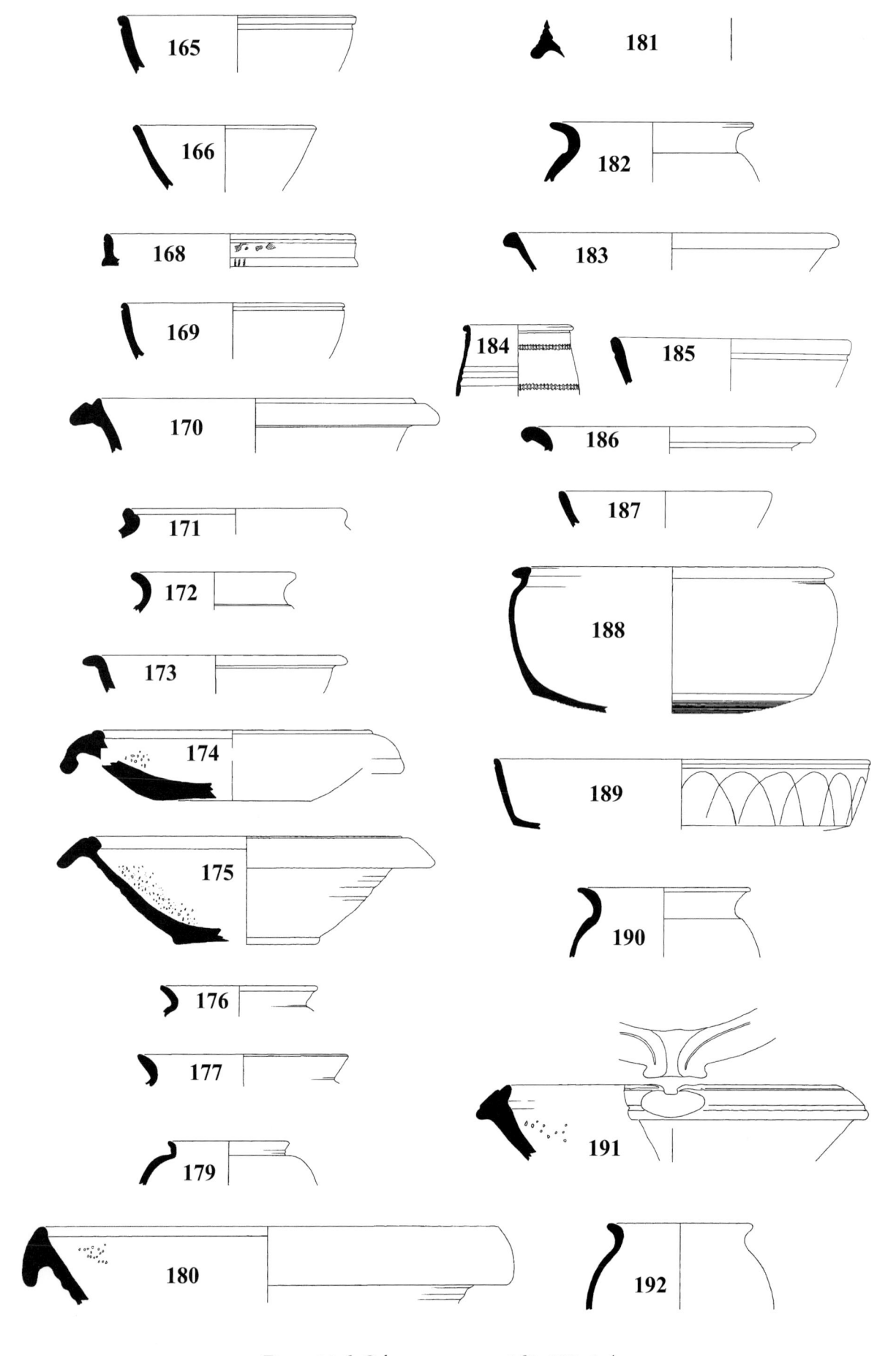

Figure 10.6. Other pottery: nos 165–192, 1:4.

Block 37

61NY
Total sherds: 11
Samian:
1 wall sherd, form unidentifiable.
Coarseware:
170) Bowl in Lower Nene Valley colour-coated ware (LNV CC).
171) Jar in a gritty fabric allied to Mucking BB2.
172) Jar in grey burnished fabric.
TPQ: 3rd C.

61OI
Total sherds: 1
The group has never been located, but the entry in the Finds Book says it contained a fragment of Huntcliff Ware.
TPQ: *c.* AD 360 on the basis of the Finds Book entry.

61OP
Total sherds: 37
Samian:
1 rim sherd Dr 37 CG.
1 rim sherd Dr 37 EG.
Coarseware:
173) Bowl in sandy grey ware.
174) Mortarium in Mancetter-Hartshill White ware (MAH WH).
175) Mortarium in Mancetter-Hartshill White ware (MAH WH).
TPQ: late 2nd C.

Block 38

61CW
Total sherds: 3
Coarseware:
176) Jar in BB2.
TPQ: mid-2nd C.

61CZ
Total sherds: 2
2 wall sherds BB2.

61DC
Total sherds: 1
Coarseware:
177) Jar in grey burnished ware.
TPQ: mid 2nd C.

61EE
Total sherds: 1

61FI
Total sherds: 12
Samian:
2 wall sherds Dr 31 CG.
Coarseware:
1 small rim sherd from a grey ware jar.
6 wall sherds amphora, form Dressel 20.
TPQ: mid-2nd C.

61GY
Total sherds: 1

Block 39

61QE
Total sherds: 6
Samian:
1 base sherd Dr 31 CG.
Coarseware:
179) Jar in BB1.
180) Mortarium in Rhineland White ware (RHL WH).
181) Reeded hammer-head mortarium in Mancetter-Hartshill White ware (MAH WH).
TPQ: 3rd C.

61QF
Total sherds: 8

61QH
Total sherds: 44
Samian:
1 rim sherd 1 wall sherd Dr 31 CG.
Coarseware:
182) Jar in BB1.
183) Bowl in BB2.
184) Beaker in Lower Nene Valley colour-coated ware (LNV CC).
185) Bowl in BB2.
TPQ: late 2nd C.

61QM
Total sherds: 24
Samian:
1 rim sherd Walters 79 EG.
1 wall sherd Dr 31R CG.
Coarseware:
186) Bowl or wide-mouth jar in hard sandy dark grey ware.
187) Dish in BB1.
TPQ: ? mid-3rd C.

61QO
Total sherds: 59
Samian:
3 rim sherds 2 wall sherds Dr 31R EG.
Coarseware:
188) Bowl or cooking casserole in a sandy orange fabric; smoothed surface. Sherds of this vessel also occurred in 61QQ. See Gillam, Type 302. The form can be routinely paralleled in north Africa (see, for example, Dore and Keay, 1989, fig. 45, Type 58 and ff.). The colour and texture of the fabric of suggests that it originated in north Africa though it is difficult to be certain on this point since the inclusions consist of little but quartz. Its date range could be 2nd–4th century.
189) Dish in BB1.
190) Jar in BB1.
TPQ: late 2nd C.

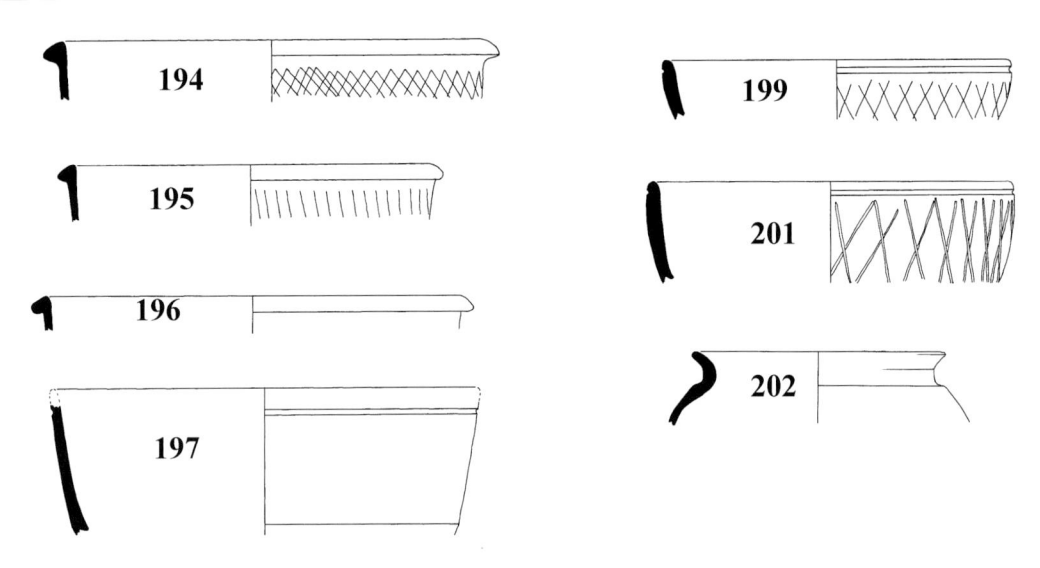

Figure 10.7. Other pottery: nos 194–202, 1:4.

61QP

Total sherds: 35
Samian:
2 rim sherds Dr 31 CG.
Coarseware:
191) Mortarium. This distinctive rim form was made by the potter Bellicus and almost certainly produced at Corbridge.
192) Jar in grey ware.
194) Bowl in BB2.
195) Bowl in BB2.
196) Bowl in BB2.
197) Bowl in BB2.
TPQ: *c.* AD 160.

61QQ

Total sherds: 5
Samian:
1 rim sherd 1 wall sherd Dr 31 CG.
1 rim sherd Dr 31R CG.
Coarseware:
188) Bowl or cooking casserole. See entry under 61QO.
TPQ: *c.* AD 160.

61RE

Total sherds: 1

Block 40

61CL

Total sherds: 3
Coarseware:
199) Bowl in BB1.
TPQ: mid-2nd C.

Block 41

61EC

Total sherds: 2
1 fragment of tile (?tegula).

61EJ

Total sherds: 4
Samian:
1 base sherd Dr 31R EG.
Coarseware:
1 wall sherd jar in calcite gritted fabric.
TPQ: late 3rd C.

11. The Small Finds (Figs 11.1–11.4)

Lindsay Allason-Jones

Illustrations by Sandra Rowntree

Introduction

The lapse in time between the excavations and work on the objects means that a number of artefacts have suffered from a lack of immediate conservation; the limited number of iron objects, for example, is particularly noticeable. Other apparent gaps in the assemblage might indicate that some groups of objects have disappeared in the intervening years rather than simply disintegrated or not been present in the first place. Despite these problems, however, the assemblage from Haltonchesters is valuable for the study of Hadrian's Wall as it includes a remarkable selection of jewellery, both locally made and imported, and a high proportion of cavalry artefacts, the latter confirming the use of the fort by cavalry units for most of the fort's history.

It has not proved possible to plot the precise findspot of most of the artefacts found during the excavations and thus it has not been feasible to assign all the individual artefacts to specific buildings with confidence. There is, however, an interesting grouping of objects which appear to relate to a barrack block on the southern edge of the *via quintana* (Block 28), which includes the pipeclay Venus statuette (No. 200), a gold strip (No. 1), a silver brooch (No. 2), and several other brooches: this may reflect the lifestyle of one, rather wealthy, individual rather than the day-to-day life of ordinary soldiers. There is a further grouping of interest from Block 5, which includes both the cannel coal armlets (apparently made from locally acquired cannel coal: Nos. 188 and 189), and the iron jeweller's anvil (No. 141), as well as an ear-ring (No. 22), a copper alloy armlet (No. 21), and a trumpet brooch (No. 4). This may suggest that the building, at some stage, was used as a jeweller's workshop. In support of the argument that jewellery of various types was being made at Haltonchesters during the Roman period, attention is drawn to a slate former for producing small sheet metal motifs, which was discovered in 1920 (Smith 1922).

The amount and quality of jewellery discovered throughout the fort is worthy of comment as this formed the largest group of objects which could be assigned to a specific purpose. These artefacts were made of precious metals, shale, jet, bone, and glass, as well as copper alloy, and vary in date from the 2nd to the 3rd century AD. Whilst the evidence cited above indicates that some of the jewellery may have been manufactured on site, the wide range of type of brooch, in particular, points to most of the jewellery being brought to the site from other provinces of the Empire.

The second largest group consisted of military artefacts of which 50% were related to cavalry equipment. The non-cavalry specific items were mostly buckles, mounts and binding fragments. The only weapon found was an unusual throwing spearhead (No. 41) and an iron spearhead (No. 144). This lack of weaponry may be the result of the poor survival of iron from the site, but is also not unusual on a Wall fort.

Domestic objects were few in number and all, including the mirror (No. 39), for example, could have been used by either men or women (see Allason-Jones 1995). The only specifically religious item is the pipeclay statuette (No. 200).

The assemblage does include a number of unusual objects. The silver brooch, for example, (No. 2) has not yet been paralleled, whilst the openwork scabbard chape (No. 48) has only one parallel known so far, from Saalburg (pers. comm. E. Deschler-Erb). The enamelled tube (No. 29) has parallels in its decoration but its precise use is unclear.

The objects discovered in the extension cover a wide spread, from a possible silver necklace fastening (No. 3) and a crossbow brooch (No. 13) to a bone needle (No. 183) and a glass inset (No. 195). There are some harness fittings, such as a terret (No. 55), which might indicate that the extension held stabling or was used in part as a corrale, but items of horse harness and cavalry equipment were found scattered throughout the site, as might be expected in a cavalry fort, and the preponderance of domestic artefacts over horse fittings might argue more forcefully for the extension being used for accommodation for people than horses.

Precious Metals (Fig. 11.1)

1. Fine strip of gold, possibly an off-cut. See Iron No. 141.
Surv.L: 30mm, Max.W: 1mm; H61 ET Db/c34

2. Hexagonal silver plate brooch which has had a repoussé silver plate fixed to its face with lead/tin alloy. Little survives of this top plate but enough to suggest that it had a large central oval hole to hold an inset within a beaded border. On the back the hinged pin and the hooked catch survive.

Although both hexagonal plate brooches (Riha 1979, taf. 59, no. 1577) and brooches with applied repoussé silver sheets (Allason-Jones and Miket 1984, no. 3.148) are known from Roman contexts, this particular form has so far defied attempts to find parallels.
W: 38mm, H: 28mm, L of pin: 28mm, L of catch: 9mm; H61 IN Da34

3. Square-sectioned rod with ridge-and-groove decoration ending in a narrow ring. Necklace fastening? Cf Beaurains: Bastien and Metzger 1977, pl. IV, B2 and B3.
Int.D of ring: 13mm, W of ring: 9mm, L of rod: 21mm, T of rod: 8mm; H61 PT

Copper Alloy Objects (Figs 11.1–11.3)

4. Small trumpet brooch. The plain oval head has a shallow groove along its upper edge. A short, circular-sectioned upper bow ends at the waist in stylized, rather angular, acanthus motifs set between transverse ridges. The lower bow is triangular in section and has marginal grooves. The disc foot is cast in one with the body of the brooch and has incised grooves around its lower edge. The catchplate turnover is missing. The spring has two coils on either side of the brooch pin. The spring pin emerges to form a very narrow wire headloop which is confined by a narrow collar decorated with two horizontal grooves. The chord is broken as is the brooch pin.

Brooches of this type are amongst the most common to be found in the Military Zone and can be dated to the late 1st to early 2nd century AD. For comments on the type and local parallels see Snape 1993, 16–7.
Total L: 50mm, W across head: 14mm, W across waist: 8mm, D of foot: 5mm, L of catchplate turnover: 11mm; H60 DQ Da25

5. Incomplete, fragmentary trumpet-and-plate brooch. The small head is decorated with two raised circles, one on either side of the short facetted bow. The waist is covered by a circular plate which is decorated with a concentric design consisting of an outer ring of enamel of unidentifiable colour separated from the inner ring of blue enamel by a ring of reserved metal. There is a reserved metal dot in the centre. The semi-oval-sectioned foot ends in a cupped end and is separated from the lower bow by a ridge. The spring has seven coils and is held within the head by a pin which fits into side lugs. The brooch pin is missing as is most of the catchplate. The whole brooch is distorted.

This form, which is a derivative of the more common trumpet brooch, has a wide distribution but a narrow date range between the mid- and late 2nd century, being most popular in the Antonine period. See Snape 1993, 17 for discussion and local parallels.
L: 52mm, W of plate: 15mm, W across head: 13mm; H61 IM Ea22

6. Incomplete knee brooch with a tubular head which has held a copper alloy spring with an iron spring pin. The bow is a curved strip. The foot, catchplate and pin are missing. This is a somewhat basic version of the late 2nd- to 3rd-century knee brooch form.
Surv.L: 22mm, W of head: 18mm; H60 MA Ec22 343

7. Foot from a knee brooch. The remains of the bow taper markedly to the small flared foot. A fragment of the short catchplate survives. See Snape 1993, 17–8 for discussion of types and dating.
Surv.L: 17mm; H61 QU Fb34 335

8. Knee brooch derivative with a cylindrical head holding an iron spring pin. The bow is short and rectangular in section; it curves forward from the head to a short ridge before curling under to the foot, tapering throughout and giving an angular S-profile. The catchplate expands behind the bow and protrudes below it, with a hooked groove cut into one edge to take the missing pin tip. Casting debris still survives at the edge of the head and bow. A close parallel known from Vindolanda, see Snape 1993, no. 196, is thought to be of 3rd-century date.
Total L: 30mm, W across head: 16mm, Total L of catchplate: 16mm, T of bow: 2mm; H61 PU De34 329

9. Knee brooch with a distorted fan-shaped head, a short hollow bow with shallow facetting, and a splayed foot which is decorated by notches along its lower edge. At the back of the head there are two lugs to take the missing spring; there are traces of rust suggesting that the spring pin was of iron. The catchplate turnover is missing.

This brooch is, strictly speaking, a knee brooch derivative of a type referred to by Snape as the 'knee and fantail' type (Snape 1993, 19, Type 5.2), which

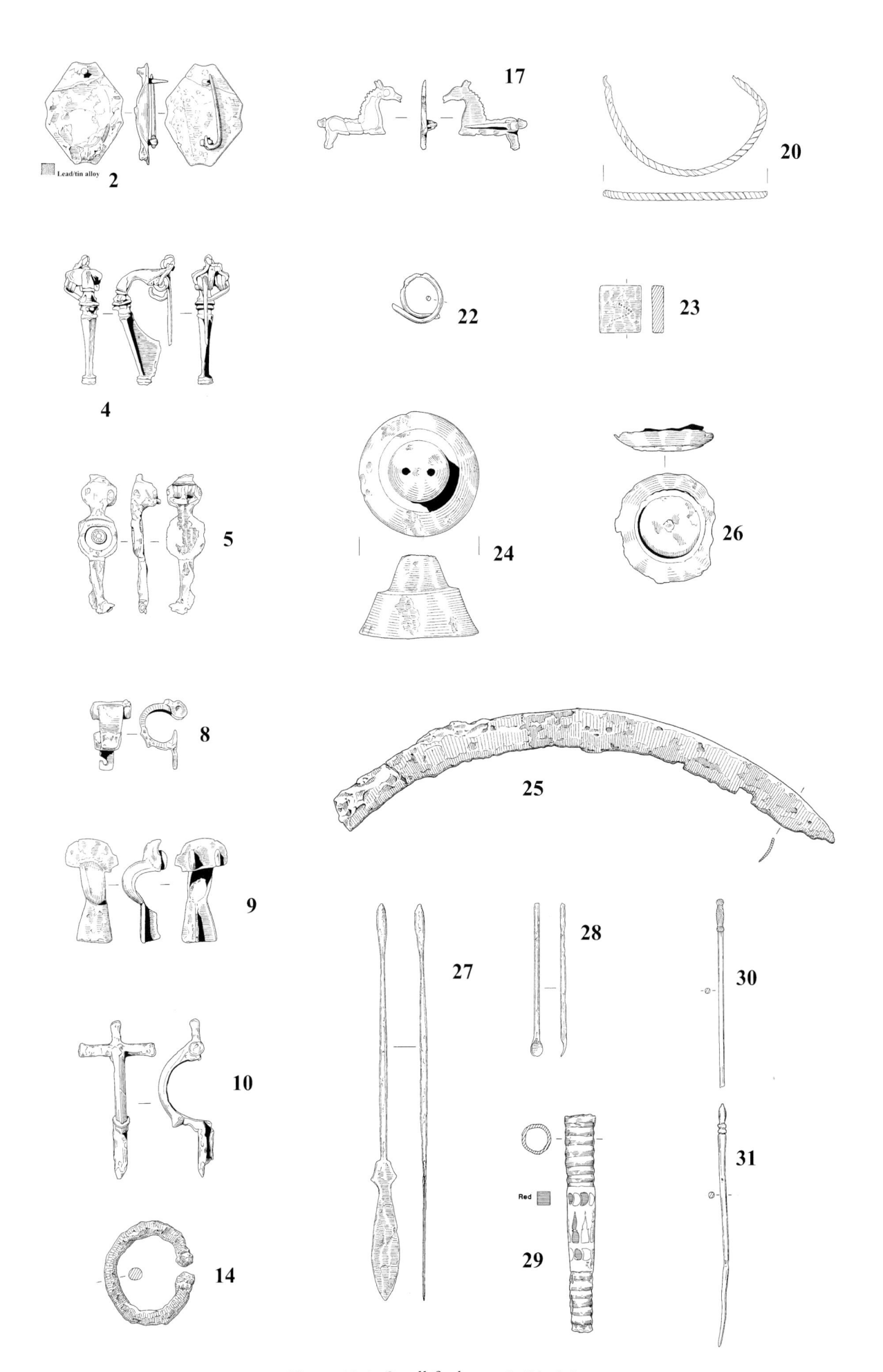

Figure 11.1. Small finds: nos 2–31, 1:2.

Collingwood included in his Group X with other fantailed brooches (Collingwood and Richmond 1969). Once considered a rare form, several examples have now been discovered in the north of England, mostly in 3rd-century contexts, although one example from Carlisle was found in a late 2nd-century context. For a discussion of the dating evidence and local examples, see Snape 1993, 19.
L: 41mm, W across head: 21mm, W across foot: 14mm; H60 GZ Eb25

10. Crossbow brooch with circular-sectioned arms and expanded terminals. The knob is collared. The bow is of semi-oval section with shallow facetting and is separated from the short ovoid foot by a transverse step. The catchplate is tightly curled and does not extend to the end of the pointed foot. Little of the hinged pin survives.
This bears a strong resemblance to a small group of brooches which Snape has included in her Type 8.6 (1993, nos. 81–3) although the shape of the foot suggests the sub-group 8.6B. The date range for the type would appear to be restricted to the 3rd century AD.
L: 61mm, W across arms: 29mm, W across bow: 4.5mm, L of catchplate: 12mm; H61 PT

11. Fragment of a crossbow brooch of a similar type to No. 10 above. The bow is narrow and triangular in section. Only one arm survives of circular section with a splayed terminal.
Surv.L: 31mm, Max.T of bow: 4mm; H61 PT

12. Small crossbow brooch lacking its tubular arms. The upper bow is semicircular in section and ends in a small flange set well down the shank. The short, lower bow flares to a bulge before ending in a narrow, blunt foot with a tubular catchplate. The pin is hinged but incomplete. There are traces of gilding on the bow.
Total L: 42mm, L of catchplate: 17.5m, W of bow: 3mm: H61 ML Ed34

13. Arm of a crossbow brooch of circular section ending in a globular terminal. The broken end has traces of rust suggesting an iron hinge pin.
L: 28mm, D of head: 10mm, T of shank: 6mm; H61 QP 339

14. Penannular brooch with a circular-sectioned shank and collared globular terminals. A groove at the midpoint of the shank indicates where the missing pin was seated. Fowler (1960) Type A3, dated to the 1st to 3rd centuries AD; see Snape 1993 for local parallels.
Int.D: 30 × 25mm, T of shank: 4mm; H61 FS Fa31

15. Fragments of a penannular brooch of circular section. Neither terminal survives but the pin with its plain wrap-around end does remain *in situ*.
Int.D: 26mm, T: 2.5mm, T of pin: 2mm; H61 CC Fa 25

16. Incomplete penannular brooch with a circular-sectioned shank and one milled knob terminal. A fragment of the wrap-around pin survives. Fowler (1960) Type A2, dated to the 1st to 4th centuries AD; see Snape 1993 for local parallels.
Int.D: 20mm, T of shank: 2mm; H60 KX Ec14 344

17. Incomplete plate brooch in the form of a stylized horse. The ears, eyes and muzzle are delineated by incised lines. A fine line also runs down the side of the denticulated mane. Part of the tail and the back leg survive but little of the front leg. The eye and most of the body have cells containing white champlevé enamel. On the back, the hinged pin is set between two small lugs. The catchplate is missing.
This forms part of a series of enamelled plate brooches of zoomorphic form, more commonly found in the south of England, which date to the 2nd and 3rd centuries. See Bateson 1981, 43, fig. 6, Group 15; Riha 1979, Taf. 67, nos. 1762–3, Type 7.25.
Total L: 32mm, Surv.H: 23mm, T of plate: 2mm, L of pin: 19mm, H of lugs: 3.5mm; H60 JN Fb23 336 Fb23

18. Fragments of a copper alloy disc brooch which has had a tin disc attached to the face. The disc is decorated with a repoussé triskele motif and a pelleted border. At the back, part of the catchplate and the spring of the pin survive.
Disc brooches with applied repoussé sheets have a wide distribution in Britain in 2nd-century contexts. The majority have a silver sheet attached by means of lead/tin solder; in analysis, however, this example showed no traces of silver and it would appear that the sheet itself was of tin. See Allason-Jones and McKay 1985, 25, no. 47, for local parallels.
No measurements possible; H61 QU Fb34 332

19. Brooch pin which tapers from a flat looped hinge with a back step.
L: 41mm; H61 FN Ce34

20. Bracelet made from three strands of wire which have been twisted together. The resulting cord has been trimmed and squashed to produce a square section. Neither terminal survives. Allason-Jones and Miket (1984) Type 12, 128.
W: 3mm; H61 QU Fb34 335

21. Narrow strip with one end flattened and rounded with incised transverse lines. Part of a strip bracelet.
Surv.L: 34mm, T: 1mm; H60 EP Ea24; *c.* AD 160

22. Loop of circular-sectioned wire with one tapered end. The whole shank is decorated by incised hoops. Ear-ring of Allason-Jones (1989) Type 2e, although its shape may suggest that this has been cut down from a bracelet of Allason-Jones and Miket (1984) Type 14.
Int.D: 13mm, T: 2mm; H60 CP Eb24

23. Small, square block weight with a V-motif picked out in incised dots on one face. The edges are bevelled.
L: 16mm, W: 18mm, T: 5mm; H61 GR Ee25

24. Bell with straight-walled skirt which meets the domed top with a pronounced step. Two small holes have been punched out of the top from the inside. No trace of the clapper survives.
D of mouth: 46mm, H: 29mm, D of holes: 3mm; H61 MW De22

25. Curved strip which thickens to the surviving edge. Traces of wood adhere to the inner face. Applied rim of a wooden vessel?
Ext.D: 280mm approx., Int.D: 250mm, approx.; H61 HL Ec33

26. Base of vessel with a circular base ring and a prominent lathe-chuck scar on both faces. Too little of the walls survive for positive identification of the form of the vessel.
D of base ring: 26mm; H61 IC Dc34

27. Medical or cosmetic instrument with an oval-sectioned shank which tapers to an olivary probe at one end and a flat, leaf-shaped blade with asymmetrical wings at the other.
  Such *spathomele* are becoming increasingly common finds in military zones throughout the Roman period but, as they are rarely found in association with other instruments, their exact use is difficult to establish: Milne considered them to be pharmaceutical rather than surgical instruments (1907, 58, pl. XII, 2 and 4). For parallels see Kunzl 1982, pls. 3, 35, 46, 57, 68, 78.
L: 170mm, W of blade: 12mm, T of probe: 4mm; H60 IR Ea25

28. Incomplete *ligula* with a circular-sectioned shank and a small, oval, cupped head. See Allason-Jones and Miket 1984, no. 3.458, for local parallels.
L: 58mm, D of shank: 2mm, W across head: 5mm; H61 QO 333; post AD 250.

29. Tapering tube with deep transverse ribs forming a wide band at both ends. The central zone is smooth with three registers of enamelled cells, the outer registers being a series of vertical crescents whilst the inner register consists of elongated triangles. The enamelling in all three registers consists of red alternating with an unknown colour, possibly white. The narrower end is filled with lead, which argues against this being a trumpet mouth-piece such as is known from Corbridge: Bishop and Dore 1989, fig. 80, no. 95. A socket at the wider end may suggest a handle or possibly part of an elaborate candlestick. See Hewitt 1968, pl. Xb, for a strigil handle of comparable type, and Henry 1930, fig. 43, 3–4, for similar enamelled motifs on perfume flasks of 2nd-century date.
L: 191mm, W: 8–13mm; H61 LA Db32

30. Pin with incomplete, circular-sectioned shank. The bead-and-reel head is decorated all over with closely spaced, incised, oblique lines. See Cool (1991) Group 5, most of which come from 2nd-century contexts.
Surv.L;72mm, T: 3mm; H61 CO Ec22/3

31. Complete pin with a circular-sectioned shank and a barrel-shaped head on a double-ridged neck. See Cool (1991) Group 3, which has a very wide date range.
L: 93mm, Max.T: 3mm; H60 BF Dc15

32. Strip of copper alloy of rectangular section, which has been flattened and curled at one end and tapered and bent at the other. Buckle pin?
L: 31mm, W: 2mm, Max.T: 1.5mm; H60 JY Ed25 34b

33. Globular bead.
Int.D: 11mm, Max.D: 19mm, H: 12mm; H61 ML Ed34

34. Group of beads consisting of two facetted barrel beads, a drum bead and a square tubular bead. One incomplete facetted barrel bead and two objects which may be drum beads are also associated.
Facetted barrel beads: L: 17mm, 15mm, 17mm, W: 9mm; drum bead: D: 11mm, L: 5mm; square bead: L: 8mm, W: 6mm; uncertain forms: D: 11mm, 12mm, L: 4.5mm, 8mm; H61 KA Fe34

35 Short ring, bead or collar with convex outer face.
Int.D: 8–10mm, L: 6mm; H60 LS Ec22 338; *c.* AD160.

36. Small barrel bead.
Int.D: 10mm, W: 1.5mm, L: 7mm; H60 KH Dd14

37. Facetted barrel bead or collar.
L: 33mm, W: 13mm; H61 FM Ee25

38. Distorted facetted barrel bead or collar.
L: 32mm, Max.W: 12mm; H61 De22

39 Two rectangular sheets of copper alloy held together by a rivet at each corner and confined by a rolled frame. One sheet is polished and plain, the other has an intricate stamped design arranged in three cells. One cell takes up one half of the sheet and is decorated by a large, lathe-turned circle with a series of smaller concentric circles in the centre around a small hole which was probably made by a compass point or the lathe. The field between the outer circle and the inner series is filled by feathered motifs. Similar motifs form a border and divide the face of the rest of the sheet into two smaller cells, each of which contains compass-drawn dot-and-ring motifs. The rolled frame is decorated by transverse grooves on the decorated face.
  This would appear to be a mirror of a similar type to Lloyd-Morgan's Group T, although the examples given are all circular (1981, 88).
L: 59mm, W: 43mm, Total T: 5mm; H60 FB Ea24

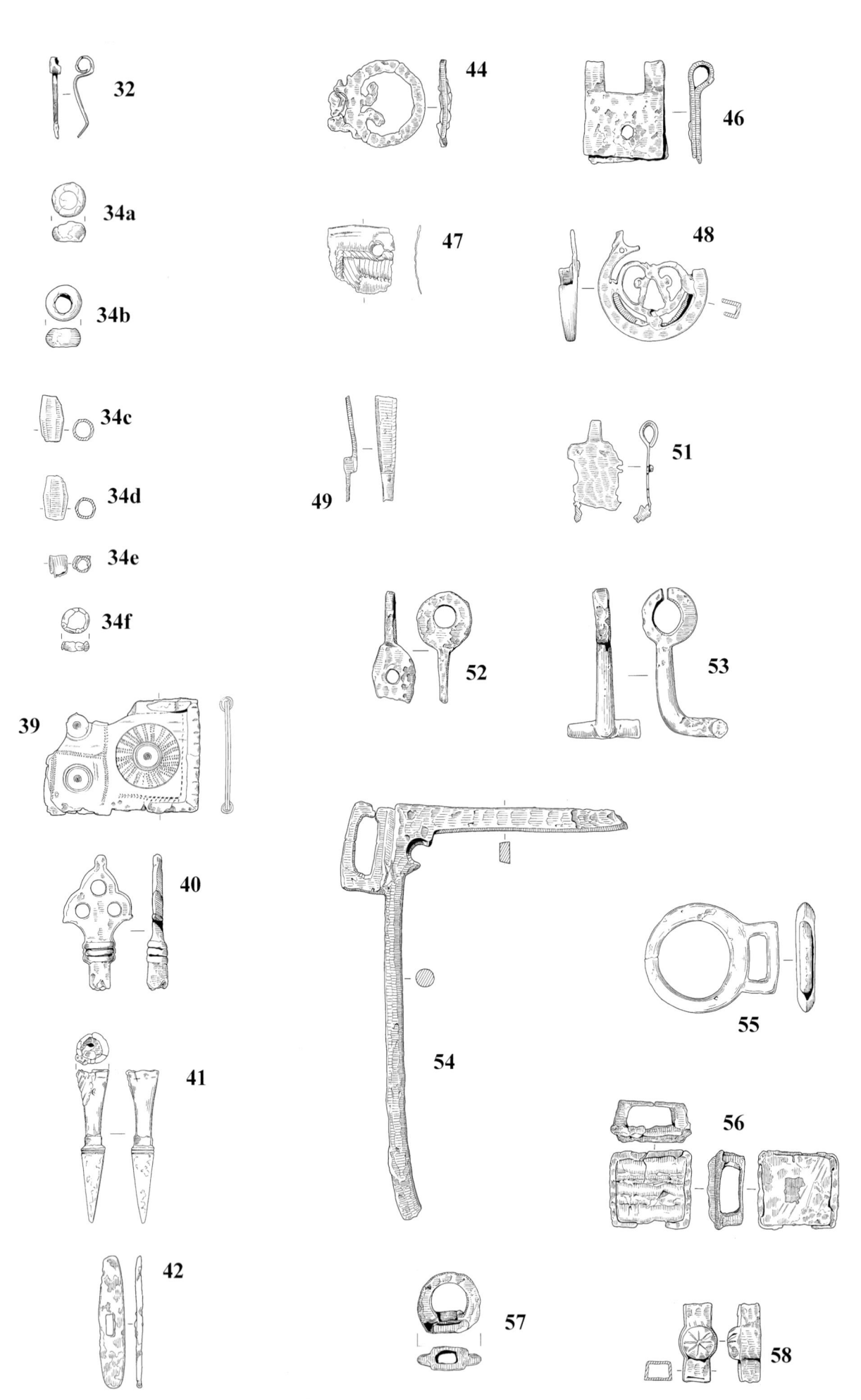

Figure 11.2. Small finds: nos 32–58, 1:2.

40. *Fleur-de-lis* key handle with a tubular shank to hold the missing key. A band of three wide ribs divides the two elements. Examples found on the German *limes* suggest that such key handles can be dated to post-AD 150: *ORL* 8, Taf. 12, 51, and locally found examples do not appear to dispute this date.
L: 52mm, W: 27mm, Max.T: 9mm; H60 spoilheap.

41. Elongated, solid pyramid with a stepped neck and a flared conical socket. Both the base of the pyramid and the socket have incised lines. The socket is filled with lead and the surface appears to have been tinned: analysis shows 3.6: 1 Cu: Pb with small amount Su and Zn. There are traces of wood adhering to the outer surface of the socket.
   Recent research by Petculescu (1991) suggests that this is the head of a throwing spear of a type rarely found outside Dacia and dateable to between 170 and 260/270 AD.
L: 56mm, Ext.D of socket: 12mm, Max.W of head: 9mm; H60 KR Dc34

42. Elliptical dagger guard with a rectangular socket cut from the back with the edges left untrimmed.
L: 50mm, W: 10mm, hole: 8 × 3mm; H61 DL Ea22

43. Incomplete oval dagger or knife guard with a rectangular socket.
W: 16mm, W of socket: 5mm, T: 1mm; H60 FS Fa31

44. Circular buckle with a rectangular-sectioned ring inlaid with squares of alternate white and blue enamel. Two curls project into the interior of the buckle. The hinge pin is of iron and fits between two very narrow projecting lugs. A fragment of bronze sheet is wrapped around the hinge pin.
   An almost exact parallel from Kaiseraugster Unterstadt has been dated to the late 1st/early 2nd century AD on literary evidence (Deschler-Erb *et al* 1991, Abb. 40, no. 26) See also a similar buckle from Richborough decorated with triangles of enamel (Bushe-Fox 1949, pl. XXXIII, no. 73).
Int.D: 24mm, Total L: 37mm, Total W: 32mm; H61 GI Ea22 South Well

45. D-shaped buckle of oval section with a narrow groove for the pin seating.
W: 40mm; H61 FS Fa31

46. Buckle plate made by folding a rectangular sheet in half and cutting a rectangle from the fold. A circular rivet hole cuts through the centre of both halves of the plate to hold a missing leather strap in position.
L: 39mm, W: 31mm; H61 EX Ee34

47. Fine sheet with one original, straight, thickened edge surviving. Repoussé decoration incorporating an outer cabled rib with incised emphasis and an inner row of dimples containing a zone of incised lines, forms a wide frame set back from the edge. The frame describes a right angle. A rough hole has been cut through with little regard for the decoration.
   Although little survives, it is possible that this may be part of a 2nd-century AD decorated breastplate for mail or scale armour: see Bishop and Coulston 1989, fig. 33.
L: 26mm, W: 25mm, T: 0.5mm; H61 DJ Ea32

48. Openwork scabbard chape of peltate shape and containing a peltate motif within a flat border. Two small rivets pierce the openwork design with a third in the surviving arm. Only part of the back survives, also pierced by a rivet hole.
   Openwork chapes are not common finds in Roman Britain although fragments are known of two from Corbridge (Corstopitum Site Museum nos. 75.619 and 75.620). On the Continent there is a type which has an openwork motto: AQUIS HE(LVETICUS) GEMELLIANUS F(ECIT), running down the front of the scabbard and into the chape; this example clearly does not form one of this group although it is in a similar tradition. For an example of the Gemellianus type see Drack and Fellmann 1988, Abb. 328.
W: 43mm, Total surv.H: 42mm, Max.T: 7mm; H61 LA Db32

49. Fragment of a scabbard runner with a tapering face with chamfered edges and two transverse grooves above the step. This is from a common form of scabbard runner used in the north-west provinces in the late 2nd-early 3rd centuries AD. See Allason-Jones and Miket 1984, no. 3.646 for local parallels.
Surv.L: 38mm, Max.W: 8mm; H61 PK Db34

50. Terminal from a scabbard runner of similar type to No. 49 above, expanding to the pointed end. A single circular-sectioned shank projects from the back.
L: 25mm, Max.W: 7mm; H61 DS Ea22

51. Incomplete pendant with a curled strip hook and a vestigial rib in the centre of the plate. Although none of the edges survive, there is enough to suggest that this was a vine-leaf harness pendant of Bishop's (1988) Type 4, possibly Type 4d.
L: 34mm, W of hook: 4mm; H60 KE Dd/e14

52. Harness link(?) consisting of a rectangular plate with a central circular hole with a circular loop projecting at right angles from one edge.
L: 40mm, W of plate: 16mm, W of ring: 20mm; H61 EX Ee34

53. Harness fastening consisting of a curved, oval-sectioned rod which ends in a T-bar with tapering arms. The other end has a large penannular ring of rectangular section, set at right angles to the shank. See Allason-

Jones and Miket 1984, no. 3.762 for German parallels.
L: 59mm, W across T-bar: 28mm, Ext.D of ring: 22mm, W of ring: 4.5mm; H60 IV Fb34.

54. Part of a hackamore. One arm is oval in section, the other rectangular. Inside the angle there is a projecting crescent whilst on the outer edge there is a projecting rectangular loop.
See Bishop 1988, fig. 25 for an illustration of how this fitted to the reins and bit. Cf Housesteads: Rushworth 2009, 2, 443–4, fig. 14.8, no. 81
L: 160mm, T of arms: 4–8mm, rectangular loop internally: 21 × 8mm; H60 GS Ee14/Fa14

55. Ring terret of triangular section which tapers away from the projecting rectangular loop.
Terrets have been discussed by Leeds 1933, 118–26, and MacGregor 1976, 38–48. Close parallels to this 1st-century example have been found at Muircleugh in Berwickshire (MacGregor 1976, no. 59) and Housesteads (museum collection, unpubl.).
Total L: 50mm, Int.D: 29mm, W of ring: 5–7.5mm, W of loop: 27mm, interior of loop: 18 × 7mm; H61 QO 331; post AD 250.

56. Rectangular rein trace with heavily ridged face set back from the rim. There are wide openings for the straps in all four walls. The back is flat and plain and has an L-shaped hole which appears to have been roughly cut out from a shallow trough but may be a casting flaw.
Face: 31 × 30mm, H: 15mm, openings: 15–19mm; H61 LA Db32

57. Swivel ring(?) of triangular section. The thick rectangular block is offset, deeper on one side and pierced by a rectangular slot.
Int.D: 14 × 11mm, plate: 9 × 12mm, slot: 9 × 4mm; H60 EN Eb44

58. Hollow tube with short, flared, rectangular-sectioned arms projecting from a central dome. The back is flat and plain. The convex face has an incised line across each end and a series of radiating grooves on the dome. The interior is filled with charcoal. Harness trace?
L: 30mm, Max.W: 15mm, Max.H: 12mm; H61 PU De34 330

59. Oval mount with an openwork triskele motif of two trumpets, flat at the back but facetted on the face. No trace survives of any means of attachment. Triskele openwork mounts have appeared in various forms on most of the Wall forts and the discovery of moulds for making such mounts have been found at Turret 26a (Allason-Jones 1988) and Newcastle fort (Allason-Jones and Dungworth 1997). Most can be dated to the end of the 2nd century or beginning of the 3rd.
L: 32mm, W: 18mm; H61 IF Fd34

60. Triskele openwork stud of heavier type than No. 59 and with three trumpets rather than two. Two shanks project from the back, each piercing a disc washer.
L: 35mm, W: 19mm; H61 DZ Ee25; late 3rd century AD.

61. Fragment of an elongated openwork belt-tag. Cf Oldenstein 1977, Taf. 41, nos. 394–5.
L: 28mm, W: 7mm; H61 De22

62. Fragment of an elliptical stud with a high central boss and one surviving trilobate terminal with a stamped dot decoration. The edge of the body has a series of notches. A short roved shank projects from the back. Cf Corbridge: Bishop and Dore 1989, no. 204 for parallels.
Surv.L: 26mm, Max.: 12mm, Total H: 10mm; H60 CS Ea14; late 2nd century AD.

63. Cylindrical stud with heavily banded wall. A rectangular-sectioned shank projects from the top and is pierced by a small circular hole. The stud is countersunk with a shallow central boss. Elaborate version of a Type 2 bell-shaped stud (Allason-Jones 1985).
L: 31mm, D: 18mm, hole: 3mm; H61 IM Ea22

64. Bell-shaped stud with a rectangular-sectioned shank cast in one with the head. The skirt is short with incised lines around the outer and inner edges. A shallow rib runs around the central boss. Allason-Jones 1985, Type 2.
L: 39mm, W of shank: 7mm, T of shank: 6mm, D of face: 18mm; H61 QO 340

65. Skirt from a bell-shaped stud of Allason-Jones (1985) Type 1. The iron shank is entirely missing. The skirt is plain with a vestigial waist. The face is concave with a central dimpled cone.
Surv.L: 9mm, D: 25mm; H60 GG Eb25

66. Tube of semi-oval section with a flat back and facetted face. The tube expands in the centre at both ends. Two stemmed loops project from one edge. Cf Oldenstein 1977, Taf. 73.
L: 38mm, W: 12mm, H: 8mm, Int.D of loops: 3.5mm; H60 HQ Fb24; post AD 160.

67. Elongated 'acorn' pendant with a large flat ring and a conical terminal. Cf Oldenstein 1977, Taf. 42, nos. 413–6.
L: 48mm, Max.W: 14mm, Max.T: 12mm; H61 IA Dc34

68. Oval terminal separated from its rectangular-sectioned strip by a shallow step. The rivet hole through the terminal has been drilled. Possibly from a helmet strengthener or harness?
L: 19mm, D of hole: 5mm; H61 DK Eb44

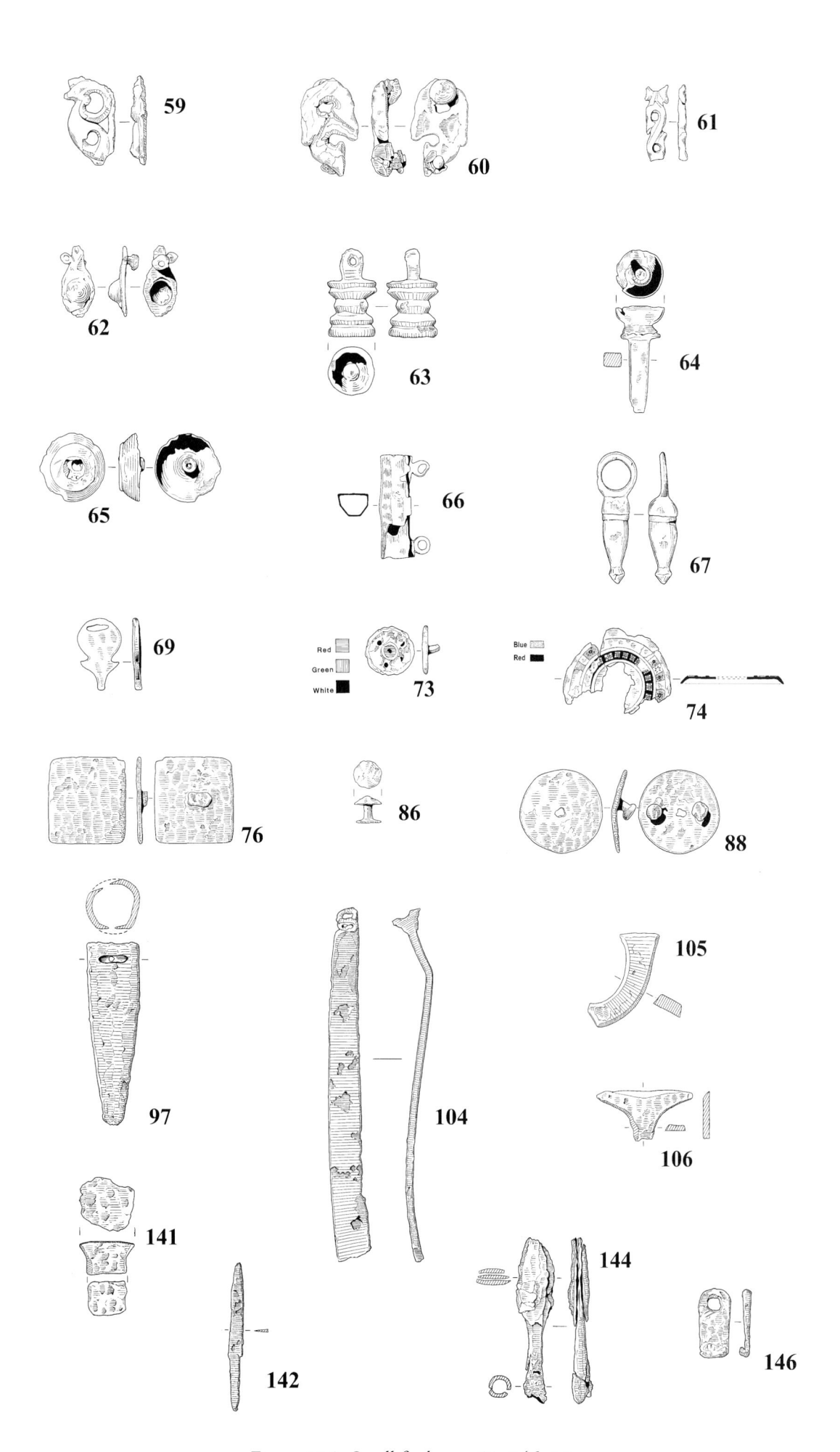

Figure 11.3. Small finds: nos 59–146, 1:2.

69. Flat oval plate with a rectangular slot cut out near the edge. From the opposing edge a winged projection leads to a broken rectangular-sectioned shank.
L: 26mm, W: 17mm, T: 2mm, slot: 8 × 2.5mm; H60 GZ Eb25

70. Fragment of U-sectioned binding.
L: 48mm, W: 5mm; H60 KI Ec14

71. Fragment of U-sectioned binding.
L: 14mm; H60 KF Ec14

72. Fragment of U-sectioned binding with traces of wood left in the channel.
L: 49mm, W: 5mm; H61 GF Db25

73. Disc stud with a short, circular-sectioned shank. The face is divided into two main zones by a circle of reserved metal which encloses red enamel with a central white enamelled dot. The outer zone has a complex enamelled motif but no reserved metal cells. The pattern appears to consist of a background of green enamel with a series of white dots contained in red/orange enamel circles. The edge of the face is raised to hold the enamel; this decorative tradition can be seen on both brooches and studs of the 2nd century. See Bateson 1981, fig. 5, no. 5.
D: 18mm, T of head: 2mm, Surv.L of shank: 4mm; H60 LS Ec22 337; post AD 160.

74. Fragmentary disc stud with a bevelled edge. The face is divided into concentric zones by reserved metal rings. The central circular field has traces of blue enamel; the second field has chequerboard motifs of blue and white set in a red background; the outer field has blue squares with red and white 'flowers' alternating with white squares with a small blue motif. No shank survives.
   See Bateson 1981, 53, who comments that 50% of the known examples have been found in the north of Britain, with the majority coming from military sites.
Est.D: 4.5mm; H Dc15

75. Small disc stud with a raised edge and a central boss. No trace of enamel or niello survives in the channel. A short shank projects from the back. See Corbridge: Bishop and Dore 1989, fig. 86, nos. 182 and 187–8, for enamelled and nielloed examples.
D: 10mm; H61 CM Db25; post AD 360

76. Square stud with rounded corners. A thick rectangular shank projects from the back but is broken close to the head. Possibly a button-and-loop fastener of Wild's (1970) Type VIb, for which he postulates a centre of manufacture near Hadrian's Wall and at Traprain Law during the 2nd century AD.
L: 30mm, W: 28mm, T: 1.5mm; H61 Db25

77. Fragments of a shallow domed stud head with lead/tin caulking and an iron shank.
D: 24mm; H60 LW Fa32

78. Small, domed head with a circular-sectioned shank.
D: 15mm, T of shank: 5mm; H61 DS Ea22

79. Domed stud head with lead/tin caulking preserving the shape of the missing rectangular-sectioned iron shank.
D: 18mm, H: 5mm; H61 CB Fa25

80. Domed stud head or boss with a flanged edge. Traces of lead survive on the inner face.
D: 32mm, H: 7mm; H61 EQ Ea22

81. Disc of copper alloy with an iron disc attached to it by corrosion. Stud?
L: 30mm, Total T: 5mm; H60 LH Ea24 348

82. Incomplete disc stud head.
D: 18mm; H61 KS Dc32

83. Incomplete, large disc stud with a short shank and traces of wood adhering to the back.
D: 45mm; H61 DM Ee25

84. Fragment of a disc stud with a broken, oval-sectioned shank.
Est.D: 24mm; H60 KE Dd/e14

85. Incomplete disc stud with a rectangular-sectioned shank.
D: 25mm; H61 MM De22

86. Small stud with a solid, conical head, oval-sectioned shank and disc rove.
H: 10mm, D of head: 10mm, D of rove: 9.5mm, D of shank: 3mm; H61 EZ Ee25

87. Small stud with conical head and a rectangular-sectioned shank.
D: 15mm, H: 17mm, T of shank: 2.5mm; H U/S

88. Disc stud with distorted head. A roughly rectangular hole has been cut through between the two disc-headed shanks.
D: 29.5mm, hole: 4 × 3mm, L of shanks: 6mm; H61 BG Ea22

89. Hollow dome with traces of lead/tin caulking inside. Studs with copper alloy domed heads and iron shanks fixed into position with lead/tin caulking are found on most of the forts on Hadrian's Wall.
D: 31mm, H: 7mm; H61 IH Db34

90. Large domed stud head which is filled with iron corrosion.
D: 26.5mm; H Ea23 349

91. Circular, domed stud with a circular-sectioned shank and lead/tin caulking.
D: 29mm; H61 De22

92. Crushed domed stud head with lead/tin caulking and an iron shank.
D: 22mm; H61 EI Ee34

93. Incomplete domed stud head with the shank torn out.
D: 24mm; H60 JC Fa24

94. Incomplete and distorted stud with a flat head and a short, tapering, rectangular-sectioned shank holding fragments of wood.
L of shank: 15mm; H60 EI Ed25

95. Fragment of a stud with a circular-sectioned shank.
H: 8mm, T of shank: 5mm; H Ea22

96. Incomplete washer with a slightly convex face.
Ext.D: 47mm, Int.D: 18mm; H61 PT

97. Conical ferrule with two opposing circular holes set in elliptical troughs.
L: 63mm, Int.D: 14mm, T: 3mm, holes: 2mm; H61 NQ Fb34; post late 3rd century AD.

98. Incomplete, oval-sectioned tube.
L: 28mm, W: 15mm; H61 PT

99. Incomplete, hexagonal-sectioned tube with one end closed.
L: 21mm, D: 14mm; H61 JZ Fd34

100. Small, incomplete, circular-sectioned tube, closed at one end.
Surv.L: 24mm, D: 10mm, T: 1mm; H61 DY Ec34

101. Squashed cone from a ferrule or barrel bead.
L: 22mm, H Ea22

102. Small loop of wire with the shanks nipped together.
L: 13mm, T: 2.5mm; H61 BR Ea22

103. Hook of elliptical section, narrowing through the curve.
L: 15mm, Max.T: 7mm; H61 BM Ea32

104. Rectangular-sectioned strip which tapers to a looped end set at right angles to the shank. Distorted.
L: 129mm, Max.W: 13mm, Max.T: 3mm; H60 QE Ea23

105. Curved bar of trapezoidal section with a splayed end. The back is flat.
L: 40mm, Max.W: 16mm, T: 5mm; H61 EY Dd34

106. Strip ending in a splayed terminal. The long edge is chamfered but the other edges are rough as if they have been cut from a sheet. Possibly an offcut rather than an object.
L: 19mm, W across terminal: 36mm, T of shank: 4mm; H61 EQ Ea22

107. Strip with parallel sides and a rounded end which is pierced by a small, off-centre, circular hole.
Surv.L: 27mm, W: 17mm, T: 1mm; H61 Fb34

108. Fragment of a rectangular(?) plate with a convex face, concave back and thickened edge.
L: 42mm, T: 2mm; H61 GM Ec34

109. Roughly circular sheet with a disc-headed rivet through the centre, bent through 90°.
W: 16mm, L of rivet: 12mm; H61 JG Ec31

110. Two fragments of copper alloy, neither of which retain their original shape, rivetted together by an iron rivet and holding fragments of leather. One sheet has part of an incised circle on the face.
Total T: 5mm; H60 FS Ea24

111. Curved strip with parallel edges and lead/tin alloy on one face.
L: 32mm, W: 19mm, T of copper alloy: 2mm; H60 KY Ec14

112. Two strips bent to enclose an object 14mm thick. Part of a collar?
T: 1mm; H61 PT

Copper alloy sheets and strips

113. H61 LC Db33 Distorted. L: 30mm, W: 12mm, T: 1mm

114. H61 HL Ec33 Distorted. L: 61mm, W: 15mm, T: 2.5mm

115. H61 DS Ea22 Irregular edges. L: 55mm, W: 8mm, T: 1mm

116. H Dc34 Two sheets. L: 34mm, 24mm

117. H61 PT Crumpled. L: 27mm

118. H61 EH Ee25 Parallel edges, rounded end. L: 20mm, W: 11mm

119. H61 GB Dd34 Curved. L: 40mm, W: 24mm, T: 1mm

120. H61 PT Crumpled. No measurements possible.

121. H61 ML Ed34 Folded. L: 24mm

Rings

122. H61 PT Incomplete, semi-circular section. Int. D: 11mm, T: 5mm

123. H61 DU De25 Annular, oval section. Int.D: 24mm, W: 4mm, T: 3.5mm

124. H61 KQ Ec31 Penannular, triangular section, one pointed terminal. Int.D: 9m, W: 22m, T: 3mm

125. H61 Ea Annular, circular section. Int.D: 16mm, W: 3.5mm, T: 3.5mm

126. H61 EX Ee34 Annular, circular section. Int.D: Fc21 21mm, T: 3mm

127. H61 LA Db32 Annular, convex face, concave back. Int.D: 20mm × 17mm, W: 7–8mm, T: 3mm

128. H61 EJ Fc21 Annular, rectangular section. Int.D: 12mm, W: 3mm, T: 2mm

129. H60 LO Ea24 Incomplete, square section. Int. D: 15mm, T: 2mm

130. H60 EK Eb44 Incomplete, rectangular section. Int.D: 15mm, W: 2.5mm, T: 3mm

Rods

131. H61 NT Ed31 Rectangular section. L: 48mm, W: 8mm, T: 4mm

132. H61 PU De34 Tapered, circular section. L: 22mm, Max.T: 2mm

133. H61 EQ Ea22 Tapered, rectangular section. L: 53mm, W: 6mm, T: 5mm

134. H61 GX Da34 Circular section. L: 19mm, T: 2.5mm

Nails

135. H61 FY Ec25 Rectangular-sectioned shank and globular head. L: 24mm, D of head: 6mm

136. H61 MV Fa34 Circular-sectioned shank and globular head. L: 27mm, D of head: 9mm

137. H60 LT Ed25 342 Rectangular-sectioned shank with solid domed head. L: 20mm, D of head: 7mm

138. H61 IJ Fb34 Headless shank of nail or rivet. L: 17mm

139. Curved rod of circular section. Possibly distorted nail shank.
Int.D: 68mm, T: 7mm; H61 NQ Fb34

140. Fragment of molten copper alloy.
H61 QH 334

Unidentified copper alloy was found in the following contexts:

H60 IY Ea14	H61 DZ Ee25
H60 KD Ec14	H61 EQ Ea22
H60 KT Ec14	H61 FI Ee23
H60 KU Ec14	H61 GI Ea22
H61 AE Ea32	H61 GN Ea22
H61 AN Ed24	H61 HJ Ed24
H61 CN Ec22/3	H61 JH Ec35
H61 CS Ea22	H61 MM De22
H61 CU Ea22	H61 PR Db34
H61 CZ Ee22	H61 PS De34
H61 DL Ea22	H61 PT QQ
H61 DS Ea22	H Ee34
H61 DZ Ea22	H61 Ed24

Iron Objects (Fig. 11.3)

Note: the condition of the iron retrieved from Haltonchesters is generally poor. In the case of the material found in 1960–1, the lack of immediate conservation has exacerbated the situation and little now survives in an identifiable state.

141. Solid iron block with a rectangular-sectioned shank which ends in a flat base. The slightly domed head is roughly rectangular in shape.

This piece appears to be complete in itself and deliberately fashioned. Its form suggests a miniature anvil and indications that the head has been struck by metal tools on a number of occasions confirms that this was not intended to be a votive miniature but usable equipment. Manning (1985, 1–4) discusses a number of large blacksmith's anvils, of which the example from Hasholme in Yorkshire is closest to this piece in shape (see Manning 1975, 67–9 for detailed description). A closer parallel in size is known from Moosberg bei Murnau (Bayerische Handelsbank 1994, 137).

The evidence of striking on the head is limited, which may indicate that this block was not used for smithing small iron objects but items in softer metals such as bronze, silver or gold. The discovery of a fine slate former for producing small sheet metal motifs at Haltonchesters in 1910 (Smith 1922) may hint at a jeweller's workshop in the area of the fort. See also the gold offcut: No. 1.
Shank: 28 × 25mm, H: 20mm, face: 42 × 36mm; H60 DM Ea24 NN

142. Knife. The narrow blade has a straight edge, which dips at the tip, and a slightly undulating cutting edge, possibly the result of regular sharpening. There is a shallow step both above and below the strip tang which tapers to a rounded end. No traces survive of the handle.
L: 107mm, Max.depth of blade: 11mm, L of blade: 67mm, L of tang: 40; H60 JU Ee/Fa14

143. Fragment of a cleaver with a straight back and cutting edge. What little survives of the shank is very wide and may indicate a socket rather than a tang.
Surv.L: 65mm, depth of blade: 32mm; H60 II Ed/Ee/Fa14 352

144. Spearhead with a narrow, leaf-shaped blade and a flared socket.
L: 118mm, Max.W of socket: 15mm, Max.W of blade: 27mm; H60 GR Eb25

145. L-shaped fragment of iron with a countersunk circular hole in the angle.
L: 42mm, W: 33mm, D of hole: 3mm; H60 EY Ea31

146. Wide strip with one surviving rounded end which encloses a circular hole.
L: 49mm, W: 23mm, Max.T: 6mm; H61 PT 350

147. Corroded annular ring.
Int.D: 34mm, W: 7mm; H60 HA Ea25

148. Fragment of a corroded ring.
No measurements possible; H60 FZ Ea14; *c*. AD 120.

149. Disc with a large rectangular hole cut from the centre. Washer?
Ext.D: 7mm, W: 1.5–2mm, T: 1.5mm; H61 PV Db34

150. Large ring of circular section.
Int.D: 46mm, W: 8mm; U/P

151. Three dome-headed hobnails arranged in a triangle.
D: 9mm, 9mm, 8mm; H60 FL Ea25/Eb25

152. Twelve dome-headed hobnails arranged in two rows.
D of each head: 10mm; H61 LG Fa23

153. Two domed hobnails.
D of each head: 10mm; H60 JO Eb25

154. Single dome-headed hobnail.
D: 9mm, L: 15mm; H60 EY Ea31

155. Small nail with an incomplete disc head and a tapering, rectangular-sectioned shank.
D of head: 14mm, L: 26mm; H60 EY Ea31

156. Nail with a disc head.
D: 16mm, L: 2mm; H60 GS Ee14/Fa14

157. Three nail shanks.
L: 19mm, 22mm, 33mm; H60 GS Ee14/Fa14

158. Fragment of a nail or stud with a disc head and a thin, square-sectioned shank.
No measurements possible; H61 HB Db33

Unidentified iron was found in the following finds groups:
H61 MB Db33
H61 HI Ea22
H61 MS Ee25

Lead Objects (Fig. 11.4)

159. Solid, spool-shaped spacer. A similar, if slightly smaller example, is known from Corbridge: Bishop and Dore 1989, fig. 93, no. 29.
H: 43mm, Max.D: 32mm; H61 EU

160. Rough cone of lead with a semicircular hole in the base. This may have been a weight but is more likely to be the caulking to hold an iron shank in a bronze stud head.
H: 24mm, D: 27mm, hole: 11 × 6mm; H61 IM Ea22

161. Well-formed disc with one raised edge. One face is rough. Infill?
D: 69mm, Max.T: 10mm; H61 AY Ee22

162. Strip of lead which has been neatly rolled into a squat tube.
L of tube: 13mm, Ext.D: 10mm; H60 EO Eb24

Strips and sheets of lead were also found in the following contexts:

163. H61 FY Fc35 Crumpled sheet. L: 90mm, T: 1mm

164. H61 CZ Ee22 Small folded sheet. W: 25mm

165. H61 FL Ec35 Large crumpled sheet. L: 115mm, T: 1–2mm

166. H61 QT Strip. L: 23mm, W: 11mm

167. H61 QB De34 Sheet. L: 28mm

168. H61 PT Large, shapeless sheet. L: 86mm

169. H61 FY Ec35 Sheet. No measurements possible

170. H61 FL Ec35 Large crumpled sheet. No measurements possible

171. H60 KT Ec14 Crumpled sheet. No measurements possible

172. H61 EX Dd34 Rod. L: 30mm, W: 5mm

173. H61 DZ Ee25 Fragment

174. H61 CS Ea22 Fragment

175. H61 CS Ea22 Waste. L: 25mm

Bone Objects (Fig. 11.4)

176. Flat, trapezoidal back plate from a scabbard chape. The sides are chamfered to enable them to slide into the missing flanged front plates and the only decoration consists of two nicks cut from the wider (open) end.
  Bone chapes were usually made in two parts with the rectangular or trapezoidal forms being the most popular. Examples from Britain and the Rhineland suggest a 3rd-century date: see MacGregor 1985, 163, fig. 86, a–e; Bishop and Coulston 1993, fig. 90, no. 10. Locally, several examples have been found at South Shields: Allason-Jones and Miket 1984, nos. 2.75–80.
L: 65mm, W: 25–35mm, T: 4mm; H60 BR Fa14

177. Counter with an irregular countersunk face and a roughly executed central dot-and-ring motif. The back has a heavily incised 'X' which reaches to the edges of the counter. According to MacGregor (1985, 133) the letter X, possibly denoting the number ten, is one of the most common symbols to be found on bone counters,

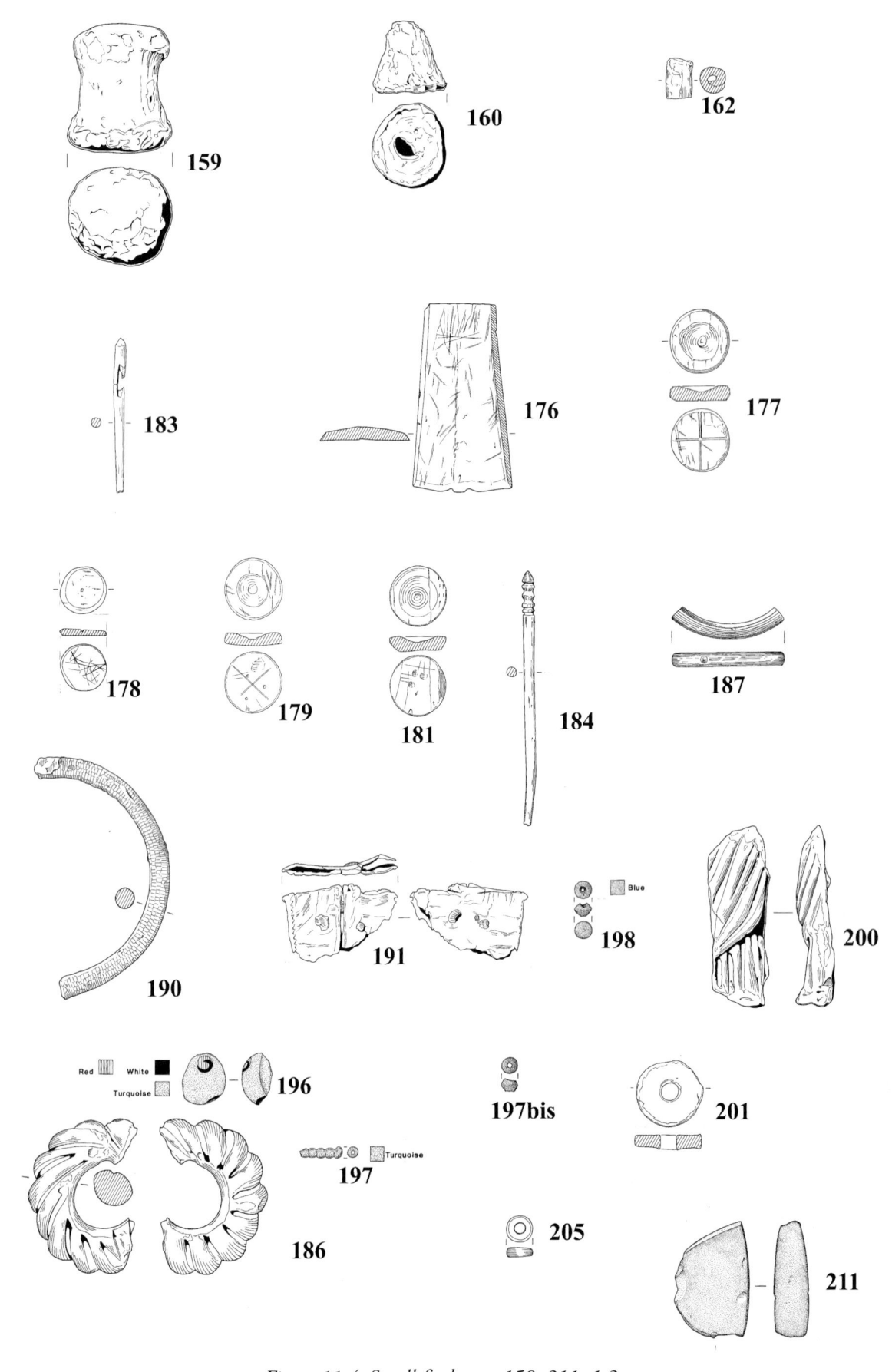

Figure 11.4. Small finds: nos 159–211, 1:2.

although he comments that these symbols are normally so faintly incised that 'it seems unlikely that they played any part in the game itself'.
D: 22mm, T: 5mm; H60 LU Ed25

178. Small counter with a flat face, central incised dot and bevelled edges. Deliberate but apparently random scratches survive on the back.
D: 16mm, T: 2mm; H60 KG Ea/Eb14; post *c.* AD 250.

179. Counter with a countersunk face which has a wide, rough, lathe-centring mark in the middle. On the back there is a roughly scratched 'H' and three drilled dots.
D: 18mm, T: 3mm; H61 CL Fa32

180. Counter with countersunk face and wide lathe-centring mark. The back is damaged but some incised lines survive.
D: 23mm, T: 4mm; H61 GH Ee25; post *c.* AD 180.

181. Counter with a countersunk face which shows clear signs of having been lathe-turned. The back has two bevelled edges: Kenyon (1948) suggested that such bevelling may indicate that the counters were used in a game like tiddlywinks; however, MacGregor (1976) has shown that these are the natural result of cutting the counters from long bones with narrow wall curvature.
D: 21mm, T: 5mm; H60 GO Ed24; post *c.* AD 160.

182. Counter with bevelled edges and countersunk face. Carelessness on the part of the craftworker has resulted in a chip being knocked out when the point of the lathe was removed. The back has similar bevelling to No. 181.
D: 23mm, T: 4.5mm; H60 HB Ed25; post late 3rd century AD.

183. Incomplete, circular-sectioned needle in two pieces. The pointed head has a countersunk, rectangular eye.
L: 53mm, Max.T: 3.5mm, L of eye: 6mm; H61 QM; post mid-3rd century AD.

184. Incomplete pin of tapering circular section with a slight curve. The conical head sits on a lathe-turned ridge-and-baluster neck.
Surv.L: 86mm, Max.T: 4.5mm; H61 GH Ee25; Hadrianic.

185. Sawn-off tip of a red deer antler.
L: 107mm; H61 EO Eb34

Shale and Cannel Coal Objects (Fig. 11.4)

The following artefacts have been analysed by Dr J.M. Jones of the Fossil Fuels and Environmental Geochemistry Institute at the University of Newcastle upon Tyne using reflectance measurements; see Allason-Jones and Jones 1994.

186. Large ring of oval section with deep grooves giving a spiral effect even though the grooves do not continue around the inner face. Incomplete.

Rings of similar size have been found on a number of sites and can be variously identified as hair-rings, *e.g.* York: Allason-Jones 1996, no. 283; or as pendants, *e.g.* South Shields and Carvoran: Allason-Jones and Jones 1994, nos. 9 and 13. However, none of these examples have cable decoration, which is more commonly found on armlets (York: Allason-Jones 1996, nos. 71–77) and finger-rings (York: Allason-Jones 1996, nos. 171–2).

Analysis has revealed this object was carved from cannel coal with a reflectance of 0.47.
Int.D: 24mm, W: 16mm, T: 12mm; H61 MD Ee34

187. Fragment of a bracelet of pentagonal section. The projecting lathe-scar on the inner face still retains its file marks indicating that this bracelet was not worn for long, if at all. Analysis has revealed this object was carved from carbargillite with a reflectance of 0.54.
Int.: 60mm, W: 6mm, T: 5mm; H60 LO Ea24

188. Fragment of a bracelet. The semicircular section may be the result of splitting. Analysis has revealed this object was carved from cannel coal with a reflectance of 0.86; this is a measurement consistent with the coal measures in the immediate vicinity of Haltonchesters. See also No. 189.
Int.D: 80mm, W: 7mm; H61 EP De34

189. Fragment of a bracelet split across its original section. Analysis has revealed this was carved from cannel coal with a reflectance measurement of 0.85; see No. 188.
Int.D: 80mm, W: 7mm; H60 FA De34

190. Two fragments of an undecorated bracelet. The outer face is convex, the inner is ridged suggesting limited removal of the lathe scar. Analysis has revealed this was carved from poor quality Kimmeridge clay with a reflectance measurement of 0.46.
Int.D: 60mm, W: 5mm, T: 7mm; H61 LA Db32

Leather (Fig. 11.4)

191. Strip of leather with one edge folded over and held by a copper-alloy rivet. A second sheet lies on top, butting up to the folded edge.
L: 38mm, W: 23mm; H61 MB Db33

Glass Objects (Fig 11.4)

192. Oval, nicolo intaglio with a bevelled edge. A female figure, either Fortuna or Concordia, has been cut through the pale blue upper stratum into the dark blue under layer. The figure faces to her left and wears long robes, probably a chiton, and holds a cornucopia in

the crook of her right arm. Her left arm is outstretched holding a patera.

Similar intaglios are discussed by Henig 1978, nos. 329–36, of which no. 330, from Chew Valley Lake, Somerset, is also nicolo.
L: 13mm, W: 10.5mm, T: 2.5mm; H61 U/S

193. Bun-shaped, opaque, white glass inset.
D: 12.5mm, H: 6mm; H60 BE Eb14

194. Bun-shaped, opaque, white glass inset with scratches from its setting around the base.
D: 21mm, T: 6.5mm; H60 FL Ea25/Eb25

195. Bun-shaped, opaque, black glass inset.
D: 13mm, H: 5mm; H61 PT

196. Fragment of a globe of 'natural' glass with two marvered ying-yang motifs of opaque red and yellow glass. Possibly a bead or the inset from a pin head.
Approx.D: 22mm; H61 EI Ee34

197. Translucent, turquoise segmented bead. See Guido 1978, 91–2, for a discussion of this type, the majority of which are of 3rd- or 4th-century date.
D: 14.5mm, W: 4mm; H61 BJ Db24/5

197 bis. Translucent, royal blue biconical bead. See Guido 1978, 95, 219.
L: 4.5mm, D: 6mm, hole: 3mm; H61 AQ Fa23

198. Translucent, dark blue, squat biconical bead. See Guido 1978, 95, 219.
D: 6mm, H: 4mm; H61 PT

199. Two black glass facetted globular beads. Modern.
D: 10mm, 7mm, H: 8mm, 6mm, holes: 1mm; H61 Fa22

Pipeclay and Pottery Objects (Fig. 11.4)

200. Fragment of a draped pipeclay figurine. Although little survives, the figure appears to be standing.

Pipeclay figurines were produced in the samian factories of Gaul from the mid-1st century AD until the centre of manufacture moved to Cologne at the end of the century. Large numbers have been found in Britain, mostly in the south-east but with a significant series from the Hadrian's Wall forts. The northern examples tend to fall into two groups: Venus figurines of the Chart Sutton type (see Jenkins 1958) and seated Dea Nutrix figures (Jenkins 1957). This fragment does not seem to belong to either type, nor does the drapery compare with that of a Minerva figurine from London (Green 1976, pl.VIIg). Comparison with bronze statuettes may suggest that this was from a depiction of Fortuna. See also Rouvier-Jeanlin 1972, nos. 426–440.
Surv.H: 62mm; H61 EY Dd34

201. Whorl cut from a sherd of black-burnished ware with cross-hatching on the face.
D: 33mm, T: 4mm, hole: 5.5mm; H61 IM Ea22

202. Counter carefully cut from a sherd of patterned samian.
D: 18mm, T: 6mm; H60 AR Eb14

203. Disc cut from a sherd of coarse grey ware.
D: 39mm, T: 7mm; H61 ES Dc22

Stone Objects (Fig. 11.4)

204. Incomplete, bun-shaped jasper inset with traces of lead/tin alloy(?) on the back for fixing it into its setting.
D: 10mm, H: 4mm; H61 LI Db32

205. Disc bead with convex edges cut from a yellow pebble.
D: 9mm, T: 3mm, hole: 4mm; H61 IQ

206. Fragment of a whetstone made from a long, rectangular-sectioned whinstone pebble which tapers to a rounded end. The other end has been sawn across.
L: 116mm, W: 43mm, T: 37mm; H60 DS

207. Whinstone pebble of rectangular section with rounded ends used as a whetstone.
L: 148mm, W: 39mm, T: 17mm; H60 CD Fa/b/c14

208. Whinstone pebble of oval section used as a whetstone.
L: 92mm, Max.W: 18mm, Max.T: 13mm; H60 ER Ed25

209. Whetstone of rectangular section with rounded corners at the surviving end. The other end has been sawn across. Sandstone.
Surv.L: 104mm, W: 28mm, T: 22mm; H60 EF Eb24

210. Fragment of a whinstone pebble of elliptical section used as a whetstone.
W: 29mm, T: 18mm; H60 FB Eb25

211. Blade of a Neolithic stone axe which has been carefully cut across the body. Neolithic axes and Bronze Age axe hammers are not unusual finds on Roman forts on Hadrian's Wall (see South Shields: Allason-Jones and Miket 1984, no. 12.69; Coventina's Well: Allason-Jones and McKay 1985, no. 27) but it is difficult to be sure if they were considered to be merely curiosities, had some religious significance or were re-used as tools. The trimming of this example, however, suggests that it has been modified for re-use, possibly for smoothing pottery.
L: 26mm, W: 40mm, Max.T: 12mm; H60 LR Fa32

Flint Objects

by C. Tolan-Smith

1. An oval cortical flake from a cobble of grey flint. There are no indications that this item is an artefact and it is more likely the result of fortuitous breakage or thermal fracturing.
39mm × 30mm; H61 JR Ec35

2. The distal fragment of a broken cortical flake of black flint. With the exception of a short length of cortex, the surviving original margins of the flake are all invasively retouched and exhibit extensive edge damage arising from utilization. The piece can be described as a composite implement, the surviving long edge having the characteristics of a knife while the more bulbous end would be better described as a scraper and exhibits characteristic scraper damage on the ventral surface. Invasive retouch of this kind is diagnostic of finds of Neolithic or earlier Bronze Age date.
65mm × 35mm, but originally at least 45mm by estimation; H61 JS Fc24

3. A plunging core rejuvenation flake of grey mottled flint with abrupt retouch and utilization damage at the proximal end. The core from which this item was struck was a blade core and such cores are typical of both the Mesolithic and Later Neolithic periods. The size of the piece itself, and that of the earlier removals of which traces are preserved on its dorsal surface, indicate the later rather than the earlier period. Abrupt retouch is often indicative of hafting, but this is unlikely in this case and it is more likely that this implement was held at the distal end while the blade-like proportions of the proximal end facilitated use in a cutting motion.
72mm × 20mm; H61 ME Ec34

Appendix I
Secondary Sources

1) An Interim Report by J. P. Gilliam: Typescript Dated June 1961

For six weeks, from May 7th until June 18th, excavations have been in progress at the Roman fort of Onnum, Haltonchesters, on Hadrian's Wall in Northumberland.

The excavation was directed for Durham University Excavation Committee by the Reader in Romano-British History and Archaeology at King's College, Newcastle upon Tyne.

In addition to professional workers, as many as one hundred and eleven volunteers took part in the excavation, for various periods at different times. The largest number of workers on the site at any one time was fifty two.

Many volunteer helpers came from such local bodies as the Society of Antiquaries of Newcastle upon Tyne, and the South Shields Archaeological Society, whilst others were recruited through the Council for British Archaeology; they came from as far afield as Invernesshire, Gloucestershire and Kent.

The fort, which lies astride Hadrian's Wall and the present Newcastle to Carlisle road, measures 460 ft from north to south and 410 from east to west. Research was concentrated in the south-western portion of the fort, which is occupied by the western part of the central administrative range, and by the barracks and stables of the rearward range.

The original fort, erected in about AD 125, under the Emperor Hadrian, was regularly planned and well built. A large granary, part of the central range, and measuring 135 ft by 34 ft, was so substantial that it survived the attacks of the northern tribes in the late second century, and required only minor repairs under the Emperor Septimius Severus, early in the third. It was finally destroyed late in the third century, when its wooden floor and the grain which stood on it were charred, and its sandstone roof collapsed.

The neighbouring building, to the west, also part of the central range, was a courtyard house 110 ft by 55 ft. By analogy it will have been the quarters of the commanding officer of the unit. At some time this house, which was of half-timbered construction, was enlarged and modified; at the same time, a wooden floor at a higher level replaced the original flagged floor. These changes, which were not reflected in either granary or barracks, were simple improvements and not the consequence of disastrous destruction. In the packing between the earlier and later floors was found a complete but worn specimen of a mixing bowl (or mortarium) with the stamp of a potter who is known to have worked in the Carlisle region between AD 130 and 160.

The enlarged half-timbered house was burnt down in the late second century. Dramatic evidence was obtained of the fire which destroyed it. Mortaria made by potters who are known to have worked at nearby Corbridge in the later second century, as well as contemporary decorated Gaulish pottery, were found in the layer of fired daub from the timber framed walls, which overlay the charred floor.

The house was so badly ruined that it required complete replacement in the early third century. The new house was similar to its predecessor though different in details of its planning. The quality of its masonry is excellent, and reflects the discipline and standing of the unit known to have been in garrison at the time, the *Ala Sabiniana*, a regiment raised from among the celtic-speaking horsemen of the plains of what is now Hungary.

At the same moment, barracks and stables were reconstructed, for the first and last time, while the west wall of the southern part of the fort, and the gate by which the military road along Hadrian's Wall entered it, were demolished, and the fort extended to the west.

While the finer products of the large Roman potteries in Northamptonshire were still on the market, that is not later than the end of the third century, the fort was burnt down a second time. This was doubtless the work of those tribes who were already coming to be referred to as the Picts. Granary, commander's house, barracks and stables were all destroyed, and all by fire.

The most striking result of the excavations however was the discovery that after this disaster the fort was not immediately reconstructed. Whereas at Birdoswald, in Cumberland, at Housesteads, further west in Northumberland, and at other forts on Hadrian's Wall, Constantius Chlorus, father of Constantine the Great, rebuilt the destroyed buildings, early in the fourth century, at Haltonchesters the fort remained a ruin and became covered with earth – *humo copertum et in labem conlapsum* – to quote a contemporary inscription from elsewhere. Haltonchesters was not reoccupied until after the latest products of the east-Yorkshire potteries had begun to reach the northern market, in the sixties of the fourth century.

The new buildings bore no kind of relationship to those which had come before. Some were of stone, or perhaps half-timbered. Others were wholly of timber, except that the main members had been held upright by being fastened in some way to long rows of massive kerb-like stones with regularly spaced holes in their upper surfaces.

After its re-occupation the fort at Haltonchesters continued long in use. The latest types and styles of pottery are as abundant, and are in significantly the same proportions, as in the latest level at Catterick, or in the late-Roman regional stations on the Yorkshire and Durham coasts. There can be little doubt that Hadrian's Wall remained in commission in some form until the very end of the fourth century or the earlier part of the fifth, though there is no evidence of still later occupation.

These conclusions are, of course, provisional; they cannot be regarded as firm until all the finds have been intensively studied, until a comparison has been made between these results and those obtained in 1958 in the extension to the fort, or even perhaps until there has been further excavation in the barrack and stable area. If the conclusions are substantiated, the implications for the history of Britain in the fourth century will be little short of revolutionary.

While no single portable find is of outstanding beauty or value, the inscribed and sculptured stones, tools, weapons, jewellery, glass, coins, and above all pottery in embarrassing abundance, are of considerable interest, especially in their contexts.

2) Roman Britain in 1960 *Journal of Roman Studies,* 51 (1961) p. 164 Info. from J. P. Gillam.

Resumed excavations at Haltonchesters took place in the angle between the Newcastle-Carlisle road and the lane to Halton. In Period I (Hadrianic) four buildings were found. (a) Next to the headquarters building lay a large granary, almost certainly of identical plan to the similarly placed granary at Rudchester. That at Haltonchesters had been founded on a massive stone raft of flagging laid on clay, itself resting on packed broken limestone. In the N part of the granary the cross wall supporting the floor ran N–S, while in the S part they ran east-west; they appeared nevertheless to be contemporary. The building continued in use till the late fourth century. (b) Next westwards was a shorter building with suspended floor like a granary, but no buttresses; it went out of use and was replaced by a different building in Period IV. (c) In the space to its S was a small building of unknown function. (d) The final building on the W, rectangular and devoid of special features, may have been a workshop. These last two buildings were replaced by others, after destruction by fire, in Period II (Severan). As yet the plan for this period is very fragmentary, but the plan for Period III (Constantian) is more complete. Period IV (Theodosian) showed an unusual method of building construction, both here and in the extension to the W. Timber uprights had evidently been attached by metal cramps in regularly spaced shallow holes in the upper surface of large kerb-like stone laid end to end in rows. These gave a firm foundation to timber-framed structures on ground covered with ruins.

3) Roman Britain in 1961 *Journal of Roman Studies,* 52 (1962) p. 164–5. Info. from J. P. Gillam.

Further work at Haltonchesters (Onnum) in the same area as the previous year (*JRS* LI 164) confirmed some provisional conclusions, while modifying others. (a) The granary of Period I (Hadrianic), 34 ft wide by a calculated 135 ft long, received minor repairs at the beginning of Period II (Severan), but was destroyed by fire at its end; it was not rebuilt, though fragments of buildings of the character of Period IV were found above its ruins. (b) What were previously interpreted as three several (*sic*) buildings W of the granary prove to be a single part-timbered courtyard house, 54 ft wide by a calculated 98 ft long, exclusive of porticoes. Enlargement and modification is dated by Antonine pottery, while reconstruction on slightly different lines took place at the beginning of Period II after destruction by fire. (c) Further investigation of the plan of the kerb-like foundations for timber buildings of Period IV (Theodosian) showed them everywhere to be mutually exclusive in plan to the ashlar building hitherto assigned to Wall-Period III (Constantian); furthermore both sets of buildings were at the same absolute and relative level. They are thus seen to be contemporary and Theodosian and it follows that Haltonchesters did not share in the Constantian restoration of Hadrian's Wall.

4) The Northern British Frontier from Antoninus Pius to Caracalla (Gillam and Mann, 1970).

p. 6

At Haltonchesters the building to the west of the west granary, whether hospital or commanding officer's house, was enlarged and re-floored, and the new flooring sealed Hadrianic and early Antonine pottery, including a mortarium stamped by MESSORIUS MARTIUS.

p. 28

"… at Haltonchesters, where the pottery from the layer of charred wattle, fired daub and burnt wooden floors which marked the close of HW IB, includes more than one type best matched in the destruction deposits at the end of VC at Corbridge, and there is no earlier destruction."

p. 43

Invaders breaking into a garrisoned province are unlikely to have attempted a detailed investment of Roman forts. They are more likely to have made straight for those sites which could be easily captured and which promised most booty. The depot-town of Corbridge will have fallen into this category, and we can date the destruction known there at this Period to the invasion attested by Herodian. The destruction at Haltonchesters probably belongs to the same invasion. It may not have been fully garrisoned when the frontier lay on the Antonine Wall, but it will have lain clear in the path of any raider approaching Corbridge.

5) The Frontier after Hadrian – A History of the Problem (Gillam, 1974)

pp. 8–9

In 1960 and 1961 at Haltonchesters there was dramatic evidence of the destruction by fire of one of the principal buildings. The unstamped pottery closely matched that from the Corbridge and Mumrills deposits, while the stamped mortaria matched those from Corbridge.

p. 10

If Corbridge was destroyed in AD 180, then so was Haltonchesters; the pottery groups are virtually identical, and Haltonchesters lies in the path of any invader making for Corbridge. With Haltonchesters go, also on pottery grounds Rudchester, certainly, and Benwell probably. And, as Richmond once thought, possibly Birdoswald itself. In fact it might be claimed that all the sites on the Wall which have produced evidence of destruction in the later second century had been overwhelmed together in AD 180.

p. 13

But, in 1960 and 1961 at Haltonchesters, and again in 1972 at Rudchester, it was found that the buildings of the second main structural phase, corresponding to Wall Period II elsewhere, had in fact been allowed to fall into ruin and became covered with earth, before the buildings of the next structural phase were erected over them. The structures to which this happened were the commanding officer's house, and barracks, which will have been part-timbered. The phenomenon was not observed in the granaries, which will have been wholly of stone. The burnt wattle and daub, in evidence at both sites at the end of Period I, was absent at the end of Period II.

p. 15

At Haltonchesters and Rudchester there was only one structural phase after Period II. At Haltonchesters this consisted of two sets of buildings, mutually exclusive in plan, at the same level, and both overlying late fourth-century pottery. Some were in rough ashlar while others consisted of stone sills with mortices for uprights. At Rudchester the single building encountered at this level was of the stone-sill type. This phase is shown by the pottery to correspond, at least approximately, to Period IV at Birdoswald. It seems to follow that for about a century. from the late 270s to the late 360s, Haltonchesters and Rudchester lay with skeleton garrisons or without garrisons at all, in grass-covered ruin, with perhaps the more substantial buildings, granaries or baths, protruding as dilapidated but unobscured masonry.

Appendix II
Selected Finds Groups

These are the finds groups whose provenance can be more or less established. They have been extracted from the Finds Books and arranged by Trench Block, Trench, Year and Group.

Block 1

Trench Dc15
60CJ In loose fallen stone outside corner of later building depth *c.* 22 ins.
60DD Built into the rough wall at the corner of the late building.
60DZ Below the late wall corner.

Block 2

Trench Db25
60HS In fallen stone to N of late wall (with holes) and at depth 37 ins.
60ID Layer of filling above clay (?natural).
60IX Immediately N of Period IV wall. Between the level of the bottom of the Period IV wall at 17 ins and the top of the clay at 42 ins.
61CM Soil below floor level with park railing stones.
61CU Layer below the flooring level with park railing stones 18–36 ins down.
61DW Cleaning fallen stones below the park railing stones. Depth *c.* 3 ft 6 ins.

Block 3

Trench Db31
60JG Towards S end above clay etc *c.* 47 ins and below latish wall at 36 ins.

Block 4

Trench Dd14
60BV North side. In second floor level.
60CK Above floor 1.
60CZ In the fallen stone on surface 4 depth *c.* 30 ins.

Trench De14
60GH Below the "flags". Depth *c.* 38 ins
60HF Cleaning below the flag level
60KN E end. In brown soil below flags and immediately above Period I wall.

Trench Ea14
60AK Below fallen stone *c.* 20 ins and below – down to 30 ins.
60CS From the clay/soil cover (or corner?) of floor depth *c.* 22 ins.
60FZ In layer below flags depth *c.* 33 ins.
60KB Burnt wattle and daub below topsoil.
60KG In dirty orange clay below burnt wattle and daub.
60KM In brown soil below heavy stones, beside Period I wall at depth 41 ins.

Trench Eb14
60AS In clay above lower level of big stones among larger stones below black soil between 22 and 28 ins.
60AY As AS.
60AZ As AS.

Trench Ec14
60KU Burnt material below topsoil.
60KX Patch of burnt material below topsoil W of Period IV wall.
60LC In rubble below topsoil, and in places below patch of burnt material (KX).

Trench Ed14
60LE Sealed in black soil below Period IV flagged floor.
60LL Black soil and rubble under Period IV flagging, on level with or below Period III flagging.
60LQ Brown soil below Period III flagging.
60MB Brown soil below Period III flagging.

Trench Fd14
60BG Black filling of robber trench of earlier N/S stone wall in W part of trench. 26 ins and on down.

Block 5

Trench Ea24
60DA Amongst fallen stone.
60EP In fallen stone.
60FJ In fallen stone at W end of trench.
60FP In fallen stone.
60GJ In clay level below the wall. Depth *c.* 32 ins.
61BF In and below the destruction layer of yellow clay.

Trench Eb24
60DP Below fallen stone to a depth of about 40 ins.
60DQ On clay surface depth 40 ins. 10 ins S of N edge. 9 ins E of wall face.
60EF Above cobble floor, depth 53 ins.
60FG Base of wall footing protruding from N side of trench. "Hadrianic" level.
60FR "Hadrianic level". max depth 60 ins.

Block 7
Trench De22
61KJ Level of Period IV stone.
61KP Stony soil below level of Period IV.
61MI S of N railings from 1 ft 6 ins depth (coin was found 3 ft 6 ins on N–S wall 3 ins from W baulk).
61PZ Filling in N end of Period I drain.

Trench Ea21
61JX Between 3 ft and 4 ft depth and under flags.
61OC Below flagging S of Period II wall.

Trench Ea22
61DL From mixed earth below level of 1st tumble of stones c. 2ft 6ins down just above the destruction level.

Trench Ea23
60JA Extreme E end from sandy mortar from Hadrianic wall below clay.

Block 9
Trench Eb31
60DG In clay layer above flags. Depth c. 30 ins.
60DO Between large flags. ?floor/fallen c. 37 ins.
60EB Clay layer above large flagstones.
60GF In flags and fallen stone c. 20 ins.

Block 10
Trench Eb34
60DY On the surface of the reddish yellow clay.
60GA In cleaning of wall.

Block 11
Trench Ea25
60IJ W of Period IV wall. Above layer of rough pitching or cobbles.
60IR W of Period IV wall. In and below layer of rough cobbles.
60JL Above long and short wall platform below removed later cobbles.
61NQ Between Period III and Period IV wall sealed by flagging recorded on 22/7/60 and removed 9/6/61.
61OB Reopened hole between Period III and IV walls, underneath flagging.
61PA Below cobble at E end of trench.
61PC In and below cobble layer at 38 ins below turf. down to 50ins, above clay. N of IA wall below its top

Trench Eb25
60EA Cleaning on clay surface below footings.
60EG Clay layer below lowest course of wall.
60EQ Below clay layer.
60EW In fallen stone and clay below it.
60FB Above clay layer.
60IG E of Period III wall from cleaning of stone surface 34/38 ins.
60IV In crevices of stone surface cleaned at 40 ins E of Period III wall.
60JO Found in removing cobble layer to E of wall face.

Block 12
Trench Ed22
60LS Black soil below topsoil around N–S wall and above associated flags.
60LV In black soil among tumbled stones below topsoil.

Block 13
Trench Ec22
61CG Mortar layer below topsoil N end of trench. Mortar only on E side N end equivalent depth elsewhere. figured samian right up against footings of N wall.
61CR Below about 2 ft below clay and mortar spreads SW and NE.
61DF Over 2 ft down in clay and fillings of questionable wall.

Block 15
Trench Ec24
61KN On mortar spread within corner of Period I wall.

Trench Ed24
60GO Destruction level 27–33 ins.
61AS From immediately under or at corresponding level to the layer of fired daub and charred wattle in SE corner at 2 ft 6 ins.
61CP Below destruction level.
61FK Under tumbled stones, W side of Period I N–S wall.

Block 16
Trench Ed25
60DU W end of trench in clay below upper layer of flagstones.
60EU Below burnt level depth c. 36 ins.
60FU Burnt level depth c. 24 ins.
60FV On flags at N end of trench depth 52 ins.
60GS Below flags 12ins down W face of wall in Fa14 "mixed bag".
60HB Above destruction level and the flag pavement.
60JU Sealed by late 4th-century flags on S side of hole above clay, above sleeper wall of W granary.

60LM In brown soil below Period III flagging and above burnt wattle and daub in S and centre of square.
60LN In burnt wattle and daub below layer LM.
60LP In burnt wattle and daub below layer LM.
60LT Grey clay below burnt wattle and daub above Period II (?) wall. below Period III (?) flagging.
60LU In mortar rubble and sandy material below layer CT. Immediately above Period II (?) wall.
60LY In sandy material and mortar below grey clay and above SW corner of Period II wall.

Block 19

Trench Fa21
60DX Within the raft.
60FA Cleaning in the structure of the raft depth 28ins.
60FO Cleaning raft to top of clay foundation.
60GI Inside raft at the E end of the trench.
60HU Between raft edge and heavy W wall depth *c.* 38 ins.
60IL Between edge of raft and the W face of the heavy (granary) wall

Block 20

Trench Eb44
60EN Clay layer below fallen stone *c.* 28 ins.

Block 21

Trench Fa24
60HQ Position of robbed W all of granary max depth 38 ins.

Block 22

Trench Ee25
61CJ In burnt level.
61DM From stone spread 18 ins below surface.
61DZ Amongst fallen stone down to the burnt level.
61EF Destruction level depth *c.* 2 ft 6 ins Dark soil overlying burnt area.
61FV In burnt layer.
61GH In tumble below burnt level.
61GR Below burnt level.
61HM Bottom level above yellow clay.
61MS Below wattle and daub level.
61NG Below level of flooring in clay on N side of E/W wall at W end of trench.

Trench Fa25
61CH Under tumbled stone S of buttress.
61CT In packing between buttress and ? portico wall at SW corner of granary, below level of top of Period I wall and above top of raft, or foundations of Period I wall.
61DE From black layer immediately above Period I foundations to E of Period III wall. Depth *c.* 3 ft 6 ins.

61DO Immediately E of Period III wall, immediately on clay foundation of E–W Period I wall.
61EA Immediately E of line of Period III wall near N end in dark soil overlying mortar and clay surface in association with early N–S wall at 48–50 ins.
61EN Clay and stones to W of wall of granary below Period III wall to W of buttress.

Block 24

Trench Fa22
61PB 3 ft in core of 2nd Period wall.

Trench Fa23
61AU Immediately below fallen roofing slates E end of trench.
61AV Filling of robber trench, centre of trench.
61BD Immediately E of PI (crossed out, PII inserted, signed JPG 5/6/51 (*sic*)) wall, between surviving foundation of granary wall or robber trench, and PI (crossed out, PII inserted) wall, below level of surviving top of PI (crossed out, PII inserted) wall, level with or slightly below, surviving top of granary wall, depth of 50 ins from edge of west end of trench. JPG.
61BT Stratified in filling low down between granary raft and Period II (JPG) wall.
61LG In clay footings between granary foundation and Period II (formerly I) wall of LD.

Trench Fb23
60JN In "Hadrianic" level.

Block 26

Trench Fd25
60JT At a depth of between 2 and 4 ft, in material of robber trench.

Block 28

Trench Da34
61NE In core of fort wall.

Trench Dc34
61HO 3ft down on clay floor.
61IU Above flagged surface at 2 ft 6 ins depth. dark soil and tumble.

Trench Dd34
61QJ In gravel and stones of *intervallum* rd.
61QK In gravel and stones of *intervallum* rd.

Trench De34
61HZ Clay occupation level.
61QA Dark earth below upper level of flags immediately under topsoil.

Block 29
Trench Db32
61MA Below road surface S of E–W wall.
61MU Below road surface.
61OG In road filling.

Trench Db33
61OU Overlying road metalling on N side of hole at 2ft depth.

Block 32
Trench Ea32
61AL Found while cleaning up in layer over cobbles. On road surface.
61BM Beneath flags.

Block 35
Trench East
61RA Trench to E of E wall of fort. In tumble of fort wall.
61RC Below cobbled layer E of E fort wall.
61RG Trench E of E fort wall at E end below burnt layer at 4ft 6ins depth.
61RI Immediately E of E fort wall in burnt layer overlying masons chipppings.

Block 36
Trench Ec33
61JV Lying on stone and lime level, under tumble of E–W wall on S side.
61MJ Below road surface and large flags.

Trench Ec34
61FU Between 3 and 3 ft 6 ins deep W of N–S wall. Below level of sandstone floor.
61JY Below burnt level.
61KG Below burnt layer.
61LV Baulk running sout (*sic*) from peg Ec34 Below flat slabs (destruction layer).

Trench Ec35
61FL Dark layer at the fourth course N–S wall.
61GV Level with and below charcoal level to E of N–S wall. About 3 ft and deeper.
61JH Below burnt level.
61JP Below burnt level next to E–W wall.

Trench Ed34
61EG Cleaning on burnt layer below fallen stones *c.* 18 ins.

Trench Ee34
61MP On flagstone 4 ft below surface.
61MX Below hearth and flagstones at 2 ft 6 ins.

Block 37
Trench Ed15
61NY Below flags.
61OI Huntcliff type rim found at a lower level than the flags which were recorded on June 10 and removed on June 11. 5 ft 6 ins East of West edge of hole. 1 ft 6 ins South of North edge of hole; 2 ft 9 ins below turf level. IMPORTANT.
61OP Between flags at 1ft depth and cobble layer at 3 ft.

Block 38
Trench Ee22
61CW In burnt layer. Depth below 3 ft 4 ins.
61CZ From clay above burnt layer. Depth 3 ft 3 ins. Above clay contained many scattered flecks of iron oxide.
61DC Cleaning on S side of E/W wall in the burnt layer – 3 ft 6 ins.
61DD In clay above burnt level – 3 ft 3 ins.
61EE N of E/W wall above burnt layer. Depth 4 ft.
61GY Below burnt layers.

Trench Ee23
61FI Burnt layer.

Block 39
Trench Ext
61QE E/W trench across N part of extension in patch of burnt wattle and daub below topsoil and to E of N–S wall.
61QF Below burnt wattle and daub.
61QH E–W trench across extension. In cobble layer to E of burnt wattle and daub (QE) at 3 ft 6 ins depth below topsoil.
61QM E–W trench across extension. Stratified below flagged floor of building E of field wall = QO QQ.
61QO E–W trench across extension. 12 ins below flagged floor of building E of field wall = QM QQ.
61QP E–W trench across extension. In clay of rampart backing of extension wall
61QQ E–W trench across extension. Below flagged floor QM and above burnt level = QM QO.
61RE W end of annexe trench from top occupation layer under flags.
61RF E–W trench across extension. Below cobbled area between walls.

Block 40
Trench Fa31
61CL Cobble layer.

Block 41
Trench Fc21
61EC In fallen tile debris.
61EJ Black filling above and between granary support walls.

Appendix III
Location of finds

Location of finds, organised by trench block, year and finds group.

Block	Year	Finds Group	Trench	Coins	Stamped Samian	Decorated Samian	Coarseware	Small Finds
1	60	BF	Dc15					31
1	60	CB	Dc15	76, 133		14, 67		
1	60	CJ	Dc15				2	
2	60	HS	Db25				1	
2	60	IX	Db25			31, 113, 124		
2	61	AO	Db25			19		
2	61	CM	Db25			70, 113	138, 139, 140, 141, 142, 143, 145, 146	75
2	61	CU	Db25	124			147, 148, 149	
2	61	DU	Dc25			10		123
2	61	FO	Dc25		19			
2	61	GF	Db25					72
3	60	HT	Db31			7		
3	60	IB	Db31	35				
3	60	JG	Db31			74		
4	60	AH	Ea14	68				
4	60	AK	Ea14				8, 9, 10	
4	60	AN	Eb14	20				
4	60	AO	Ea14	37				
4	60	AR	Eb14					202
4	60	AS	Eb14				14	
4	60	AZ	Eb14	119				
4	60	BE	Eb14					193
4	60	BM	Fd14	89				
4	60	BR	Fa14					176
4	60	CD	Fa14					207
4	60	CK	Dd14				4	
4	60	CM	Ee14	129				
4	60	CS	Ea14					62
4	60	EL	Eb14	128				
4	60	ES	Ea14	7				
4	60	FP	Eb14		23	9		
4	60	FZ	Ea14					148
4	60	GH	De14				5	
4	60	GQ	De14			40		
4	60	GS	Ec14					54, 156, 157

Appendices

Block	Year	Finds Group	Trench	Coins	Stamped Samian	Decorated Samian	Coarseware	Small Finds
4	60	HF	De14				6, 7	
4	60	II	Ed14					143
4	60	JU	Ea14					142
4	60	KE	Dd14					51, 84
4	60	KF	Ee14			86		71
4	60	KG	Ea14					178
4	60	KH	Dd14		8			36
4	60	KI	Ec14	1				70
4	60	KO	De14			85		
4	60	KR	Ec14					41
4	60	KT	Ec14					171
4	60	KX	Ec14					16
4	60	KY	Ec14					111
4	60	LC	Ec14	57				
4	60	LQ	Ed14				15	
4	60	MB	Ed14				17, 18, 19, 20, 21	
4	61	AM	Ec14	33, 51				
5	60	BW	Ea24			97		
5	60	CL	Eb24			15		
5	60	CP	Eb24					22
5	60	DM	Ea24					141
5	60	DP	Eb24				34, 35, 36, 61	
5	60	DQ	Eb24				37, 38	4
5	60	EF	Eb24				62	209
5	60	EH	Ea24			98		
5	60	EO	Eb24					162
5	60	EP	Ea24			59	23, 26	21
5	60	FS	Ea24					43, 110
5	60	IP	De24			42		
5	60	LB	De24			88		
5	60	LH	Ea24					81
5	60	LO	Ea24					129, 187
5	61	BF	Ea24			69	27, 28, 29, 30, 31, 32, 33	
7	60	GX	Eb23		11	41, 124		
7	60	HI	Ea23	79				
7	61	AB	Ea22			75		
7	61	AR	Ea22			75, 125		
7	61	AY	Ea22			69		161
7	61	BG	Ea22		26			88
7	61	BR	Ea22					102
7	61	CF	Ea22	122		119		
7	61	CS	Ea22					174, 175
7	61	DL	Ea22	23		57, 101	54, 55, 56	42
7	61	DS	Ea22	21				50, 78, 115
7	61	EQ	Ea22					80, 106, 133
7	61	FM	Ea22					37
7	61	GZ	Ea22			47		
7	61	HI	Ea22			48		

Block	Year	Finds Group	Trench	Coins	Stamped Samian	Decorated Samian	Coarseware	Small Finds
7	61	IK	Ea22			90		
7	61	IM	Ea22	15				5, 63, 160, 201
7	61	JX	Ea21				51, 52	
7	61	KJ	De22				41, 42, 43, 44	
7	61	KP	De22			92	45, 46	
7	61	MI	De22	42		54, 57	47, 48	
7	61	MK	De22			11, 29		
7	61	MM	De22					85
7	61	NO	De22			94		
7	61	OQ	De22			95		
7	61	PZ	De22				49, 50	
8	61	JB	De23		21			
9	60	DG	Eb31				57	
9	60	DO	Eb31				58	
9	60	EJ	Ea31	121				
9	60	EY	Ea31					154, 155, 145
9	60	GF	Eb31				58	
10	60	GA	Eb34				63	
10	61	EO	Eb34	108, 120				185
11	60	CW	Ea25		9			
11	60	EA	Eb25				60	
11	60	EW	Eb25			38	76, 77	
11	60	FB	Eb25				78	39, 210
11	60	FL	Ea25					151, 194
11	60	GG	Eb25					65
11	60	GR	Eb25					144
11	60	GU	Ea25		27			
11	60	GZ	Eb25					9, 69
11	60	HA	Ea25					147
11	60	HP	Ea25		30			
11	60	IJ	Ea25			16	64, 65	
11	60	IR	Ea25					27
11	60	JL	Ea25				66	
11	60	JO	Eb25				201, 202	153
11	60	JW	Ea25			121		
11	61	IS	Ec25			50, 80		
11	61	NQ	Ea25				69	97, 139
11	61	NZ	Eb25			130		
11	61	OB	Ea25			61	70, 71	
11	61	PC	Ea25				72, 73, 74, 75	
12	60	LS	Ec22				79	35, 73
12	60	LV	Ec22	4			81, 82, 83, 85, 100	
13	60	MA	Ec22					6
13	61	BO	Ec22			69		
13	61	CG	Ec22			13		
13	61	CO	Ec22					30
13	61	CR	Ec22		5		85, 86	
13	61	DF	Ec22			3		

Block	Year	Finds Group	Trench	Coins	Stamped Samian	Decorated Samian	Coarseware	Small Finds
14	60	IV	Ed21					53
14	61	OA	Ed21		20			
15	60	GO	Ed24				87	181
15	60	GP	Ed24			39		
15	61	AN	Ed24	112		68		
15	61	AS	Ed24			53, 69	88, 89, 90, 91	
15	61	AX	Ed24			63		
15	61	BB	Ed24	25	15			
15	61	CP	Ed24			2, 12	92, 93, 94	
15	61	EL	Ed24			21		
15	61	HJ	Ed24			71		
15	61	HY	Ed24			49		
15	61	IE	Ed24					92
15	61	KL	Ec24		16			
15	61	LB	Ec24			134		
16	60	EI	Ed25					94
16	60	ER	Ed25					208
16	60	EU	Ed25				96	
16	60	GD	Ed25			126		
16	60	HB	Ed25				98, 99	182
16	60	IQ	Ed25			17, 18		
16	60	JY	Ed25					32
16	60	LT	Ed25					137
16	60	LU	Ed25					177
18	60	CC	Fa13	75, 77, 117				
19	60	DX	Fa21				101	
19	60	FA	Fa21				102	189
20	60	EK	Eb44					130
20	60	EN	Eb44					57
21	60	EV	Fb24	53				
21	60	HQ	Fa24					66
21	60	JC	Fa24					93
22	61	BL	Ee25			120		
22	61	BP	Ee25			1, 46		
22	61	CB	Fa25					79
22	61	CC	Fb25					15
22	61	CT	Fa25				127	
22	61	DE	Fa25				128, 129	
22	61	DM	Ee25				103, 104, 105, 106, 107, 108, 109	83
22	61	DZ	Ee25			33	110, 111, 112, 113, 114, 115	60, 173
22	61	EA	Fa25			64		
22	61	EF	Ee25				116	
22	61	EH	Ee25			35		118
22	61	EN	Fa25			76		
22	61	EZ	Ee25					86
22	61	FV	Ee25			22, 44, 90	117	
22	61	GH	Ee25			45	118, 119, 120, 122, 123, 124	180, 184

Block	Year	Finds Group	Trench	Coins	Stamped Samian	Decorated Samian	Coarseware	Small Finds
22	61	GR	Ee25					23
22	61	HM	Ee25				124	
22	61	LI	Fa25					204
22	61	MC	Ee25		22			
22	61	MS	Ee25				126	
23	60	LR	Fa32	26, 41				211
23	60	LW	Fa32			60		
23	60	LX	Fa32	12				
23	61	MG	Fa32			8		
24	60	JN	Fb23					17
24	61	AG	Fa23			6		
24	61	AQ	Fa23					197
24	61	AU	Fa23				131	
24	61	AV	Fa23		1	89		
24	61	BD	Fa23			99, 127		
24	61	BT	Fa23				132, 133, 134, 136, 137	
24	61	LD	Fa23		17	129		
24	61	LG	Fa23					152
24	61	NT	Fa22					131
24	61	PB	Fa22				130	
28	61	EP	De34					188
28	61	ET	Db34	73		132		1
28	61	EY	Dd34					105, 200
28	61	FN	Ce34					19
28	61	GA	Db34			111		
28	61	GB	Dd34			39		119
28	61	GX	Da34					134
28	61	HG	Dc34		28			
28	61	HP	Ce34			56		
28	61	HZ	De34			77		
28	61	IA	Dc34			65		67
28	61	IB	Db34			105		
28	61	IC	Dc34					26
28	61	IH	Db34			78		89
28	61	IN	Da34			72, 115		2
28	61	JL	Da34		3	24, 51		
28	61	JM	Ce34		6			
28	61	KB	Dc34	113		91		
28	61	LE	Dc34	91		65, 116		
28	61	PK	Db34	65				49
28	61	PL	Dc34	110		52		
28	61	PN	Db34	95				
28	61	PU	De34					8, 58, 132
28	61	PV	Db34					149
28	61	PY	Dc34			27		
28	61	QA	De34			39		

Appendices

Block	Year	Finds Group	Trench	Coins	Stamped Samian	Decorated Samian	Coarseware	Small Finds
28	61	QB	De34					167
28	61	QJ	Dd34				150	
29	61	KS	Dc32					82
29	61	LA	Db32	66		133		29, 48, 56, 127, 190
29	61	LC	Db33					113
29	61	LK	Da32		13, 29	30		
29	61	LQ	Db33			25, 93		
29	61	LZ	Db32			131		
29	61	MA	Db32				152, 153, 154	
29	61	MB	Db33					191
29	61	OU	Db33		7			
30	61	ES	Dc22					203
30	61	FZ	Dc22			104		
30	61	PD	Dc22	52				
31	61	JJ	Dc23			4		
32	61	AL	Ea32			43		
32	61	BM	Ea32			43, 100	155, 156, 157	103
32	61	DJ	Ea32			34		47
34	61	JG	Ec31					109
34	61	JQ	Ec31			107		
34	61	KQ	Ec31			36, 66		124
35	61	QR	East			84		
35	61	QT	East			28, 128		166
36	61	DR	Ee34			117		
36	61	DY	Ec34					100
36	61	EG	Ed34				168	
36	61	EI	Ee34			20		196
36	61	EM	Fa34	84				
36	61	EV	Ec35			103		
36	61	EX	Ee34	82				46, 52, 126, 172
36	61	FL	Ec35			77		165, 170
36	61	FY	Ec35	62				135, 163, 169
36	61	GV	Ec35		10		166	
36	61	HL	Ec33					25, 114
36	61	HR	Fb34					Flint (1)
36	61	IF	Fd34					59
36	61	IJ	Fb34					138
36	61	IV	Fb34	92, 98				
36	61	JD	Fd34		25			
36	61	JV	Ec33				158	
36	61	JY	Ec34				160, 161	
36	61	JZ	Fd34		18	5		99
36	61	KA	Fc34					34
36	61	LV	Ec34				163, 164, 165	
36	61	MD	Ec34					186
36	61	ME	Ec34			26		Flint (3)
36	61	MJ	Ec33				159	
36	61	ML	Ed34					121

Block	Year	Finds Group	Trench	Coins	Stamped Samian	Decorated Samian	Coarseware	Small Finds
36	61	MV	Fa34					136
36	61	MX	Ee34				169	
36	61	NS	Fc34			115		
36	61	QL	Ed34			83		
36	61	QU	Fb34			122		7, 18, 20
36	61	QV	Fc34	2				
37	61	NY	Ed15				170, 171, 172	
37	61	OP	Ed15				173, 174, 175	
38	61	CD	Ee22			69		
38	61	CW	Ee22				176	
38	61	CZ	Ee22					164
38	61	DC	Ee22				177	
38	61	FI	Ee23			44		
39	61	PT		50, 87, 123, 134	14	61, 73, 96, 108, 109, 118		3, 10, 11, 96, 98, 112, 117, 120, 122, 146, 168, 195, 198
39	61	QE	Ext				179, 180, 181	
39	61	QH	Ext				182, 183, 184	140
39	61	QM	Ext			58, 123	186, 187	183
39	61	QO	Ext				188, 189, 190	28, 55, 64
39	61	QP	Ext				191, 192, 194, 195, 196, 197	13
39	61	QQ	Ext				188	
40	61	CL	Fa31				199	179
40	61	DK	Fa31					68
40	61	EK	Fa31			102, 114		
40	61	FE	Fa31			55		
40	61	FR	Fb31			110		
40	61	FS	Fa31					14, 45
41	61	EJ	Fc21					128
42	61	JS	Fc24		12	81		

Unprovenenced Material

Block	Year	Finds Group	Trench	Coins	Stamped Samian	Decorated Samian	Coarseware	Small Finds
	60	BY				37		
	60	DS						206
	60	JM				32		
	60	KQ		97				
	61	BJ	Db24			135		
	61	EU	Dd					159
	61	HB						158
	61	HS	CC34			23		
	61	IQ				49, 79, 106		205
	61	OZ				82		

Bibliography

Abbreviations
BM   British Museum
CAJ   *Chester Archaeological Journal*
D.   Déchelette, 1904 (Figure Type in)
JRS   *Journal of Roman Studies*
MAN   Musée des Antiquités Nationales, St-Germain-en-Laye.
O.   Oswald, 1964 (Figure Type in)

Abbatt, R. 1849 *A History of the Picts' or Romano-British Wall, and of the Roman Stations and Vallum*. London.

Allason-Jones, L. 1985 Bell-shaped studs, in Bishop, M. C., ed. *The Production and Distribution of Roman Military Equipment: Proceedings of the Roman Military Equipment Research Seminar*. Oxford: BAR International Series 275, 95–108.

Allason-Jones, L. 1988 Small Finds from Turrets on Hadrian's Wall, in *Military Equipment and the Identity of Roman Soldiers: Proceedings of the Fourth Roman Military Equipment Conference* ed. J. C.Coulston, 197–233. Oxford.

Allason-Jones, L. 1989 *Ear-rings in Roman Britain*, Oxford.

Allason-Jones, L. 1995 'Sexing' small finds, in *Theoretical Roman Archaeology: Second Conference Proceedings,* Aldershot.

Allason-Jones, L. 1996 *Roman Jet in the Yorkshire Museum*, York.

Allason-Jones, L. and Dungworth, D. B. 1997 Metalworking on Hadrian's Wall, in Groenman-van Waateringe, W., van Beek, B. L., Willems, W. J. H. and Wynia, S. L. (eds), *Roman Frontier Studies 1995. Proceedings of the XVIth International Congress of Roman Frontier Studies,* 317–21. Oxford.

Allason-Jones, L. and Jones, J. M. 1994 Jet and other materials in Roman artefact studies, *Archaeol. Aeliana* 5 ser, 22, 265–72.

Allason-Jones, L. and Miket, R. F. 1984 *Catalogue of Small Finds from South Shields Roman Fort,* Newcastle upon Tyne.

Atkinson, D. 1942 Report on Excavations at Wroxeter, 1923–1927. Oxford.

Bastien, P. and Metzger, C. 1977 *Le Trésor de Beaurains,* Arras.

Bateson, J. D. 1981 *Enamel-working in Iron Age, Roman, and Sub-Roman Britain,* Oxford.

Bayerische Handelsbank 1994 *Romische alltag in Bayern. Das Leben vor 2000 Jahr,* Munich.

Berry, J. and Taylor, D. J. A. 1997 The Roman fort at Halton Chesters: A geophysical survey, *Archaeologia Aeliana* 5 ser, 25, 51–60.

Bidwell, P. and Speak, S. 1994 *Excavations at South Shields Roman Fort Volume 1* Newcastle upon Tyne (Society of Antiquaries of Newcastle upon Tyne with Tyne and Wear Museums).

Bishop, M. C. 1988 Cavalry equipment of the Roman army in the first century AD, in Coulston, J. C., ed. *Military Equipment and the Identity of Roman Soldiers. Proceedings of the Fourth Roman Military Equipment Conference*, 67–96. Oxford

Bishop, M. C. and Coulston, J. 1989 *Roman Military Equipment,* Princes Risborough

Bishop, M. C. and Coulston, J. C. N. 1993 *Roman Military Equipment from the Punic Wars to the Fall of Rome,* London.

Bishop, M. C. and Dore, J. N. 1989 *Corbridge: Excavations of the Roman Fort and Town, 1944–80,* London.

Blood, K. and Bowden, M. C. B. 1990 The Roman fort at Halton Chesters, *Archaeologia Aeliana* 5 ser, 18, 55–62.

Brickstock, R. J. (forthcoming) The coins from Chesters Bridge Abutment, in Bidwell, P. T., ed. Excavations at Chesters Bridge, *Archaeologia Aeliana*.

Brickstock, R. J. and Dungworth, D. B. (forthcoming) A casual find from Chesters Bridge Abutment, *Archaeologia Aeliana*.

Bruce, J. C. 1851 *The Roman Wall*, 1st edn. London & Newcastle upon Tyne.

Bruce, J. C. 1867 *The Roman Wall*, 3rd edn. London & Newcastle upon Tyne.

Bushe-Fox, J. P. 1949 *Fourth report on the Excavation of the Roman fort at Richborough, Kent,* London.

Carson, R. A. G. and Kent, J. P. C. 1960 *Late Roman Bronze Coinage, part II.* London.

Casey, P. J. 1994a *Roman coinage in Britain*, 2 edn. Princes Risborough: Shire Publications.

Casey, P. J. 1994b *Carausius and Allectus: the British usurpers.* London.

Collingwood, R. G. and Richmond, I. A. 1969 *The Archaeology of Roman Britain,* London.

Cool, H. E. M. 1991 Roman metal hairpins from southern Britain, *Archaeol. Journ.* 147 (1990), 148–82.

Craster, H. H. E. 1914 *A History of Northumberland*, 10, 457–522.

Daniels, C. M. 1978 *Handbook to the Roman Wall* (J C Bruce), 13th edn, Newcastle upon Tyne.

Déchellette, J. 1904 *Les Vases Céramiques Ornés de la Gaule Romaine.* Paris.

Deschler-Erb, E., Peter, M. and Deschler-Erb, S. 1991 *Das frühkaiserzeitliche Militärlager in der Kaiseraugster Unterstadt,* Augst.

Dore, J. N. and Keay, N. 1989 *Excavations at Sabratha 1948–1951, Volume II The Finds, Part 1 The Amphorae, Coarse Pottery and Building Materials.* London (Society for Libyan Studies).

Dore, J. N. and Wilkes, J. J. 1999 Excavations directed by J. D. Leach and J. J. Wilkes on the site of a Roman fortress at Carpow, Perthshire, 1964–79, *Proc Soc Ant Scot* 129, 481–575.

Drack, W. and Fellmann, R. 1988 *Die Römer in der Schweiz.* Stuttgart

Fölzer, E. 1913 Die Bilderschüsseln der ostgallischen Sigillata-Manufakturen. Bonn.

Fowler, E. 1960 The origins and development of the penannular brooch in Europe, *Proc.Prehistoric Soc* 26,149–77.

Gillam, J. P. 1974 The Frontier after Hadrian – A History of the Problem. *Archaeologia Aeliana,* 5 ser, 2, 1–15.

Gillam, J. P. 1976 Coarse Fumed Ware in North Britain and Beyond. *Glasgow Archaeological Journal*, 4, (Studies in Roman Archaeology for Anne S. Robertson), 57–80.

Gillam, J. P. and Mann, J. C. 1970 The Northern British Frontier from Antoninus Pius to Caracalla. *Archaeologia Aeliana*, 4 ser, 48, 1–44.

Green, M. 1976 *A Corpus of Religious Material from the Civilian Areas of Roman Britain*, Oxford.

Guido, M. 1978 *The Glass Beads of the Prehistoric and Roman Periods in Britain and Ireland*, London.

Hartley, B. R. 1972 The Roman Occupation of Scotland: The Evidence of the Samian Ware. *Britannia*, 3, 1–55.

Hartley, K. F. 2002a Mortarium stamps from Catterick Bypass, Catterick 1972 (Sites 433 and 434), and other excavations. In Wilson, P. R., 2002, 338–43.

Hartley, K. F. 2002b 9.5.9.2. Stamped Mortaria from Catterick Bridge (Site 240). In Wilson, 2002, 467–8.

Henig, M. 1978 *Corpus of Roman Engraved Gemstones*, ed. 2, Oxford.

Henry, F. 1930 Émailleurs d'Occident, in *Préhistoire*, 2:1, 65–146.

Hermet, F. 1934 *La Graufesenque (Condatomago)*. Paris.

Hewitt, A. T. M. 1968 *Roman Villa, West Park, Rockbourne, Nr. Fordingbridge, Hants. Illustrated Report*. Privately printed.

Hill, P. V. and Kent, J. P. C. 1960 *Late Roman Bronze Coinage, part 1*. London.

Hodgson, J. 1840 *History of Northumberland, Part 2, vol III*. Newcastle upon Tyne.

Hodgson, N. 1999 Wallsend – Segedunum, in Bidwell, P. T. ed. *Hadrian's Wall 1989–1999: A Summary of Recent Excavations and Research*. Carlisle: Cumberland and Westmorland Antiquarian and Archaeological Society and the Society of Antiquaries of Newcastle upon Tyne, 83–94.

Hodgson, N. 2003 *Excavations at Wallsend Roman Fort*. Newcastle upon Tyne: Tyne and Wear Museums.

Huld-Zetsche, I. 1972 *Trierer Reliefsigillata Werkstatt I, Materialen zur römische-germanisch Keramik 9*. Bonn.

Jacobs, J. 1913 Sigillatafunde aus einem römischen Keller zu Bregenz. *Jahrbuch für Altertumskunde 6 (1912)*. Wien.

Jarrett, M. G. 1959 The Defences of the Roman Fort at Halton Chesters. *Archaeologia Aeliana* 4 ser., 37, 177–90.

Jarrett, M. G. 1960 Roman Coins and Potters' Stamps from Halton Chesters. *Archaeologia Aeliana* 4 ser., 38, 153–60.

Jenkins, F. 1957 The cult of the Dea Nutrix in Kent, *Archaeol. Cantiana* 71, 38–46

Jenkins, F. 1958 The cult of the pseudo-Venus in Kent, *Archaeol. Cantiana* 72, 62–76.

Karnitsch, P. 1959 *Die Reliefsigillata von Ovilava*. Linz.

Karnitsch, P. 1960 *Die Reliefsigillata von Veldidena: Archäologische Forschungen in Tirol, I*. Innsbruck.

Kenyon, K. M. 1948 *Excavations at the Jewry Wall site, Leicester*, London.

Knorr, R. 1919 *Töpfer und Fabriken verzierter Terra-Sigillata des ersten Jahrhunderts*. Stuttgart.

Knorr, R. and Sprater, Fr. 1927 *Die westpfälzischen Sigillata-Töpferein von Blickweiler und Eschweiler Hof*. Speyer.

Kunzl, E. 1982 Medizinische Instrumente aus Sepulkralfunde der römischen Kaiserzeit, in *Bonner Jahrbuch*.

Leeds, E. T. 1933 *Celtic Ornament*, Oxford.

Lloyd-Morgan, G. 1981 *Description of the collections in the Rijksmuseum G M Kam at Nijmegen. X. The Mirrors*, Nijmegen.

MacGregor, A. 1976 *Finds from a Roman Sewer System and Adjacent Building in Church Street*, York.

MacGregor, A. 1985 *Bone, Antler, Ivory and Horn*, London.

MacGregor, M. 1976 *Early Celtic Art in North Britain*, Leicester.

Manning, W. H. 1975 An iron anvil from Hasholme, Yorkshire, *East Riding Archaeologist*, 2, 67–9.

Manning, W. H. 1985 *Catalogue of the Romano-British Iron Tools, Fittings and Weapons in the British Museum*, London.

Mattingly, H., Sydenham, E. A., Sutherland, C. H. V., Carson, R. A. G., Kent, J. P. C. and Burnett, A. M. (eds) 1926–1994 *The Roman Imperial Coinage*, volumes 1–10, London.

Milne, J. 1907 *Surgical Instruments in Greek and Roman Times*, Oxford.

Oldenstein, J. 1976 Zur Ausrüstung römischer Auxiliareinheiten, *Bericht der Römisch-Germanischen Kommission* 57, 49–284.

Oswald, F. 1945 Decorated Ware from Lavoye. *Journal of Roman Studies*, 35, 49–57.

Oswald, F. 1964 *Index of Figure Types on Terra Sigillata ("Samian Ware")*. London (Gregg Press Ltd). Originally published as a Supplement to the Annals of Archaeology and Anthropology; 1936–37 (University Press of Liverpool).

Petculescu, L. 1991 Bronze spearheads and spearbutts from Dacia, *Journ. Roman Military Equipment Studies*, 2, 35–58.

Richmond, I. A. and Gillam, J. P. 1950 Excavations on the Roman Site at Corbridge 1946–1949. *Archaeologia Aeliana*, 4 Ser, 27, 152–201.

Ricken, H. 1934 Die Bilderschüsseln der Kastelle Saalburg un Zugmantel. *Saalburg Jahrbuch*, 8, 130–83.

Ricken, H. 1948 *Die Bilderschüsseln der römischen Töpfer von Rheinzabern, Tafelband*. Speyer.

Ricken, H. and Fischer, C. 1963 *Die Bilderschüsseln der römischen Töpfer von Rheinzabern, Texband*. Bonn.

Riha, E. 1979 *Die romischen Fibeln aus Augst und Kaiseraugst*, Augst.

Rogers, G. B. 1974 *Poteries Sigillées de la Gaule Centrale I. Les Motifs non figurés*. Paris (CNRS).

Rouvier-Jeanlin, M. 1972 *Les figurines gallo-romains en terre cuite au Musée des Antiquités Nationales*, Paris.

Rushworth, A. (2009) *Housesteads Roman Fort. The Grandest Station: Excavation and Survey 1954–95*. (English Heritage Archaeological Report). 2 vols.

Simpson, F. G. and Richmond, I. A. 1937 The Fort on Hadrian's Wall at Halton. *Archaeologia Aeliana* 4 Ser, 14, 151–71.

Simpson, G. and Rogers, G. 1969 Cinnamus de Lezoux. *Gallia*, 27, 3–14.

Smith, R. A. 1922 On some recent exhibits, *Antiq.Journ*.2, 199–200.

Snape, M. 1993 *Roman Brooches from Northern Britain*, Oxford

Stanfield, J. A. 1935 A Samian Bowl from Bewcastle, with a note on the potters Casurius and Apolauster. *Trans. Cumberland and Westmorland Architectural and Archaeological Society*, N. Ser., 35, 182–205.

Stanfield, J. A. and Simpson, G 1958 *Central Gaulish Potters*. London (OUP).

Tomber, R. and Dore, J. N. 1998 *The National Roman Fabric Reference Collection: A Handbook* (MoLAS Monogr 2). London: Museum of London Archaeology Service.

Wheeler, R. E. M. 1923 *Segontium, Y Cymmrodor*, 33.

Wild, J. P. 1970 Button-and-loop fasteners in the Roman Provinces, *Britannia* 1, 137–55.

Wilmott, T. 1997 *Birdoswald. Excavations of a Roman Fort on Hadrian's Wall and its successor settlements: 1987–92* (EH Archaeological Report 14). London: English Heritage.

Wilmott, T. 2001 *Birdoswald Roman Fort: 1800 years on Hadrian's Wall*. Stroud: Tempus.

Wilson, P. R. 2002 *Cataractonium: Roman Catterick and its hinterland. Excavations and Research, 1958–1997. Part l*. CBA Research Report 128. York (Council for British Archaeology).

Index

Advocisus, 113
Aestivus, 120
ala Sabiniana, xii, 39, 161
Albens, 115
Albinus iv, 120
Albucianus, 120
Albucius ii, 120–121
Alcester, 124
Anaus, stamped mortarium, 20, 134
annona militaris, 93
Antonine (potter), 116, 118
Antonine Wall, 38, 163
antoniniani, 92
Antoninus Pius, 92, 163
Anunus, 109
Aper ii, 108, 121
Aquincum Hoard, 120, 121
archive plans (PI), 4, 7
Argonne ware, 118
Augustus, 92
Aulus Platorius Nepos, 1, 38

ballistaria, 1
Banuus, 113
Bar Hill, 121
barracks, xii, 1, 3, 34, 37, 38, 81, 143, 161, 163
    see also stable-barracks
basilica equestris exercitatoria, 3
bathhouse, 1
    extension/Severan/third-century bathhouse, 1, 3
    Hadrianic bathhouse, 1
    north-west corner bathhouse, 1
Baylham Mill, 109
BB1, 66, 126, 127, 129, 131, 133, 134, 136, 137, 139, 141, 142
BB2, 44, 126, 127, 129, 131, 133, 134, 136, 137, 139, 141
Beliniccus iii, 108, 121
Bellicus-type mortarium, 37
Belsa Arve(rnicus?), 121
Benwell, 121
Binchester, 120
Birdoswald, 3, 108, 162, 163
Blickweiller ware, 118
bone objects, 155, 157
Bregenz Cellar, 108
brooches, *see* jewellery
Bruce, J. C., 1
Brunt (Burnt) Ha'penny Field, 91, 92

Camelon, 121
Capellianus, 121

Caracalla, 163
Carausius, 93
Cardurnock, 109
Carpow, vii
Carrawburgh, 115
Cassius Dio, 38
Castleford, 124
Casurius ii, 108, 109, 116
Catterick, 108, 116, 120, 121
Catullus ii, 121
Catussa, 118
cavalry, 3, 143
    drill hall, 3
    equipment, xii, 143–144, 149–150, 152
Cavannus, 121
Central Gaulish ware, 38, 108–109, 118, 120
Cerialis iii, 111
Cerialis v, 118
Chester, 108, 111
Chester-le-Street, 121
Chesters, 116, 121
Chesterholm, 120, 121, 124
Cinnamus ii, 109, 111, 113, 116, 118
Claudius Gothicus, 93
Clermont-Ferrand, 115
coarseware, xii, 38, 40, 126–142
Cobnertus iv, 120, 121
coins, xii, 38, 40, 91–93
    coin periods, 91
    copies, 92
    counterfeits, 92, 93
    denominations, 92, 93
Colchester, 13
Colchester Colour-coated ware, 136
Commodus, 38
Constantine, 91, 162
Constantius Caesar, 3
Constantius Chlorus, 162
contubernia, 3
copper alloy objects, 144, 146–147, 149
Corbridge, vii, xii, 3, 111, 113, 115, 116, 149, 155, 161, 163
    destruction deposit, xii, 19, 20, 38, 163
Corbridge Training Excavation, 6
courtyard building, xii, 15–24, 161
    dating evidence, 19
    destruction deposit, 16, 19, 20, 39, 161
    Period I, 16–19, 38, 49, 69, 88
        modifications to Period I, 16, 18, 19
    Period II, 16– 19, 38

Crambeck mortarium, 25, 45
Crambeck Parchment ware, 127, 129, 131, 139
Crambeck Reduced ware, 126, 129, 131, 136
Criciro v, 109
Cuccillus i, 121

Decentius, 91
denarii, 92, 93
Derbyshire coarseware, 133
destruction deposits, 49, 50–51, 55, 62, 83
    see also courtyard building, fort (curtain) wall, granary building
Dickinson, Brenda, 4, 38, 126
Dobson, John, 1
Docilis i, 109, 116
Dore, John/J. N. (JND), vii, viii, 4, 12, 127
Do(v)eccus i, 116, 121
Dressel 20 amphora, 131, 133, 134, 136, 141
dupondii, 92
Durham University Excavation Committee, 1

east gate, 1
East Gaulish ware, 118, 120
Ebchester, 121
Elginhaugh, vii
English Heritage, viii, 4, 40
extension, the/fort extension/west extension, xii, 1, 3, 39, 92
extension west wall, 1, 37

Fences Burn, 1
Finds Book, xii, 4, 6, 7, 19
Finds Groups, 4
flint objects, 159
forehall, 3
fort (curtain) wall, 34, 36
    demolition/destruction of, xii, 34, 35, 39, 44
    east wall, 35–36, 79
    west wall, 9, 44
fourth-century buildings, xii, 39–40, 162
    dating evidence, 25, 27, 29, 30, 39–40
    Fragment A, 25
        B, 25, 27
        C, 27–29
        D, 29
        E, 29–30
        F, 30
        G, 30

garrison, xii
    see also ala Sabiniana
gateways, 1
Geminus iv, 108
geophysical survey, 1
Gillam, John/J. P. (JPG), vii, viii, xii, 1, 3, 4, 6, 7, 9, 11, 12, 16, 18, 19, 37, 39, 92
'Gillam system' of recording, 6
glass objects, 157–158
granary, xii, 39, 161
    buttresses, 9, 11, 46, 66, 68, 74
    dating evidence, 11, 12–13, 38
    destruction deposits, 11–12, 39, 161, 162

    extensions, 9, 11
    kerb, 9, 68, 162
    Period I, 11, 69, 72, 86, 88, 90, 162
        modifications to Period I, 38
    Period II, 11, 68, 74, 86, 162
    Porticoes/Loading Bays, 11, 13, 39, 66, 68, 70, 86
    raft/foundation raft, 9, 12, 46, 68, 69, 74, 90, 162
    roof/roofing material, 11, 12, 13, 72–73
    sleeper walls, 9, 46, 48, 65, 66, 70, 72, 73, 74, 88, 90
    vent, 9
Great Chesterford, 113

Hadrian, 92
Hadrian's Wall, 1, 38, 93, 108, 109, 124, 143, 152, 158, 161, 162
Hadrian's Wall ditch, 1
Hadrian's Wall periods/Wall Period chronology, 38–40
Haltonchesters excavations,
    1823 and 1827, 1
    1935–6, 1, 3
    1956–8, 3, 40
    1960–61, xii, 1, 3–4, 15, 16, 19
Hartley, Brian, 4, 126
Hartshill Mancetter mortarium, 25, 39, 85
Hasholme, Yorks, 154
Heiligenberg ware, 118
Hodgson, John, 1
Housesteads, vii, 39, 150, 162
Hunnum, 93
Huntcliff-type ware, 25, 29, 30, 78, 83, 126, 129, 131, 136, 139, 141

Ianus ii, 118, 120
inscriptions,
    RIB 1060, 92
    RIB 1280, 1
    RIB 1281, 1
    RIB 1427, 1, 38
    RIB 1433, xii, 39
intervallum road, 16, 35, 49
iron objects, 143, 154–155
Iullinus ii, 113, 121
Iustus ii, 115

Jarrett, M. G., 3, 25, 34, 39, 44, 92
jewellery, xii, 143, 144, 146–147, 149, 150, 153–154, 157
    workshop, xii, 143, 154
    see also copper alloy, bone objects, shale and cannel coal objects

La Graufesenque, 108
La Madeleine ware, 118
late second-century destruction, 38
late third-century destruction, 39
lead objects, 155
leather object, 157
Les Martres-de-Veyre, 12, 108, 121
Lezoux, 108, 109, 113, 115, 120, 121
Little Chester, 115
London, 108, 111, 115, 116, 158
Lower Nene Valley Colour-coated ware, 39, 129, 131, 133, 134, 136, 137, 139, 141

Index

Magnentius, 91
Mainz, 116
Maior i, 121
Malluro i, 121
Malton, 121
Mammius, 121
Mancetter-Hartshill White ware, 126, 129, 133, 136, 141
Mansuetus ii, 121
Marcus Aurelius, 92, 93
Maryport, 108
Mercator iv, 115
Messorius Martius, stamped mortarium, 18, 38, 59, 133, 163
mints, *see* coin catalogue p. 94–107
   see also coins
Moselkeramik Blackslipped ware, 126
Muxtullus, 108, 124

Newstead, 111
North of England Excavation Committee, 1
north gate, 1
Notitia Dignitatum, xii, 39, 93

'Park Railings', 3, 51
'park railing stones', xii, 29, 39, 51
Paternus v, 109, 115–116, 121
Patricius i, 108
Paullus v, 124
phase plans, 40
pipeclay and pottery objects, 158
porta quintana, xii, 1, 35, 36–37, 75, 76, 77
Pottacus, 124
praetentura, 1, 92, 93
Primary Archive, vii, xii, 4, 6, 7, 8
Pudding Pan Rock, 120, 121, 124
Pugnus ii, 109, 113

Quintilianus i, 109, 124
Quintus v, 124

recording methodology, xii, 6
   see also Finds Book, Primary Archive, Trench Block
Red House, vii
Reginus vi, 120
retentura, xii, 1, 92, 93
Rheinland, 121, 155
Rheinland White ware, 141
Rheinzabern, 108, 118
Richborough, 116, 149
Richmond, I. A., 1, 7, 39, 92
Rouen, 113
Rudchester, 162, 163
Rufianus, 124

Sacer i, 109
samian ware, xii, 38, 126–142
   decorated, 108–109, 111–120
   stamped, 4, 108, 120–125

Secondary Excavation Archive, 6
section drawings, 4
Secundus v, 109, 113, 118, 124
Segontium, 111
Senilis iii, 124
Septimius Severus, 39, 161
Servus iv, 113, 115
Severus Alexander, 92
shale and cannel coal objects, 143, 157
Silchester, 116
Silver Hill, 91
Simpson, F. G., 92
Sissus ii, 109
Sommer, Sebastian, 3
South Gaulish ware, 108
South Shields, vii, 92, 115, 121, 124, 155, 157
Spanish Dressel amphora, 133, 134
stable-barracks, 3
stables, 1, 161
Stanwix, 121
stone objects, 158
Structural Synopsis xii, 7, 8, 34, 44–90
Swan, Mrs V. G., 4

Tác, 121
Tetricus I, 93
Tetricus II, 93
Trajan, 92
Trajan Decius, 92
Trench Block (Blocks), xii, 7, 34
Trench Identifier, 7
Trier ware, 120

Upchurch Fine Reduced ware, 134
Ulpius Marcellus, 38

via principalis, 3, 16
via quintana, 34, 36, 37, 38, 39, 81, 143
Vindolanda 144

wall backing, 34, 35, 44
Wallsend, 3
Watercrook, 116
weaponry, *see* cavalry equipment
Wels, 111, 116
west gate (*porta principalis sinistra*), 1, 9, 16, 34, 38
Wilderspool ware, 127, 129, 133
Wilten, 115
Wingham, Kent, 115
workshop, 3, 16, 162
   see also jewellery
Wroxeter, 111, 115, 121, 124

York, 113